This past August I took a trip to Arizona. I went to visit my grandmother on my father's side, and while I was there, I came across a comic shop where I discovered **Toriko** (the English version)! They only had volume 1, but I bought it right away! It came in handy when I introduced myself. It reminded me of how happy I am that I chose to become a manga artist. (My current weight is…71 kg!! Gyaaar!)

—Mitsutoshi Shimabukuro, 2010

Mitsutoshi Shimabukuro made his debut in **Weekly Shonen Jump** in 1996. He is best known for **Seikimatsu Leader Den Takeshi!** for which he won the 46th Shogakukan Manga Award for children's manga in 2001. His current series, **Toriko**, began serialization in Japan in 2008.

TORIKO

TORIKO VOL. 12
SHONEN JUMP Manga Edition

STORY AND ART BY **MITSUTOSHI SHIMABUKURO**

Translation/Christine Dashiell
Adaptation/Hope Donovan
Touch-Up Art & Lettering/Maui Girl
Design/Matt Hinrichs
Editor/Hope Donovan

Printed in Canada

Published by VIZ Media, LLC
P.O. Box 77010
San Francisco, CA 94107

10 9 8 7 6 5 4 3 2 1
First printing, October 2012

www.viz.com

RATED T FOR TEEN

PARENTAL ADVISORY
TORIKO is rated T for Teen and is recommended for ages 13 and up. This volume contains realistic and fantasy violence.
ratings.viz.com

THE WORLD'S MOST POPULAR MANGA
SHONEN JUMP
www.shonenjump.com

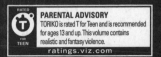

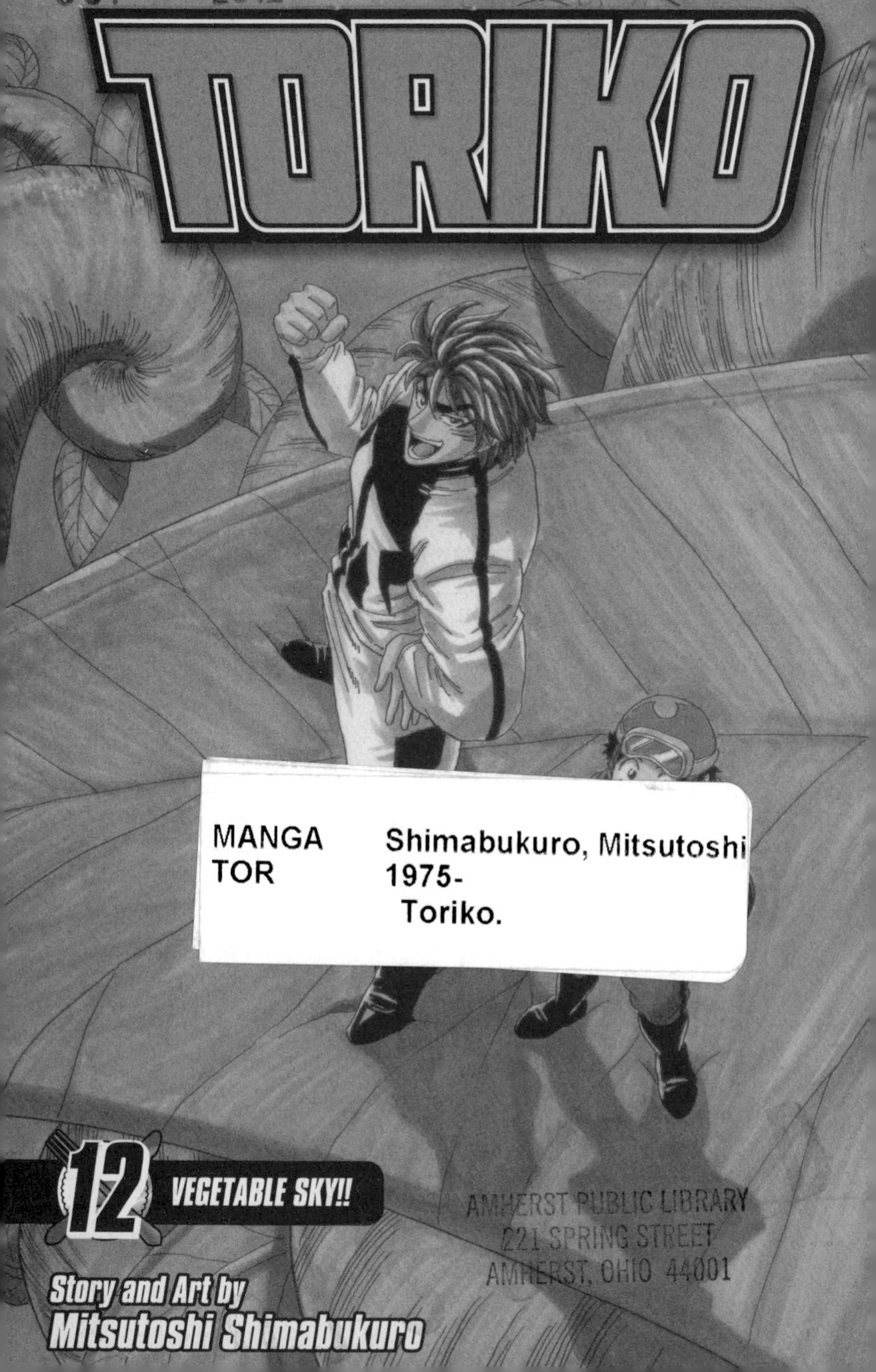
TORIKO
12
VEGETABLE SKY!!
Story and Art by
Mitsutoshi Shimabukuro

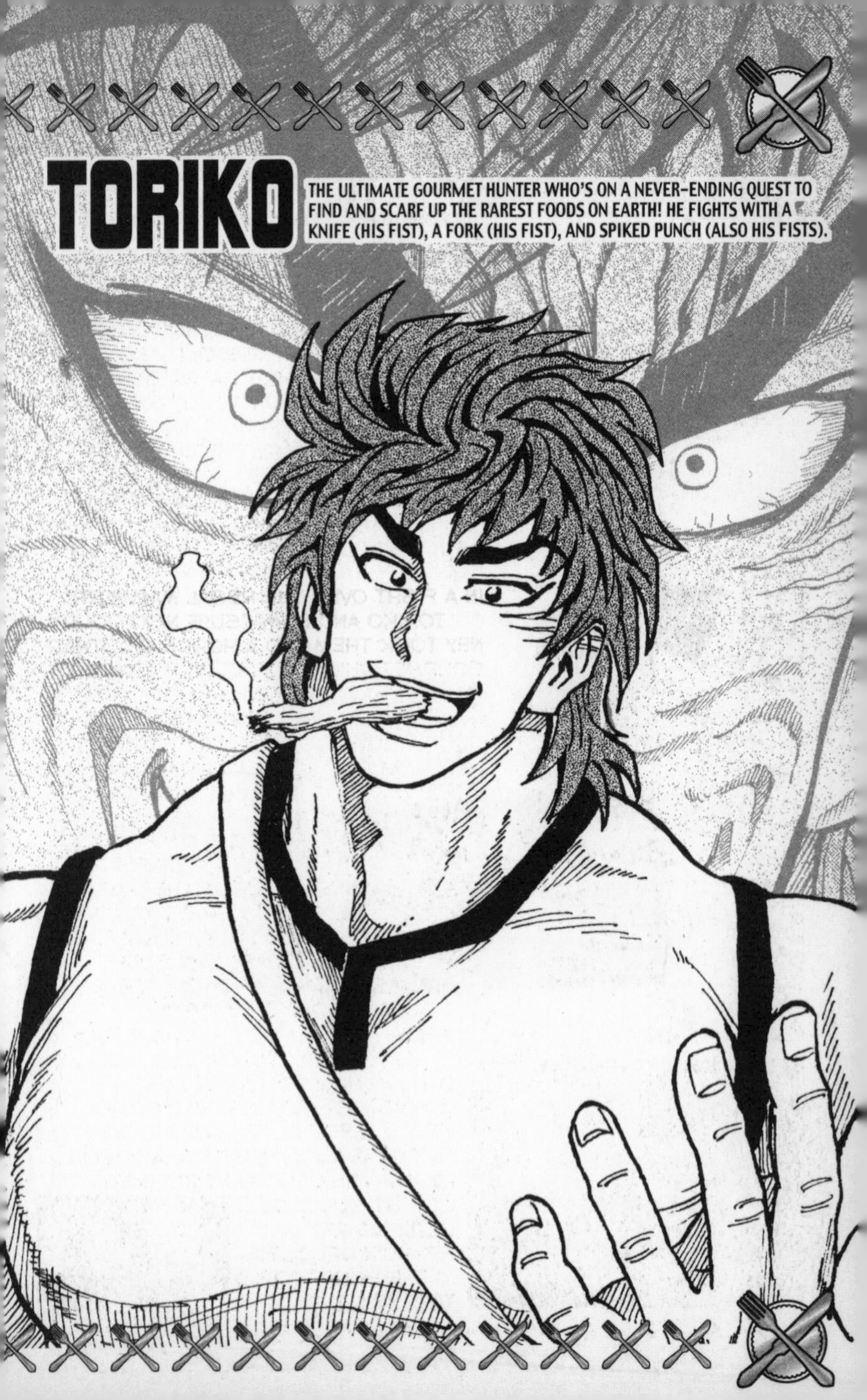
TORIKO
THE ULTIMATE GOURMET HUNTER WHO'S ON A NEVER-ENDING QUEST TO FIND AND SCARF UP THE RAREST FOODS ON EARTH! HE FIGHTS WITH A KNIFE (HIS FIST), A FORK (HIS FIST), AND SPIKED PUNCH (ALSO HIS FISTS).

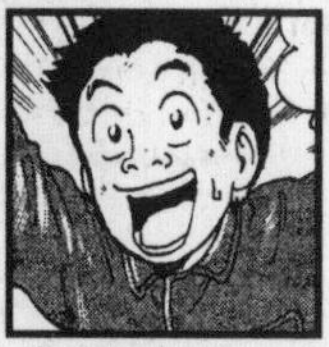

●KOMATSU
TALENTED IGO HOTEL CHEF AND TORIKO'S #1 FAN.

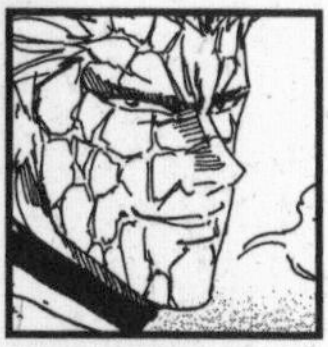

●MATCH
TRIPLE SLICIN' LIEUTENANT OF THE GOURMET MAFIA.

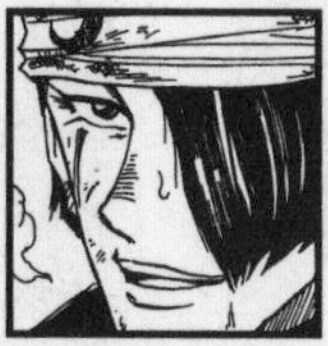

●TAKIMARU
A GOURMET KNIGHT, A GROUP OF GOURMET HUNTERS WHO ADHERE TO THE GOURMET FAITH.

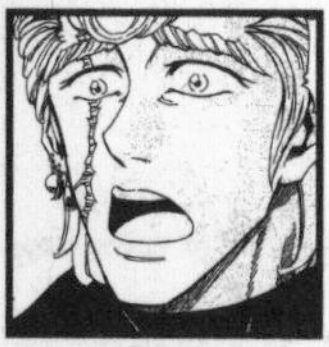

●TEPPEI
A GOURMET REVIVER. PROTECTS RARE FOODS FROM GOURMET HUNTERS.

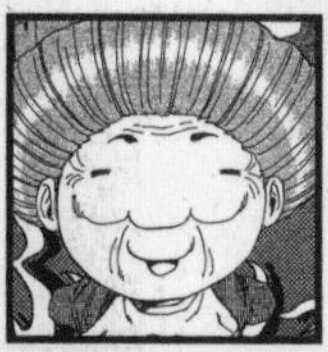

●SETSUNO
AKA GRANNY SETSU. FAMOUS CHEF AND GOURMET LIVING LEGEND.

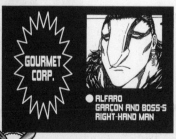

GOURMET CORP.

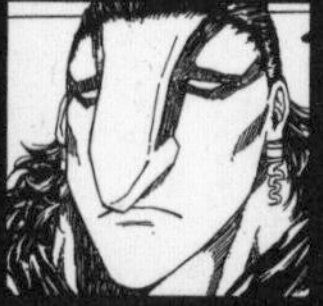

●ALFARO
GARÇON AND BOSS'S RIGHT-HAND MAN

WHAT'S FOR DINNER

IT'S THE AGE OF GOURMET! KOMATSU, THE HEAD CHEF AT THE HOTEL OWNED BY THE IGO (INTERNATIONAL GOURMET ORGANIZATION), BECAME FAST FRIENDS WITH THE LEGENDARY GOURMET HUNTER TORIKO WHILE GATOR HUNTING. NOW KOMATSU ACCOMPANIES TORIKO ON HIS LIFELONG QUEST TO CREATE THE PERFECT FULL-COURSE MEAL.

RECENTLY, THE IGO'S RIVAL ORGANIZATION, GOURMET CORP., HAS BEEN GOING AFTER THE SAME FOODS AS TORIKO! BUT HE DEALT THEIR STRONGEST GT ROBOT A SWIFT DEFEAT IN A FIGHT OVER THE REGAL MAMMOTH.

TORIKO AND KOMATSU'S NEXT JOURNEY TOOK THEM AND A HORDE OF OTHER GOURMET HUNTERS, INCLUDING MATCH AND TAKIMARU, TO ICE HELL IN SEARCH OF CENTURY SOUP. BUT A TRIO FROM

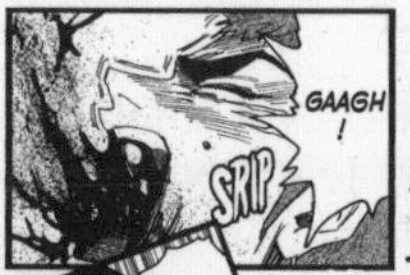
GAAGH!
SRIP

GOURMET CORP. SHOWED UP AND FOUGHT TORIKO AND FRIENDS TO THE DEATH! LUCKILY, TEPPEI THE REVIVER

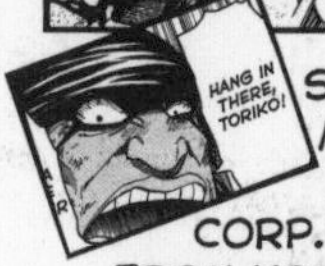
HANG IN THERE, TORIKO!

SHOWED UP AT THE LAST MINUTE TO SAVE TORIKO.

NOT SO LUCKILY, GOURMET CORP. SNATCHED THE SOUP FROM KOMATSU. HOWEVER, TEPPEI SQUEEZED ONE FINAL DROP FROM THE GOURMET SHOWCASE.

AFTERWARD, TORIKO AND THE OTHERS HEADED TO LIFE, THE COUNTRY OF HEALING, FOR SOME VERY INTENSE RECUPERATION. AT THE SAME TIME, KOMATSU SET ABOUT RE-CREATING THE CENTURY SOUP WITH NO SUCCESS... UNTIL HIS PET PENGUIN DROOLED IN THE SOUP! COULD THIS BE IT?!

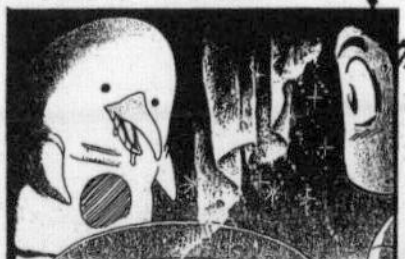

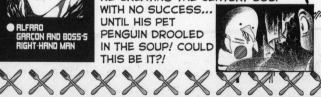

Contents

TORIKO

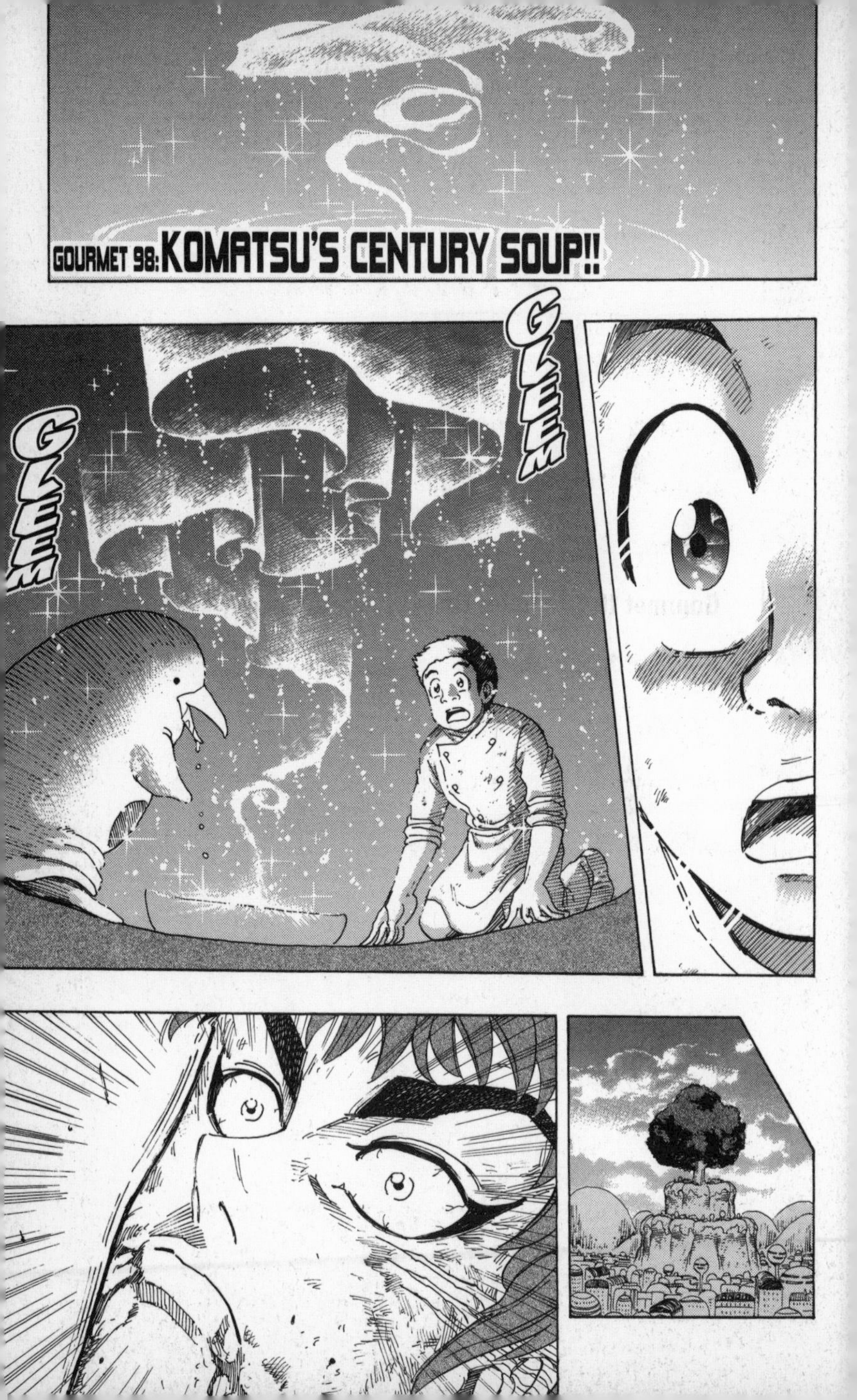
GOURMET 98: KOMATSU'S CENTURY SOUP!!
GLEEM
GLEEM

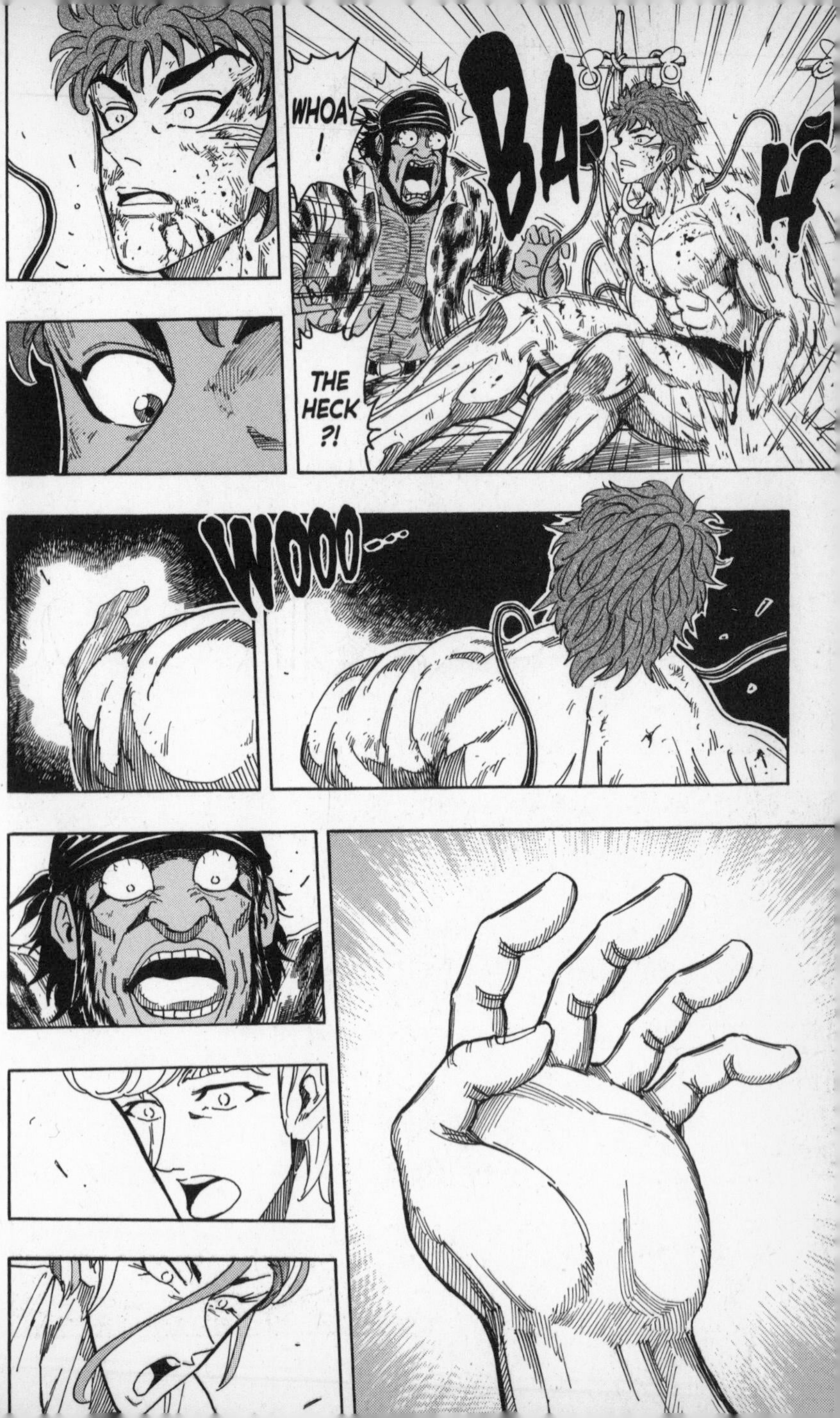
BA-H
WHOA!
THE HECK?!
WOOO...

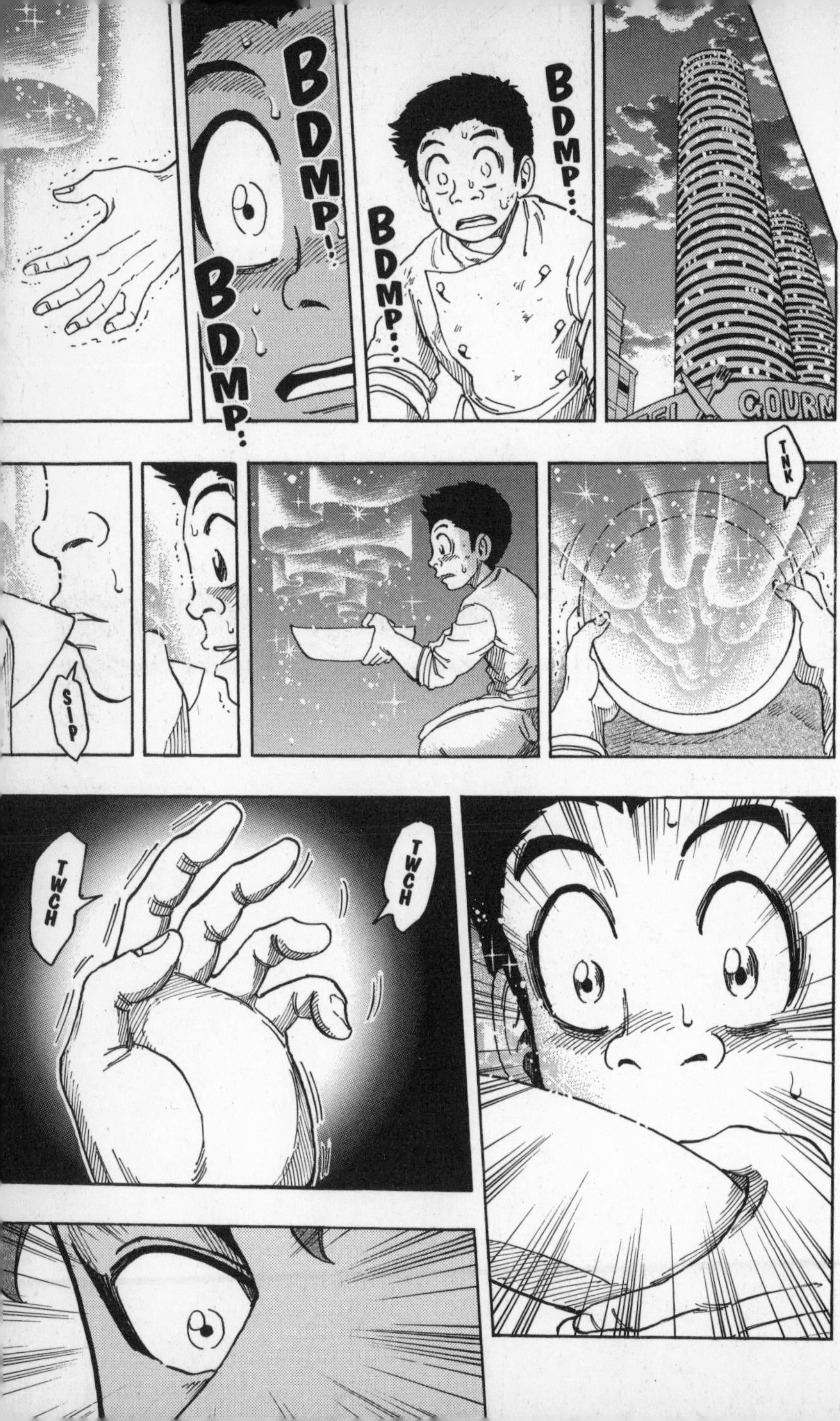
GOURM
BDMP...
BDMP...
BDMP!
BDMP...
TNK
SIP
TWCH
TWCH

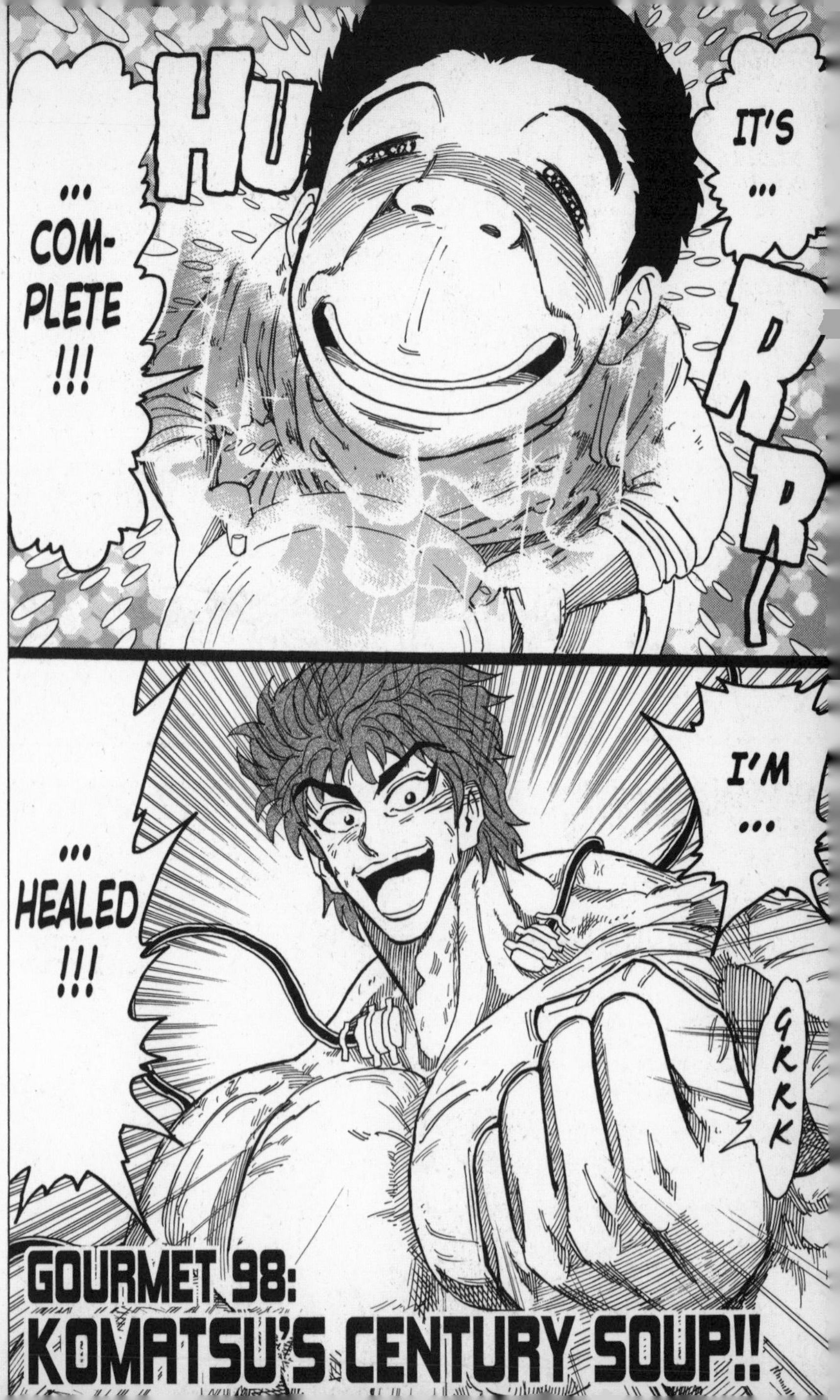
IT'S ...
HURR
... COM-PLETE !!!
I'M ...
... HEALED !!!
GRKK
GOURMET 98:
KOMATSU'S CENTURY SOUP!!

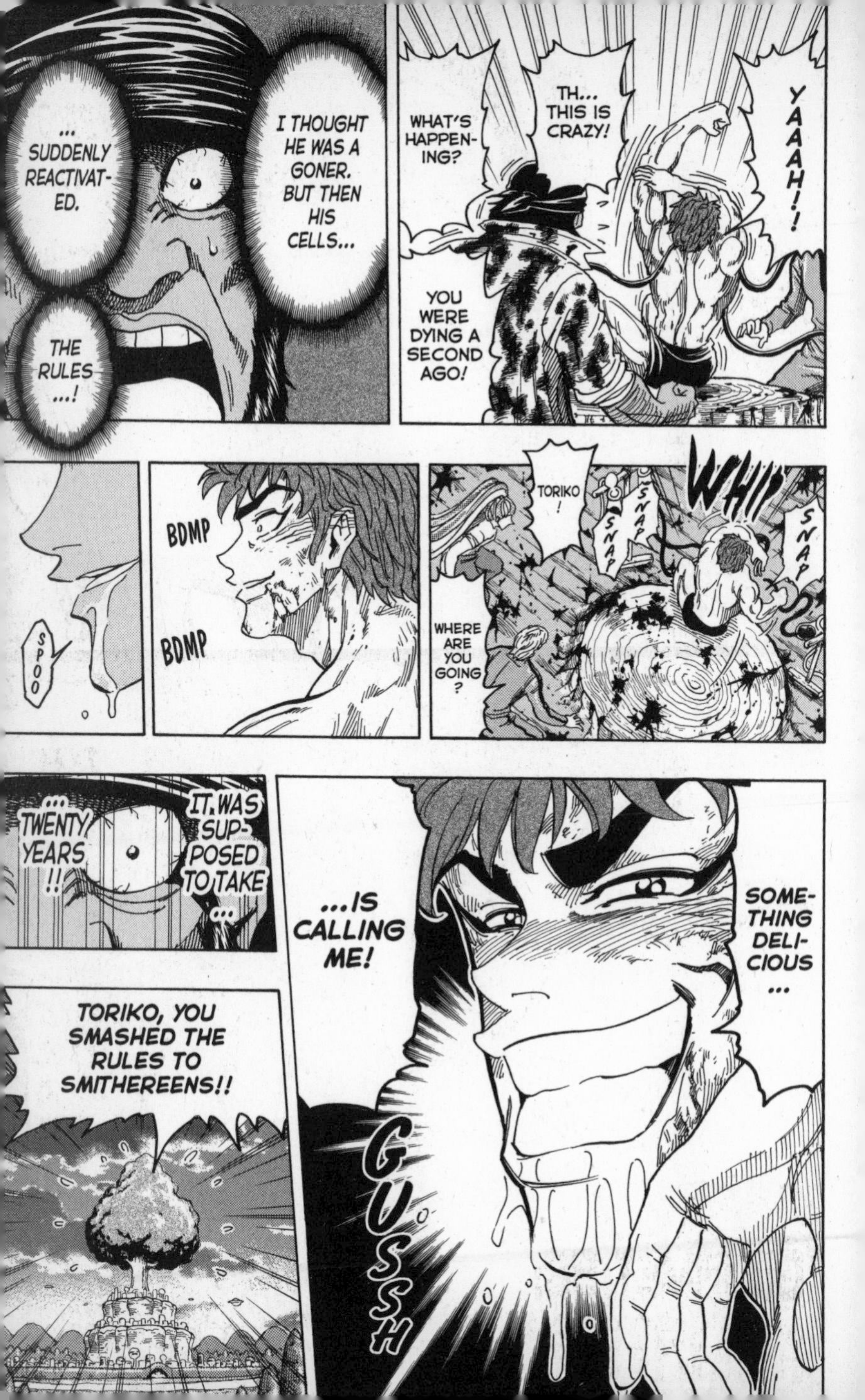
YAAAH!!
TH... THIS IS CRAZY!
WHAT'S HAPPEN-ING?
YOU WERE DYING A SECOND AGO!
I THOUGHT HE WAS A GONER. BUT THEN HIS CELLS...
... SUDDENLY REACTIVAT-ED.
THE RULES ...!
WHIP
SNAP
SNAP
TORIKO!
SNAP
WHERE ARE YOU GOING?
BDMP
BDMP
SPOO
SOME-THING DELI-CIOUS ...
...IS CALLING ME!
GUSSH
IT WAS SUP-POSED TO TAKE ...
... TWENTY YEARS!!
TORIKO, YOU SMASHED THE RULES TO SMITHEREENS!!

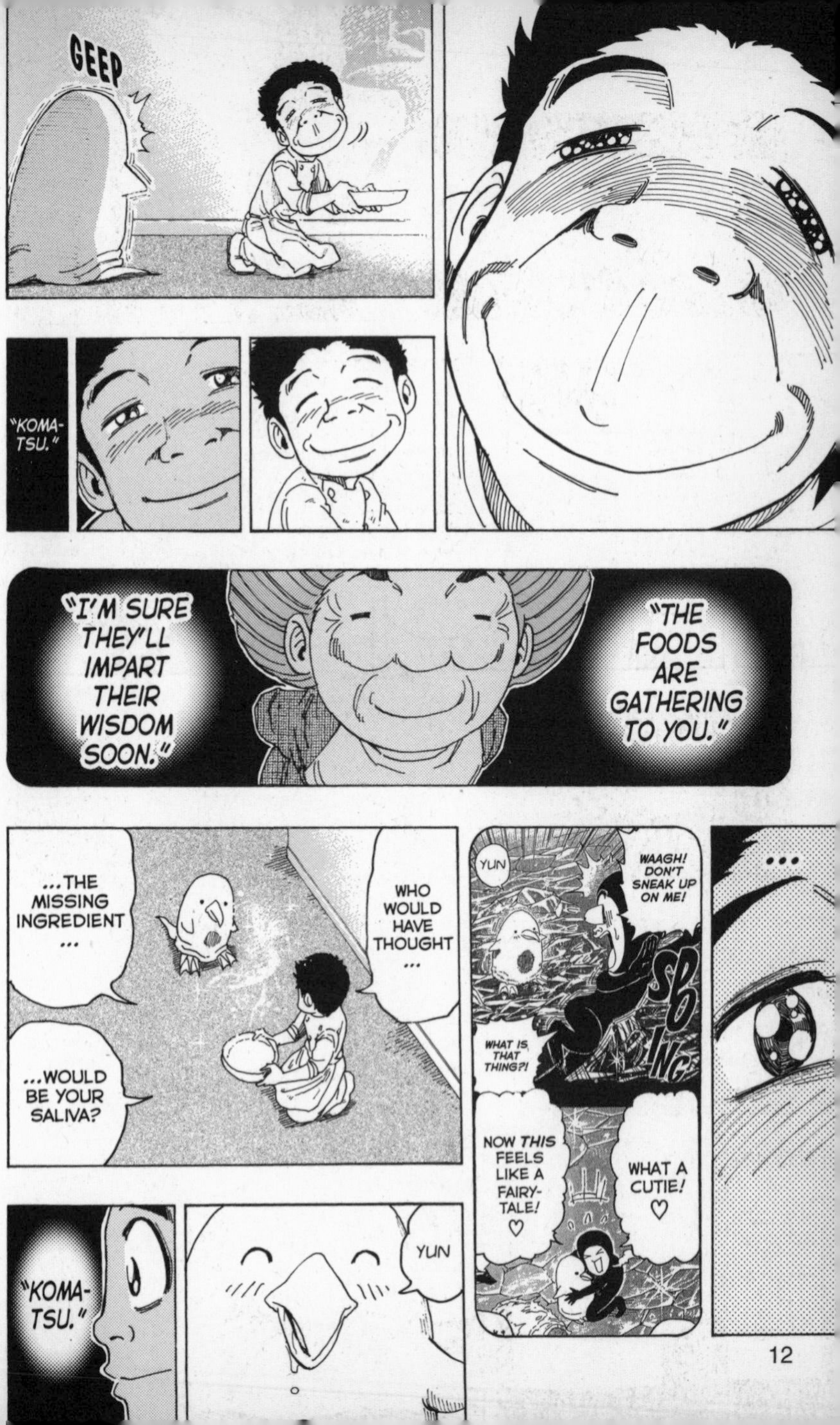
GEEP
"KOMA-TSU."
"THE FOODS ARE GATHERING TO YOU."
"I'M SURE THEY'LL IMPART THEIR WISDOM SOON."
...
YUN
WAAGH! DON'T SNEAK UP ON ME!
SBING
WHAT IS THAT THING?!
WHAT A CUTIE! ♡
NOW *THIS* FEELS LIKE A FAIRY-TALE! ♡
WHO WOULD HAVE THOUGHT...
...THE MISSING INGREDIENT...
...WOULD BE YOUR SALIVA?
YUN
"KOMA-TSU."

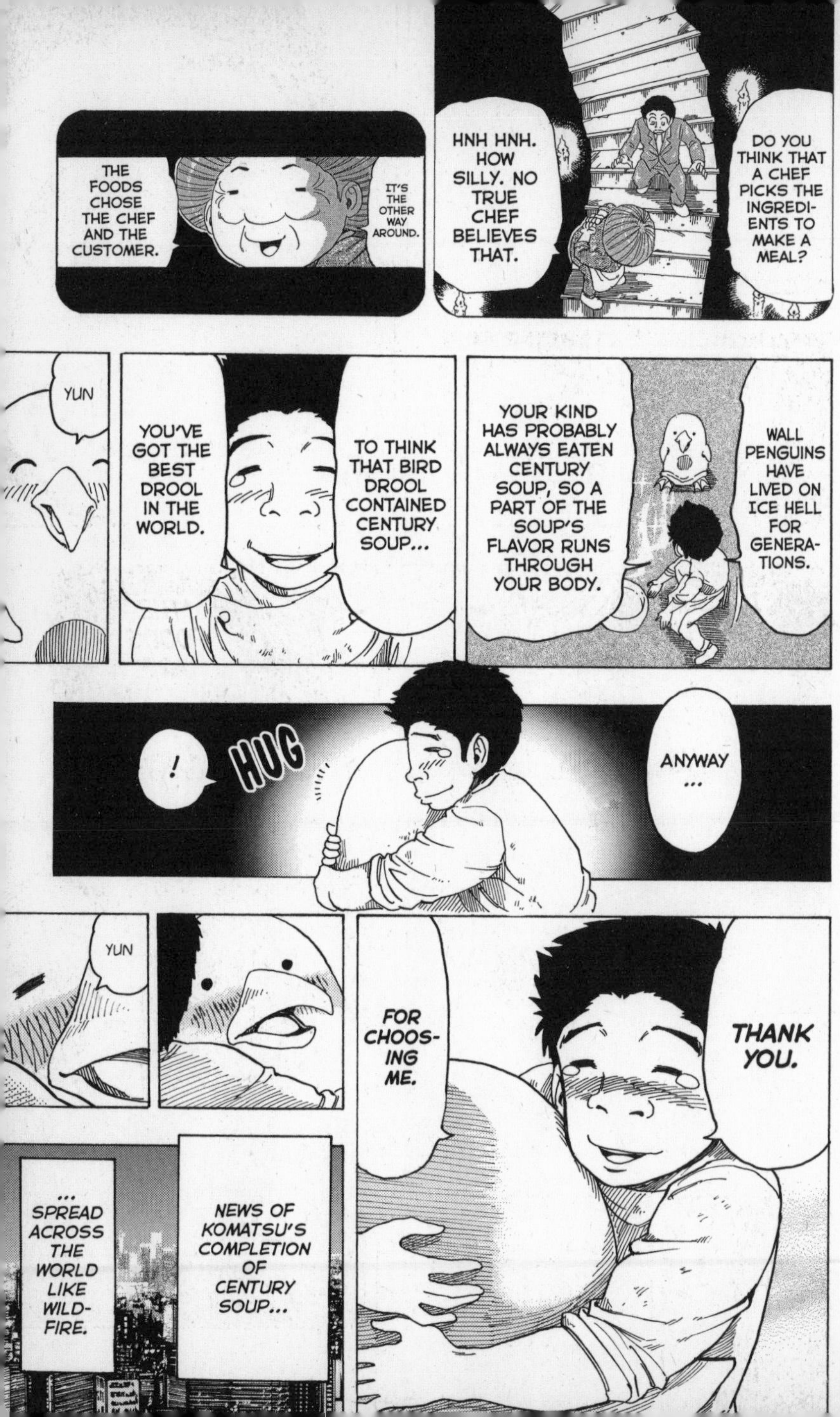
DO YOU THINK THAT A CHEF PICKS THE INGREDIENTS TO MAKE A MEAL?
HNH HNH. HOW SILLY. NO TRUE CHEF BELIEVES THAT.
IT'S THE OTHER WAY AROUND.
THE FOODS CHOSE THE CHEF AND THE CUSTOMER.
WALL PENGUINS HAVE LIVED ON ICE HELL FOR GENERATIONS.
YOUR KIND HAS PROBABLY ALWAYS EATEN CENTURY SOUP, SO A PART OF THE SOUP'S FLAVOR RUNS THROUGH YOUR BODY.
TO THINK THAT BIRD DROOL CONTAINED CENTURY SOUP...
YOU'VE GOT THE BEST DROOL IN THE WORLD.
YUN
ANYWAY ...
HUG
!
THANK YOU.
FOR CHOOSING ME.
YUN
NEWS OF KOMATSU'S COMPLETION OF CENTURY SOUP...
... SPREAD ACROSS THE WORLD LIKE WILDFIRE.

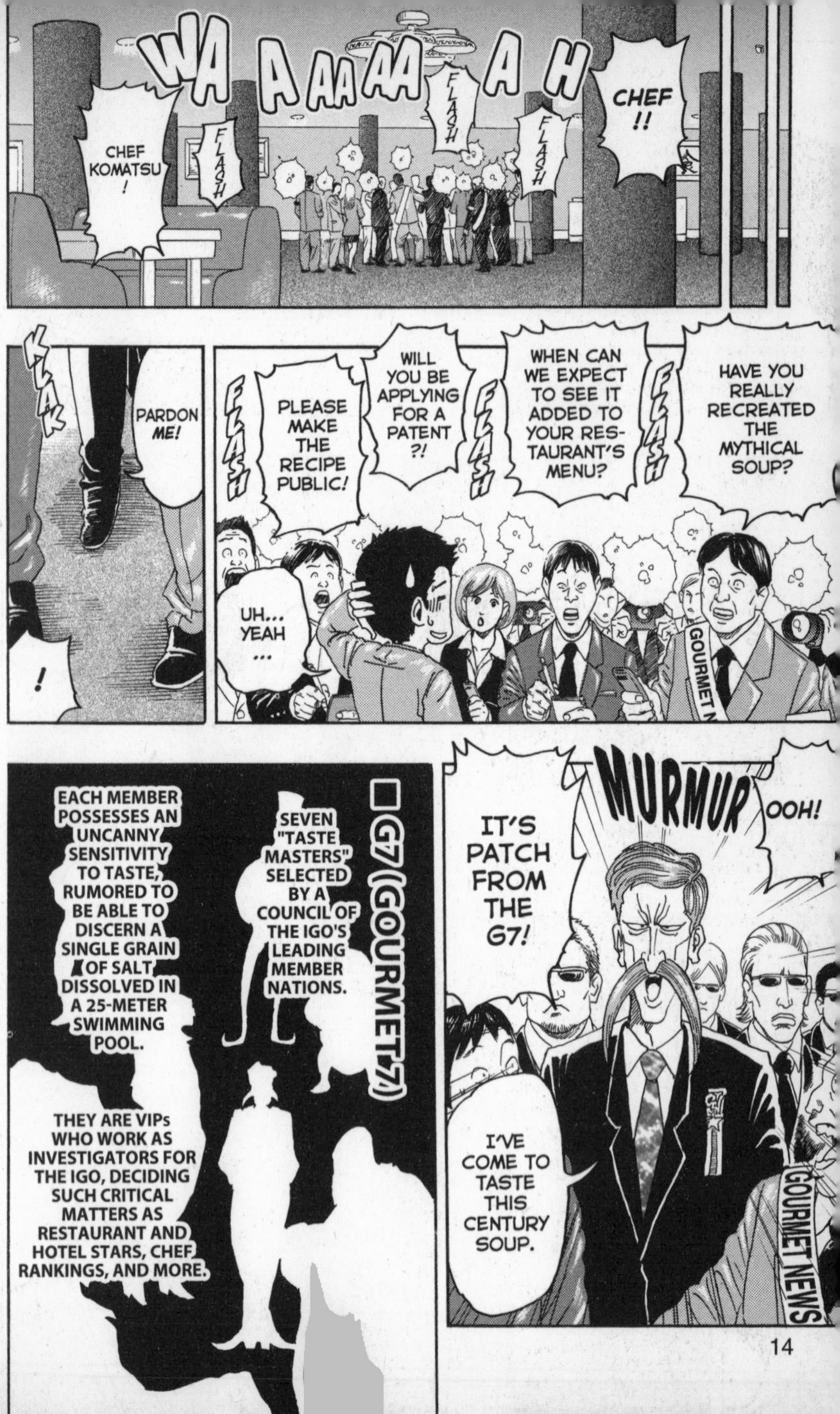
CHEF !!
FLASH
FLASH
WAAAAAAAH
FLASH
CHEF KOMATSU !
HAVE YOU REALLY RECREATED THE MYTHICAL SOUP?
FLASH
WHEN CAN WE EXPECT TO SEE IT ADDED TO YOUR RESTAURANT'S MENU?
FLASH
WILL YOU BE APPLYING FOR A PATENT ?!
PLEASE MAKE THE RECIPE PUBLIC!
FLASH
UH... YEAH ...
KLAK
PARDON ME!
!
OOH!
MURMUR
IT'S PATCH FROM THE G7!
I'VE COME TO TASTE THIS CENTURY SOUP.
GOURMET NEWS
G7 (GOURMET 7)
SEVEN "TASTE MASTERS" SELECTED BY A COUNCIL OF THE IGO'S LEADING MEMBER NATIONS.
EACH MEMBER POSSESSES AN UNCANNY SENSITIVITY TO TASTE, RUMORED TO BE ABLE TO DISCERN A SINGLE GRAIN OF SALT DISSOLVED IN A 25-METER SWIMMING POOL.
THEY ARE VIPs WHO WORK AS INVESTIGATORS FOR THE IGO, DECIDING SUCH CRITICAL MATTERS AS RESTAURANT AND HOTEL STARS, CHEF RANKINGS, AND MORE.

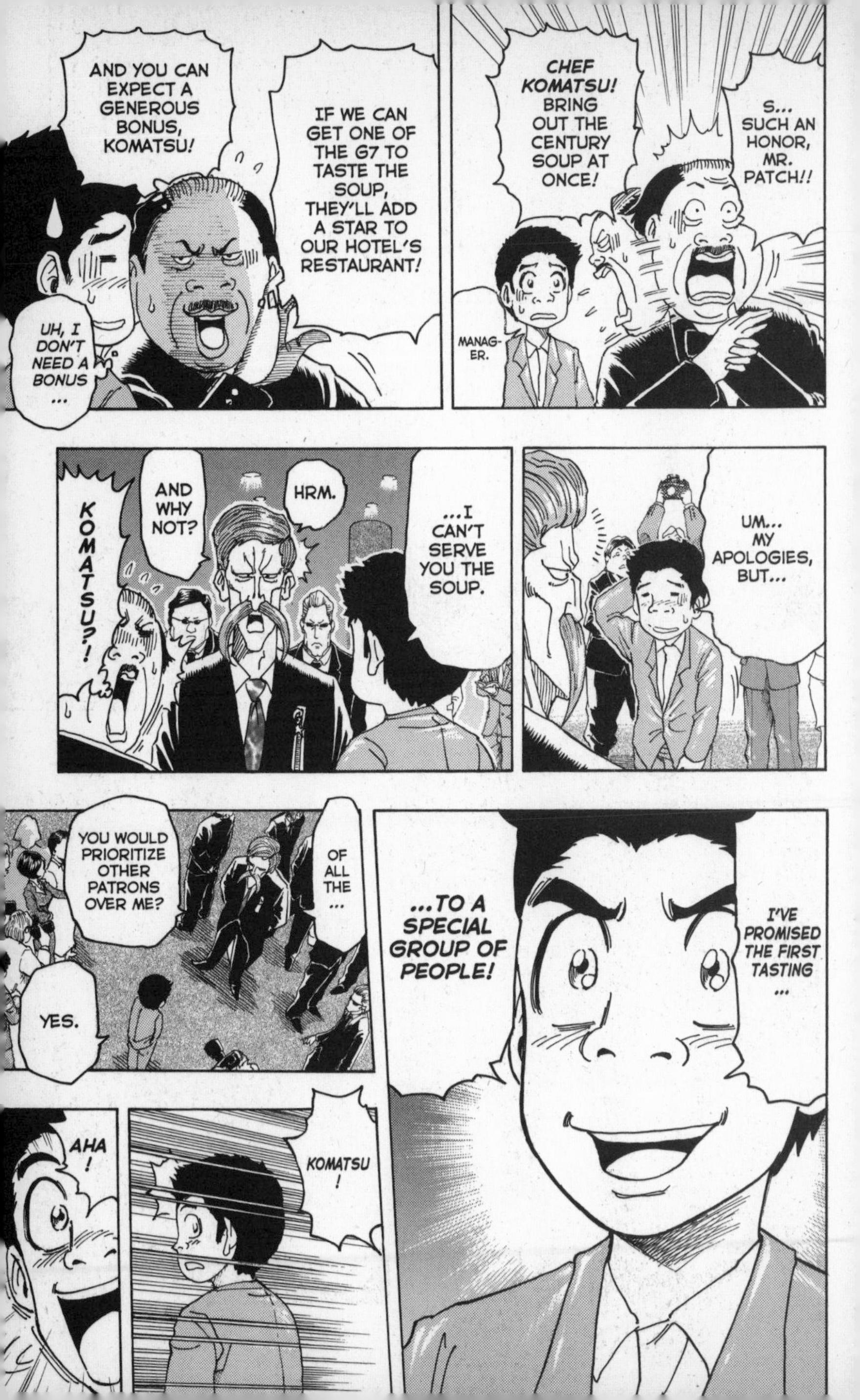
S... SUCH AN HONOR, MR. PATCH!!
CHEF KOMATSU! BRING OUT THE CENTURY SOUP AT ONCE!
MANAGER.
IF WE CAN GET ONE OF THE G7 TO TASTE THE SOUP, THEY'LL ADD A STAR TO OUR HOTEL'S RESTAURANT!
AND YOU CAN EXPECT A GENEROUS BONUS, KOMATSU!
UH, I DON'T NEED A BONUS...
UM... MY APOLOGIES, BUT...
...I CAN'T SERVE YOU THE SOUP.
HRM.
AND WHY NOT?
KOMATSU?!
I'VE PROMISED THE FIRST TASTING...
...TO A SPECIAL GROUP OF PEOPLE!
OF ALL THE...
YOU WOULD PRIORITIZE OTHER PATRONS OVER ME?
YES.
KOMATSU!
AHA!

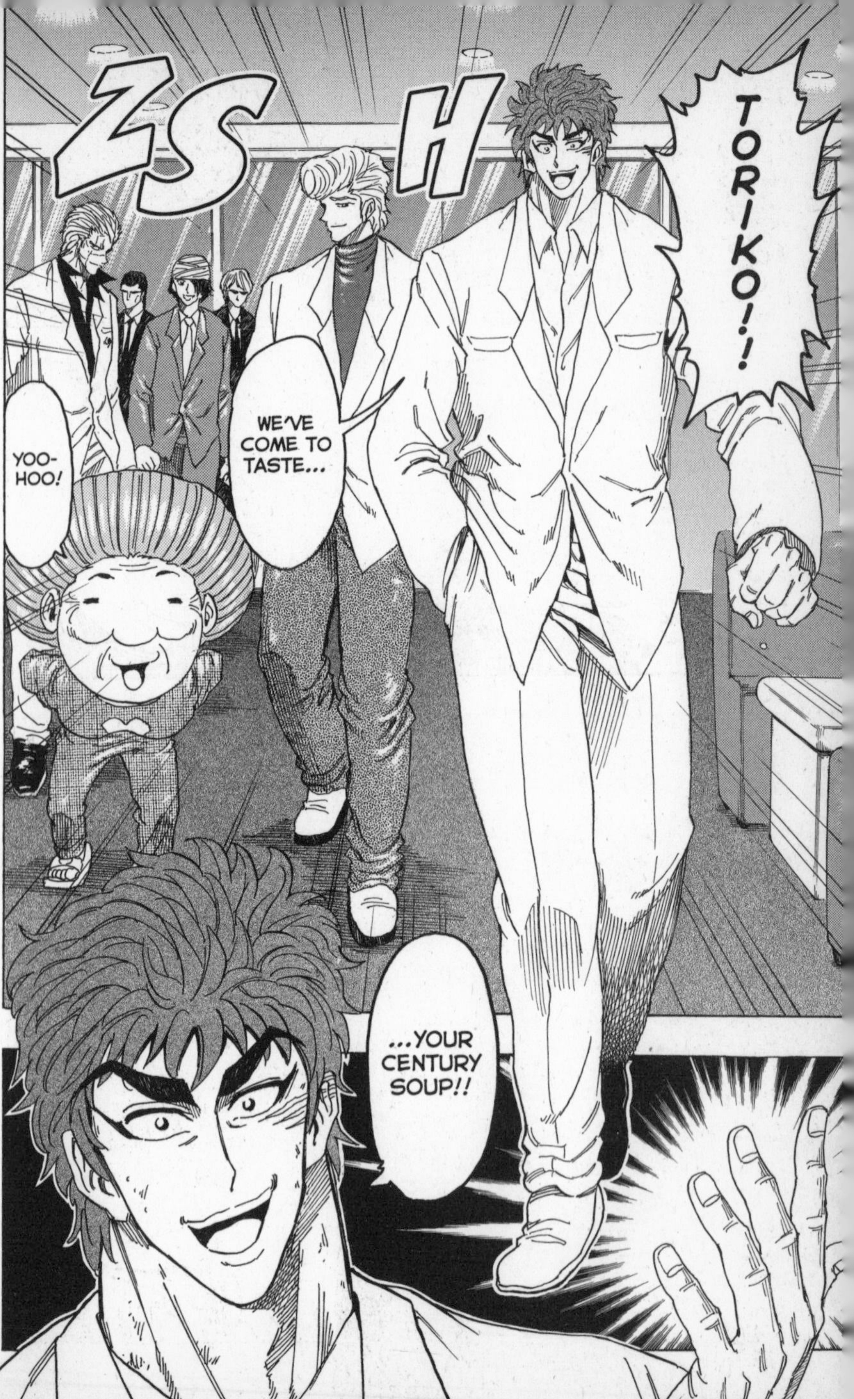
TORIKO!!
ZSH
WE'VE COME TO TASTE...
YOO-HOO!
...YOUR CENTURY SOUP!!

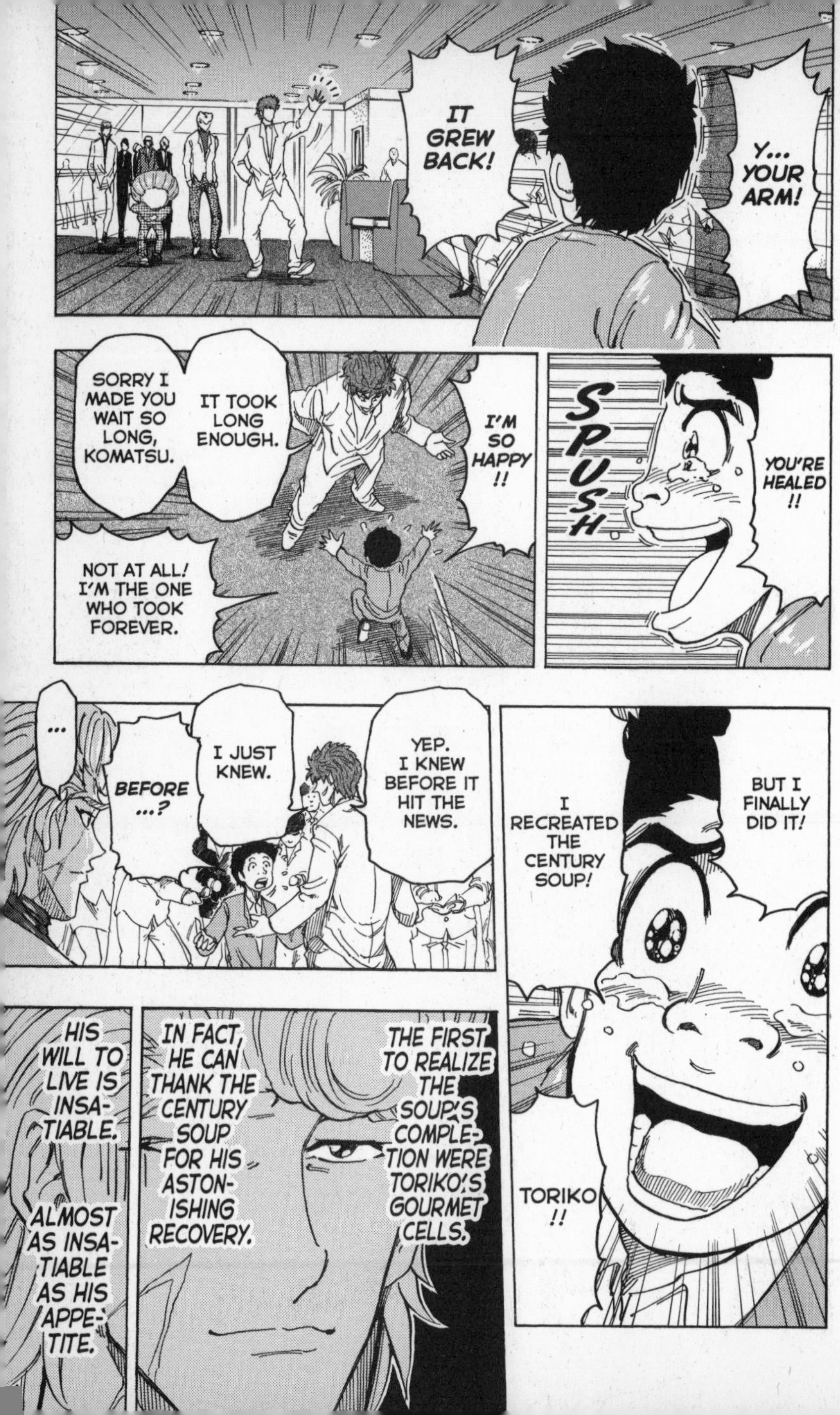
Y... YOUR ARM!
IT GREW BACK!
YOU'RE HEALED!!
SPUSH
I'M SO HAPPY!!
IT TOOK LONG ENOUGH.
SORRY I MADE YOU WAIT SO LONG, KOMATSU.
NOT AT ALL! I'M THE ONE WHO TOOK FOREVER.
BUT I FINALLY DID IT!
I RECREATED THE CENTURY SOUP!
TORIKO!!
YEP. I KNEW BEFORE IT HIT THE NEWS.
I JUST KNEW.
BEFORE...?
...
THE FIRST TO REALIZE THE SOUP'S COMPLETION WERE TORIKO'S GOURMET CELLS.
IN FACT, HE CAN THANK THE CENTURY SOUP FOR HIS ASTONISHING RECOVERY.
HIS WILL TO LIVE IS INSATIABLE.
ALMOST AS INSATIABLE AS HIS APPETITE.

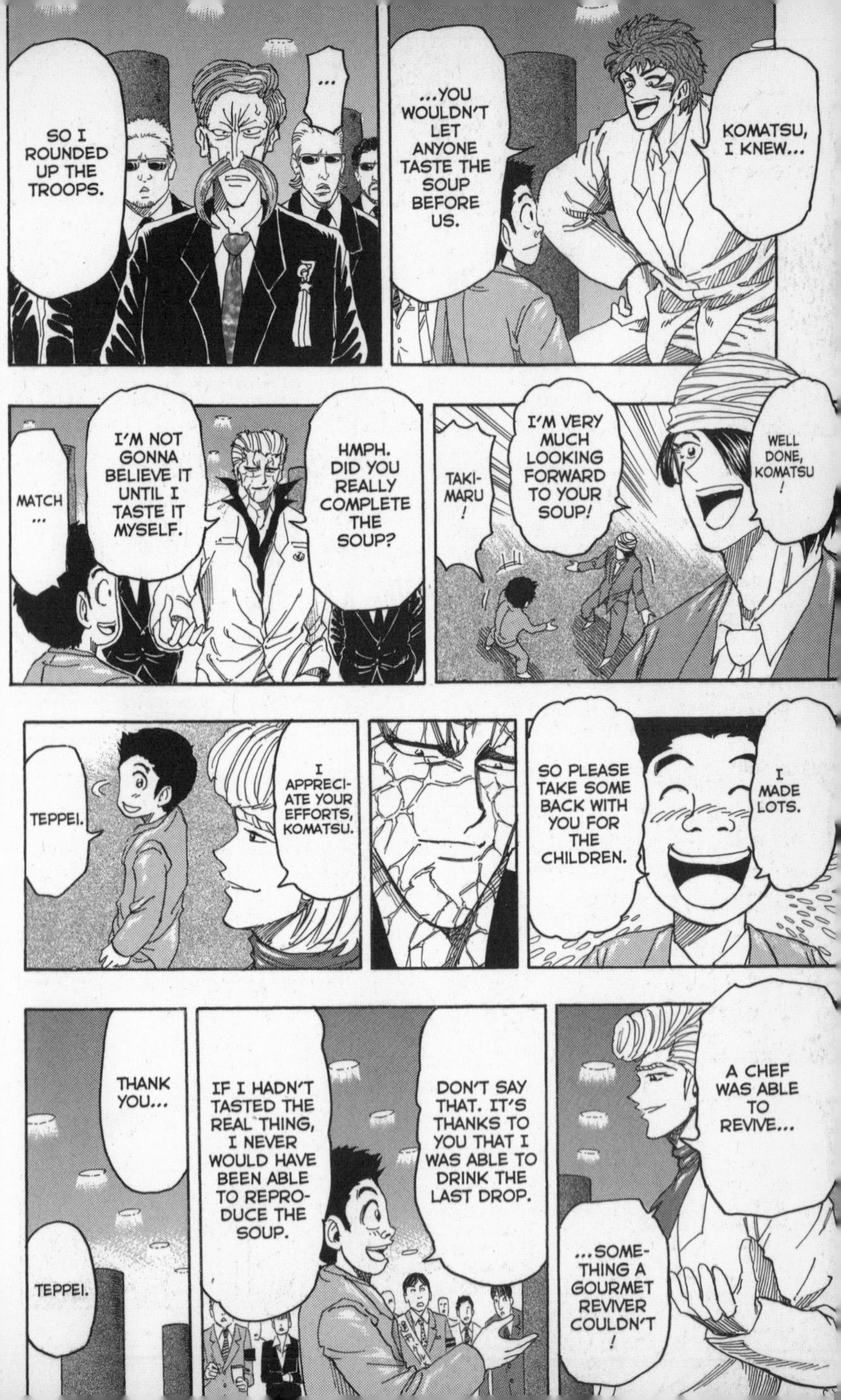
KOMATSU, I KNEW...
...YOU WOULDN'T LET ANYONE TASTE THE SOUP BEFORE US.
...
SO I ROUNDED UP THE TROOPS.
WELL DONE, KOMATSU!
I'M VERY MUCH LOOKING FORWARD TO YOUR SOUP!
TAKI-MARU!
HMPH. DID YOU REALLY COMPLETE THE SOUP?
I'M NOT GONNA BELIEVE IT UNTIL I TASTE IT MYSELF.
MATCH...
I MADE LOTS.
SO PLEASE TAKE SOME BACK WITH YOU FOR THE CHILDREN.
I APPRECIATE YOUR EFFORTS, KOMATSU.
TEPPEI.
A CHEF WAS ABLE TO REVIVE...
...SOMETHING A GOURMET REVIVER COULDN'T!
DON'T SAY THAT. IT'S THANKS TO YOU THAT I WAS ABLE TO DRINK THE LAST DROP.
IF I HADN'T TASTED THE REAL THING, I NEVER WOULD HAVE BEEN ABLE TO REPRODUCE THE SOUP.
THANK YOU...
TEPPEI.

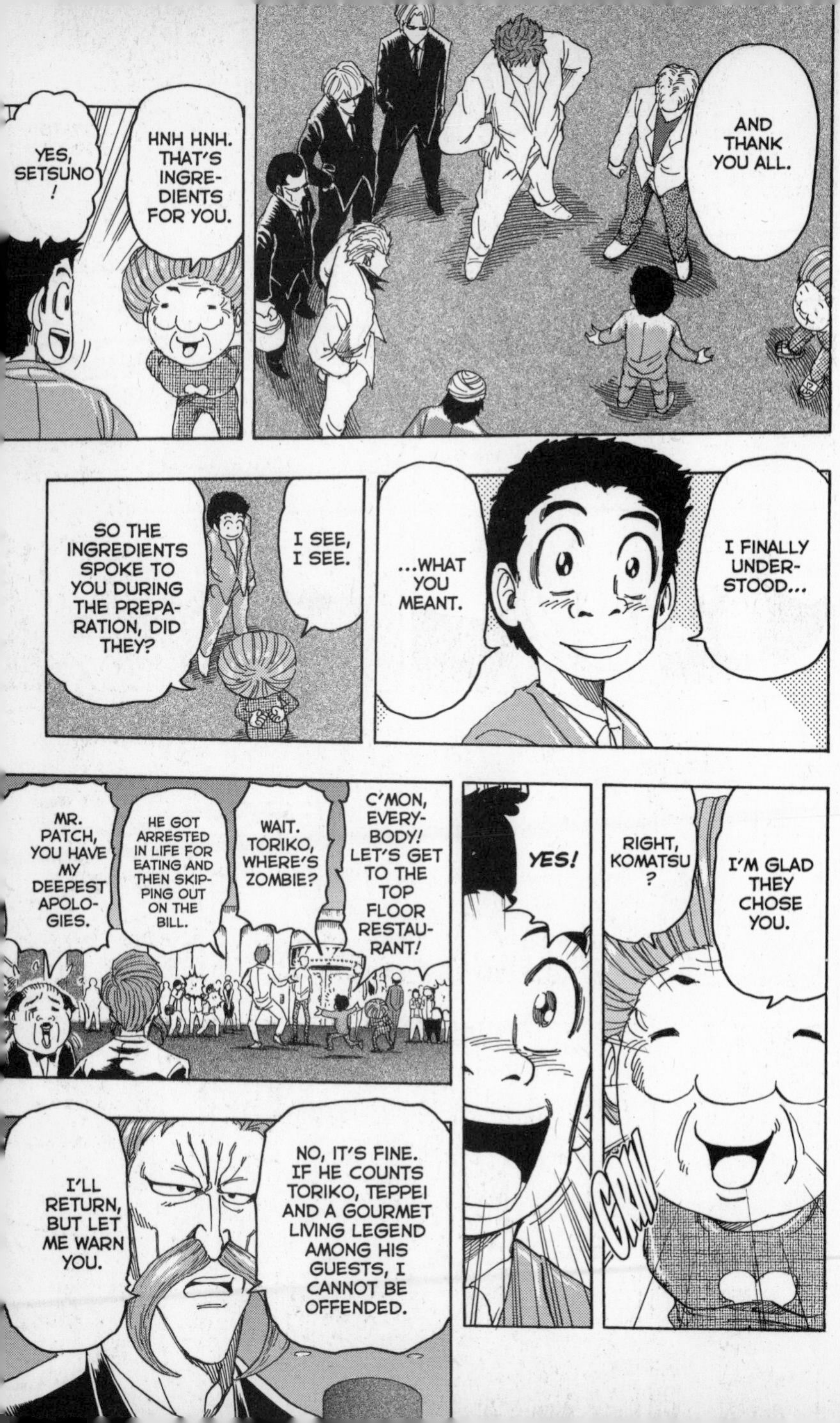
AND THANK YOU ALL.
HNH HNH. THAT'S INGREDIENTS FOR YOU.
YES, SETSUNO!
I FINALLY UNDERSTOOD...
...WHAT YOU MEANT.
I SEE, I SEE.
SO THE INGREDIENTS SPOKE TO YOU DURING THE PREPARATION, DID THEY?
I'M GLAD THEY CHOSE YOU.
RIGHT, KOMATSU?
YES!
C'MON, EVERYBODY! LET'S GET TO THE TOP FLOOR RESTAURANT!
WAIT. TORIKO, WHERE'S ZOMBIE?
HE GOT ARRESTED IN LIFE FOR EATING AND THEN SKIPPING OUT ON THE BILL.
MR. PATCH, YOU HAVE MY DEEPEST APOLOGIES.
NO, IT'S FINE. IF HE COUNTS TORIKO, TEPPEI AND A GOURMET LIVING LEGEND AMONG HIS GUESTS, I CANNOT BE OFFENDED.
I'LL RETURN, BUT LET ME WARN YOU.

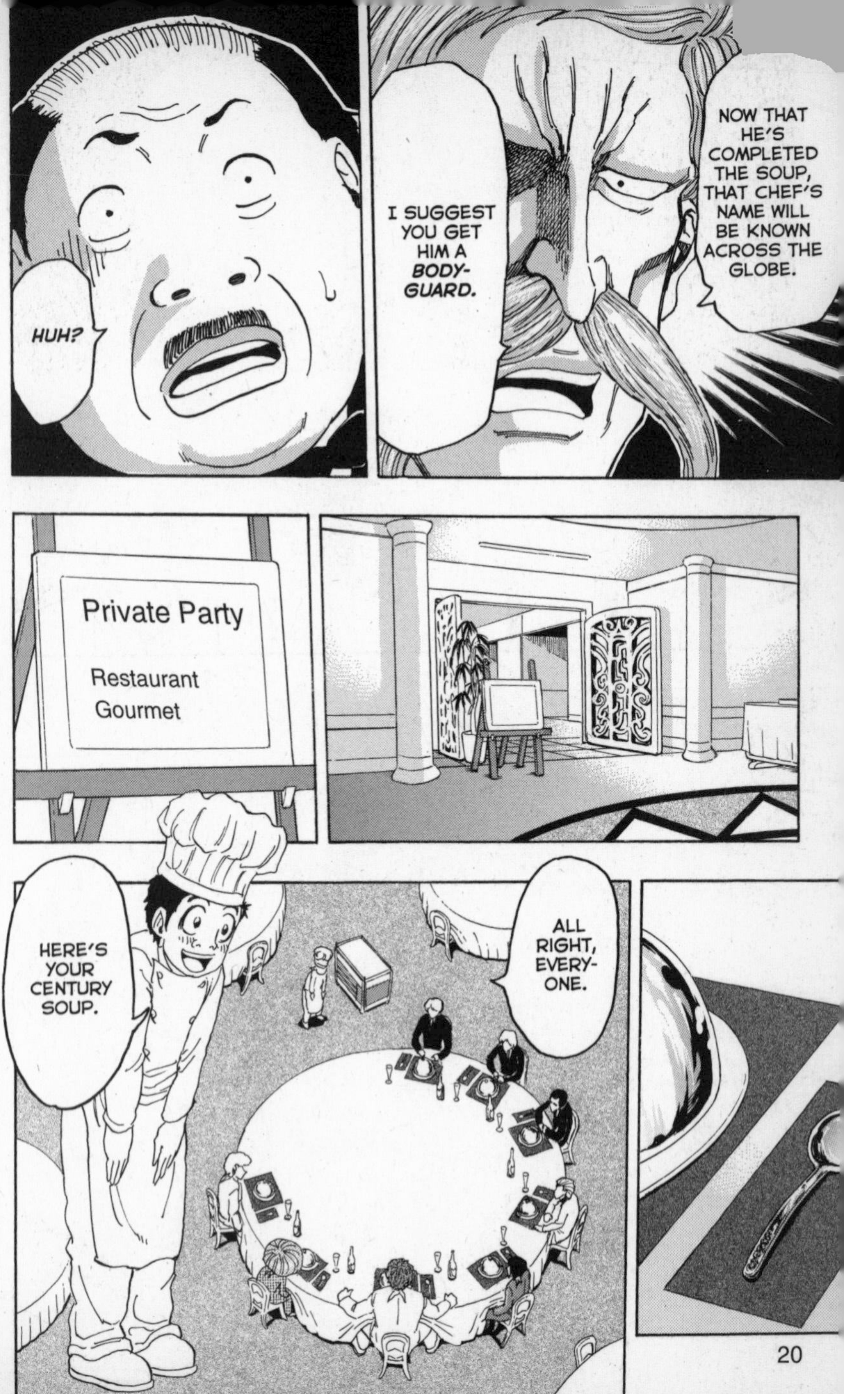
NOW THAT HE'S COMPLETED THE SOUP, THAT CHEF'S NAME WILL BE KNOWN ACROSS THE GLOBE.
I SUGGEST YOU GET HIM A *BODY-GUARD.*
HUH?
Private Party
Restaurant Gourmet
ALL RIGHT, EVERY-ONE.
HERE'S YOUR CENTURY SOUP.

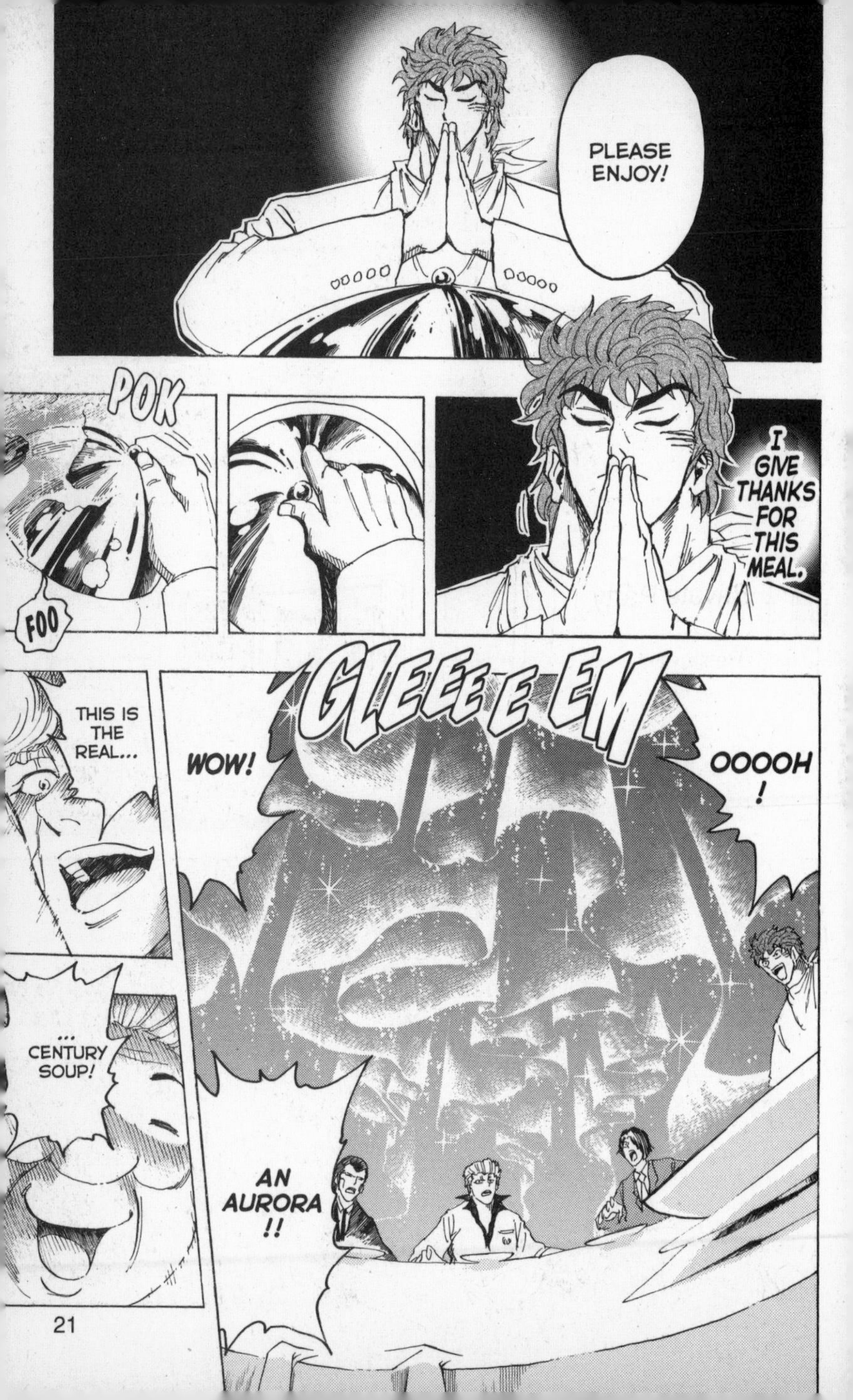
PLEASE ENJOY!
I GIVE THANKS FOR THIS MEAL.
POK
FOO
GLEEE E EM
OOOOH!
WOW!
AN AURORA!!
THIS IS THE REAL...
... CENTURY SOUP!

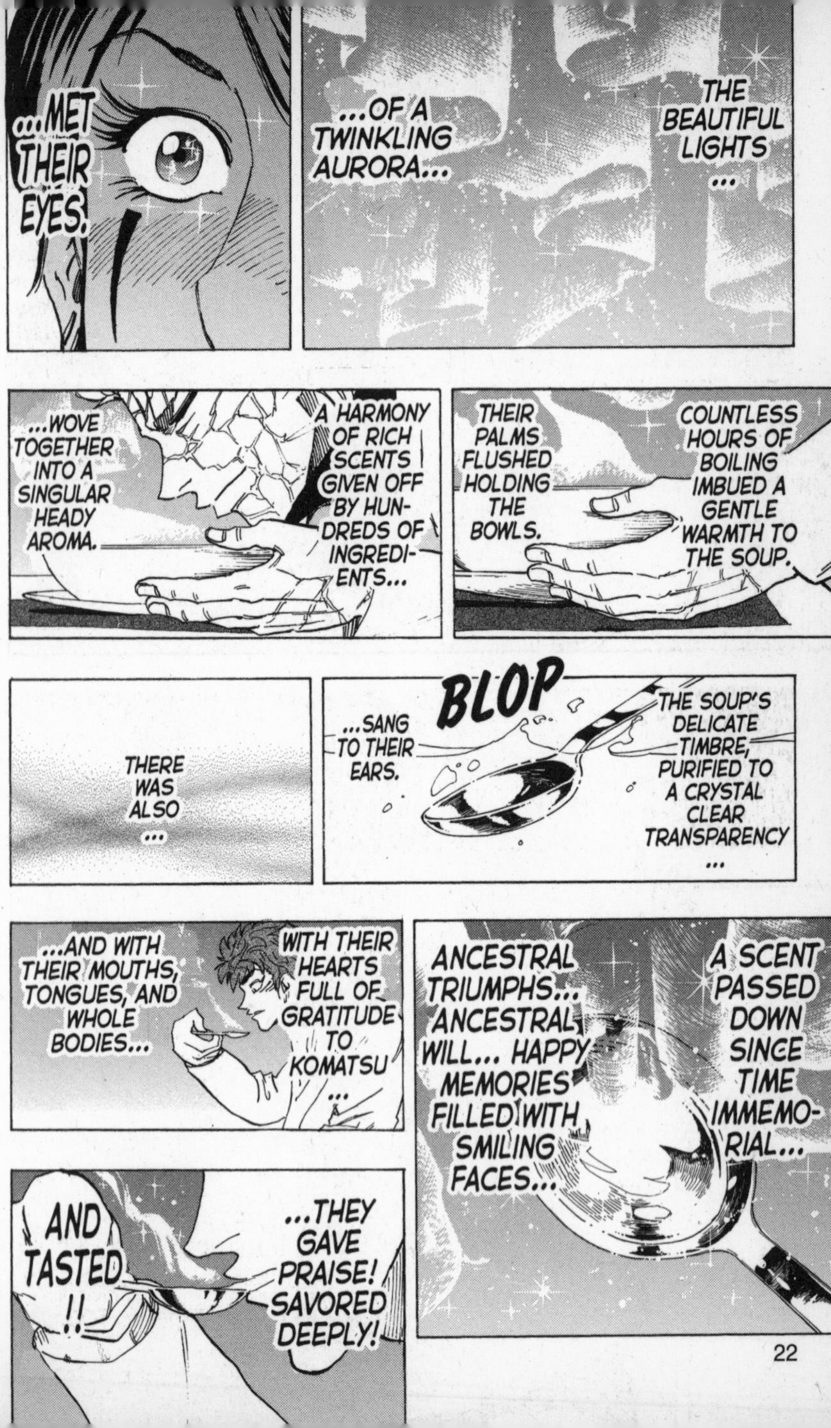
THE BEAUTIFUL LIGHTS...
...OF A TWINKLING AURORA...
...MET THEIR EYES.
COUNTLESS HOURS OF BOILING IMBUED A GENTLE WARMTH TO THE SOUP.
THEIR PALMS FLUSHED HOLDING THE BOWLS.
A HARMONY OF RICH SCENTS GIVEN OFF BY HUNDREDS OF INGREDIENTS...
...WOVE TOGETHER INTO A SINGULAR HEADY AROMA.
THE SOUP'S DELICATE TIMBRE, PURIFIED TO A CRYSTAL CLEAR TRANSPARENCY...
BLOP
...SANG TO THEIR EARS.
THERE WAS ALSO...
A SCENT PASSED DOWN SINCE TIME IMMEMORIAL...
ANCESTRAL TRIUMPHS... ANCESTRAL WILL... HAPPY MEMORIES FILLED WITH SMILING FACES...
WITH THEIR HEARTS FULL OF GRATITUDE TO KOMATSU...
...AND WITH THEIR MOUTHS, TONGUES, AND WHOLE BODIES...
...THEY GAVE PRAISE! SAVORED DEEPLY!
AND TASTED!!

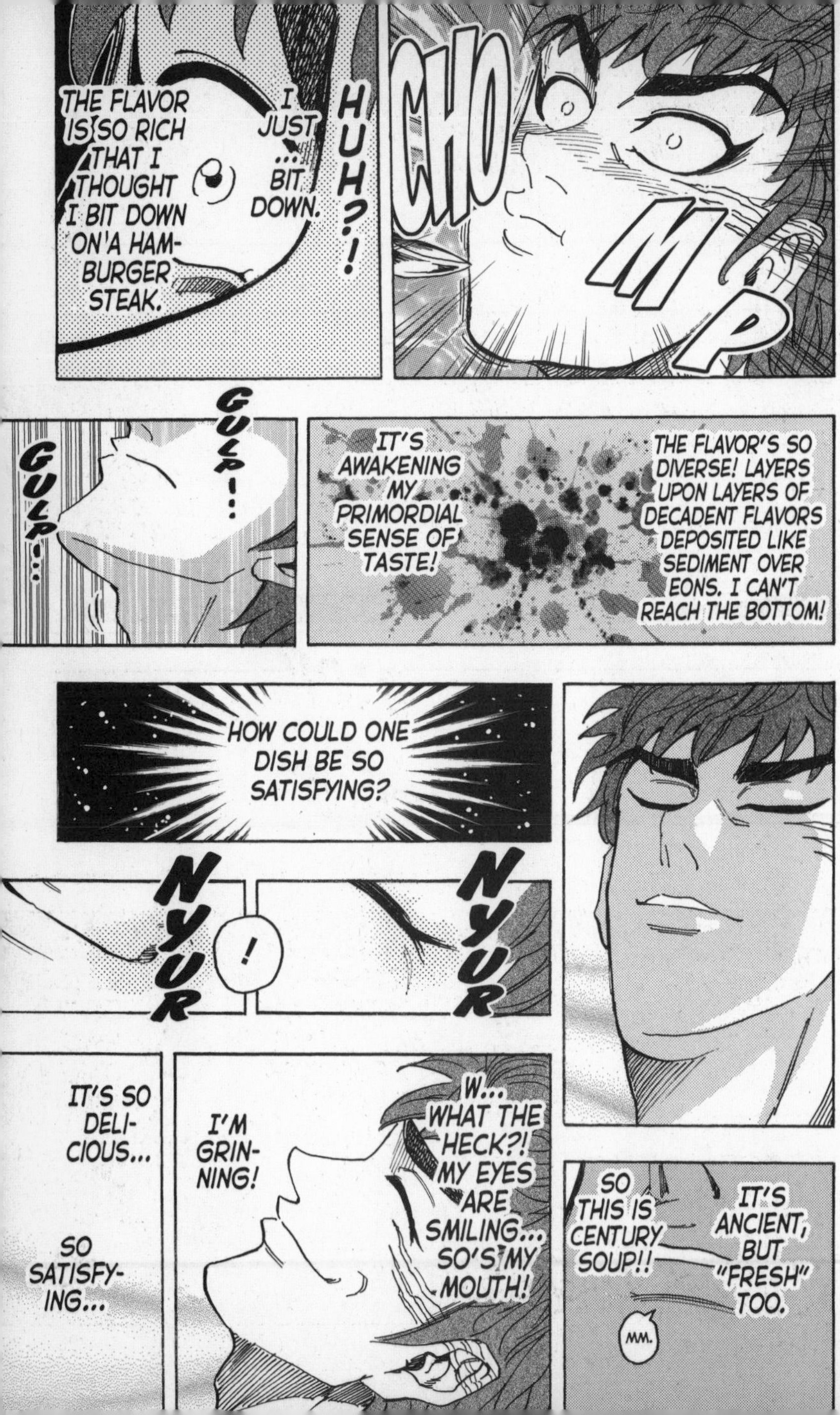
CHOMP
HUH?!
I JUST ... BIT DOWN.
THE FLAVOR IS SO RICH THAT I THOUGHT I BIT DOWN ON A HAMBURGER STEAK.
THE FLAVOR'S SO DIVERSE! LAYERS UPON LAYERS OF DECADENT FLAVORS DEPOSITED LIKE SEDIMENT OVER EONS. I CAN'T REACH THE BOTTOM!
IT'S AWAKENING MY PRIMORDIAL SENSE OF TASTE!
GULP...
GULP...
HOW COULD ONE DISH BE SO SATISFYING?
NYUR
!
NYUR
IT'S ANCIENT, BUT "FRESH" TOO.
SO THIS IS CENTURY SOUP!!
MM.
W... WHAT THE HECK?! MY EYES ARE SMILING... SO'S MY MOUTH!
I'M GRINNING!
IT'S SO DELICIOUS...
SO SATISFYING...

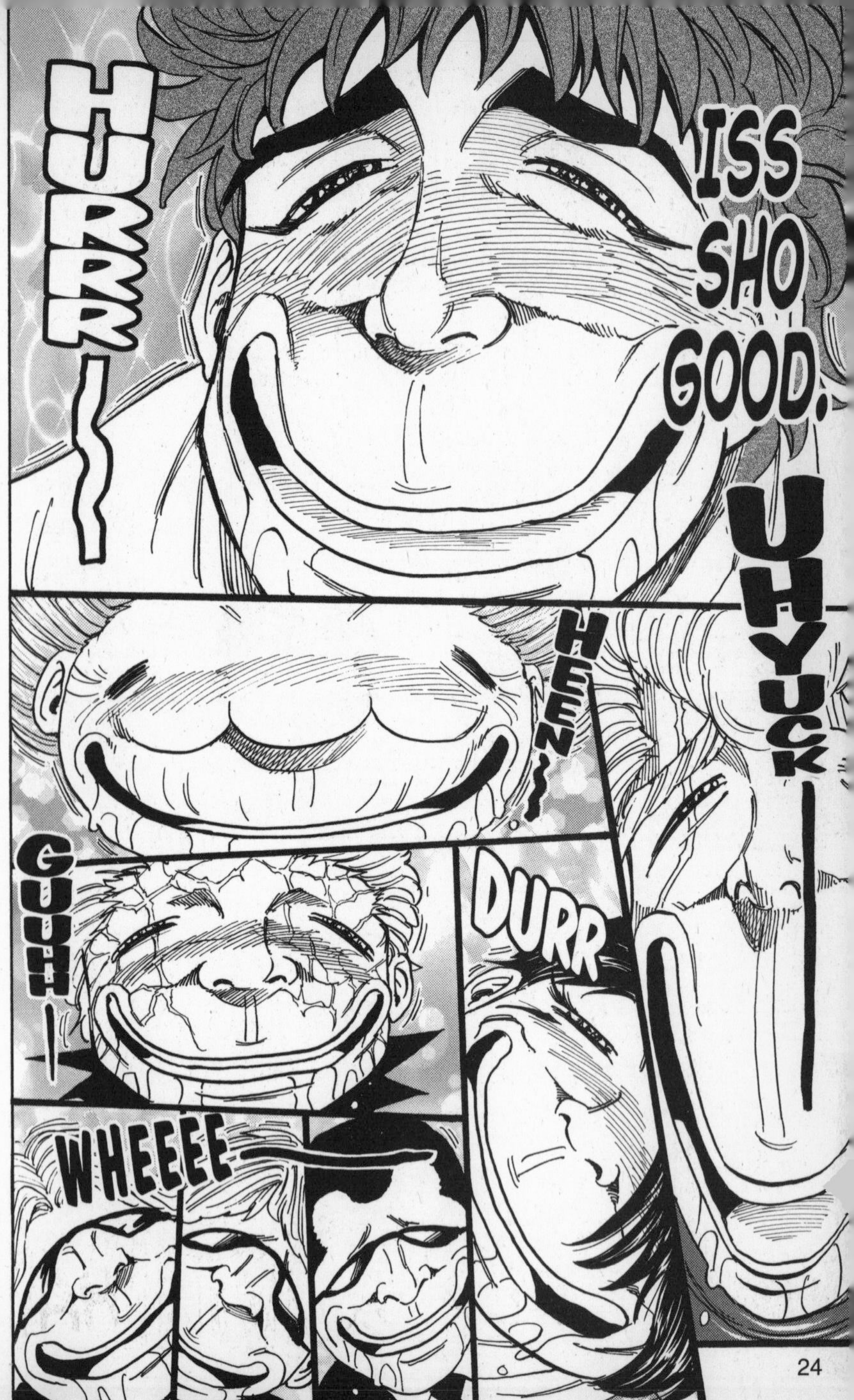
ISS SHO GOOD.
HURRR~
UHYUCK—
HEEN~
DURR
GUUH—
WHEEEE—

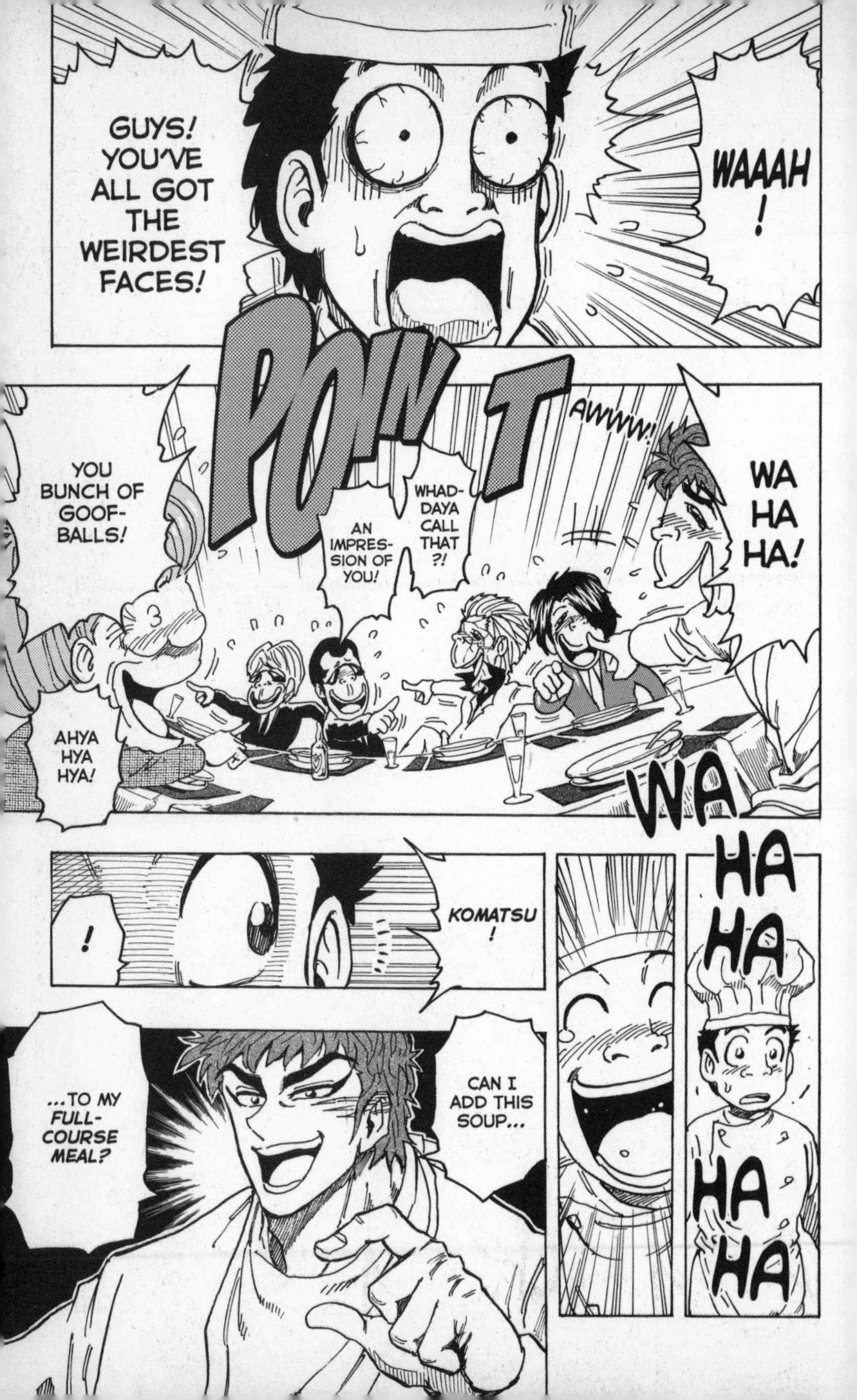

WAAAH!
GUYS! YOU'VE ALL GOT THE WEIRDEST FACES!
POIN T
AWWW!
WA HA HA!
WHAD-DAYA CALL THAT?!
AN IMPRES-SION OF YOU!
YOU BUNCH OF GOOF-BALLS!
AHYA HYA HYA!
WA HA HA HA HA HA HA
KOMATSU!
...!
!
CAN I ADD THIS SOUP...
...TO MY FULL-COURSE MEAL?

TORIKO

GOURMET CHECKLIST

Vol. 107

PARASITE EMPEROR
(INSECT)

CAPTURE LEVEL: 81

HABITAT: TOMMYROD'S INSIDES

LENGTH: 10 METERS

HEIGHT: ---

WEIGHT: 7 TONS

PRICE: NO VALUE AS A FOODSTUFF

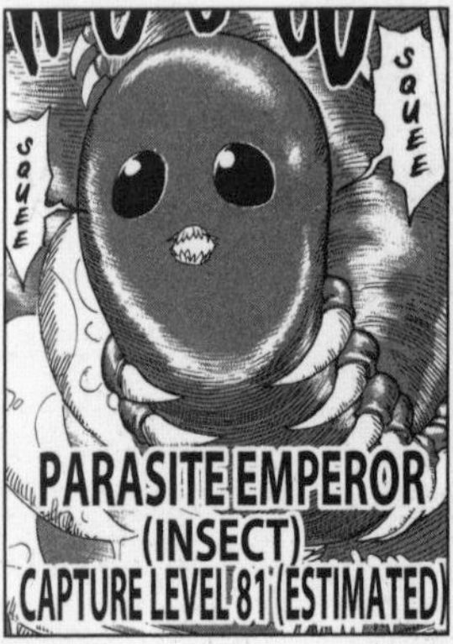

SQUEE
SQUEE
PARASITE EMPEROR
(INSECT)
CAPTURE LEVEL 81 (ESTIMATED)

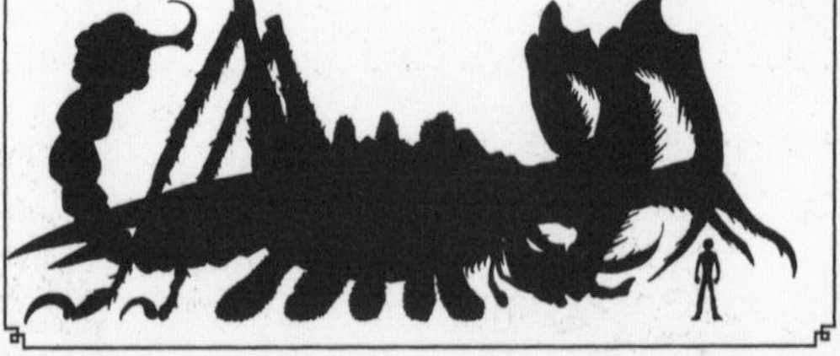

SCALE

THE HYBRID SPAWN OF DOZENS OF VIOLENT INSECTS THAT RESIDE WITHIN TOMMYROD, VICE-CHEF OF GOURMET CORP. TOMMY MUST EXERT HALF OF HIS STRENGTH JUST TO KEEP THIS LIVING TERROR FROM BEING BORN. IT IS A TRULY AMORAL CREATURE THAT ATTACKS INDISCRIMINATELY. IT IS CAPABLE OF UTTERLY ANNIHILATING EVERYTHING AROUND IT BY SPEWING SUB-ZERO BREATH, FIERY GASES, SPIDER'S WEBBING, AND SCORPION VENOM--MAKING IT ONE OF THE SINGLE MOST DANGEROUS INSECTS IN THE HUMAN WORLD.

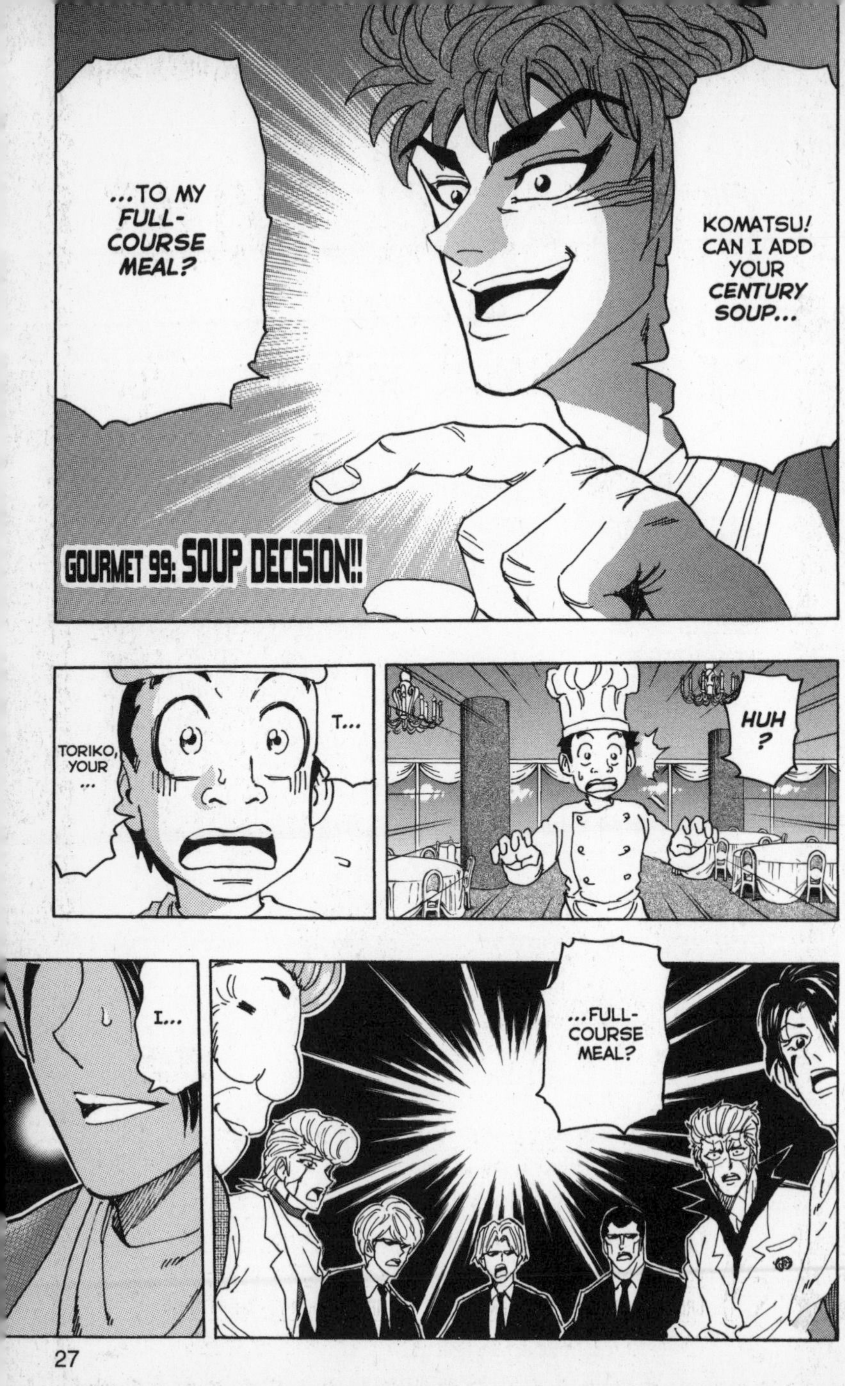
KOMATSU! CAN I ADD YOUR CENTURY SOUP...
...TO MY FULL-COURSE MEAL?
GOURMET 99: SOUP DECISION!!
HUH?
T...
TORIKO, YOUR ...
...FULL-COURSE MEAL?
I...

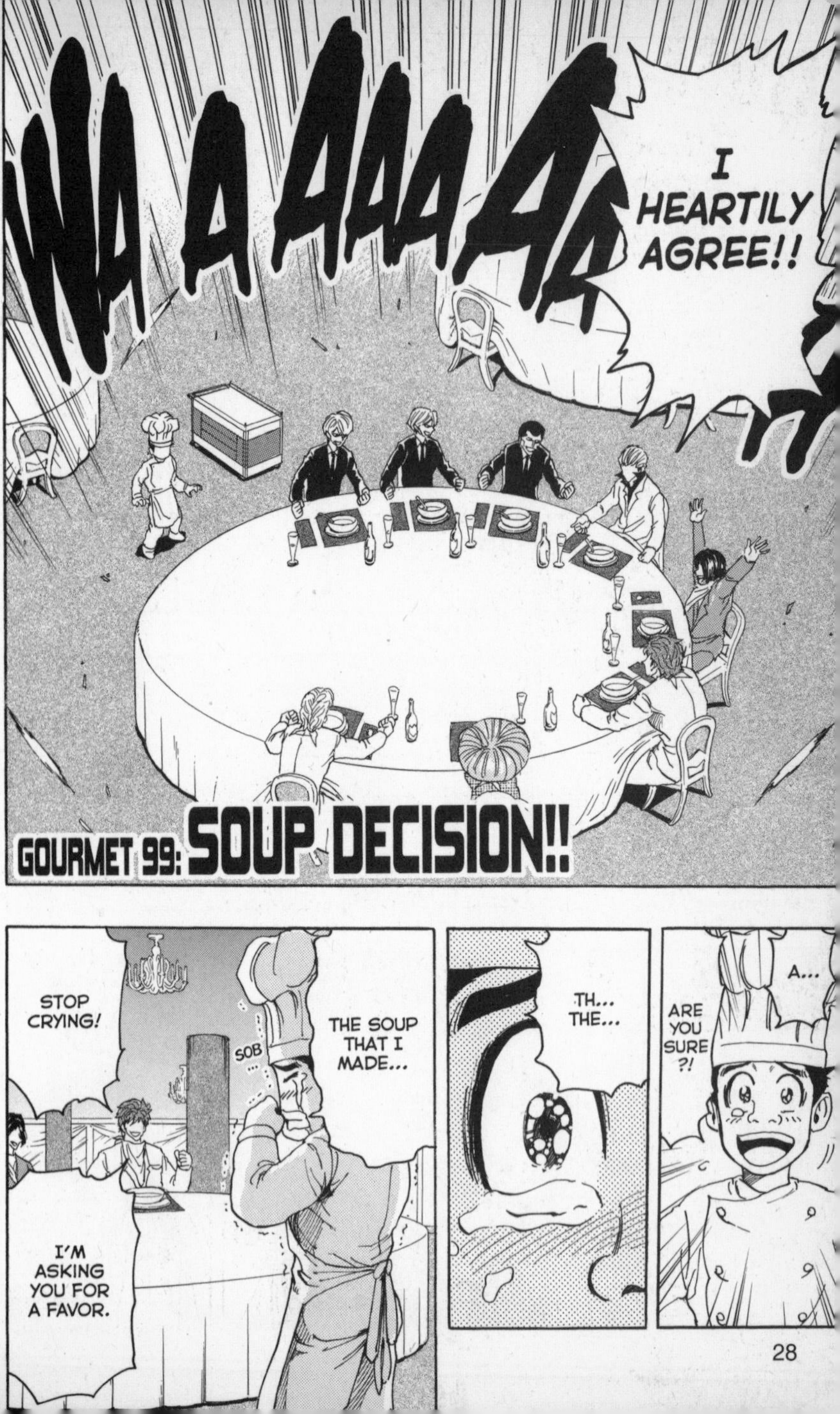

WAAAAAAA
I HEARTILY AGREE!!
GOURMET 99: SOUP DECISION!!
A...
ARE YOU SURE?!
TH... THE...
THE SOUP THAT I MADE...
SOB...
STOP CRYING!
I'M ASKING YOU FOR A FAVOR.

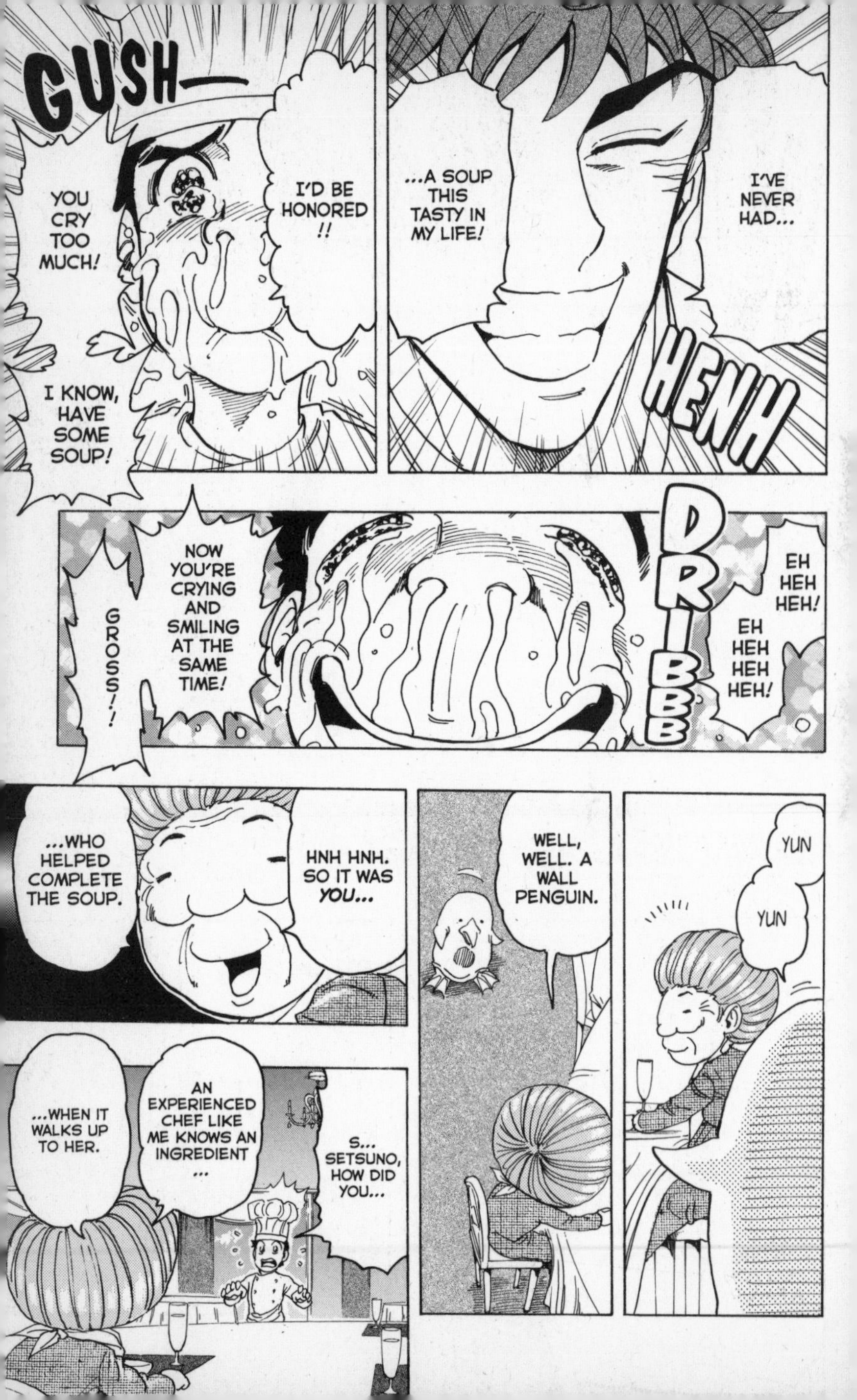
I'VE NEVER HAD...
...A SOUP THIS TASTY IN MY LIFE!
HENH
GUSH—
I'D BE HONORED!!
YOU CRY TOO MUCH!
I KNOW, HAVE SOME SOUP!
DRIBBB
EH HEH HEH!
EH HEH HEH HEH!
NOW YOU'RE CRYING AND SMILING AT THE SAME TIME!
GROSS!!
YUN
YUN
WELL, WELL. A WALL PENGUIN.
HNH HNH. SO IT WAS *YOU*...
...WHO HELPED COMPLETE THE SOUP.
S... SETSUNO, HOW DID YOU...
AN EXPERIENCED CHEF LIKE ME KNOWS AN INGREDIENT...
...WHEN IT WALKS UP TO HER.

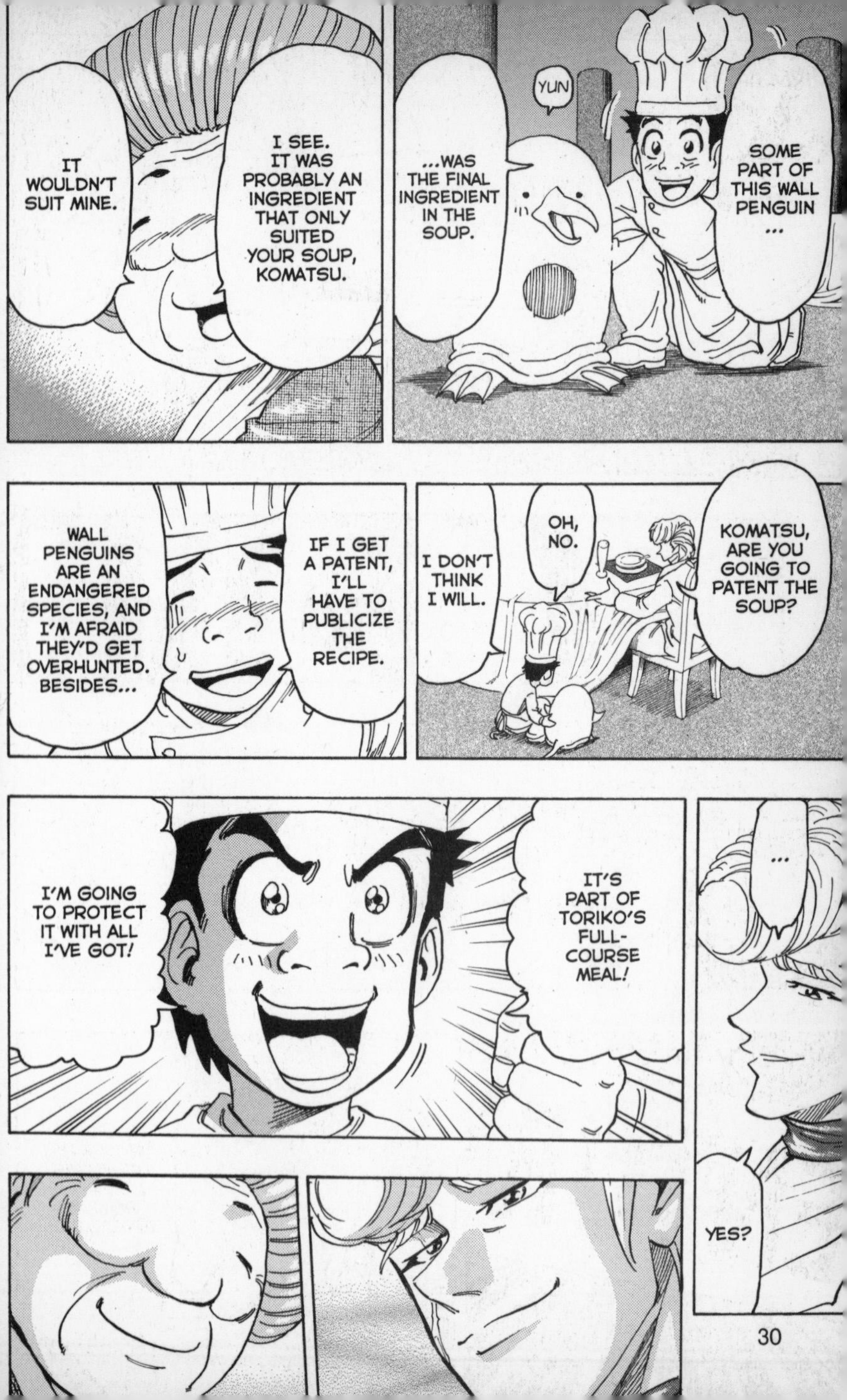
SOME PART OF THIS WALL PENGUIN...
YUN
...WAS THE FINAL INGREDIENT IN THE SOUP.
I SEE. IT WAS PROBABLY AN INGREDIENT THAT ONLY SUITED YOUR SOUP, KOMATSU.
IT WOULDN'T SUIT MINE.
KOMATSU, ARE YOU GOING TO PATENT THE SOUP?
OH, NO.
I DON'T THINK I WILL.
IF I GET A PATENT, I'LL HAVE TO PUBLICIZE THE RECIPE.
WALL PENGUINS ARE AN ENDANGERED SPECIES, AND I'M AFRAID THEY'D GET OVERHUNTED. BESIDES...
...
YES?
IT'S PART OF TORIKO'S FULL-COURSE MEAL!
I'M GOING TO PROTECT IT WITH ALL I'VE GOT!

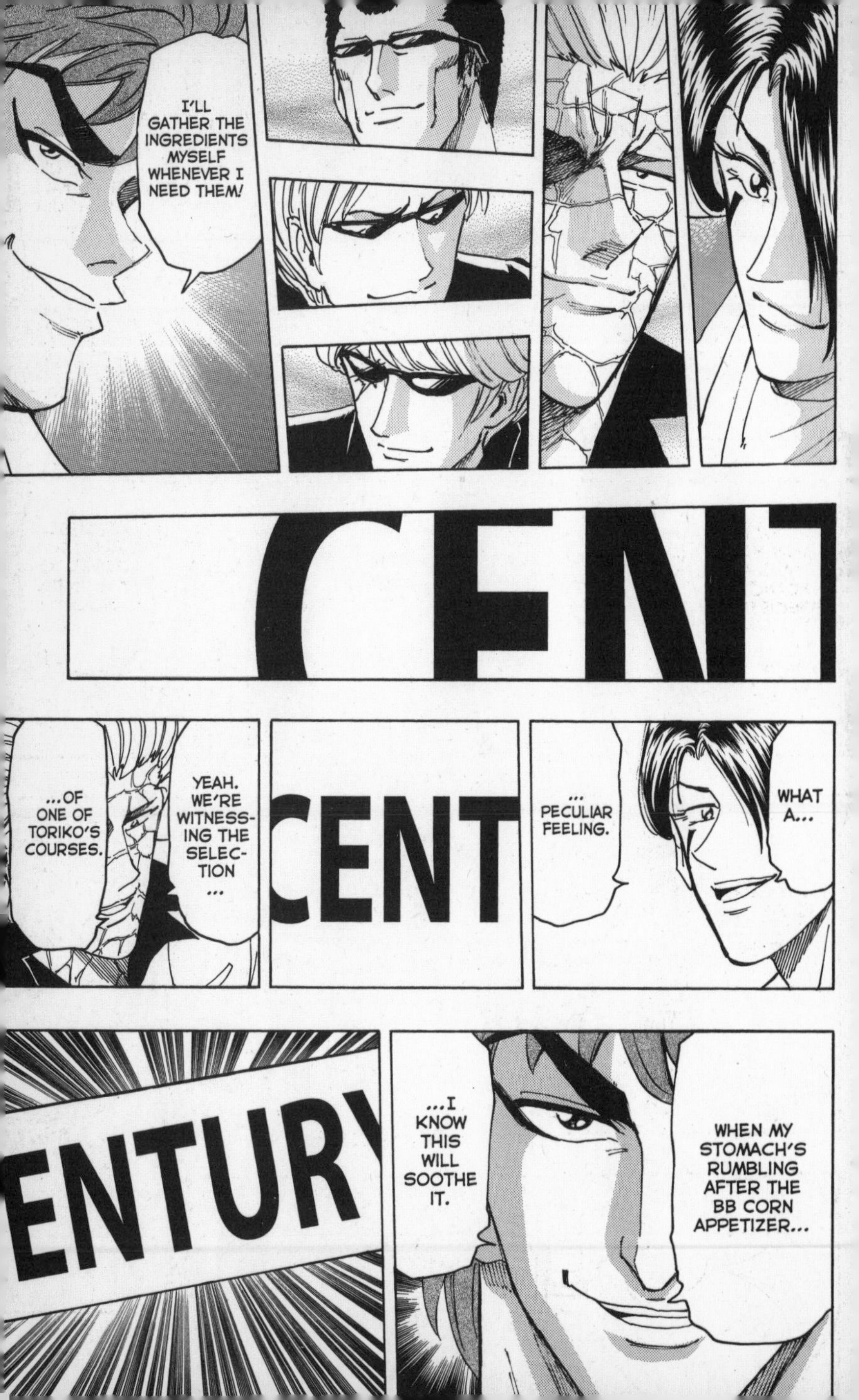
I'LL GATHER THE INGREDIENTS MYSELF WHENEVER I NEED THEM!
CENT
WHAT A...
...PECULIAR FEELING.
CENT
YEAH. WE'RE WITNESSING THE SELECTION...
...OF ONE OF TORIKO'S COURSES.
WHEN MY STOMACH'S RUMBLING AFTER THE BB CORN APPETIZER...
...I KNOW THIS WILL SOOTHE IT.
ENTURY

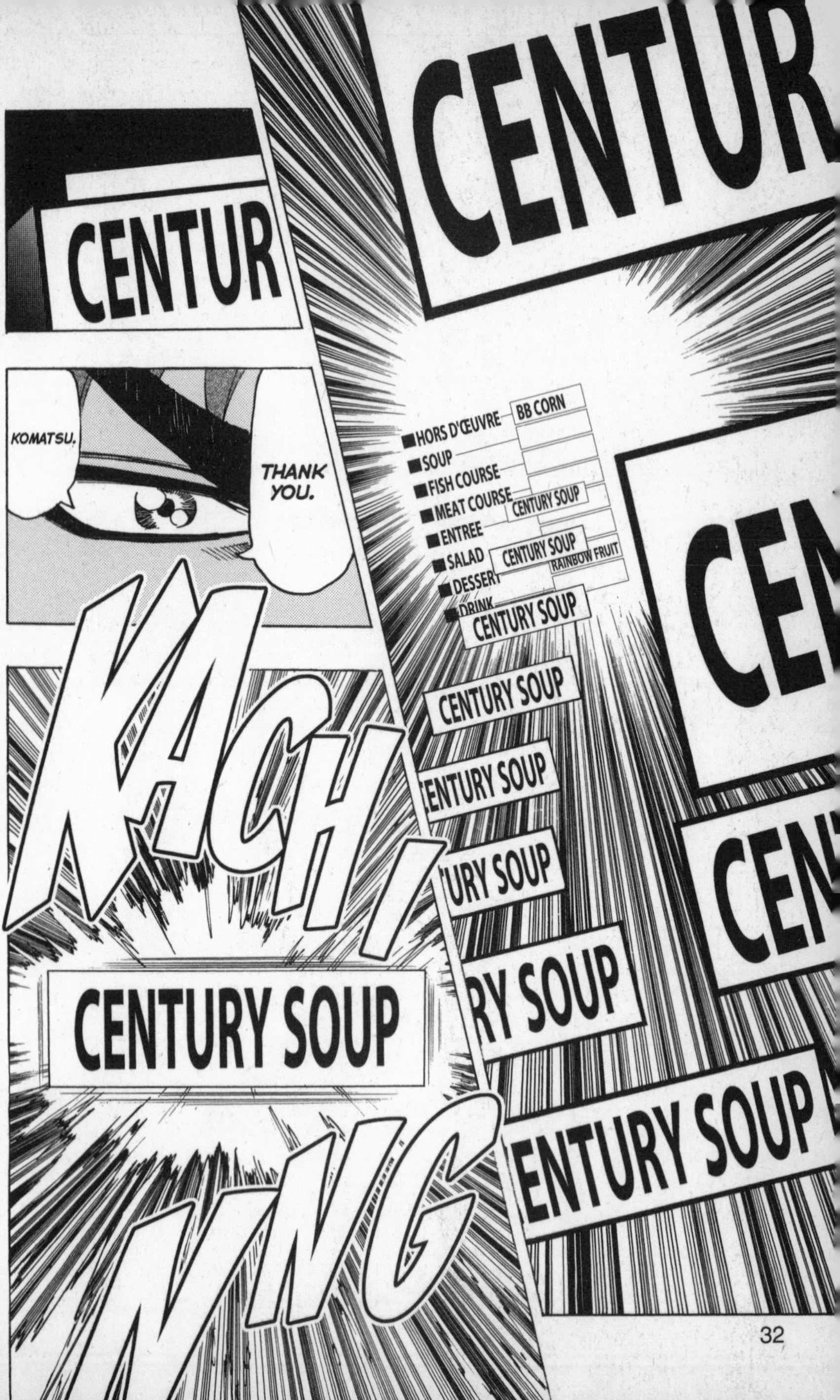
CENTUR
HORS D'ŒUVRE
SOUP
FISH COURSE
MEAT COURSE
ENTREE
SALAD
DESSERT
DRINK
BB CORN
CENTURY SOUP
CENTURY SOUP
RAINBOW FRUIT
CENTURY SOUP
CENTURY SOUP
ENTURY SOUP
TURY SOUP
RY SOUP
ENTURY SOUP
CEN
CEN
CENTUR
KOMATSU.
THANK YOU.
KACHING
CENTURY SOUP

TORIKO'S FULL-COURSE MEAL

■ HORS D'ŒUVRE	BB CORN
■ SOUP	CENTURY SOUP
■ FISH COURSE	
■ MEAT COURSE	
■ ENTREE	
■ SALAD	
■ DESSERT	RAINBOW FRUIT
■ DRINK	

CHEERS!!

RAAAA HAA

AND THE PLACE WAS FLOODED WITH RESERVATIONS.

CENTURY SOUP ADDED AN EXTRA SPARKLE TO THE HOTEL RESTAURANT'S MENU.

...CONTINUED ON INTO THE MORNING.

THE FEAST...

...TO A SIX-STAR HOTEL.

THANKS TO KOMATSU'S TREMENDOUS FEAT, HOTEL GOURMET ROSE FROM A FIVE-STAR...

AFTERWARD, KOMATSU'S CENTURY SOUP WAS OFFICIALLY RECOGNIZED BY THE G7.

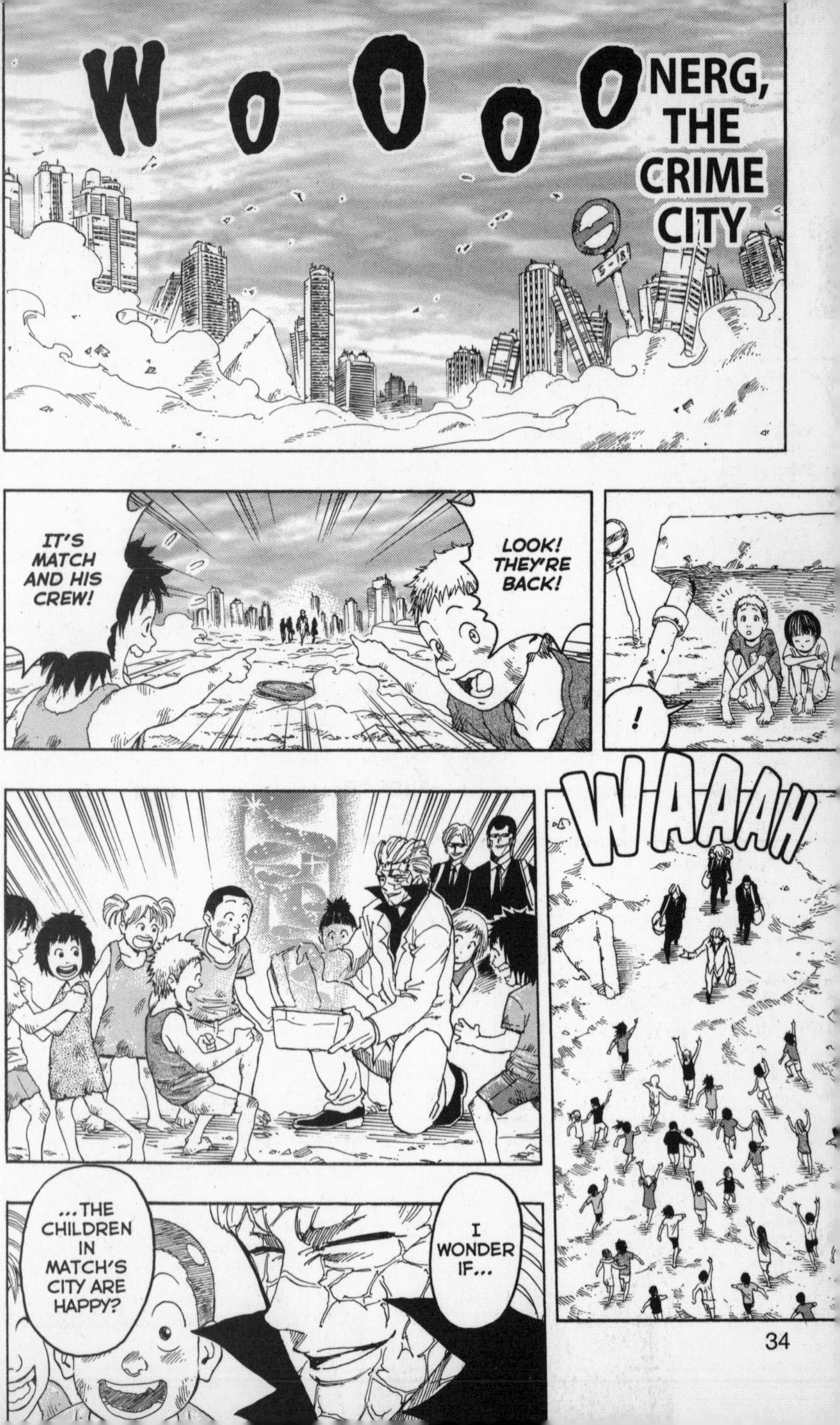
WOOOONERG, THE CRIME CITY
!
LOOK! THEY'RE BACK!
IT'S MATCH AND HIS CREW!
WAAAH
I WONDER IF...
...THE CHILDREN IN MATCH'S CITY ARE HAPPY?

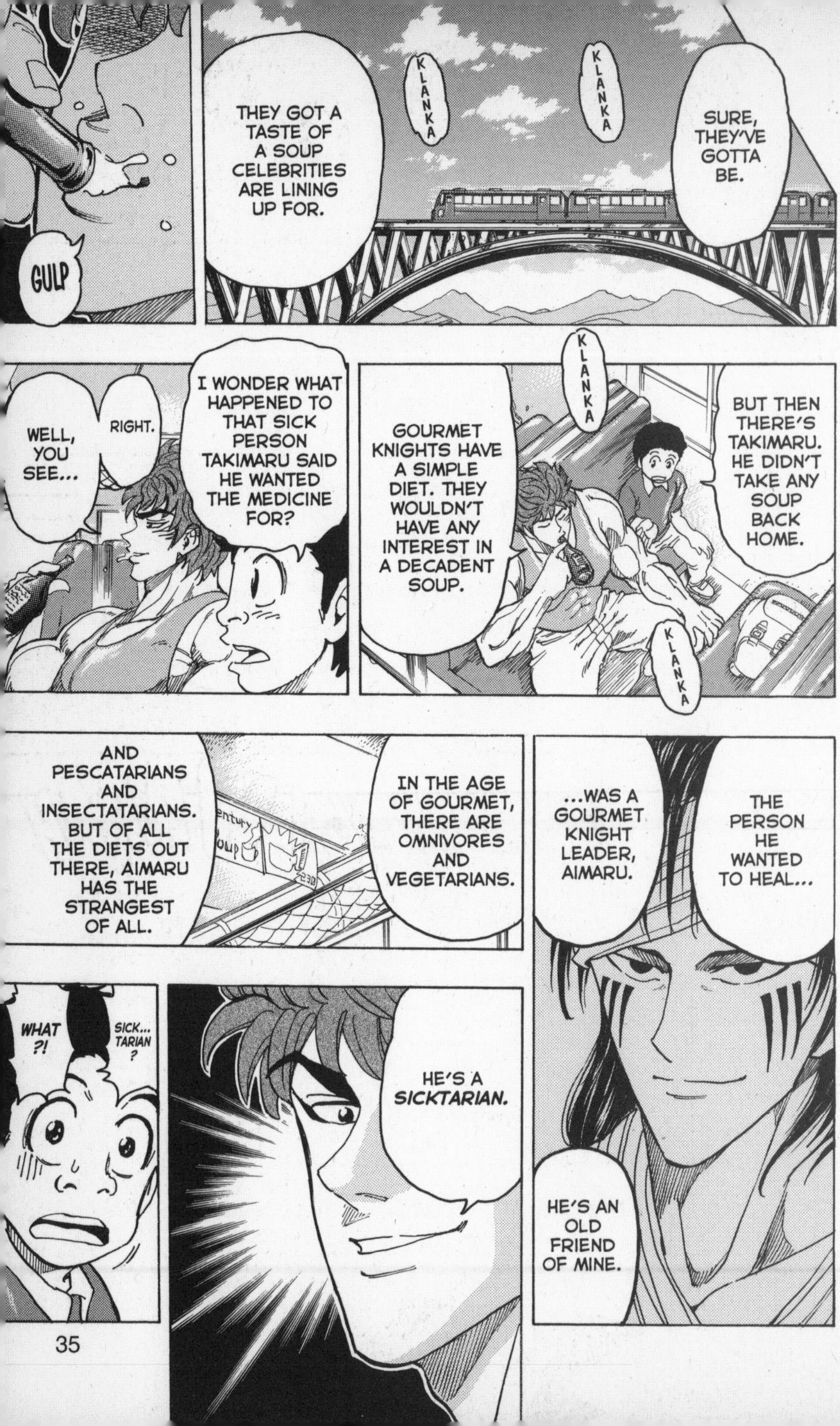
SURE, THEY'VE GOTTA BE.
KLANKA
KLANKA
THEY GOT A TASTE OF A SOUP CELEBRITIES ARE LINING UP FOR.
GULP
KLANKA
BUT THEN THERE'S TAKIMARU. HE DIDN'T TAKE ANY SOUP BACK HOME.
GOURMET KNIGHTS HAVE A SIMPLE DIET. THEY WOULDN'T HAVE ANY INTEREST IN A DECADENT SOUP.
KLANKA
I WONDER WHAT HAPPENED TO THAT SICK PERSON TAKIMARU SAID HE WANTED THE MEDICINE FOR?
RIGHT.
WELL, YOU SEE...
THE PERSON HE WANTED TO HEAL...
...WAS A GOURMET KNIGHT LEADER, AIMARU.
HE'S AN OLD FRIEND OF MINE.
IN THE AGE OF GOURMET, THERE ARE OMNIVORES AND VEGETARIANS.
AND PESCATARIANS AND INSECTATARIANS. BUT OF ALL THE DIETS OUT THERE, AIMARU HAS THE STRANGEST OF ALL.
HE'S A *SICKTARIAN.*
SICK... TARIAN?
WHAT ?!

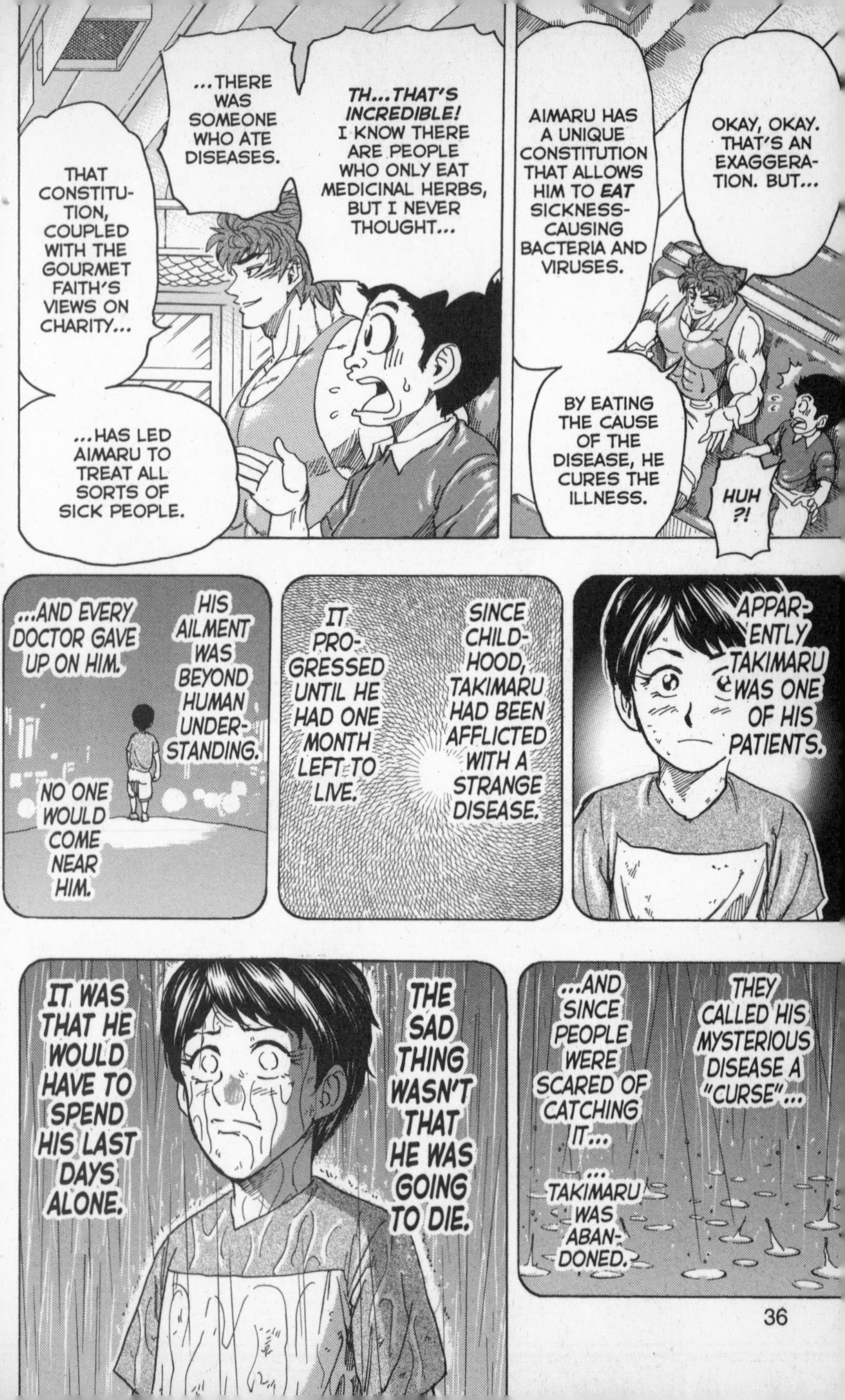
OKAY, OKAY. THAT'S AN EXAGGERATION. BUT...
AIMARU HAS A UNIQUE CONSTITUTION THAT ALLOWS HIM TO *EAT* SICKNESS-CAUSING BACTERIA AND VIRUSES.
HUH ?!
BY EATING THE CAUSE OF THE DISEASE, HE CURES THE ILLNESS.
...THERE WAS SOMEONE WHO ATE DISEASES.
TH...THAT'S INCREDIBLE! I KNOW THERE ARE PEOPLE WHO ONLY EAT MEDICINAL HERBS, BUT I NEVER THOUGHT...
THAT CONSTITUTION, COUPLED WITH THE GOURMET FAITH'S VIEWS ON CHARITY...
...HAS LED AIMARU TO TREAT ALL SORTS OF SICK PEOPLE.
APPARENTLY TAKIMARU WAS ONE OF HIS PATIENTS.
SINCE CHILDHOOD, TAKIMARU HAD BEEN AFFLICTED WITH A STRANGE DISEASE.
IT PROGRESSED UNTIL HE HAD ONE MONTH LEFT TO LIVE.
HIS AILMENT WAS BEYOND HUMAN UNDERSTANDING.
...AND EVERY DOCTOR GAVE UP ON HIM.
NO ONE WOULD COME NEAR HIM.
THEY CALLED HIS MYSTERIOUS DISEASE A "CURSE"...
...AND SINCE PEOPLE WERE SCARED OF CATCHING IT...
...TAKIMARU WAS ABANDONED.
THE SAD THING WASN'T THAT HE WAS GOING TO DIE.
IT WAS THAT HE WOULD HAVE TO SPEND HIS LAST DAYS ALONE.

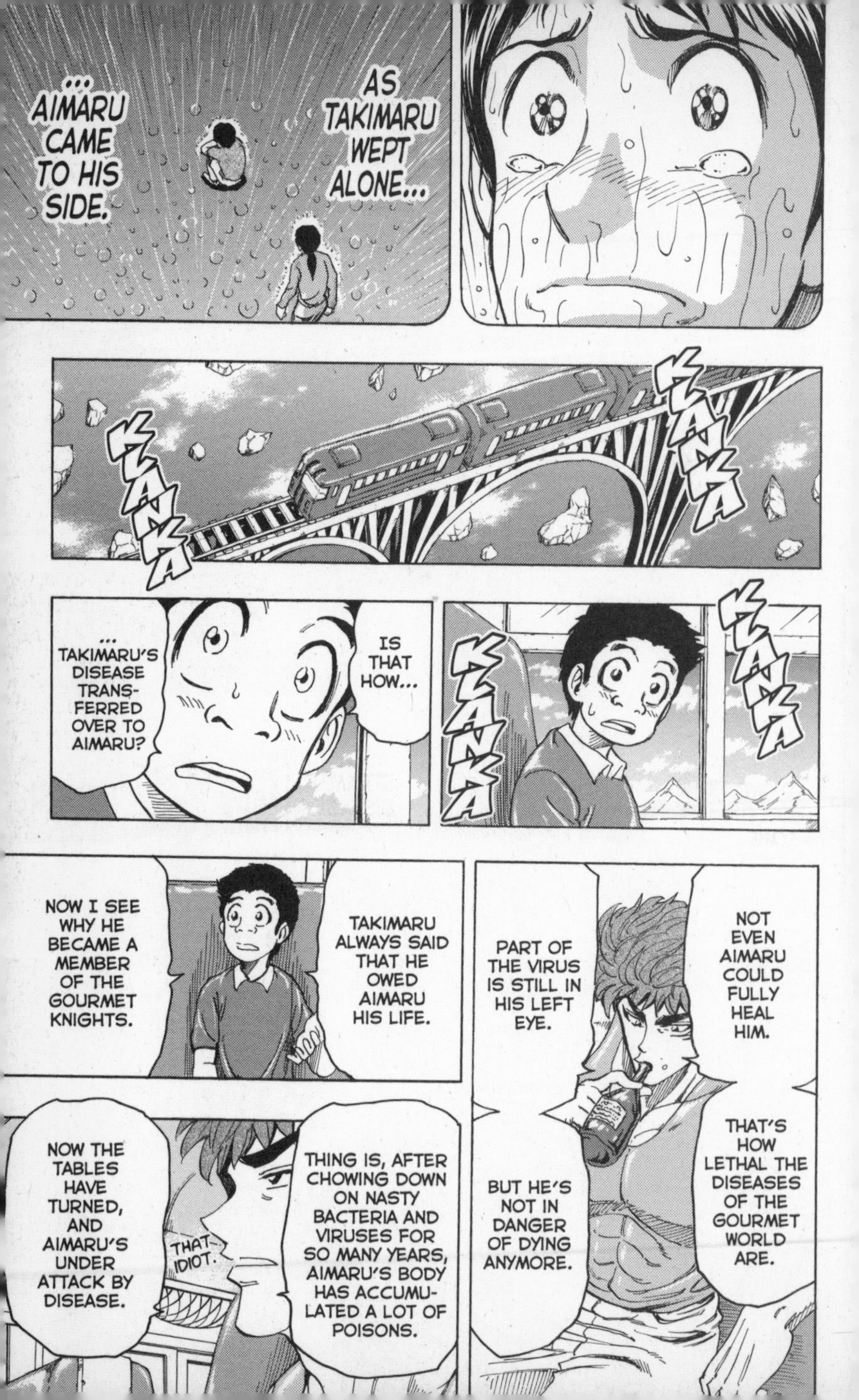
AS TAKIMARU WEPT ALONE...
...AIMARU CAME TO HIS SIDE.
KLANKA
KLANKA
KLANKA
KLANKA
IS THAT HOW...
...TAKIMARU'S DISEASE TRANSFERRED OVER TO AIMARU?
NOT EVEN AIMARU COULD FULLY HEAL HIM.
PART OF THE VIRUS IS STILL IN HIS LEFT EYE.
THAT'S HOW LETHAL THE DISEASES OF THE GOURMET WORLD ARE.
BUT HE'S NOT IN DANGER OF DYING ANYMORE.
TAKIMARU ALWAYS SAID THAT HE OWED AIMARU HIS LIFE.
NOW I SEE WHY HE BECAME A MEMBER OF THE GOURMET KNIGHTS.
THING IS, AFTER CHOWING DOWN ON NASTY BACTERIA AND VIRUSES FOR SO MANY YEARS, AIMARU'S BODY HAS ACCUMULATED A LOT OF POISONS.
NOW THE TABLES HAVE TURNED, AND AIMARU'S UNDER ATTACK BY DISEASE.
THAT IDIOT.

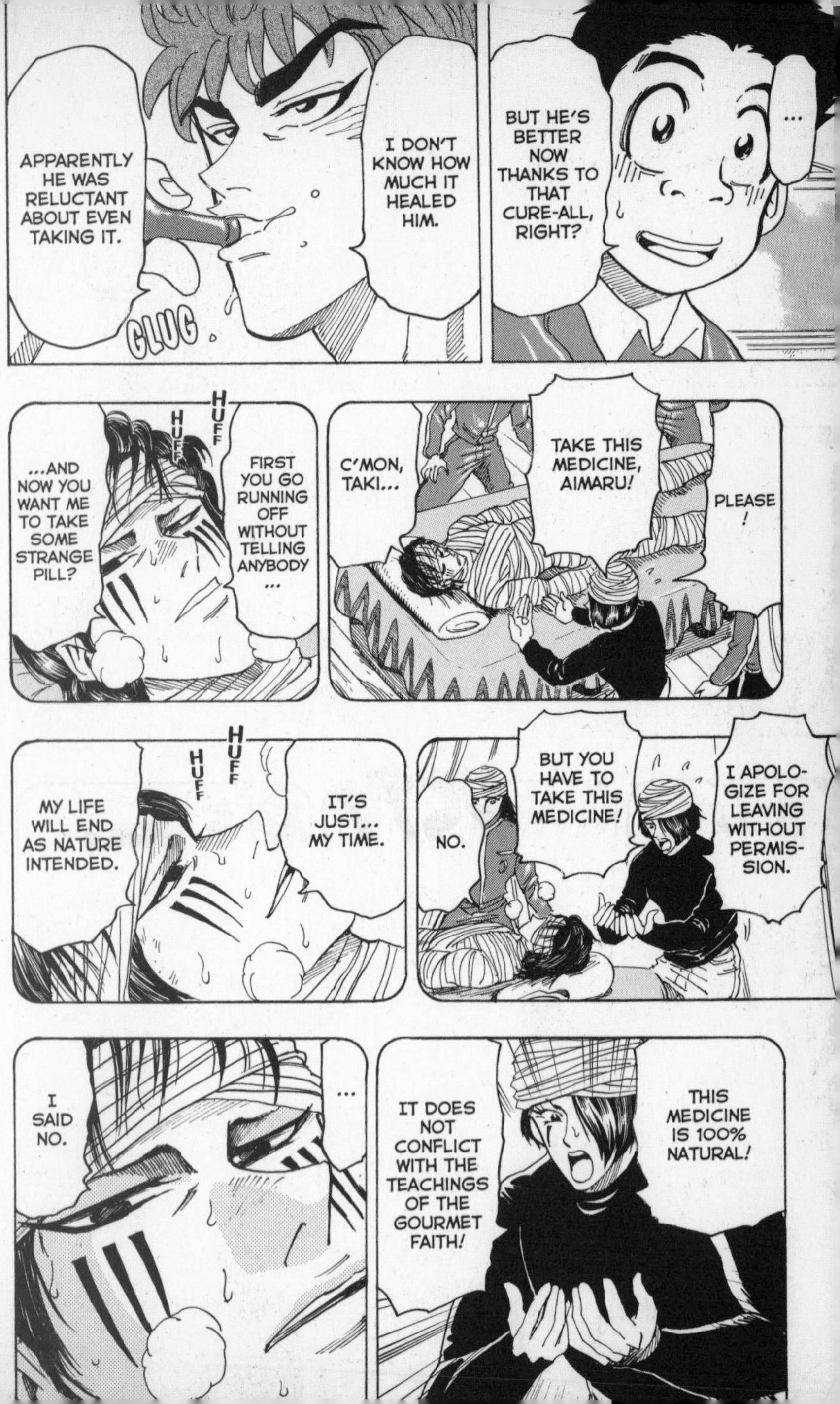
...
BUT HE'S BETTER NOW THANKS TO THAT CURE-ALL, RIGHT?
I DON'T KNOW HOW MUCH IT HEALED HIM.
APPARENTLY HE WAS RELUCTANT ABOUT EVEN TAKING IT.
GLUG
TAKE THIS MEDICINE, AIMARU!
PLEASE!
C'MON, TAKI...
HUFF
HUFF
FIRST YOU GO RUNNING OFF WITHOUT TELLING ANYBODY...
...AND NOW YOU WANT ME TO TAKE SOME STRANGE PILL?
I APOLO-GIZE FOR LEAVING WITHOUT PERMIS-SION.
BUT YOU HAVE TO TAKE THIS MEDICINE!
NO.
HUFF
HUFF
IT'S JUST... MY TIME.
MY LIFE WILL END AS NATURE INTENDED.
THIS MEDICINE IS 100% NATURAL!
IT DOES NOT CONFLICT WITH THE TEACHINGS OF THE GOURMET FAITH!
...
I SAID NO.

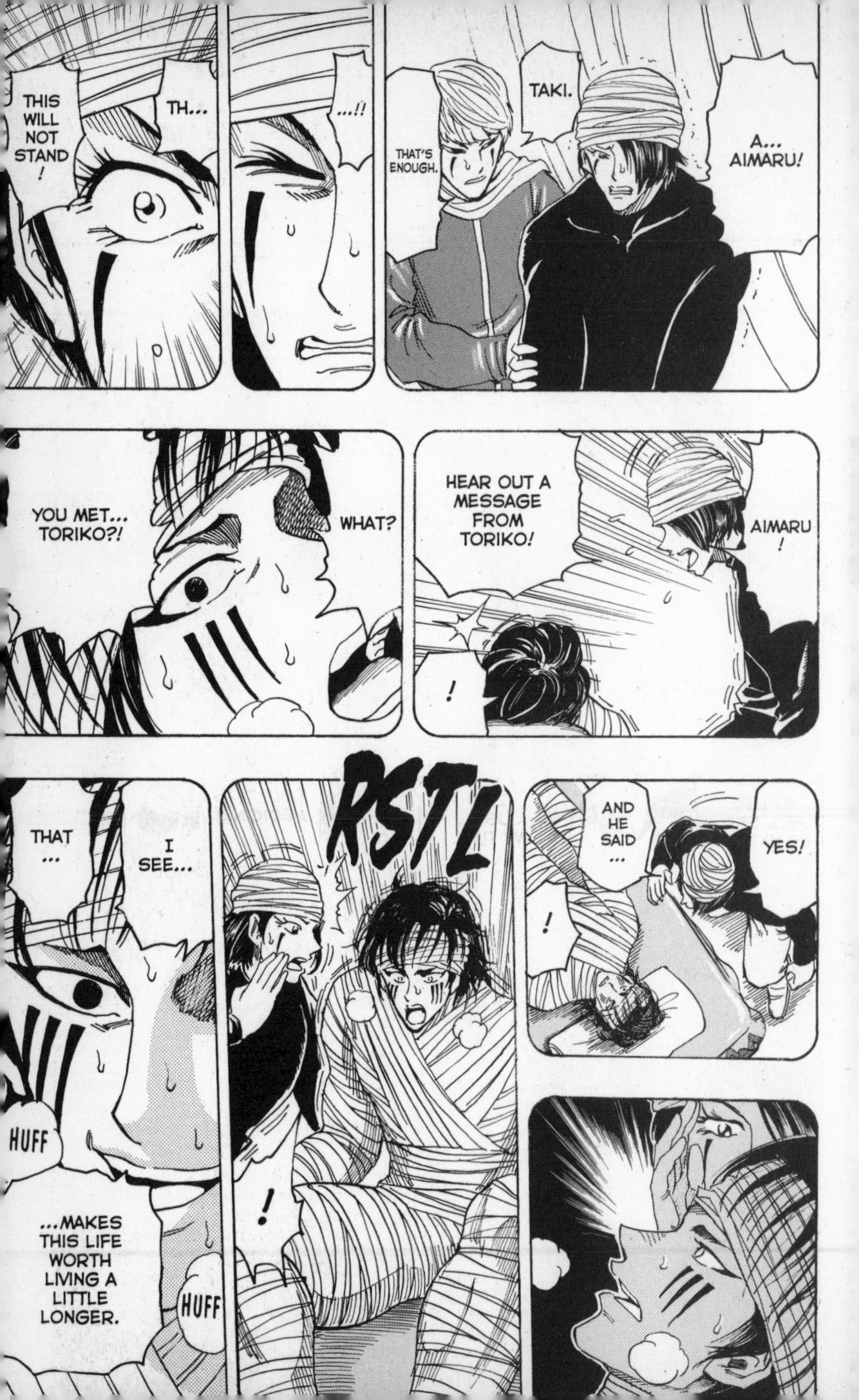
A... AIMARU!
TAKI.
THAT'S ENOUGH.
...!!
TH...
THIS WILL NOT STAND!
AIMARU!
HEAR OUT A MESSAGE FROM TORIKO!
!
WHAT?
YOU MET... TORIKO?!
YES!
AND HE SAID...
!
RSTL
!
I SEE...
THAT...
HUFF
...MAKES THIS LIFE WORTH LIVING A LITTLE LONGER.
HUFF

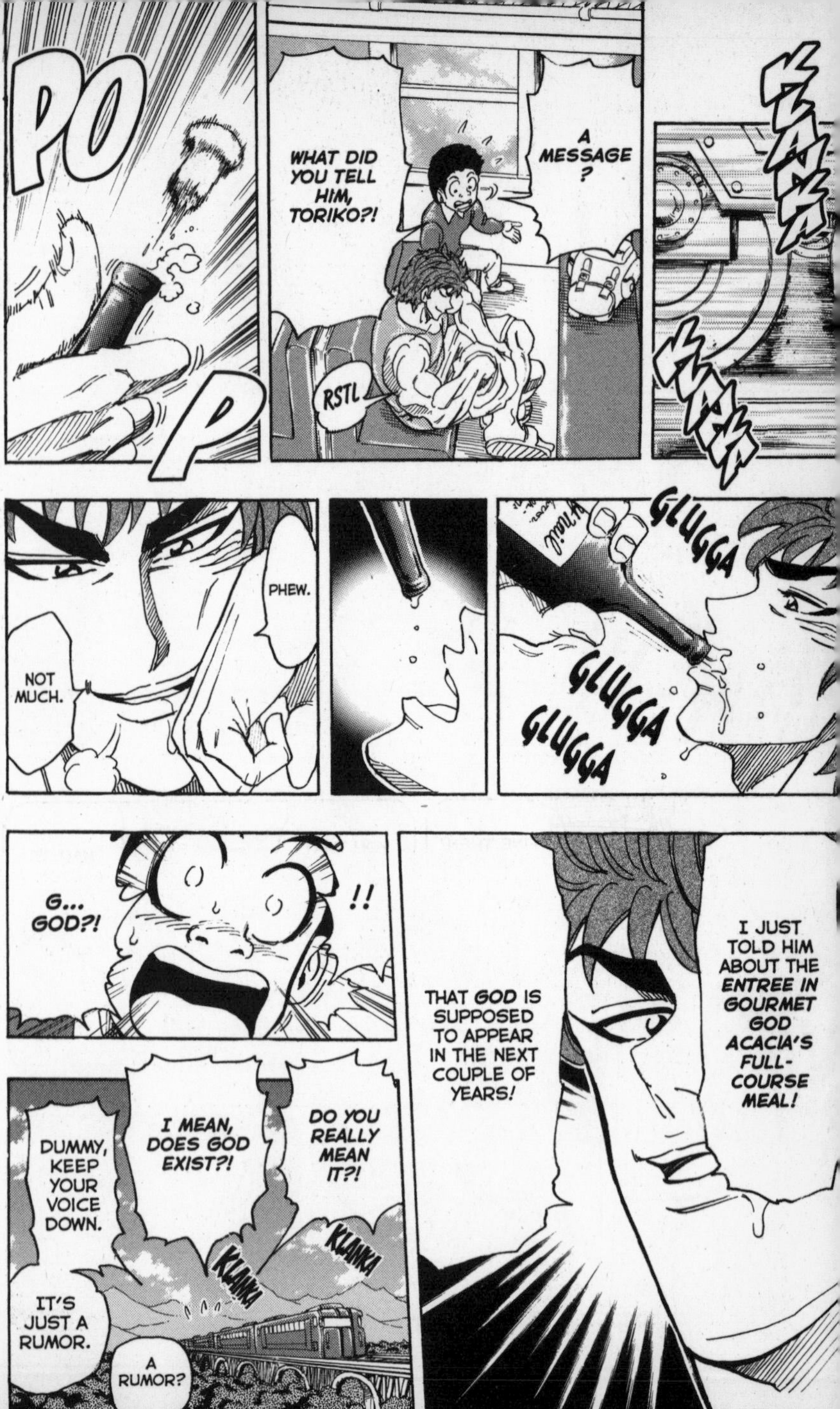
KLANKA
KLANKA
A MESSAGE?
WHAT DID YOU TELL HIM, TORIKO?!
RSTL
PO
P
GLUGGA
GLUGGA
GLUGGA
PHEW.
NOT MUCH.
I JUST TOLD HIM ABOUT THE ENTREE IN GOURMET GOD ACACIA'S FULL-COURSE MEAL!
THAT GOD IS SUPPOSED TO APPEAR IN THE NEXT COUPLE OF YEARS!
!!
G... GOD?!
DO YOU REALLY MEAN IT?!
I MEAN, DOES GOD EXIST?!
DUMMY, KEEP YOUR VOICE DOWN.
KLANKA
KLANKA
IT'S JUST A RUMOR.
A RUMOR?

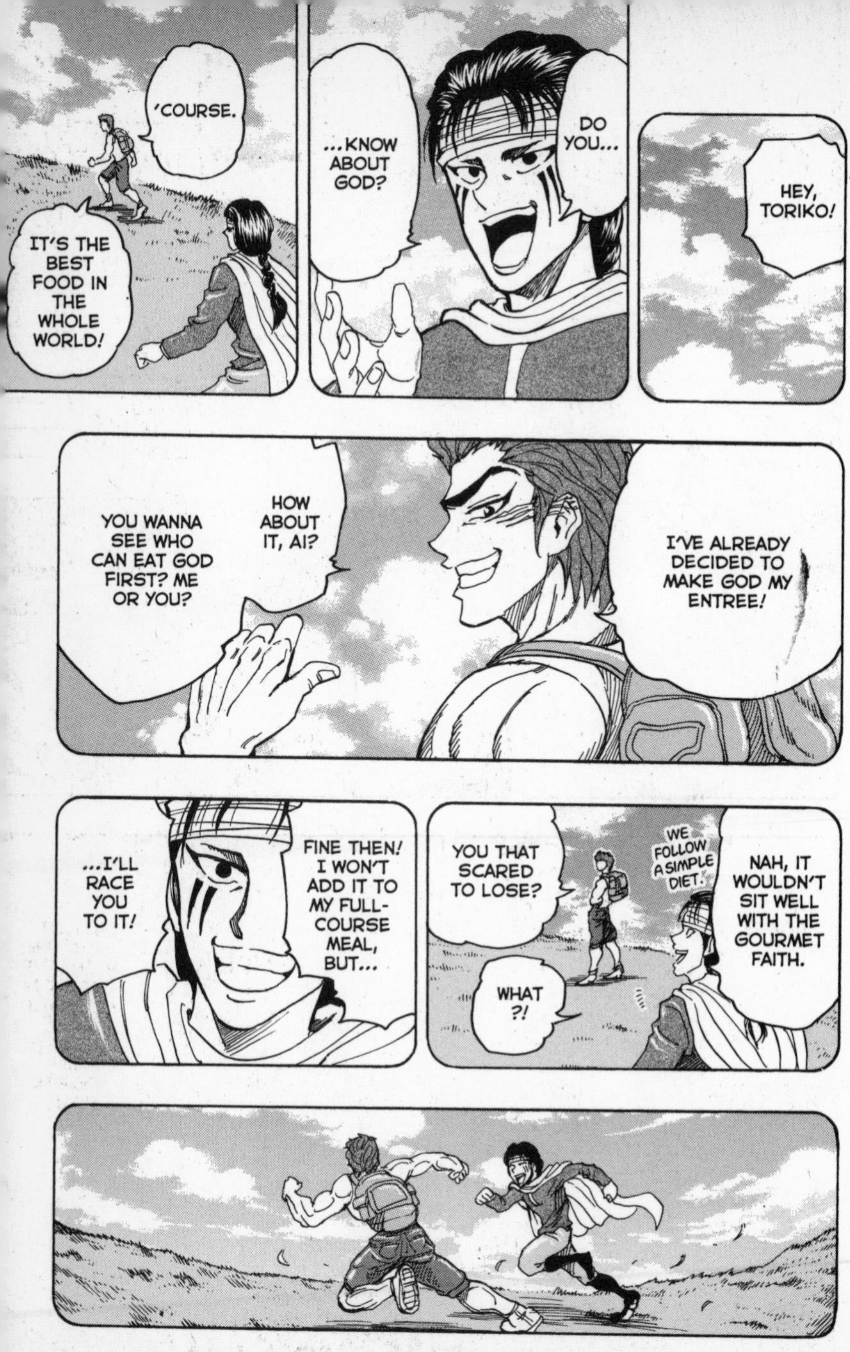
HEY, TORIKO!
DO YOU...
...KNOW ABOUT GOD?
'COURSE.
IT'S THE BEST FOOD IN THE WHOLE WORLD!
I'VE ALREADY DECIDED TO MAKE GOD MY ENTREE!
HOW ABOUT IT, AI?
YOU WANNA SEE WHO CAN EAT GOD FIRST? ME OR YOU?
NAH, IT WOULDN'T SIT WELL WITH THE GOURMET FAITH.
WE FOLLOW A SIMPLE DIET.
YOU THAT SCARED TO LOSE?
WHAT?!
FINE THEN! I WON'T ADD IT TO MY FULL-COURSE MEAL, BUT...
...I'LL RACE YOU TO IT!

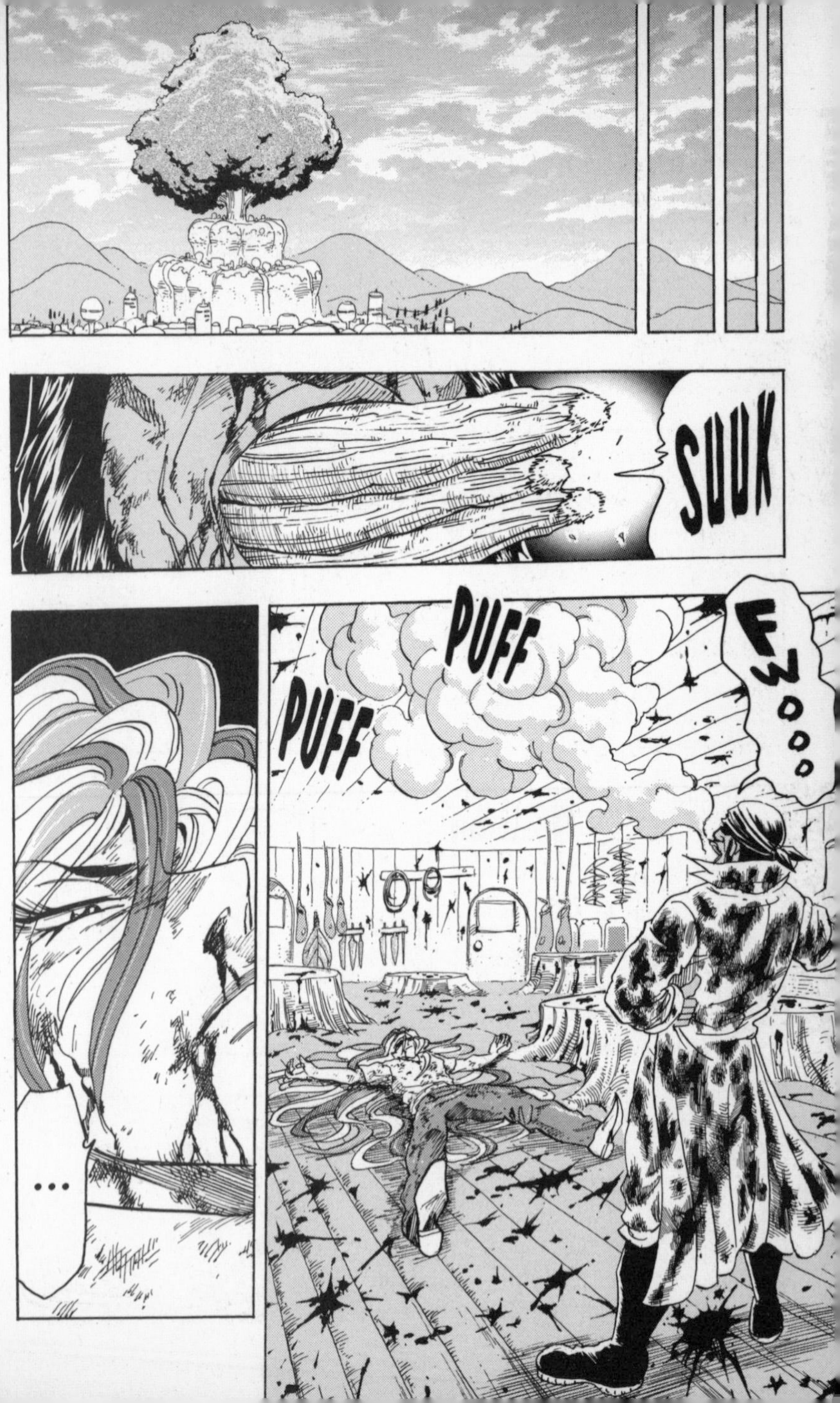
SUUK
FWOOO
PUFF
PUFF
...

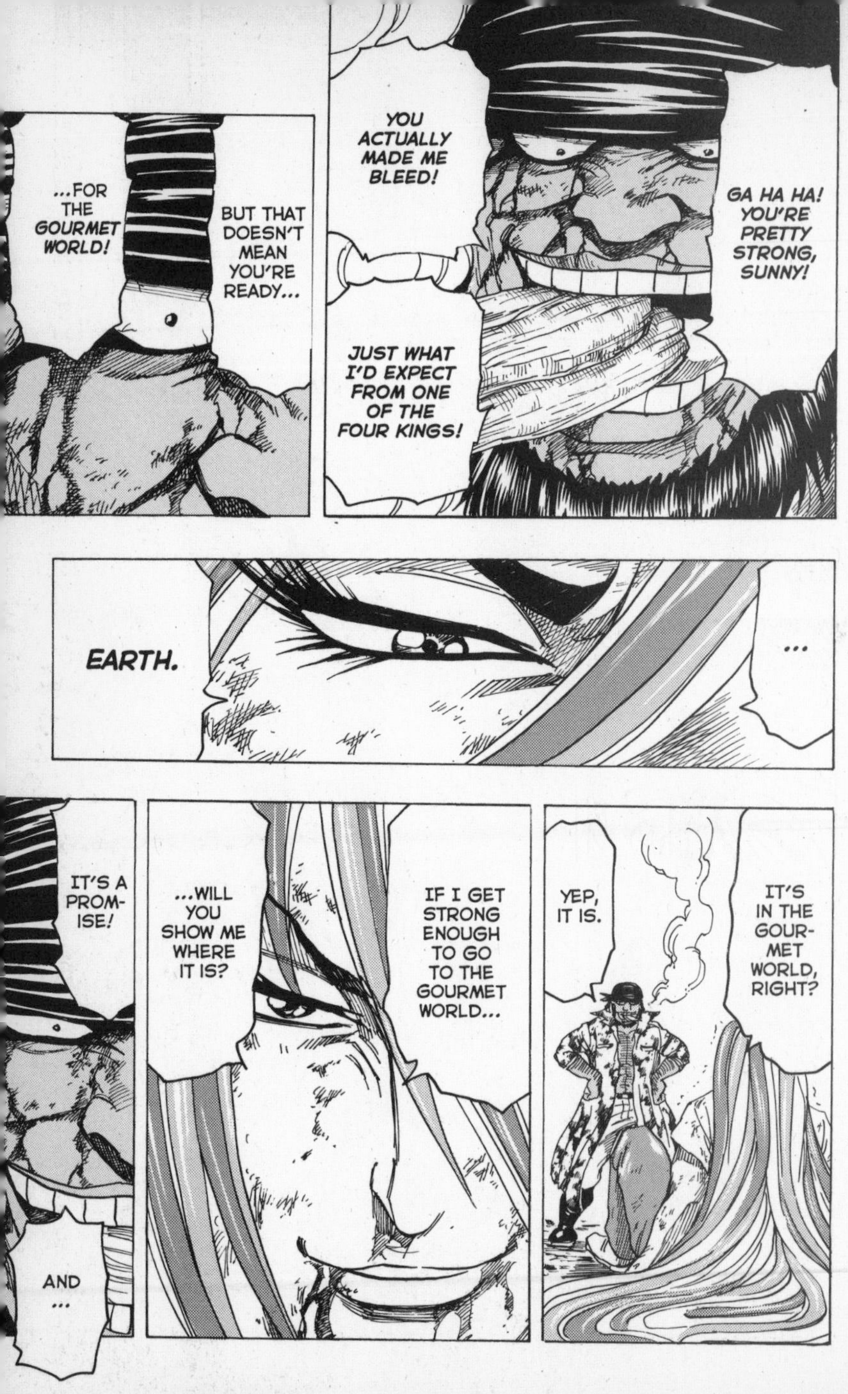
GA HA HA! YOU'RE PRETTY STRONG, SUNNY!
YOU ACTUALLY MADE ME BLEED!
JUST WHAT I'D EXPECT FROM ONE OF THE FOUR KINGS!
BUT THAT DOESN'T MEAN YOU'RE READY...
...FOR THE GOURMET WORLD!
...
EARTH.
IT'S IN THE GOURMET WORLD, RIGHT?
YEP, IT IS.
IF I GET STRONG ENOUGH TO GO TO THE GOURMET WORLD...
...WILL YOU SHOW ME WHERE IT IS?
IT'S A PROMISE!
AND ...

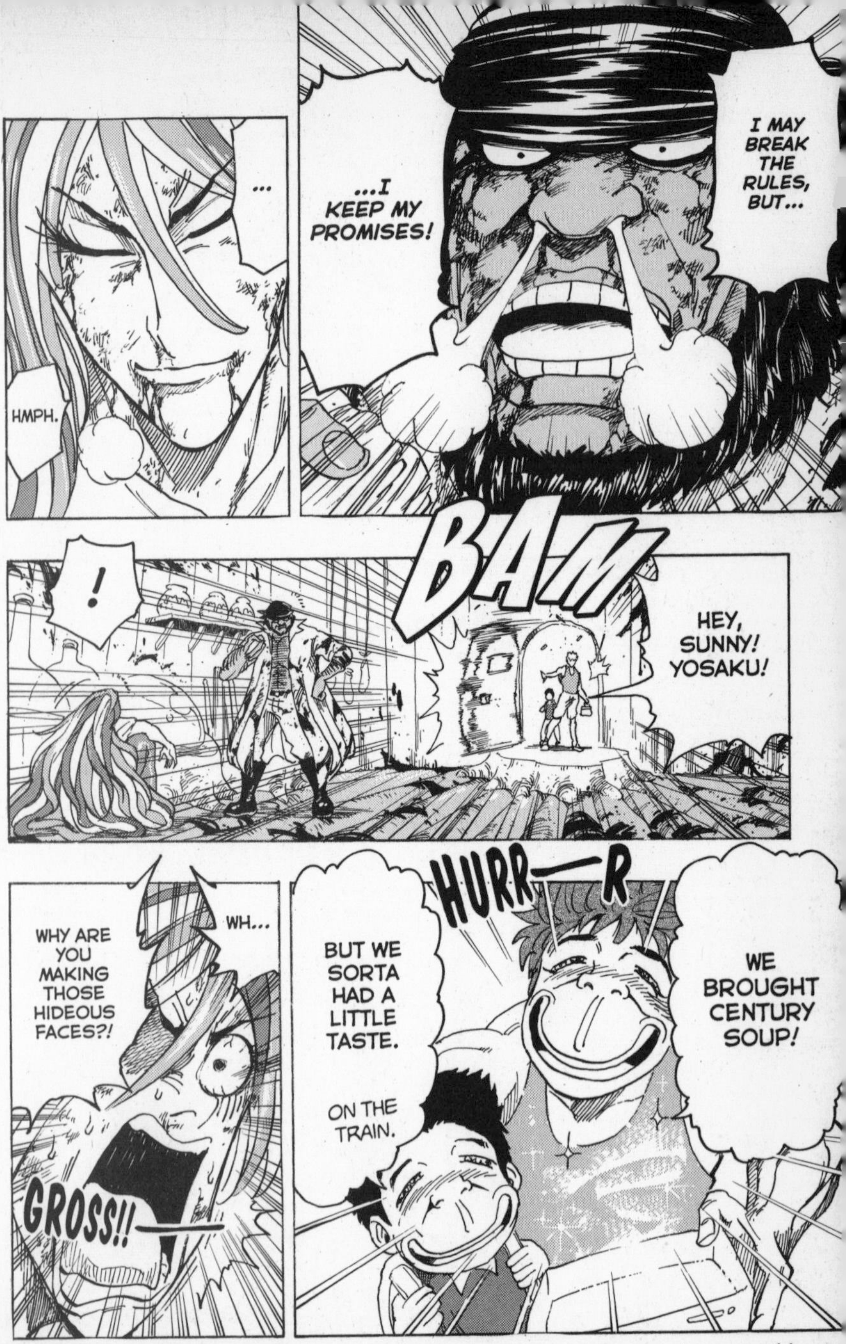
I MAY BREAK THE RULES, BUT...
...I KEEP MY PROMISES!
...
HMPH.
BAM
HEY, SUNNY! YOSAKU!
!
WE BROUGHT CENTURY SOUP!
HURR—R
BUT WE SORTA HAD A LITTLE TASTE.
ON THE TRAIN.
WH...
WHY ARE YOU MAKING THOSE HIDEOUS FACES?!
GROSS!!—

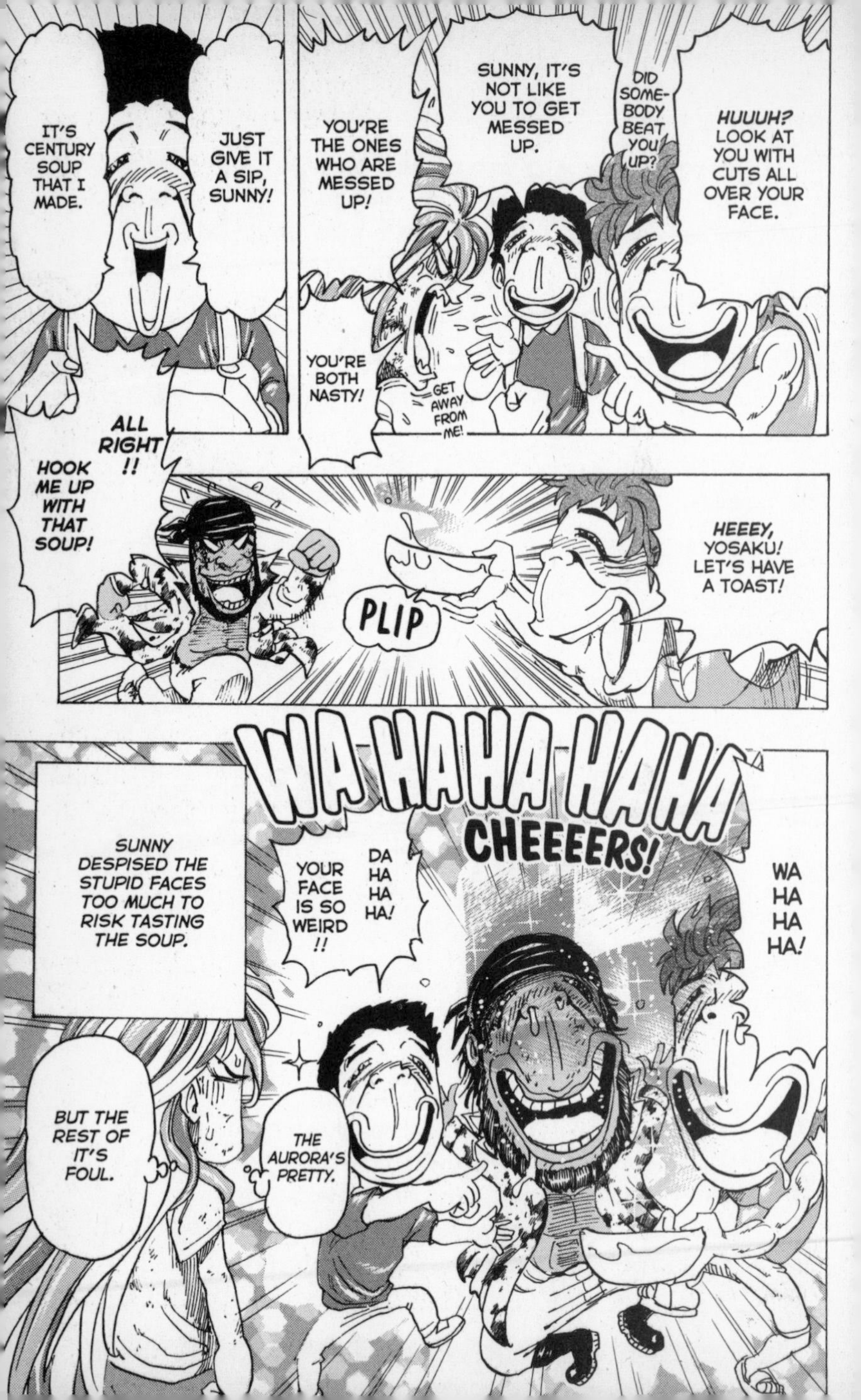
HUUUH? LOOK AT YOU WITH CUTS ALL OVER YOUR FACE.
DID SOMEBODY BEAT YOU UP?
SUNNY, IT'S NOT LIKE YOU TO GET MESSED UP.
YOU'RE THE ONES WHO ARE MESSED UP!
GET AWAY FROM ME!
YOU'RE BOTH NASTY!
JUST GIVE IT A SIP, SUNNY!
IT'S CENTURY SOUP THAT I MADE.
HEEEY, YOSAKU! LET'S HAVE A TOAST!
PLIP
ALL RIGHT!!
HOOK ME UP WITH THAT SOUP!
WA-HAHA-HAHA
CHEEEERS!
WA HA HA HA!
DA HA HA HA!
YOUR FACE IS SO WEIRD!!
SUNNY DESPISED THE STUPID FACES TOO MUCH TO RISK TASTING THE SOUP.
THE AURORA'S PRETTY.
BUT THE REST OF IT'S FOUL.

TORIKO

GOURMET CHECKLIST

Vol. 108

HELLBOROS
(REPTILE)

CAPTURE LEVEL: 72

HABITAT: ICE HELL

LENGTH: 42 METERS

HEIGHT: ---

WEIGHT: 60 TONS

PRICE: MEAT TOO FOUL TO EAT

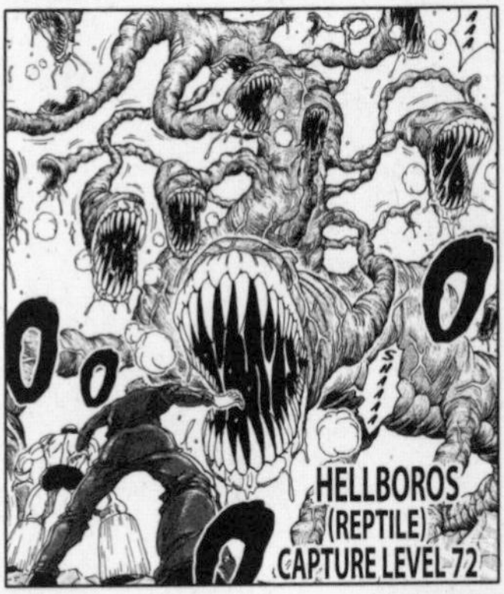
HELLBOROS
(REPTILE)
CAPTURE LEVEL 72

SCALE

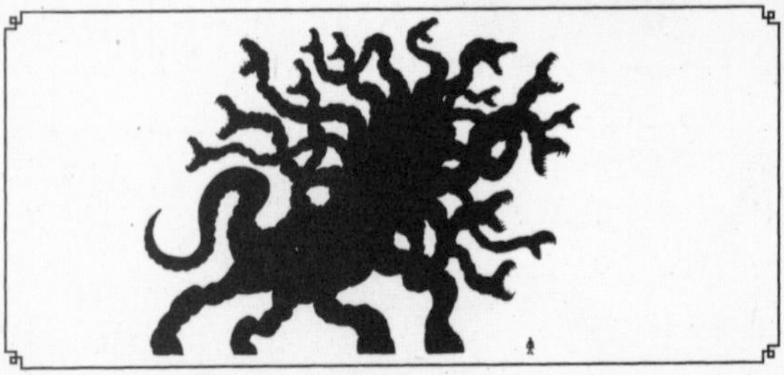

ONE HUNDRED YEARS AGO, KNOCKING MASTER JIRO DEEPLY SEDATED THIS RULER OF ICE HELL. THE HELLBOROS EVOLVED FOR THE SOLE PURPOSE OF EATING, EVEN LOSING ITS EYES ALONG THE WAY. IT TRACKS ITS PREY WITH PIT ORGANS. GREEDY AND FEROCIOUS, IT WILL CONSUME EVERYTHING AND ANYTHING, CEMENTING ITS PLACE ON THE TOP OF THE FOOD CHAIN.

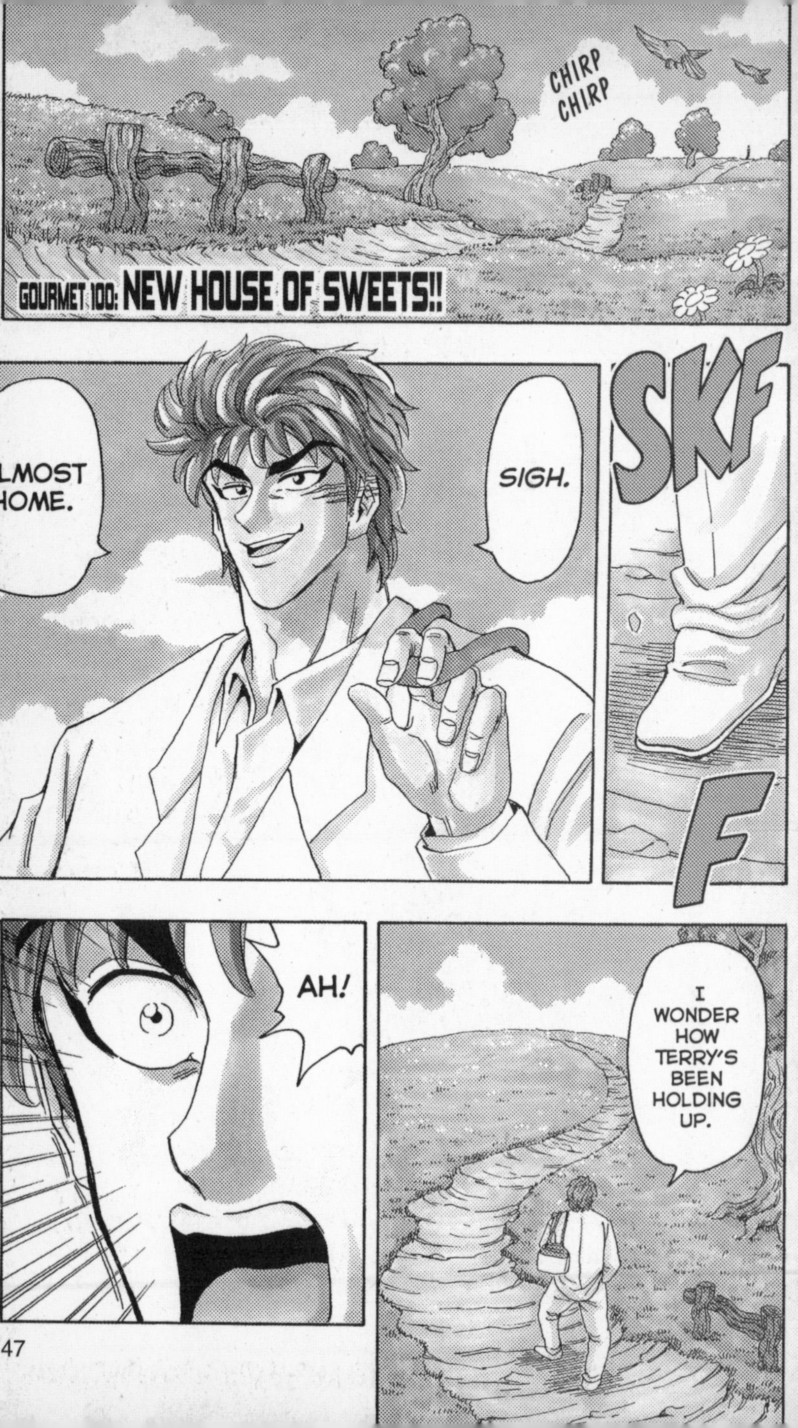
CHIRP CHIRP
GOURMET 100: NEW HOUSE OF SWEETS!!
SKF F
SIGH.
ALMOST HOME.
I WONDER HOW TERRY'S BEEN HOLDING UP.
AH!

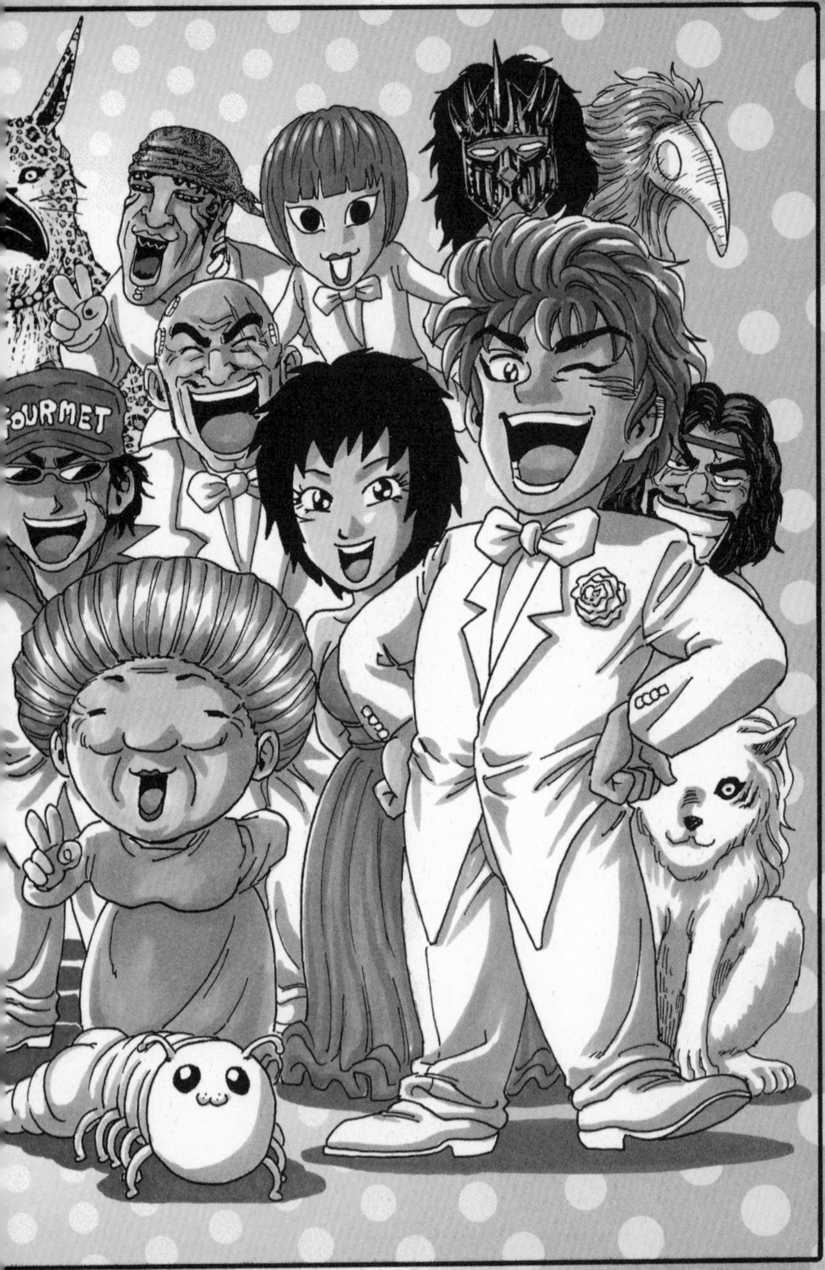
OURMET

GOURMET 100:
NEW HOUSE OF SWEETS!!

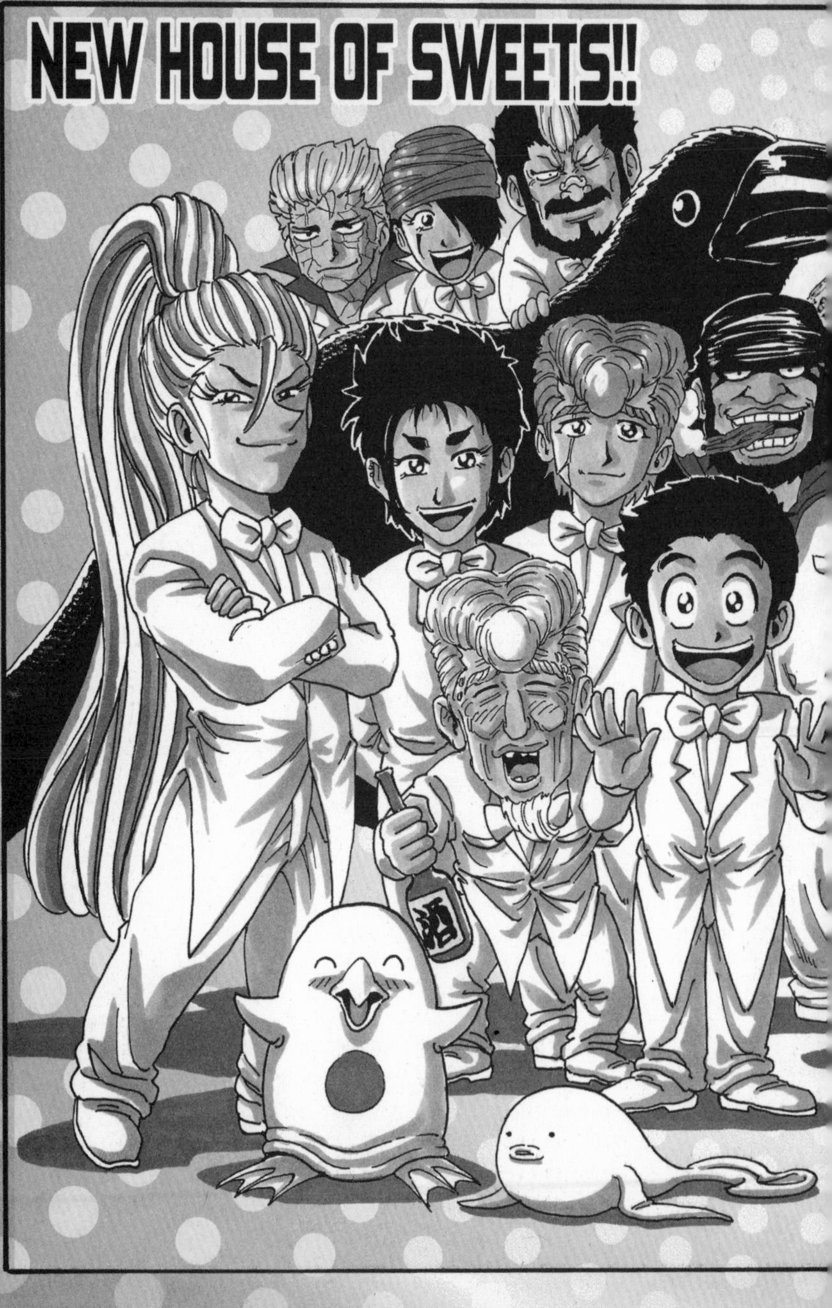
酒

TORIKO

GOURMET CHECKLIST

Vol.109

FORESTRY SEED
(SEED OF THE PROTECTION TREE)

CAPTURE LEVEL: ---

HABITAT: PROPERTY OF TEPPEI

(DETAILS UNKNOWN)

LENGTH: 3 CM

HEIGHT: ---

WEIGHT: 100 G

PRICE: 9,500,000 YEN PER SEED

OKAY, LITTLE FORESTRY SEED!

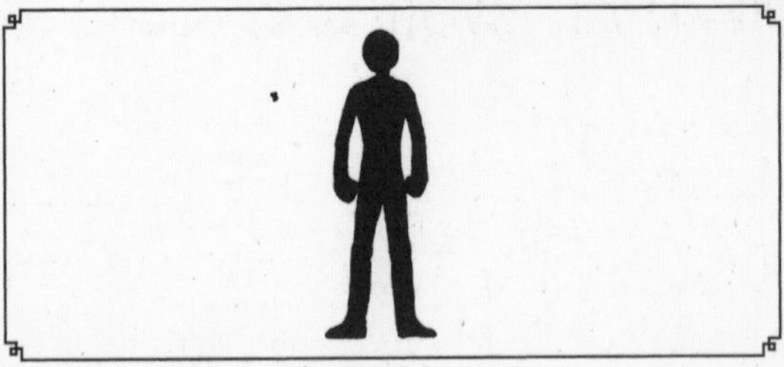

SCALE

THE INCREDIBLE PROTECTION TREE GROWS AT LIGHTNING SPEED. IT WILL FORM AROUND WHATEVER IT GROWS NEAR, AN ABILITY WHICH CAN BE UTILIZED TO OTHER ENDS BESIDES PRESERVATION, SUCH AS MOVING ROCK FACES OR CREATING SCAFFOLDING. THE POSSIBILITIES ARE ENDLESS! FURTHERMORE, THE PROTECTION TREE'S LEAVES CONTAIN A CARDIO STIMULANT, WHICH CAN BE USED TO RESTART A HUMAN HEART. CAREFUL THOUGH! IT'S REALLY POTENT!

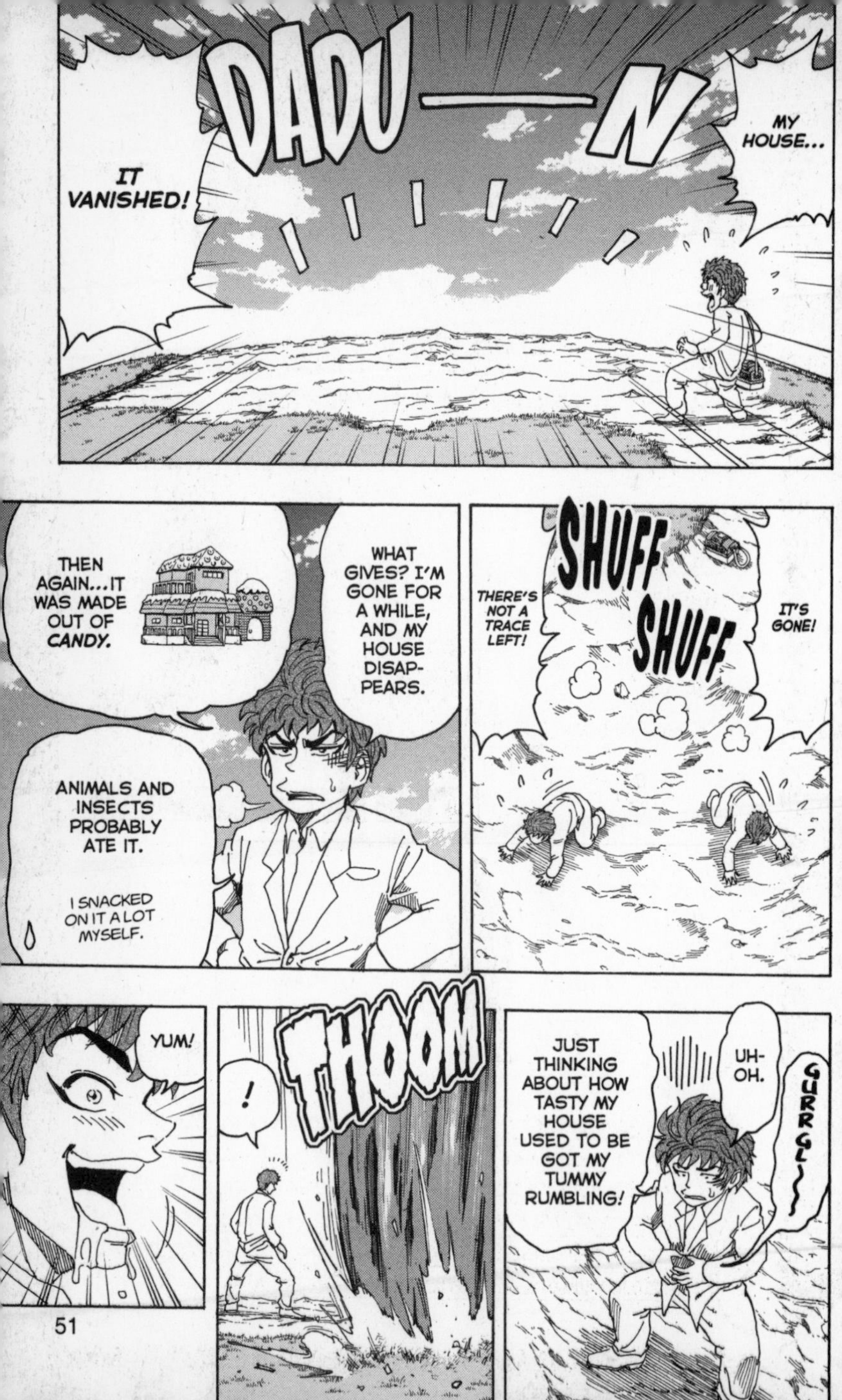
MY HOUSE...
DADU—N
IT VANISHED!
SHUFF SHUFF
IT'S GONE!
THERE'S NOT A TRACE LEFT!
WHAT GIVES? I'M GONE FOR A WHILE, AND MY HOUSE DISAP-PEARS.
THEN AGAIN...IT WAS MADE OUT OF CANDY.
ANIMALS AND INSECTS PROBABLY ATE IT.
I SNACKED ON IT A LOT MYSELF.
GURRGL~
UH-OH.
JUST THINKING ABOUT HOW TASTY MY HOUSE USED TO BE GOT MY TUMMY RUMBLING!
THOOM
!
YUM!

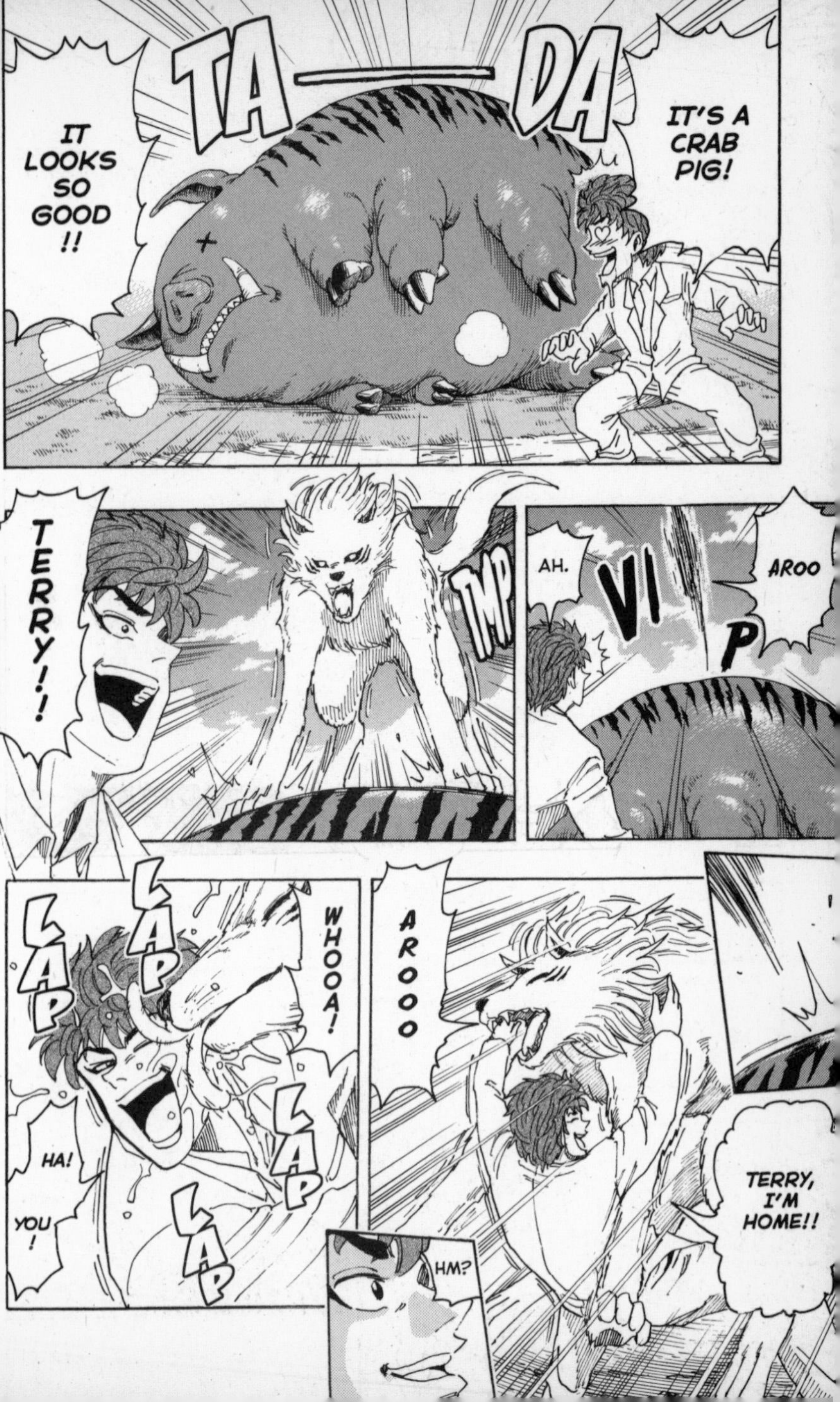
TA——DA
IT'S A CRAB PIG!
IT LOOKS SO GOOD!!
AROO
VIP
AH.
TMP
TERRY!!!
TERRY, I'M HOME!!
AROOOO
HM?
WHOOA!
LAP LAP
LAP LAP
LAP
HA!
YOU!

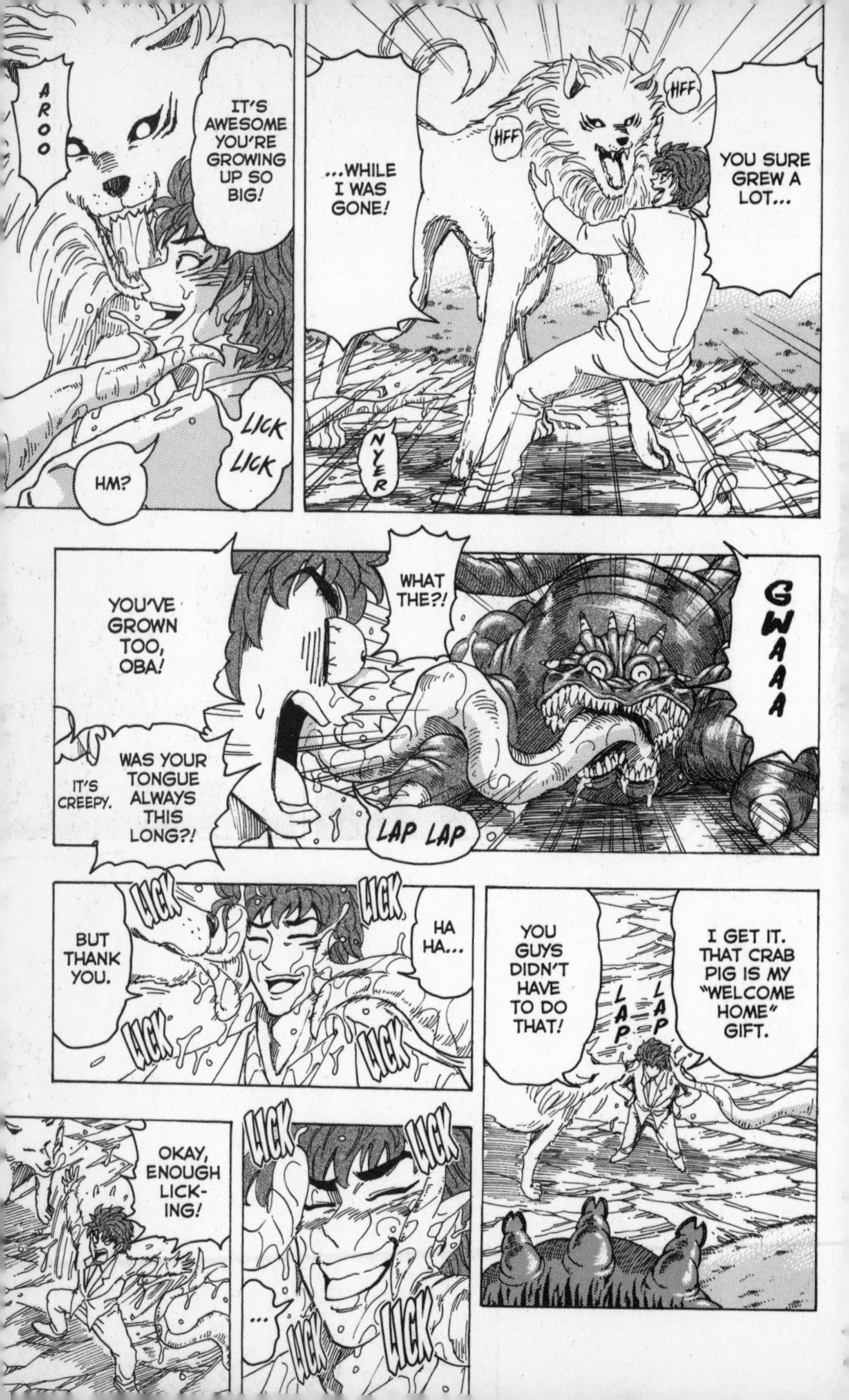
YOU SURE GREW A LOT...
HFF
HFF
...WHILE I WAS GONE!
NYER
IT'S AWESOME YOU'RE GROWING UP SO BIG!
AROO
LICK LICK
HM?
GWAAAA
WHAT THE?!
YOU'VE GROWN TOO, OBA!
WAS YOUR TONGUE ALWAYS THIS LONG?!
IT'S CREEPY.
LAP LAP
I GET IT. THAT CRAB PIG IS MY "WELCOME HOME" GIFT.
LAP LAP
YOU GUYS DIDN'T HAVE TO DO THAT!
LICK
HA HA...
LICK
BUT THANK YOU.
LICK
LICK
LICK
LICK
...
LICK
LICK
OKAY, ENOUGH LICK-ING!

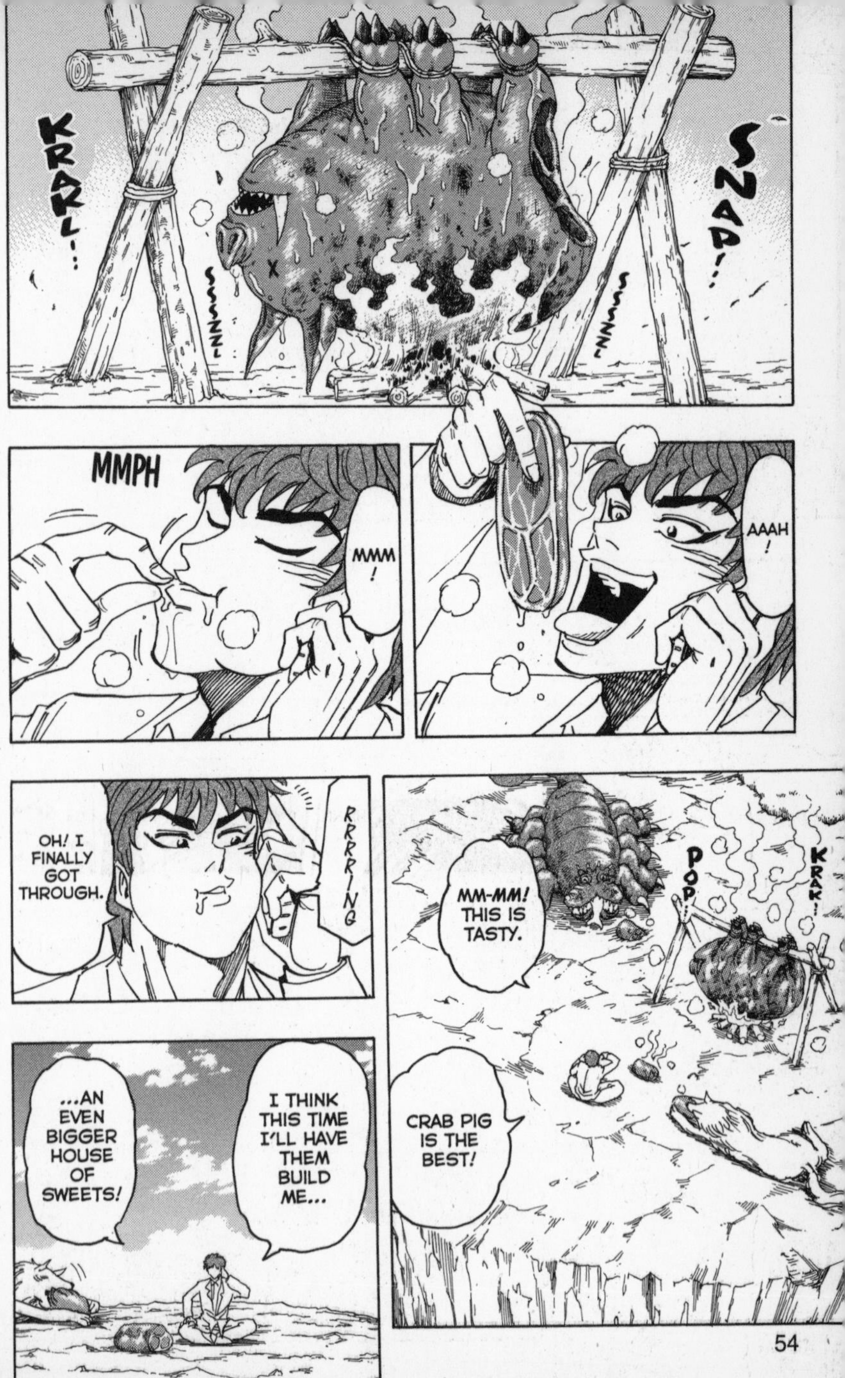
SNAP!!
SSSSZZZ
SSSSZZZ
KRAKL!!
AAAH!
MMPH
MMM!
KRAK!
POP!
MM-MM! THIS IS TASTY.
CRAB PIG IS THE BEST!
RRRRING
OH! I FINALLY GOT THROUGH.
I THINK THIS TIME I'LL HAVE THEM BUILD ME...
...AN EVEN BIGGER HOUSE OF SWEETS!

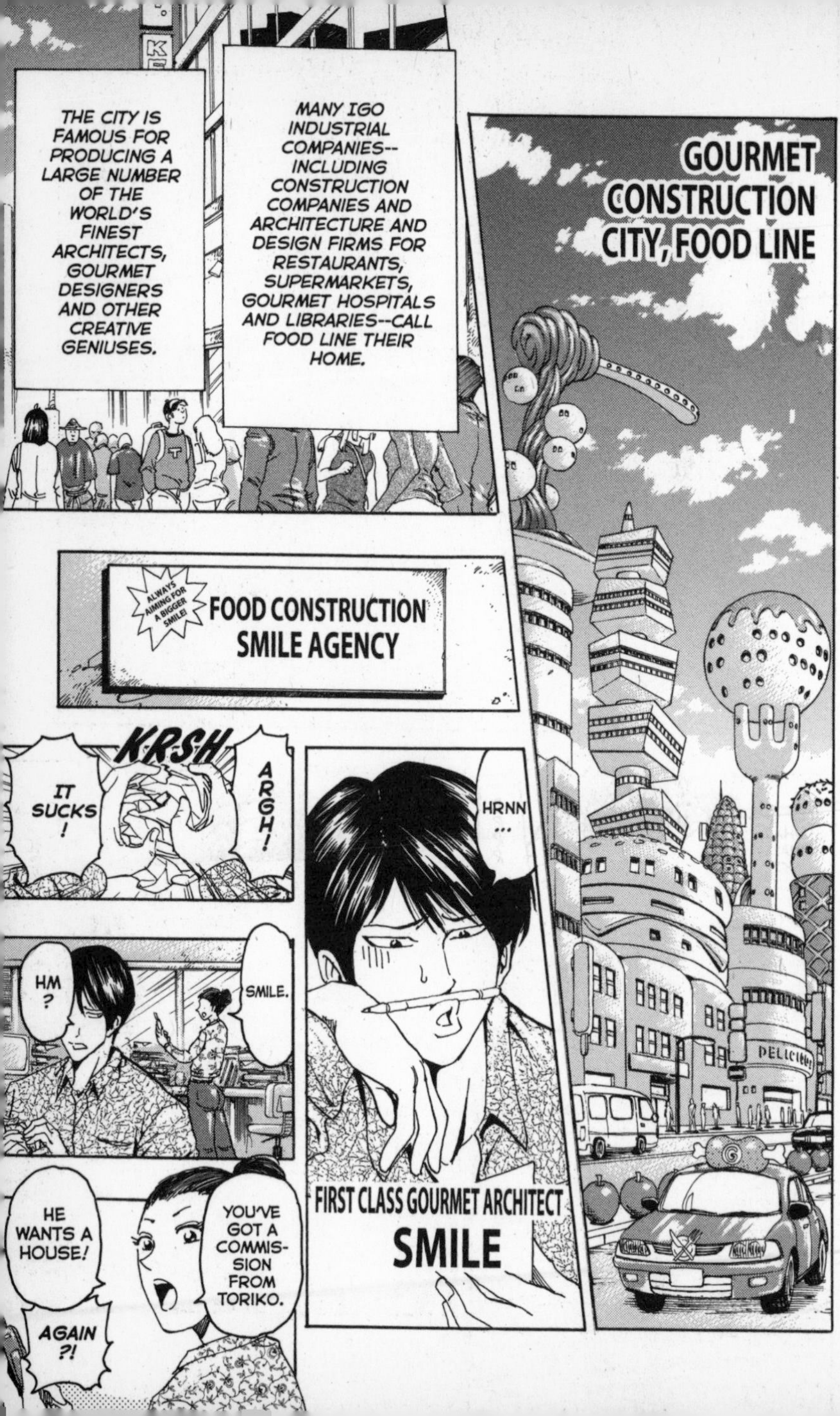
GOURMET CONSTRUCTION CITY, FOOD LINE
MANY IGO INDUSTRIAL COMPANIES-- INCLUDING CONSTRUCTION COMPANIES AND ARCHITECTURE AND DESIGN FIRMS FOR RESTAURANTS, SUPERMARKETS, GOURMET HOSPITALS AND LIBRARIES--CALL FOOD LINE THEIR HOME.
THE CITY IS FAMOUS FOR PRODUCING A LARGE NUMBER OF THE WORLD'S FINEST ARCHITECTS, GOURMET DESIGNERS AND OTHER CREATIVE GENIUSES.
ALWAYS AIMING FOR A BIGGER SMILE!
FOOD CONSTRUCTION SMILE AGENCY
HRNN...
FIRST CLASS GOURMET ARCHITECT
SMILE
ARGH!
K-R-S-H
IT SUCKS!
SMILE.
HM?
YOU'VE GOT A COMMISSION FROM TORIKO.
HE WANTS A HOUSE!
AGAIN?!

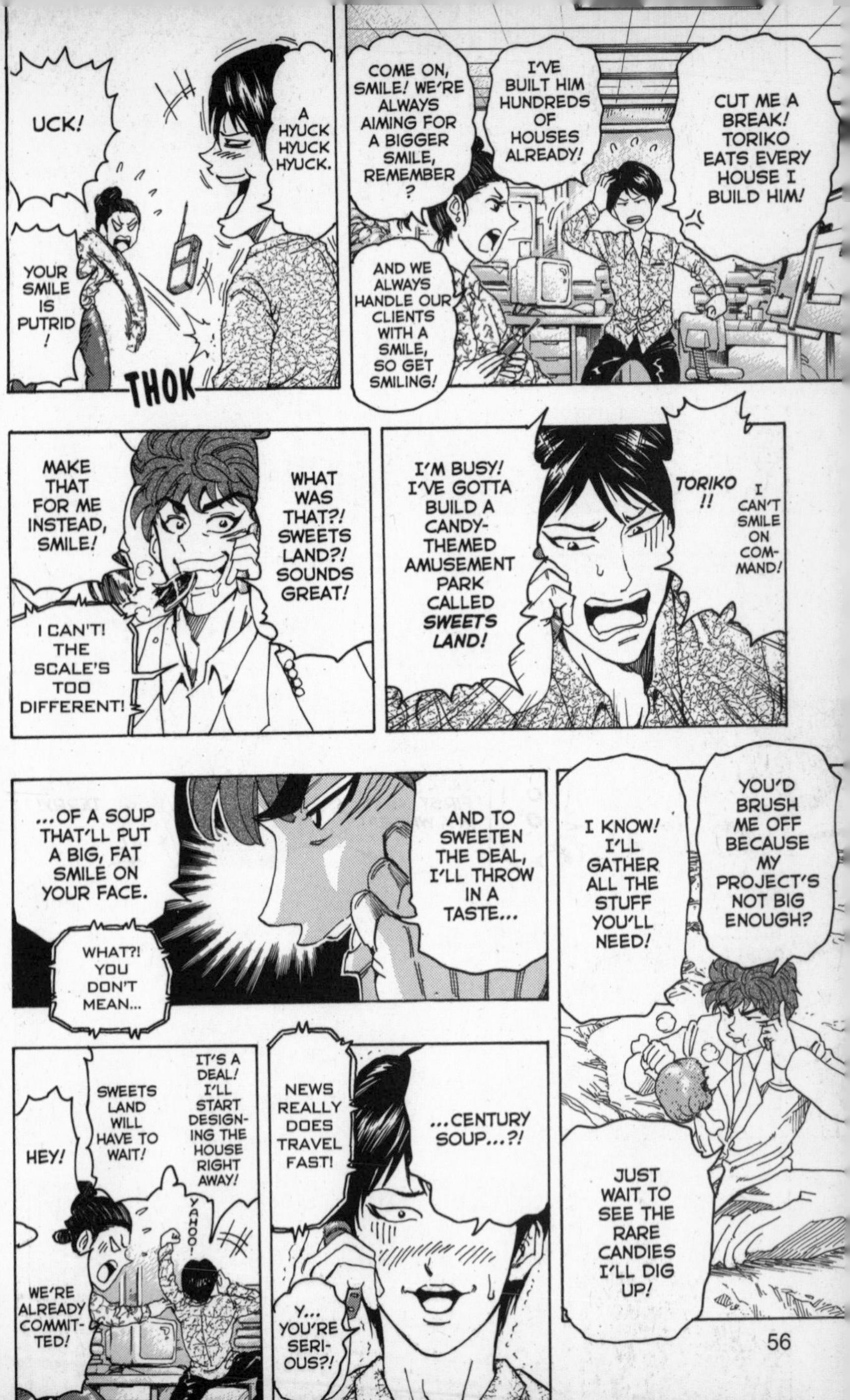
CUT ME A BREAK! TORIKO EATS EVERY HOUSE I BUILD HIM!
I'VE BUILT HIM HUNDREDS OF HOUSES ALREADY!
COME ON, SMILE! WE'RE ALWAYS AIMING FOR A BIGGER SMILE, REMEMBER?
AND WE ALWAYS HANDLE OUR CLIENTS WITH A SMILE, SO GET SMILING!
A HYUCK HYUCK HYUCK.
UCK!
YOUR SMILE IS PUTRID!
THOK
TORIKO!!
I CAN'T SMILE ON COMMAND!
I'M BUSY! I'VE GOTTA BUILD A CANDY-THEMED AMUSEMENT PARK CALLED SWEETS LAND!
WHAT WAS THAT?! SWEETS LAND?! SOUNDS GREAT!
MAKE THAT FOR ME INSTEAD, SMILE!
I CAN'T! THE SCALE'S TOO DIFFERENT!
YOU'D BRUSH ME OFF BECAUSE MY PROJECT'S NOT BIG ENOUGH?
I KNOW! I'LL GATHER ALL THE STUFF YOU'LL NEED!
JUST WAIT TO SEE THE RARE CANDIES I'LL DIG UP!
AND TO SWEETEN THE DEAL, I'LL THROW IN A TASTE...
...OF A SOUP THAT'LL PUT A BIG, FAT SMILE ON YOUR FACE.
WHAT?! YOU DON'T MEAN...
...CENTURY SOUP...?!
NEWS REALLY DOES TRAVEL FAST!
Y... YOU'RE SERIOUS?!
IT'S A DEAL! I'LL START DESIGNING THE HOUSE RIGHT AWAY!
YAHOO!
SWEETS LAND WILL HAVE TO WAIT!
HEY!
WE'RE ALREADY COMMITTED!

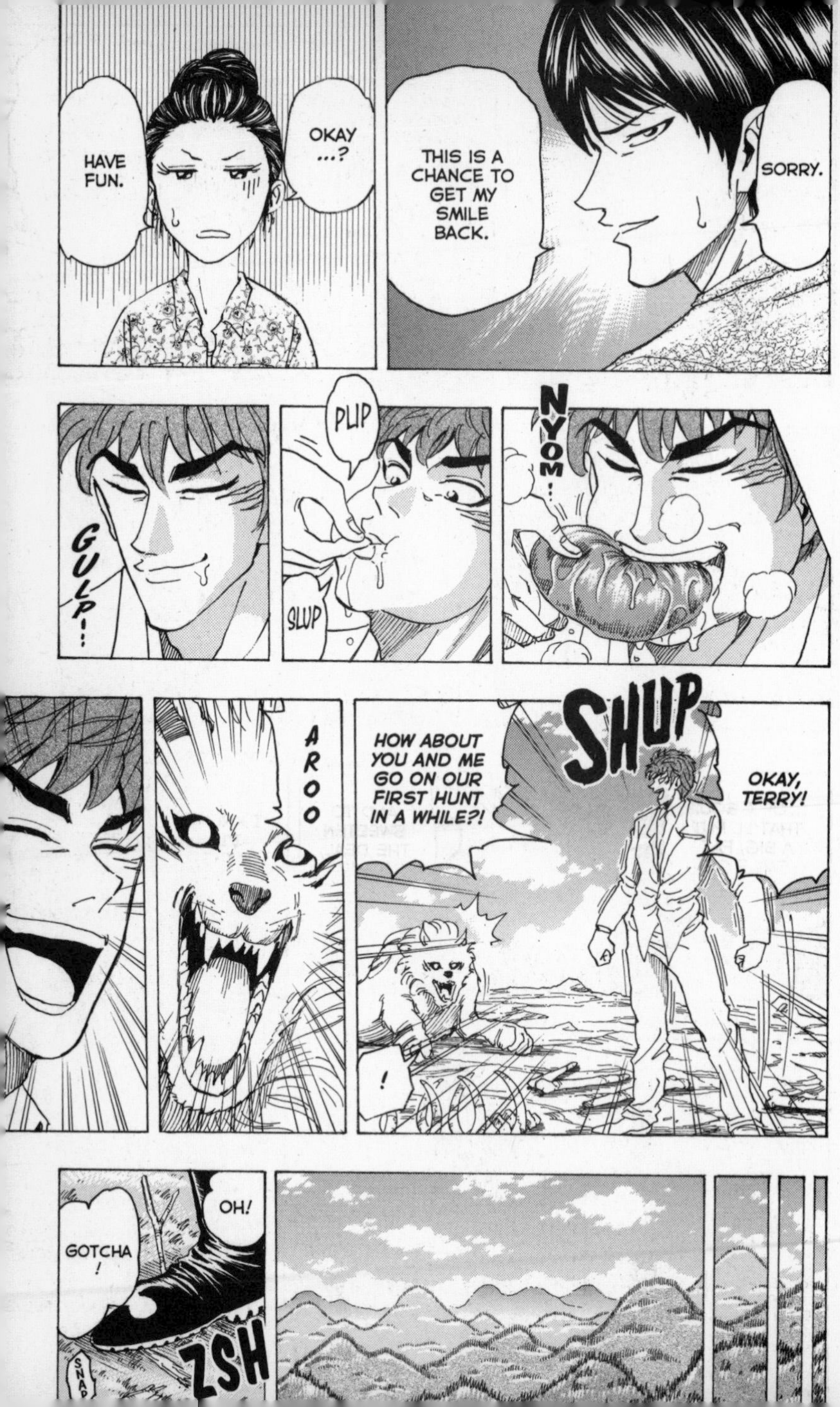
SORRY.
THIS IS A CHANCE TO GET MY SMILE BACK.
OKAY ...?
HAVE FUN.
NYOM!
PLIP
SLUP
GULP!!
SHUP
OKAY, TERRY!
HOW ABOUT YOU AND ME GO ON OUR FIRST HUNT IN A WHILE?!
!
AROO
OH!
GOTCHA!
ZSH
SNAP

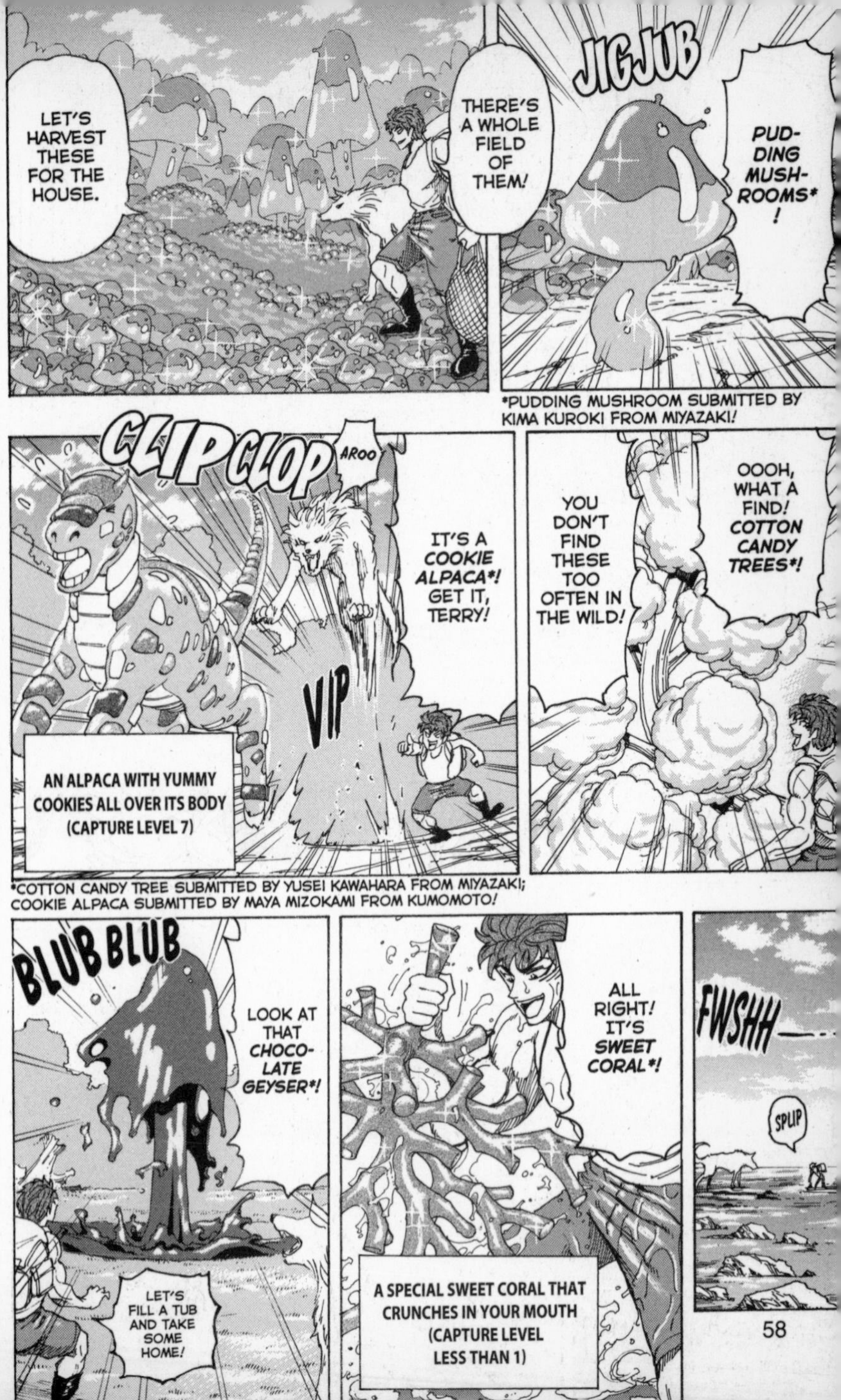
JIG JUB
PUDDING MUSHROOMS*!
THERE'S A WHOLE FIELD OF THEM!
LET'S HARVEST THESE FOR THE HOUSE.
*PUDDING MUSHROOM SUBMITTED BY KIMA KUROKI FROM MIYAZAKI!
OOOH, WHAT A FIND! COTTON CANDY TREES*!
YOU DON'T FIND THESE TOO OFTEN IN THE WILD!
CLIP CLOP
AROO
IT'S A COOKIE ALPACA*! GET IT, TERRY!
VIP
AN ALPACA WITH YUMMY COOKIES ALL OVER ITS BODY (CAPTURE LEVEL 7)
*COTTON CANDY TREE SUBMITTED BY YUSEI KAWAHARA FROM MIYAZAKI; COOKIE ALPACA SUBMITTED BY MAYA MIZOKAMI FROM KUMOMOTO!
FWSHH
SPLIP
ALL RIGHT! IT'S SWEET CORAL*!
A SPECIAL SWEET CORAL THAT CRUNCHES IN YOUR MOUTH (CAPTURE LEVEL LESS THAN 1)
BLUB BLUB
LOOK AT THAT CHOCOLATE GEYSER*!
LET'S FILL A TUB AND TAKE SOME HOME!

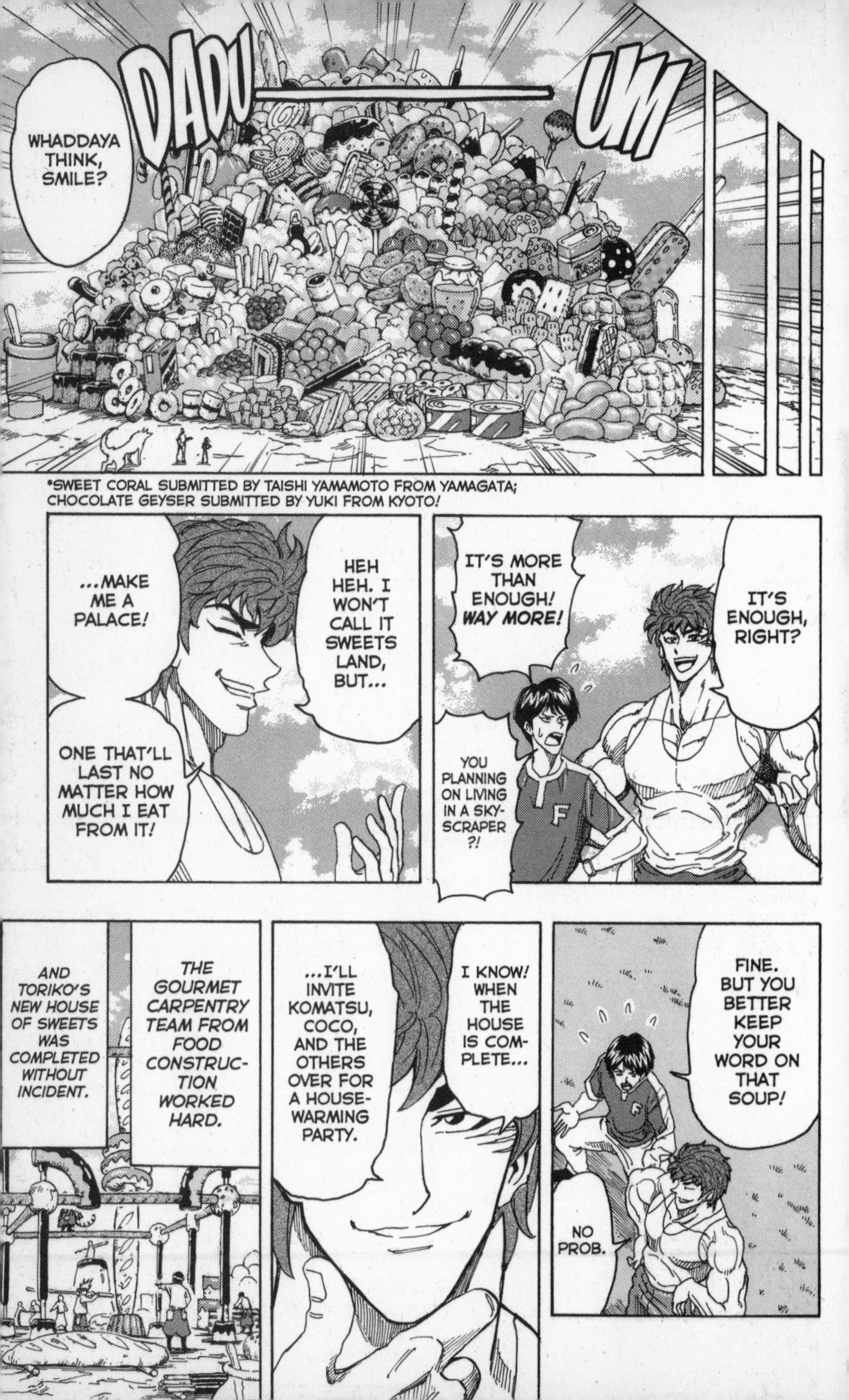
DADU—UM
WHADDAYA THINK, SMILE?
IT'S ENOUGH, RIGHT?
IT'S MORE THAN ENOUGH! *WAY MORE!*
YOU PLANNING ON LIVING IN A SKY-SCRAPER?!
HEH HEH. I WON'T CALL IT SWEETS LAND, BUT...
...MAKE ME A PALACE!
ONE THAT'LL LAST NO MATTER HOW MUCH I EAT FROM IT!
FINE. BUT YOU BETTER KEEP YOUR WORD ON THAT SOUP!
NO PROB.
I KNOW! WHEN THE HOUSE IS COM-PLETE...
...I'LL INVITE KOMATSU, COCO, AND THE OTHERS OVER FOR A HOUSE-WARMING PARTY.
THE GOURMET CARPENTRY TEAM FROM FOOD CONSTRUC-TION WORKED HARD.
AND TORIKO'S NEW HOUSE OF SWEETS WAS COMPLETED WITHOUT INCIDENT.

*SWEET CORAL SUBMITTED BY TAISHI YAMAMOTO FROM YAMAGATA; CHOCOLATE GEYSER SUBMITTED BY YUKI FROM KYOTO!

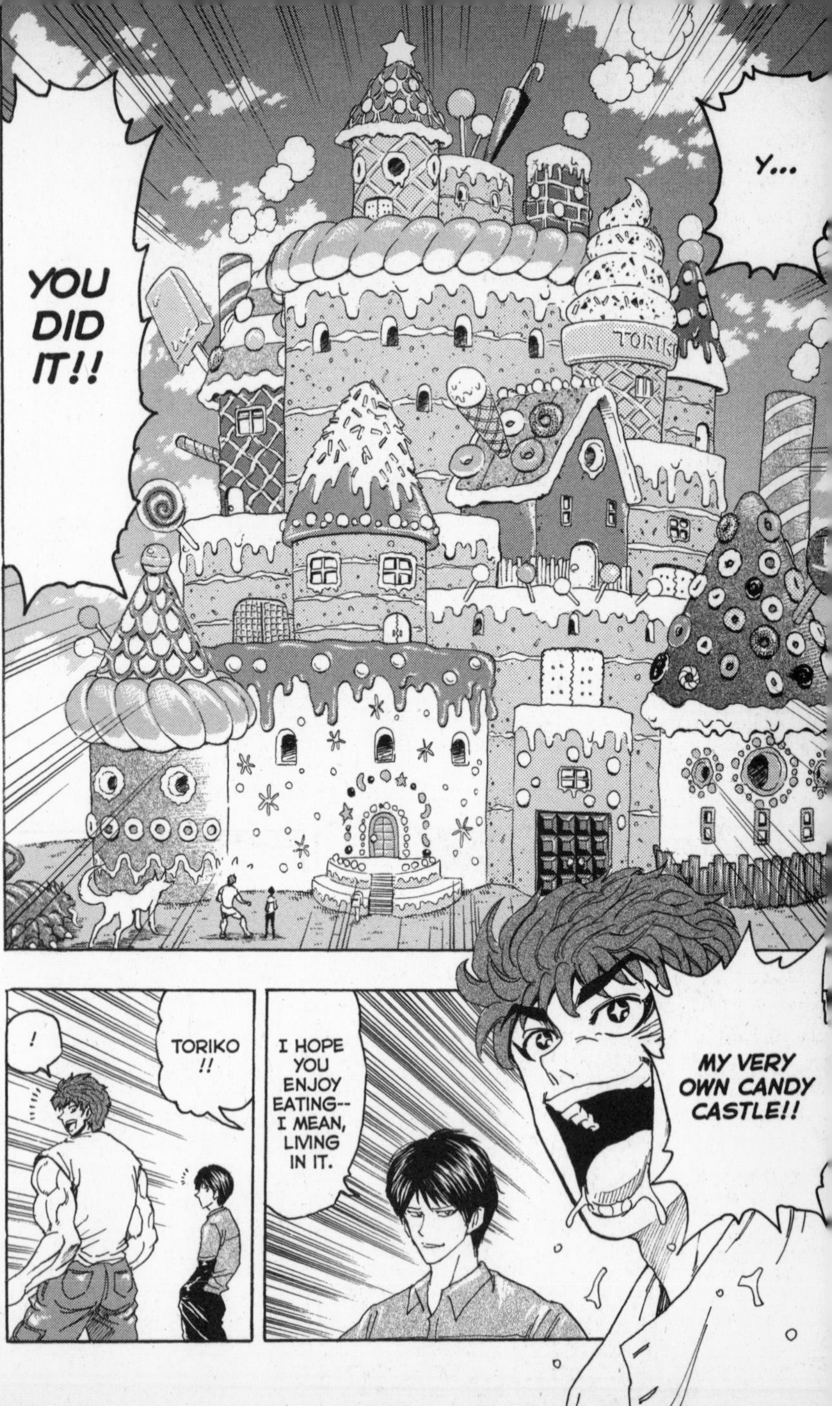
Y...
YOU DID IT!!
MY VERY OWN CANDY CASTLE!!
I HOPE YOU ENJOY EATING-- I MEAN, LIVING IN IT.
TORIKO !!
!

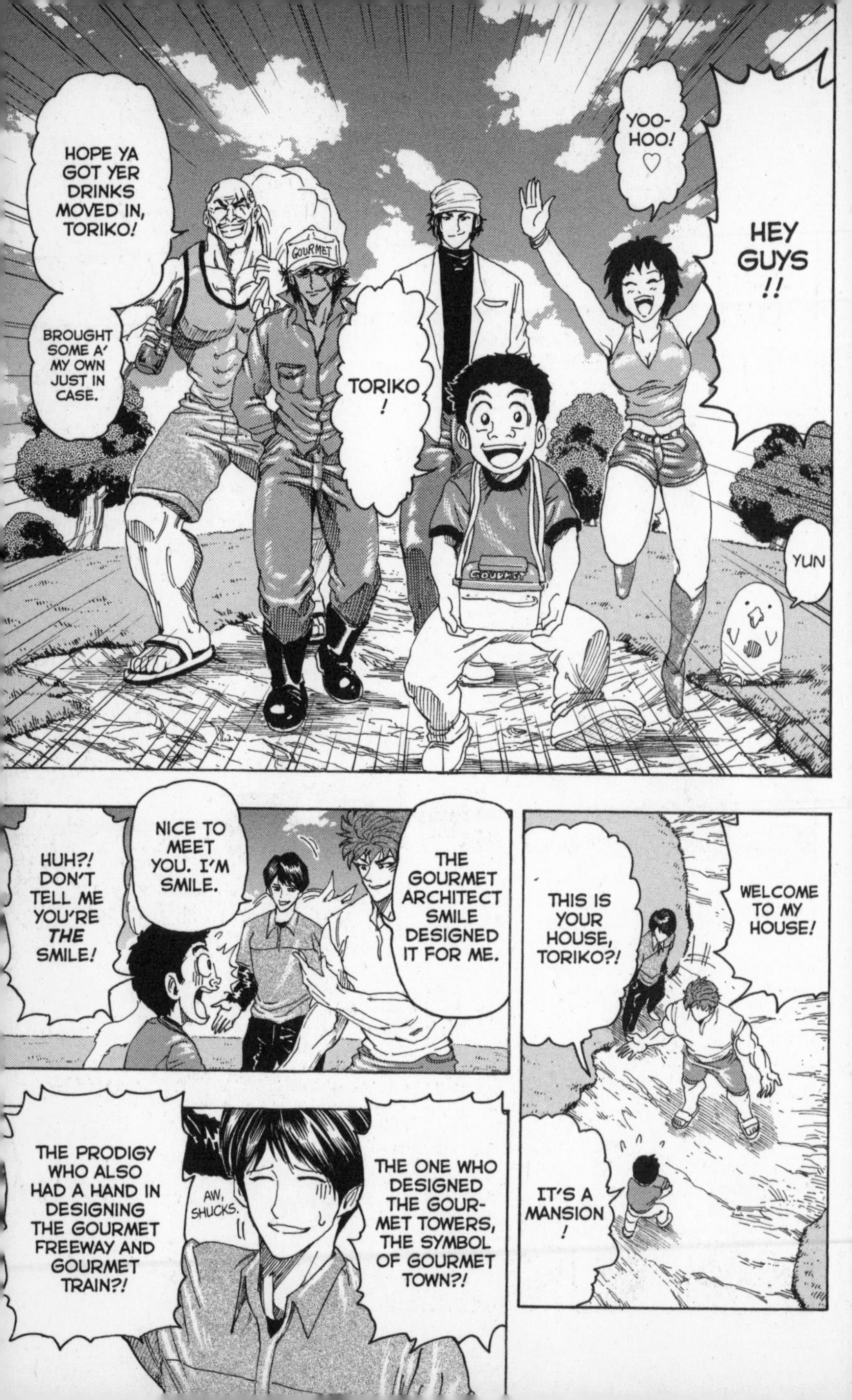
HEY GUYS!!
YOO-HOO! ♡
YUN
TORIKO!
HOPE YA GOT YER DRINKS MOVED IN, TORIKO!
BROUGHT SOME A' MY OWN JUST IN CASE.
WELCOME TO MY HOUSE!
THIS IS YOUR HOUSE, TORIKO?!
IT'S A MANSION!
THE GOURMET ARCHITECT SMILE DESIGNED IT FOR ME.
NICE TO MEET YOU. I'M SMILE.
HUH?! DON'T TELL ME YOU'RE *THE* SMILE!
THE ONE WHO DESIGNED THE GOURMET TOWERS, THE SYMBOL OF GOURMET TOWN?!
AW, SHUCKS.
THE PRODIGY WHO ALSO HAD A HAND IN DESIGNING THE GOURMET FREEWAY AND GOURMET TRAIN?!

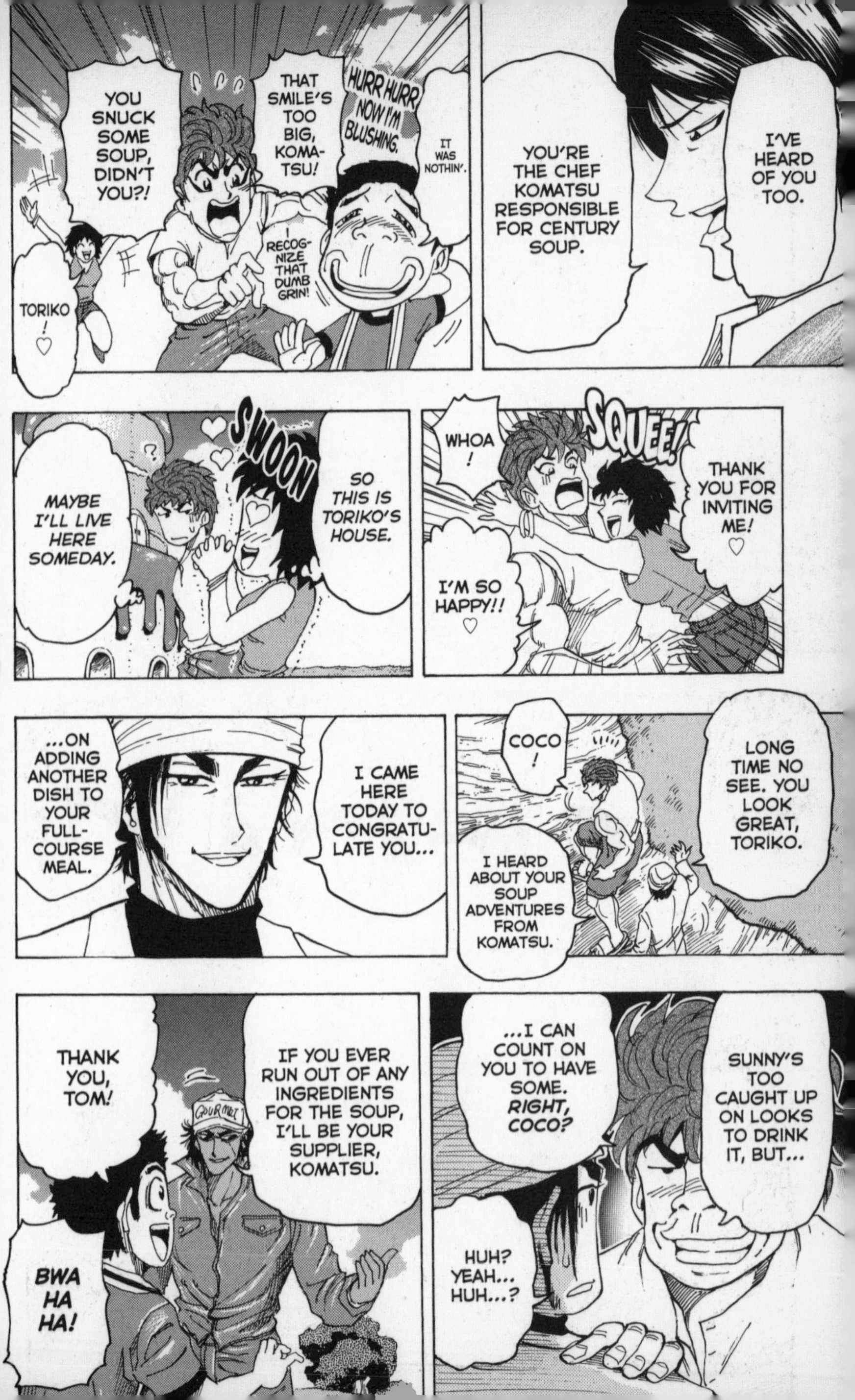
I'VE HEARD OF YOU TOO.
YOU'RE THE CHEF KOMATSU RESPONSIBLE FOR CENTURY SOUP.
HURR HURR NOW I'M BLUSHING.
IT WAS NOTHIN'.
THAT SMILE'S TOO BIG, KOMATSU!
I RECOGNIZE THAT DUMB GRIN!
YOU SNUCK SOME SOUP, DIDN'T YOU?!
TORIKO! ♡
SQUEE!
THANK YOU FOR INVITING ME! ♡
WHOA!
I'M SO HAPPY!! ♡
SWOON
SO THIS IS TORIKO'S HOUSE.
MAYBE I'LL LIVE HERE SOMEDAY.
LONG TIME NO SEE. YOU LOOK GREAT, TORIKO.
COCO!
I HEARD ABOUT YOUR SOUP ADVENTURES FROM KOMATSU.
I CAME HERE TODAY TO CONGRATULATE YOU...
...ON ADDING ANOTHER DISH TO YOUR FULL-COURSE MEAL.
SUNNY'S TOO CAUGHT UP ON LOOKS TO DRINK IT, BUT...
...I CAN COUNT ON YOU TO HAVE SOME. RIGHT, COCO?
HUH? YEAH... HUH...?
IF YOU EVER RUN OUT OF ANY INGREDIENTS FOR THE SOUP, I'LL BE YOUR SUPPLIER, KOMATSU.
THANK YOU, TOM!
BWA HA HA!

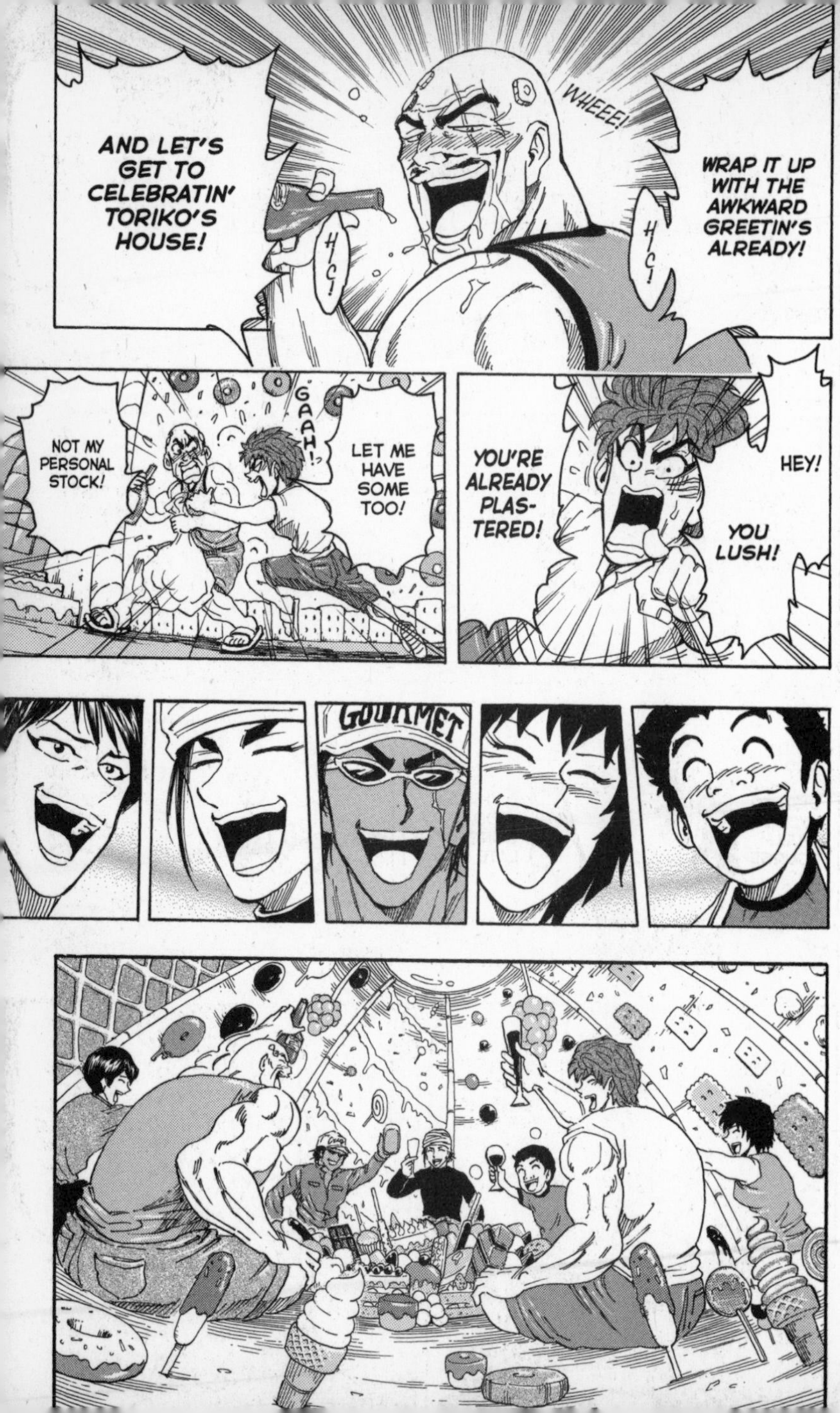
WRAP IT UP WITH THE AWKWARD GREETIN'S ALREADY!
HIC!
WHEEE!
HIC!
AND LET'S GET TO CELEBRATIN' TORIKO'S HOUSE!
HEY!
YOU LUSH!
YOU'RE ALREADY PLAS-TERED!
LET ME HAVE SOME TOO!
GAAAH!?
NOT MY PERSONAL STOCK!
GOURMET

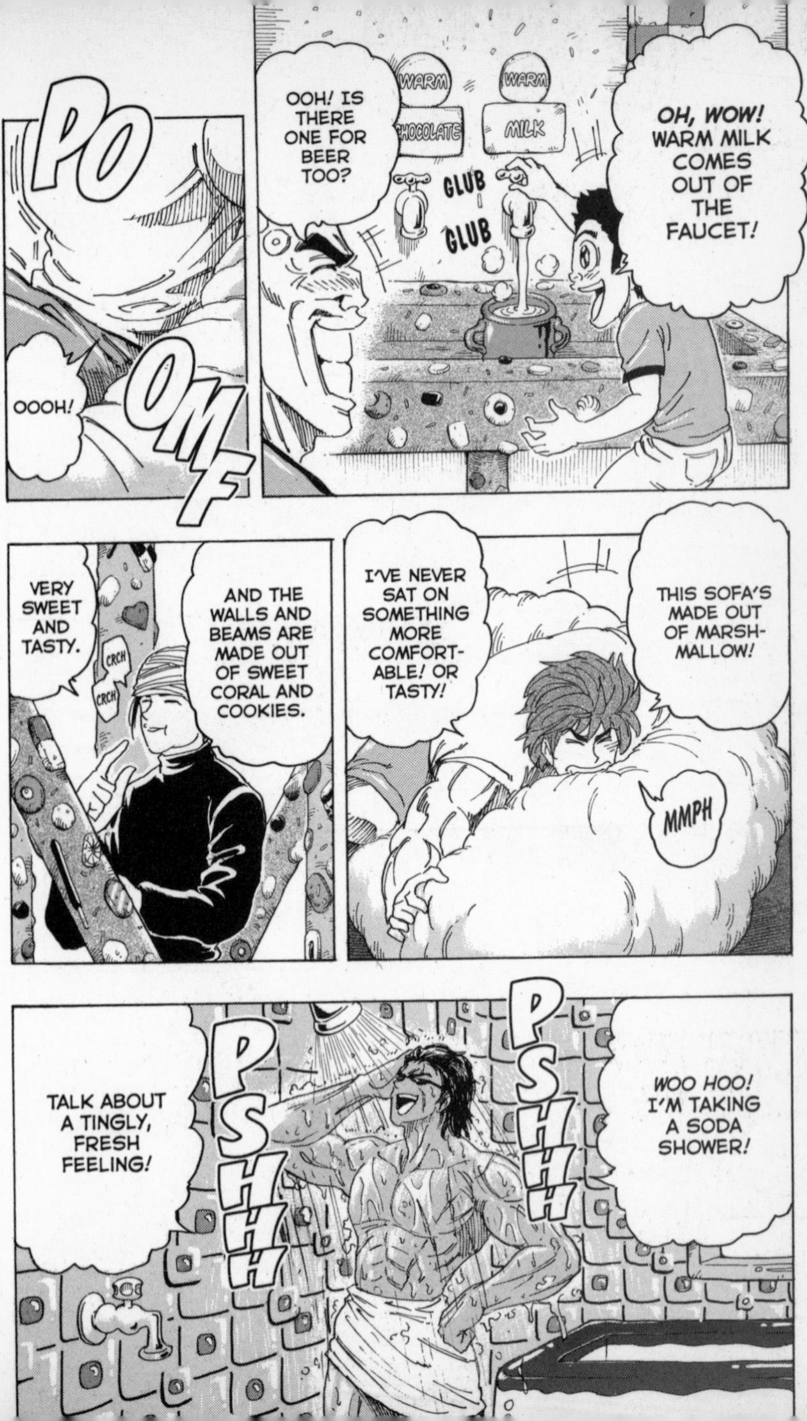
OH, WOW! WARM MILK COMES OUT OF THE FAUCET!
WARM
MILK
WARM
CHOCOLATE
GLUB GLUB
OOH! IS THERE ONE FOR BEER TOO?
POOMF
OOOH!
THIS SOFA'S MADE OUT OF MARSHMALLOW!
MMPH
I'VE NEVER SAT ON SOMETHING MORE COMFORTABLE! OR TASTY!
AND THE WALLS AND BEAMS ARE MADE OUT OF SWEET CORAL AND COOKIES.
VERY SWEET AND TASTY.
CRCH CRCH
WOO HOO! I'M TAKING A SODA SHOWER!
PSHHH
PSHHH
TALK ABOUT A TINGLY, FRESH FEELING!

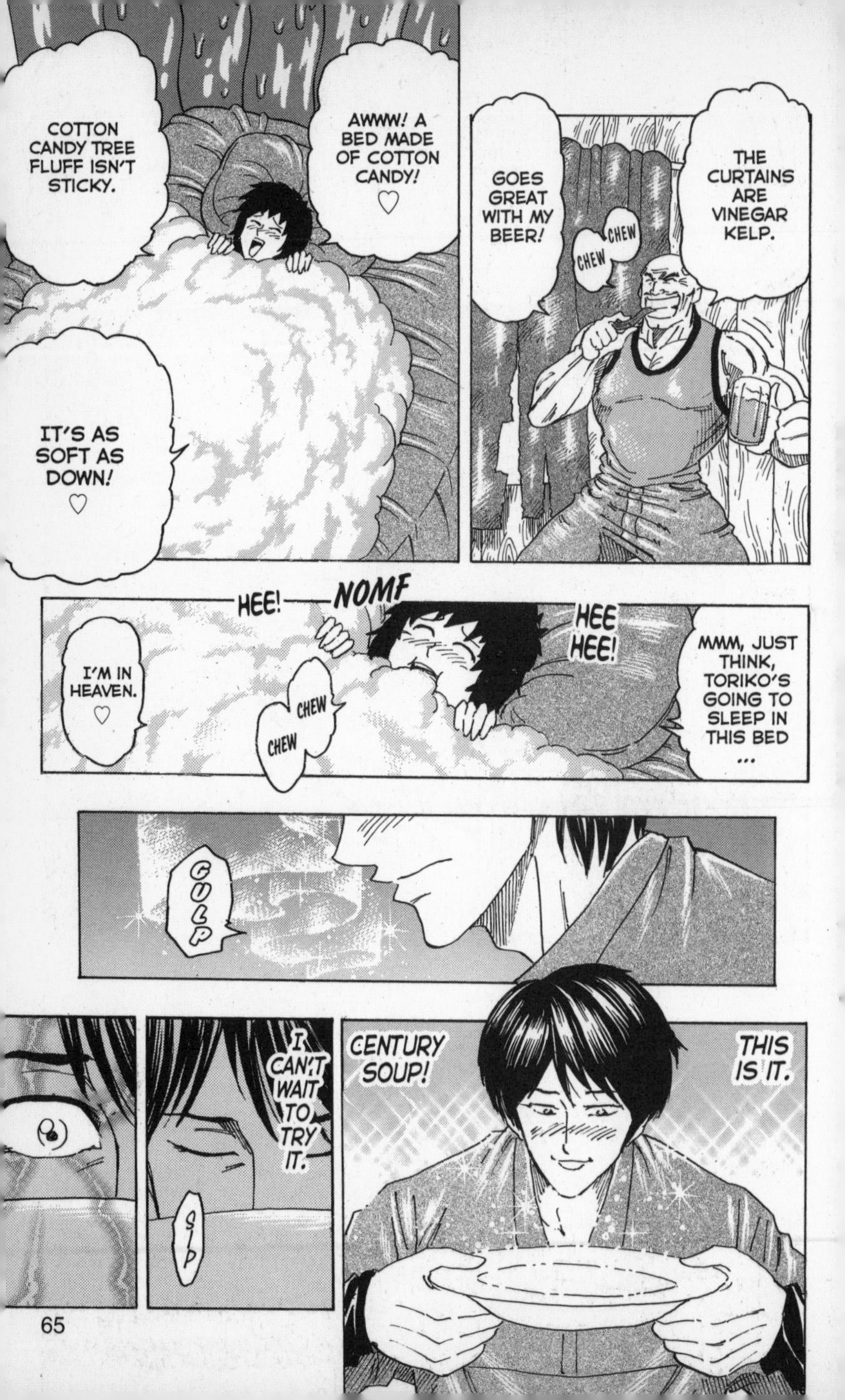
THE CURTAINS ARE VINEGAR KELP.
CHEW CHEW
GOES GREAT WITH MY BEER!
AWWW! A BED MADE OF COTTON CANDY! ♡
COTTON CANDY TREE FLUFF ISN'T STICKY.
IT'S AS SOFT AS DOWN! ♡
MMM, JUST THINK, TORIKO'S GOING TO SLEEP IN THIS BED ...
HEE HEE!
NOMF
HEE!
CHEW CHEW
I'M IN HEAVEN. ♡
GULP
THIS IS IT.
CENTURY SOUP!
I CAN'T WAIT TO TRY IT.
SIP

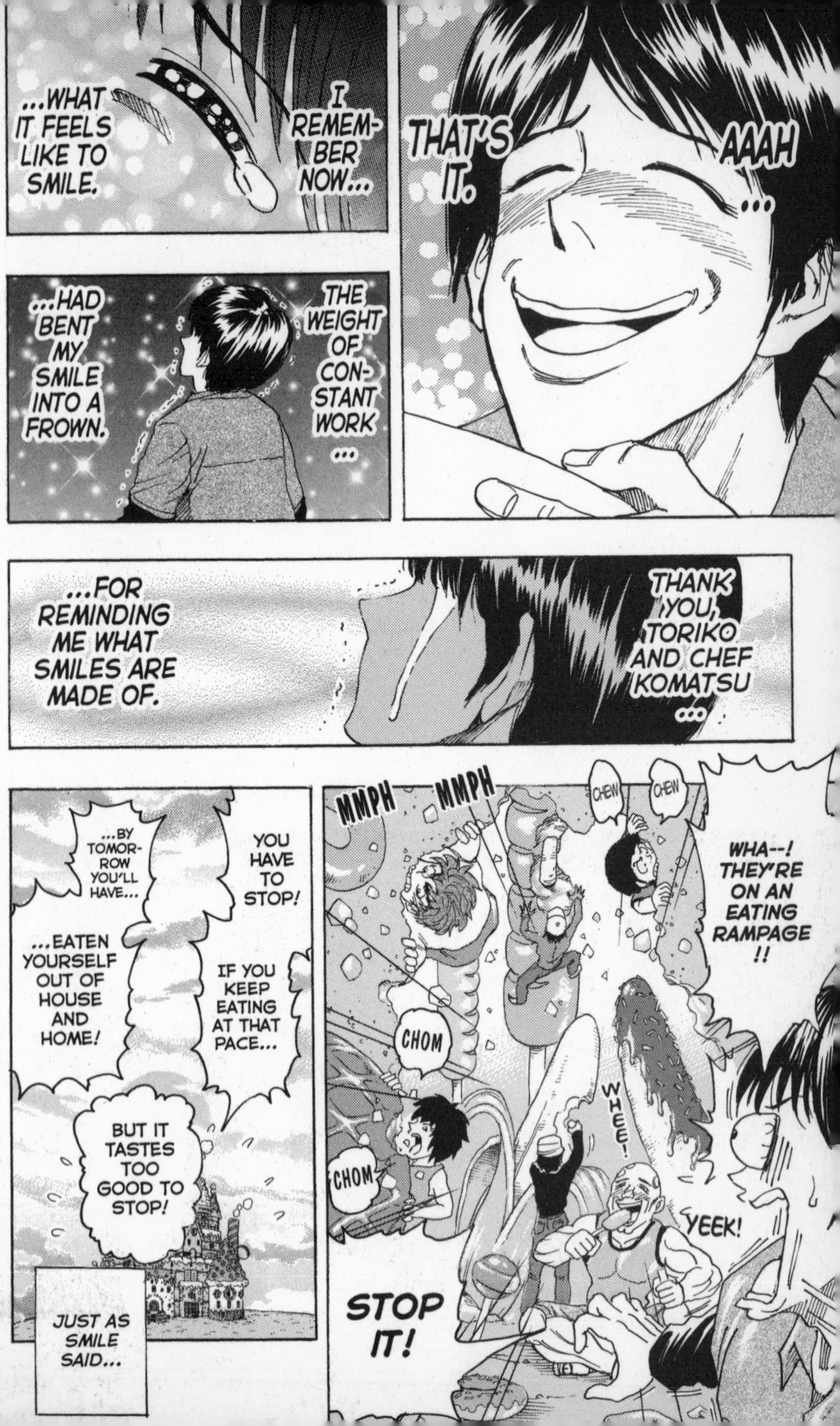
AAAH...
THAT'S IT.
I REMEMBER NOW...
...WHAT IT FEELS LIKE TO SMILE.
THE WEIGHT OF CONSTANT WORK...
...HAD BENT MY SMILE INTO A FROWN.
THANK YOU, TORIKO AND CHEF KOMATSU...
...FOR REMINDING ME WHAT SMILES ARE MADE OF.
CHEW
CHEW
MMPH
MMPH
WHA--! THEY'RE ON AN EATING RAMPAGE!!
CHOM
WHEE!
CHOM
YEEK!
STOP IT!
YOU HAVE TO STOP!
IF YOU KEEP EATING AT THAT PACE...
...BY TOMORROW YOU'LL HAVE...
...EATEN YOURSELF OUT OF HOUSE AND HOME!
BUT IT TASTES TOO GOOD TO STOP!
JUST AS SMILE SAID...

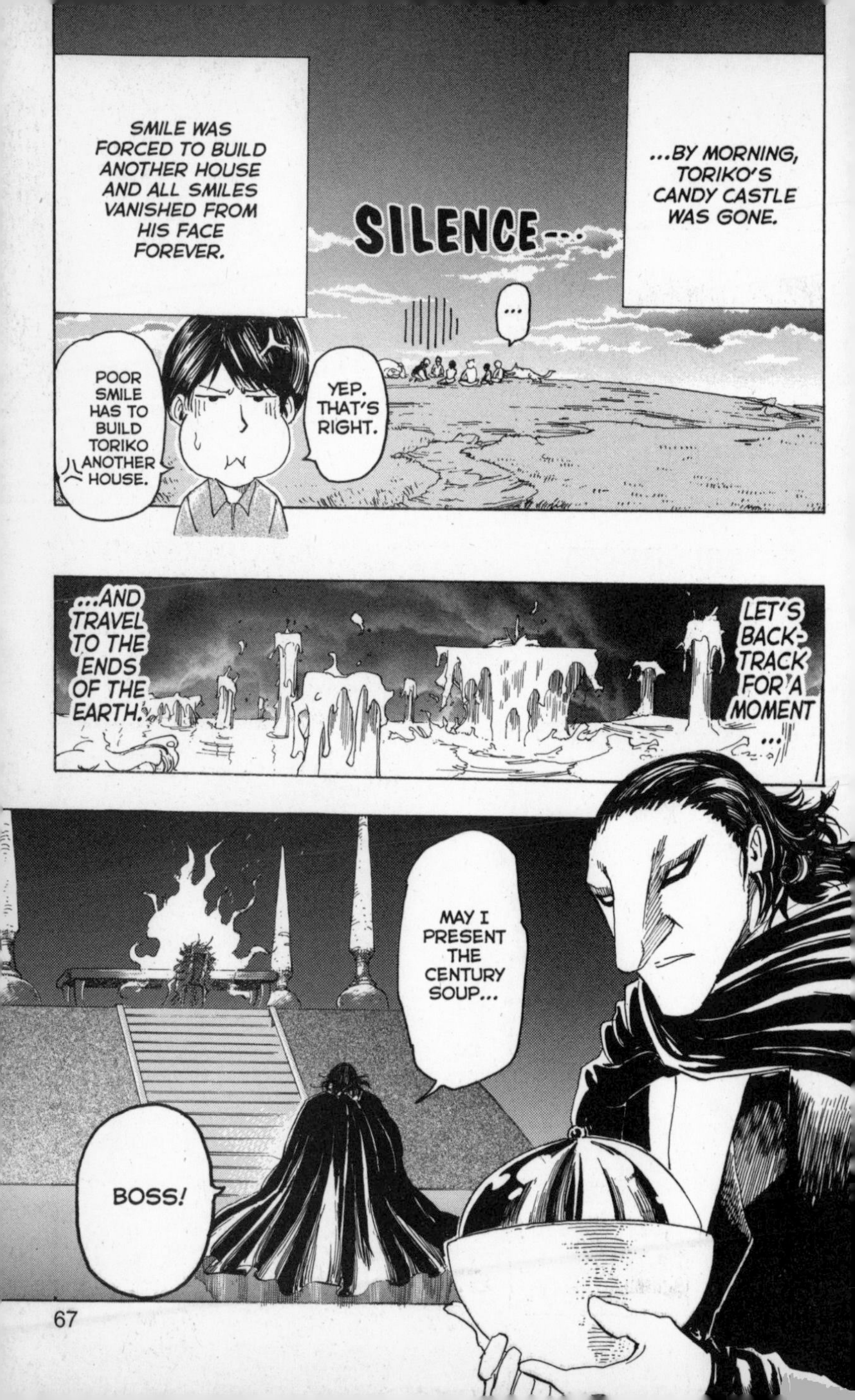
...BY MORNING, TORIKO'S CANDY CASTLE WAS GONE.
SILENCE...
...
SMILE WAS FORCED TO BUILD ANOTHER HOUSE AND ALL SMILES VANISHED FROM HIS FACE FOREVER.
YEP. THAT'S RIGHT.
POOR SMILE HAS TO BUILD TORIKO ANOTHER HOUSE.
LET'S BACKTRACK FOR A MOMENT...
...AND TRAVEL TO THE ENDS OF THE EARTH.
MAY I PRESENT THE CENTURY SOUP...
BOSS!

GOURMET CHECKLIST

Vol. 110

FERTILITY SEED
(SEED)

CAPTURE LEVEL: ---

HABITAT: PROPERTY OF TEPPEI (DETAILS UNKNOWN)

LENGTH: 1 CM

HEIGHT: ---

WEIGHT: 50 G

PRICE: 5,000,000 YEN PER SEED

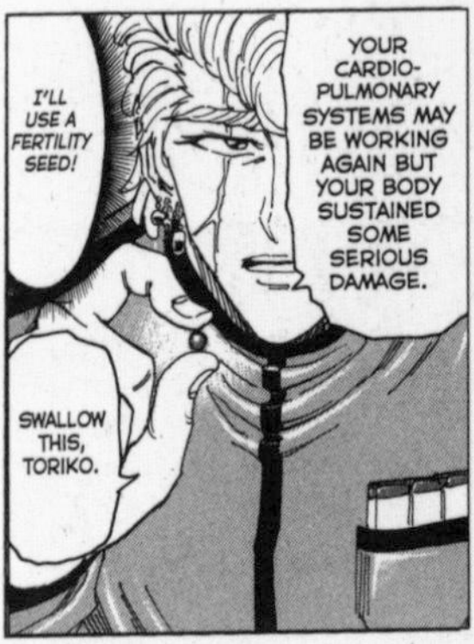
YOUR CARDIO-PULMONARY SYSTEMS MAY BE WORKING AGAIN BUT YOUR BODY SUSTAINED SOME SERIOUS DAMAGE.
I'LL USE A FERTILITY SEED!
SWALLOW THIS, TORIKO.

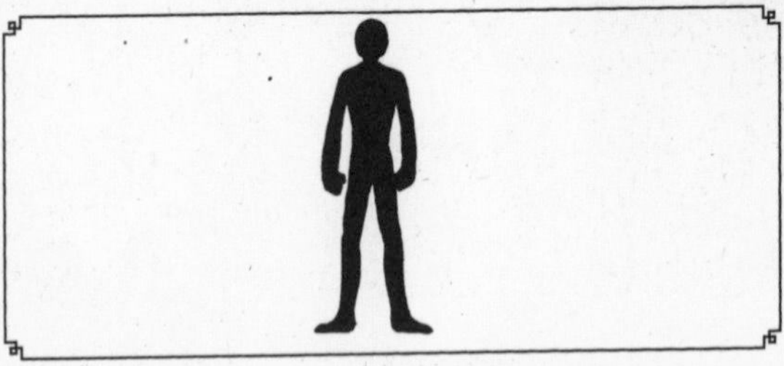

SCALE

A SEED THAT JUMP-STARTS THE BODY'S NATURAL HEALING PROCESS. ITS POISON KILLS JUST ENOUGH CELLS TO TRIGGER A SWIFT RECOVERY IN THE OTHERS. INDIVIDUALS WHO HAVE HAD THEIR ENERGY STORES SEVERELY DEPLETED RUN THE RISK OF DYING IF ADMINISTERED THIS SEED. THEREFORE, THE UTMOST CAUTION IS NEEDED WHEN HANDLING IT. ITS USE IS RESTRICTED UNDER GOURMET LAW.

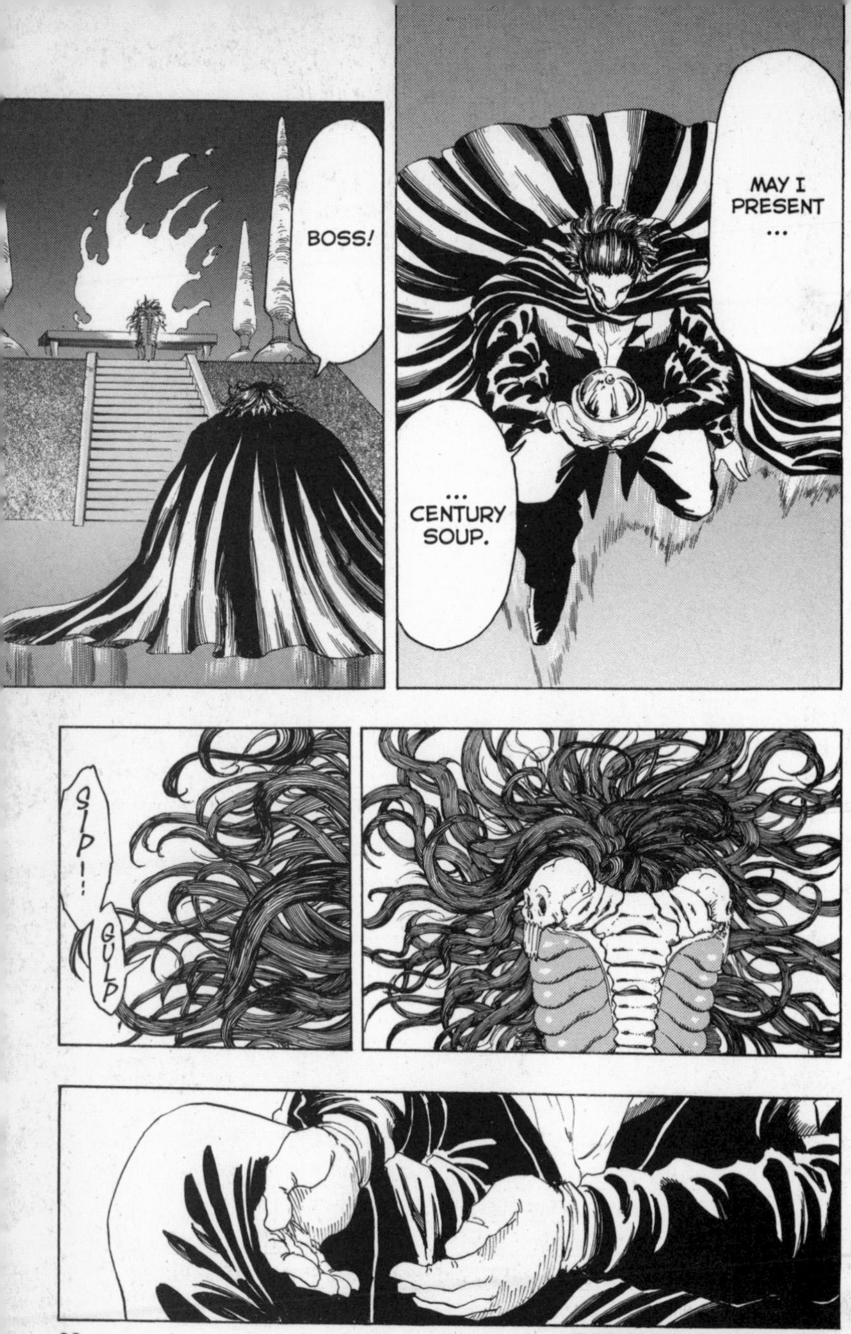
MAY I PRESENT ...
... CENTURY SOUP.
BOSS!
SIP!!
GULP

GOURMET 101: ACACIA'S DISCIPLES!!

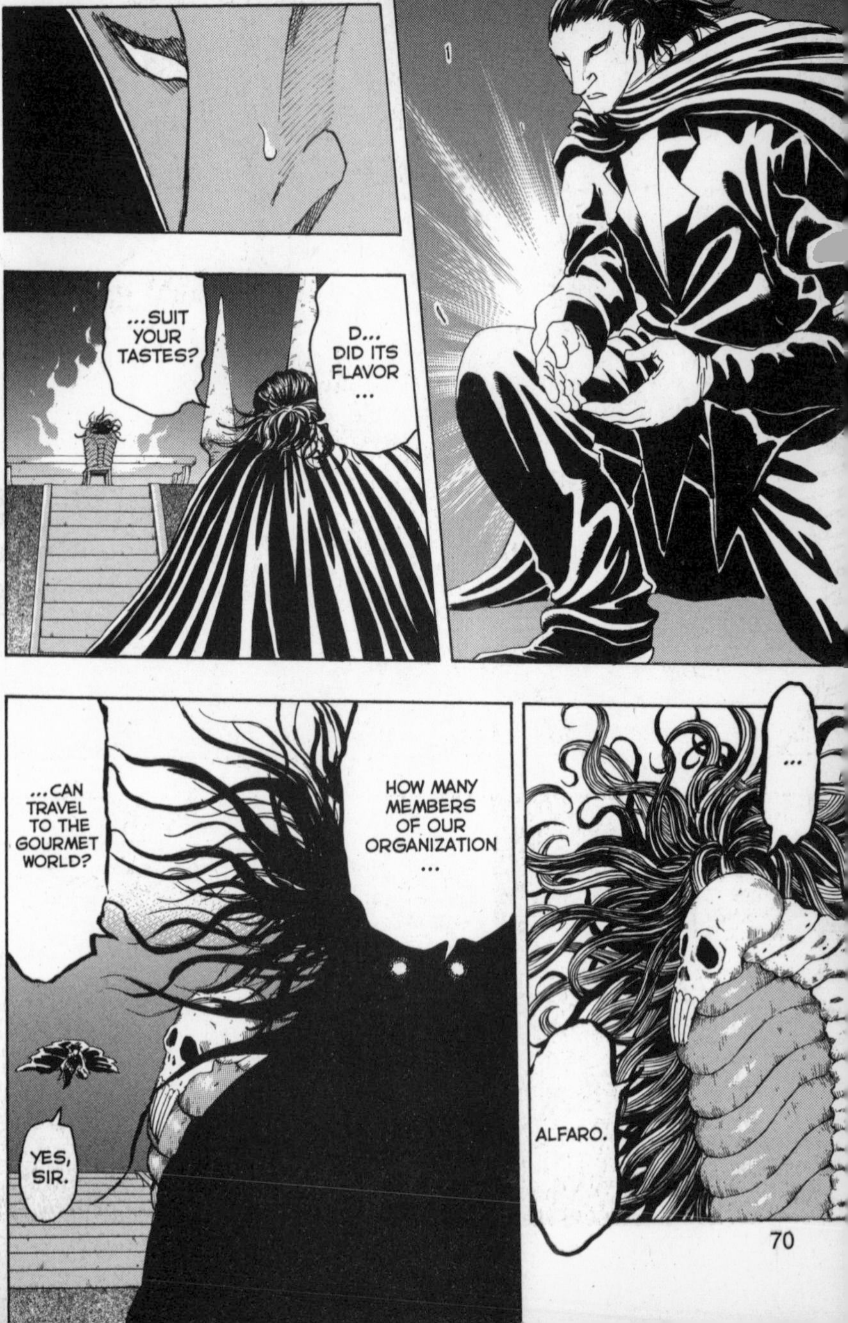
D... DID ITS FLAVOR ...
...SUIT YOUR TASTES?
...
ALFARO.
HOW MANY MEMBERS OF OUR ORGANIZATION ...
...CAN TRAVEL TO THE GOURMET WORLD?
YES, SIR.

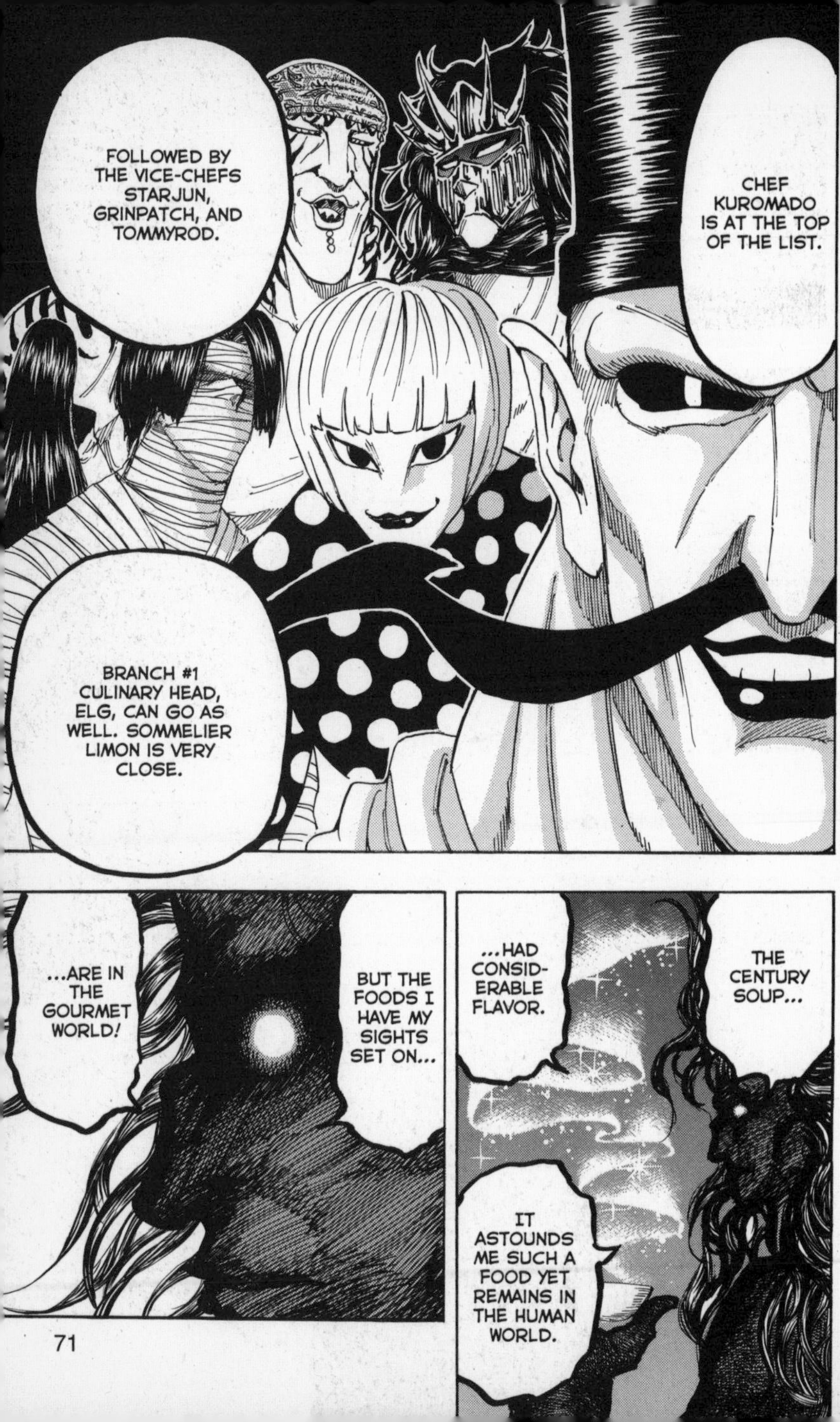
CHEF KUROMADO IS AT THE TOP OF THE LIST.
FOLLOWED BY THE VICE-CHEFS STARJUN, GRINPATCH, AND TOMMYROD.
BRANCH #1 CULINARY HEAD, ELG, CAN GO AS WELL. SOMMELIER LIMON IS VERY CLOSE.
THE CENTURY SOUP...
...HAD CONSID-ERABLE FLAVOR.
IT ASTOUNDS ME SUCH A FOOD YET REMAINS IN THE HUMAN WORLD.
BUT THE FOODS I HAVE MY SIGHTS SET ON...
...ARE IN THE GOURMET WORLD!

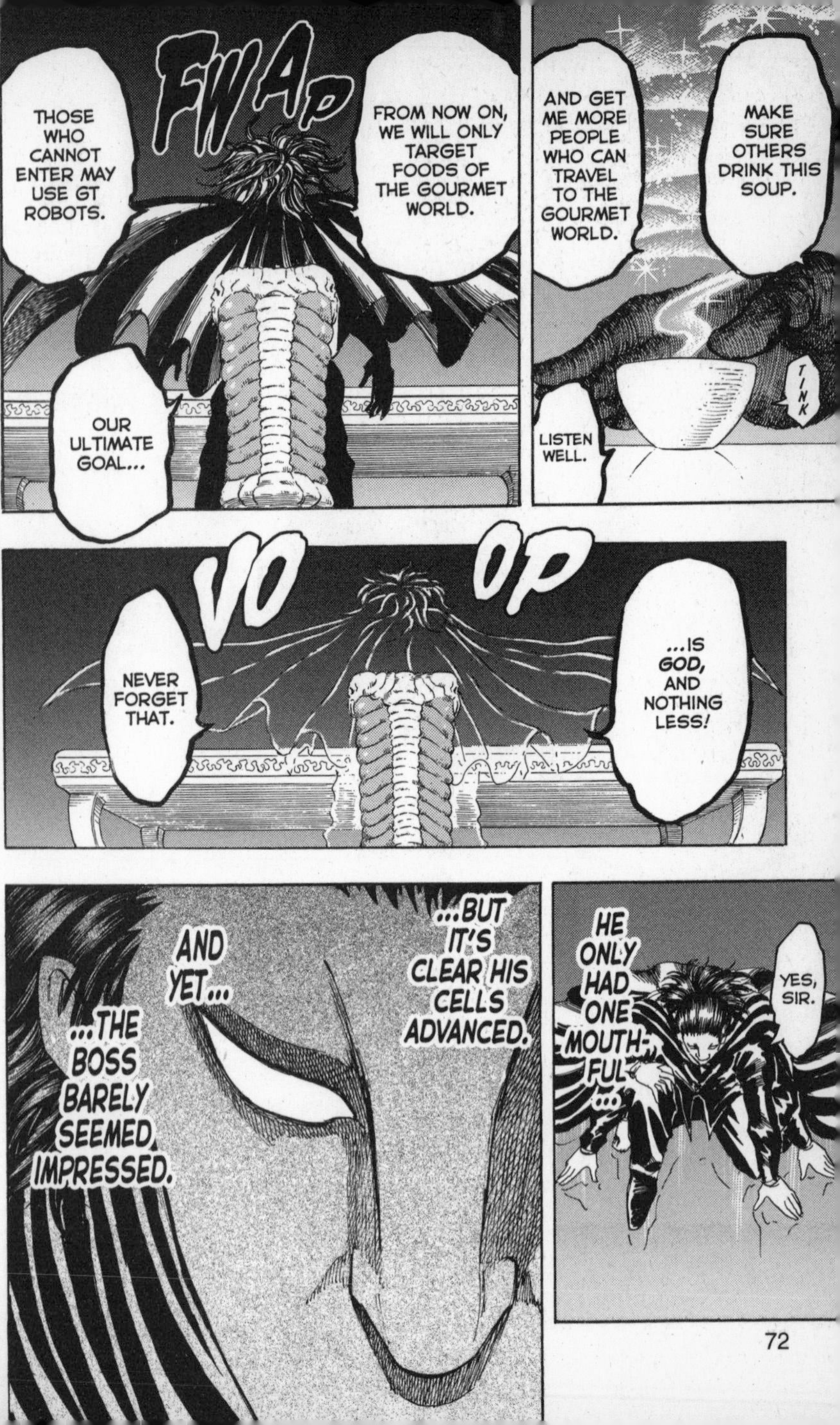

MAKE SURE OTHERS DRINK THIS SOUP.
AND GET ME MORE PEOPLE WHO CAN TRAVEL TO THE GOURMET WORLD.
TINK
LISTEN WELL.
FROM NOW ON, WE WILL ONLY TARGET FOODS OF THE GOURMET WORLD.
FWAP
THOSE WHO CANNOT ENTER MAY USE GT ROBOTS.
OUR ULTIMATE GOAL...
...IS *GOD*, AND NOTHING LESS!
VOOP
NEVER FORGET THAT.
YES, SIR.
HE ONLY HAD ONE MOUTHFUL...
...BUT IT'S CLEAR HIS CELLS ADVANCED.
AND YET...
...THE BOSS BARELY SEEMED IMPRESSED.

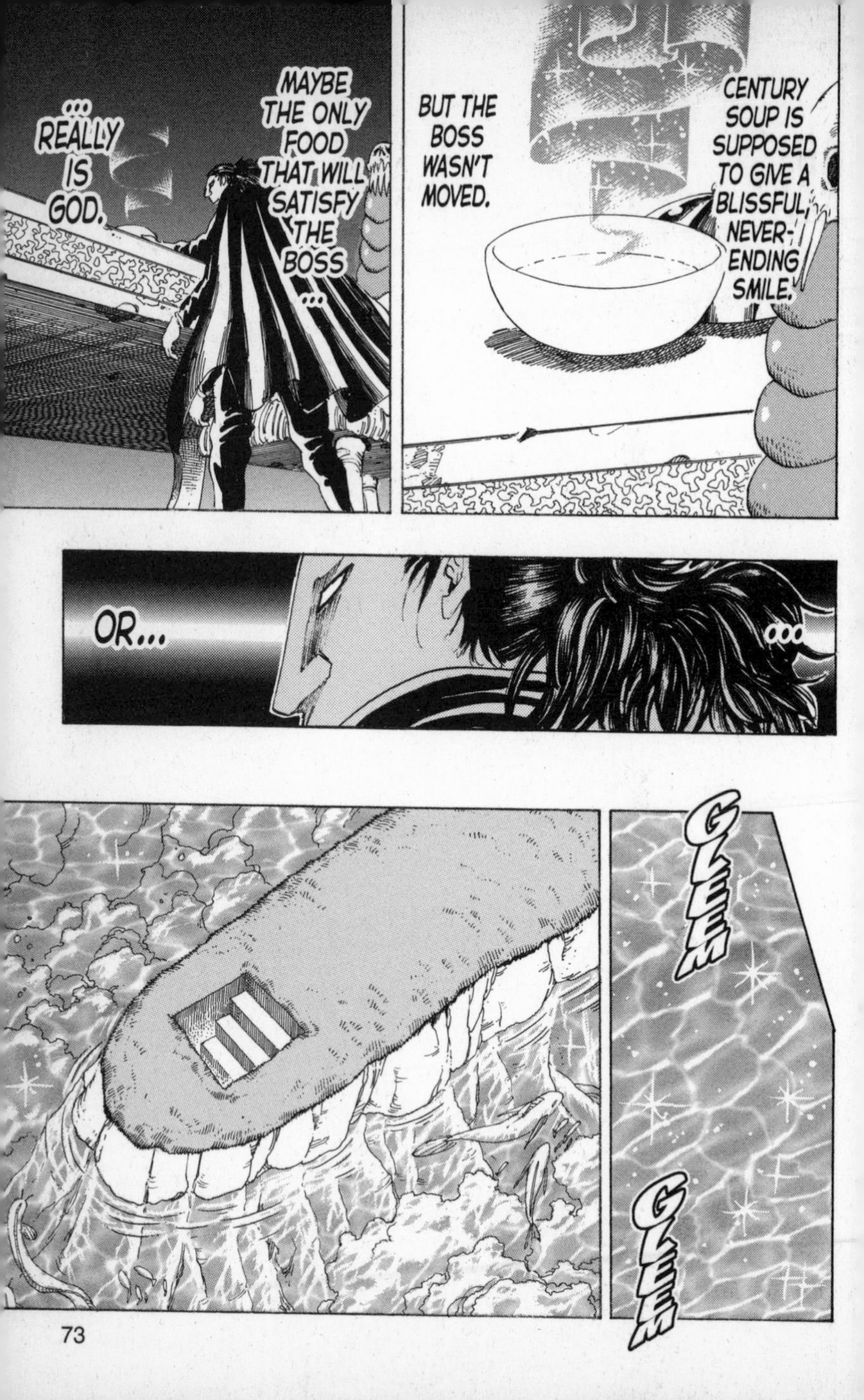
CENTURY SOUP IS SUPPOSED TO GIVE A BLISSFUL, NEVER-ENDING SMILE.
BUT THE BOSS WASN'T MOVED.
MAYBE THE ONLY FOOD THAT WILL SATISFY THE BOSS ...
... REALLY IS GOD.
...
OR...
GLEEM
GLEEM

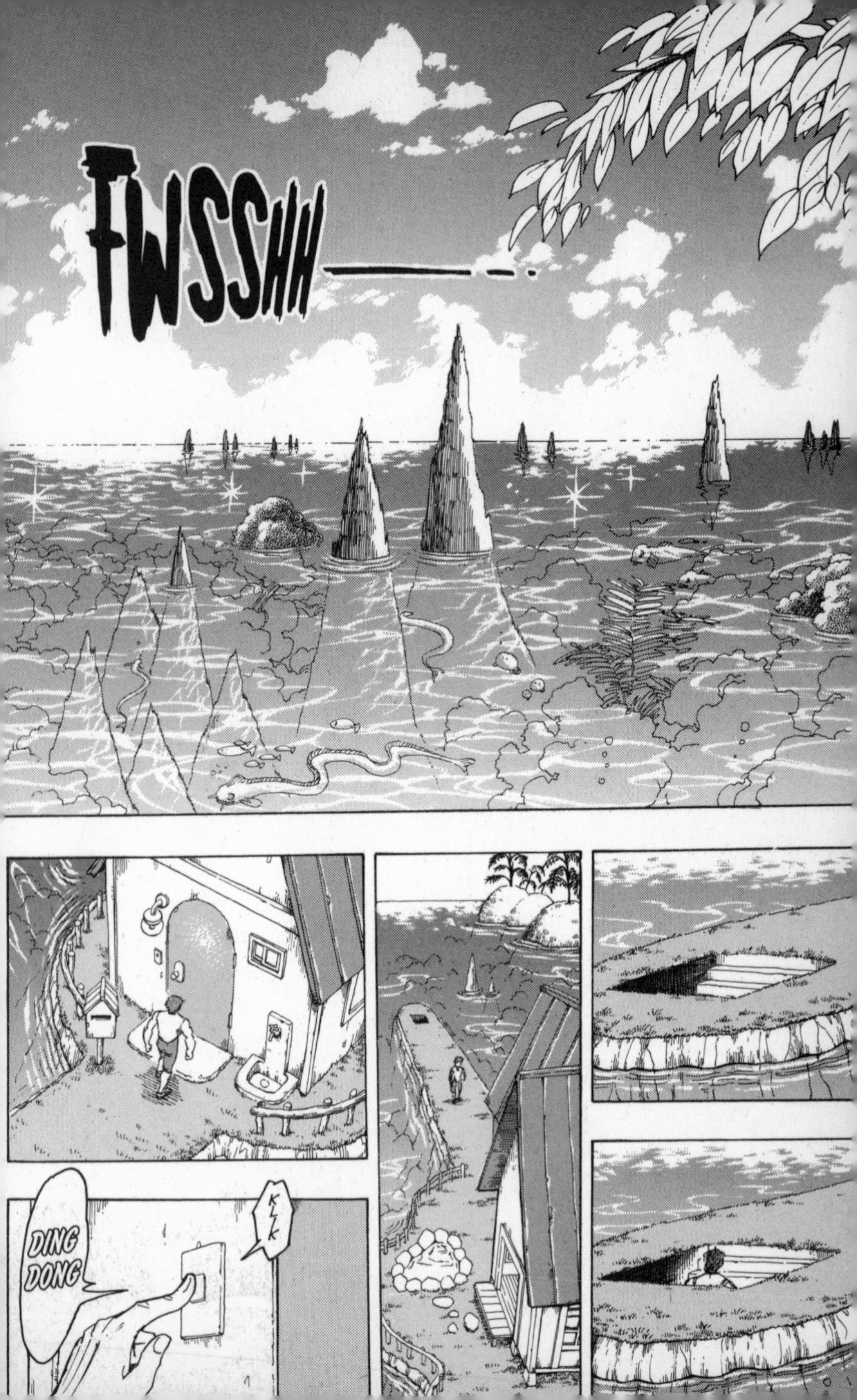
FWSSHH
KLIK
DING DONG

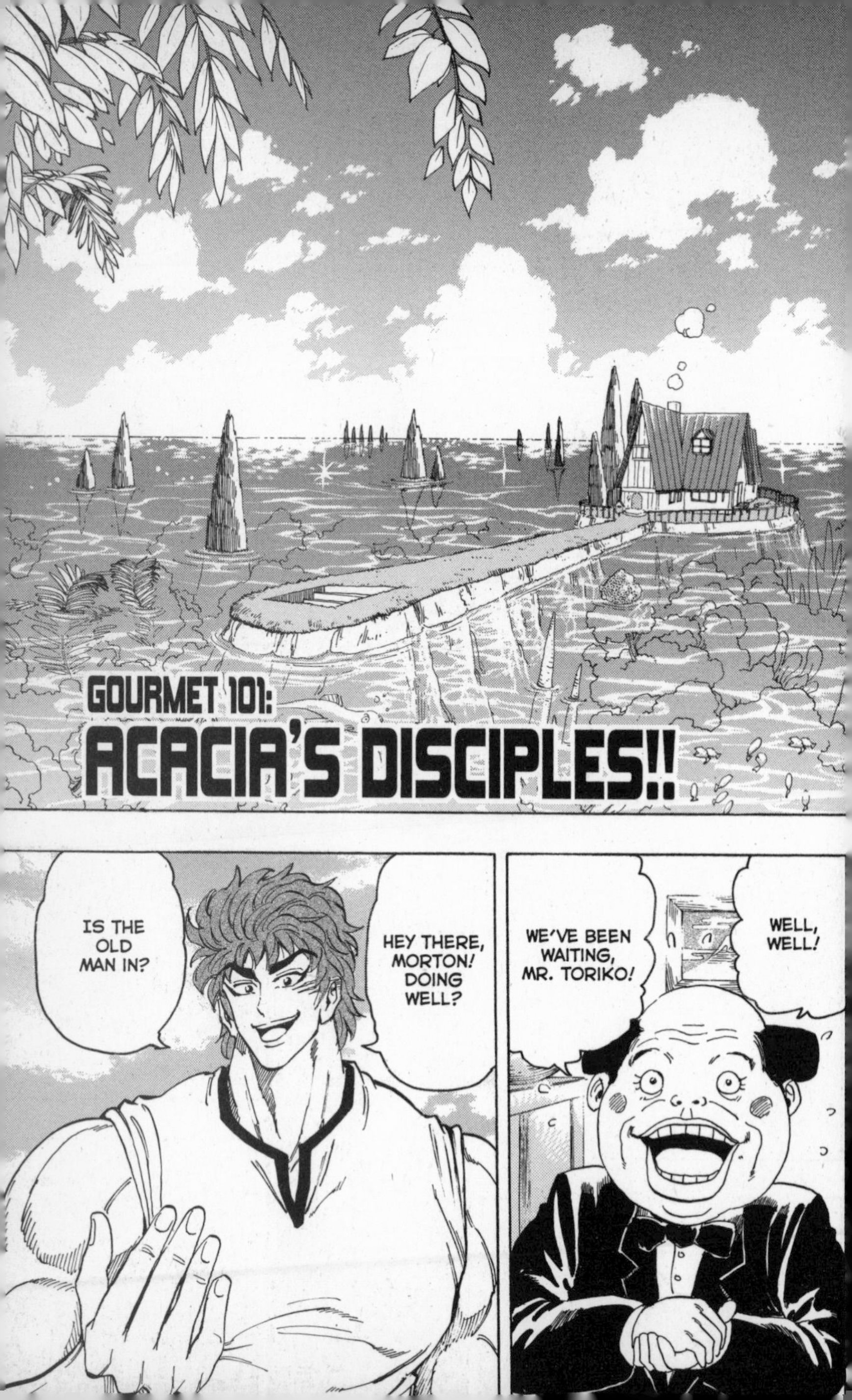
GOURMET 101:
ACACIA'S DISCIPLES!!
WELL, WELL!
WE'VE BEEN WAITING, MR. TORIKO!
HEY THERE, MORTON! DOING WELL?
IS THE OLD MAN IN?

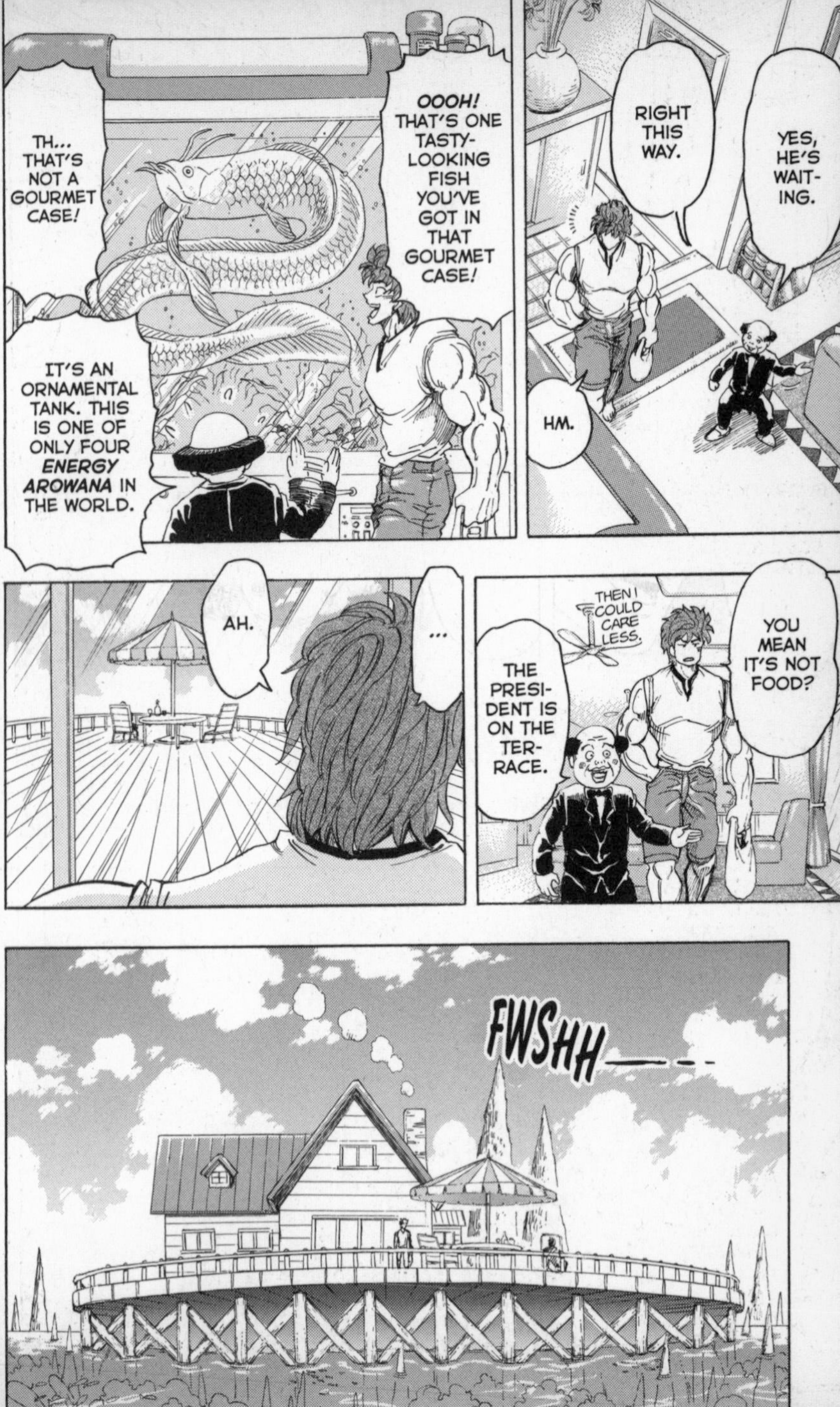
YES, HE'S WAITING.
RIGHT THIS WAY.
HM.
OOOH! THAT'S ONE TASTY-LOOKING FISH YOU'VE GOT IN THAT GOURMET CASE!
TH... THAT'S NOT A GOURMET CASE!
IT'S AN ORNAMENTAL TANK. THIS IS ONE OF ONLY FOUR ENERGY AROWANA IN THE WORLD.
YOU MEAN IT'S NOT FOOD?
THEN I COULD CARE LESS.
THE PRESIDENT IS ON THE TERRACE.
...
AH.
FWSHH—

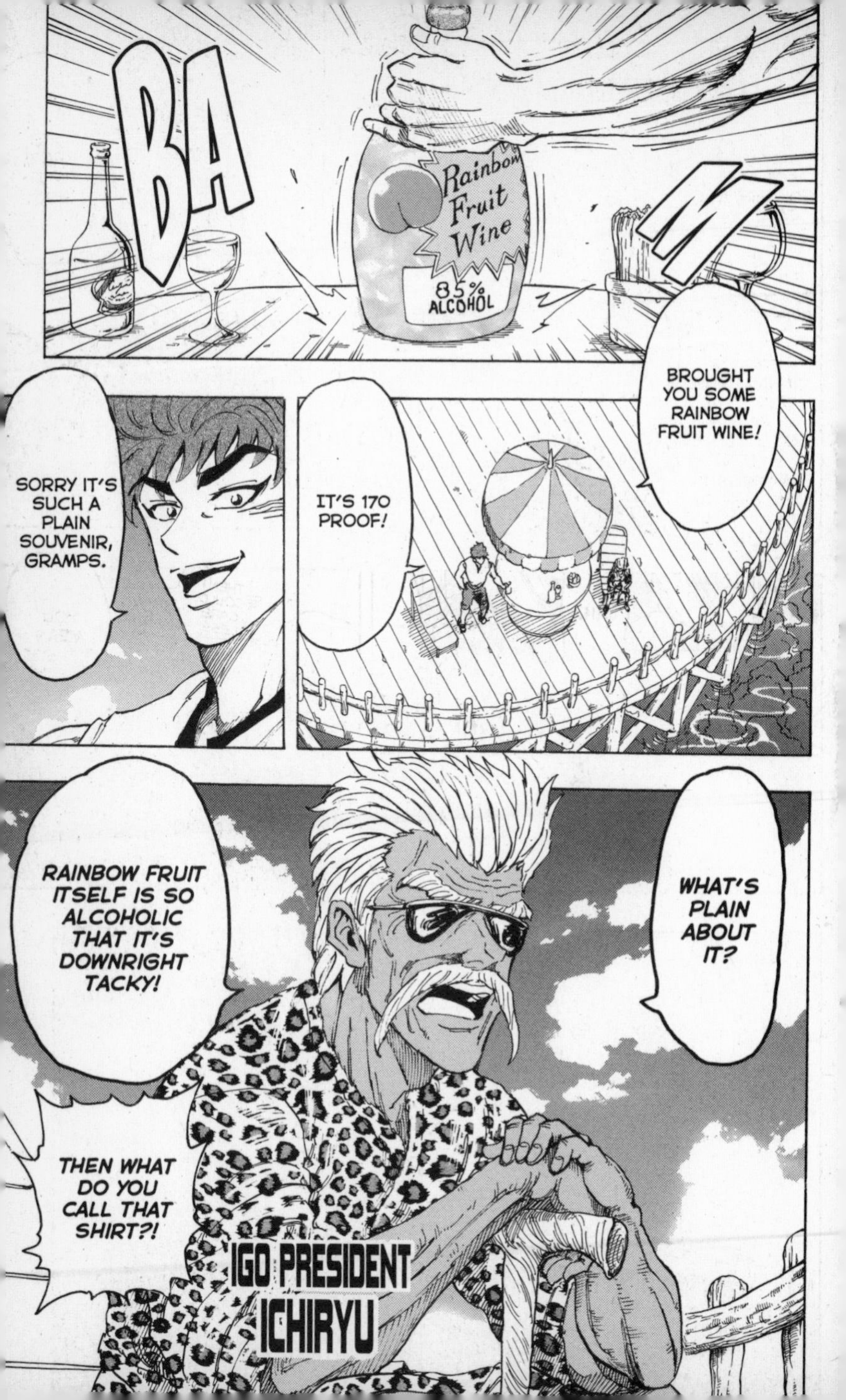
BAM
Rainbow Fruit Wine
85% ALCOHOL
BROUGHT YOU SOME RAINBOW FRUIT WINE!
IT'S 170 PROOF!
SORRY IT'S SUCH A PLAIN SOUVENIR, GRAMPS.
WHAT'S PLAIN ABOUT IT?
RAINBOW FRUIT ITSELF IS SO ALCOHOLIC THAT IT'S DOWNRIGHT TACKY!
THEN WHAT DO YOU CALL THAT SHIRT?!
IGO PRESIDENT ICHIRYU

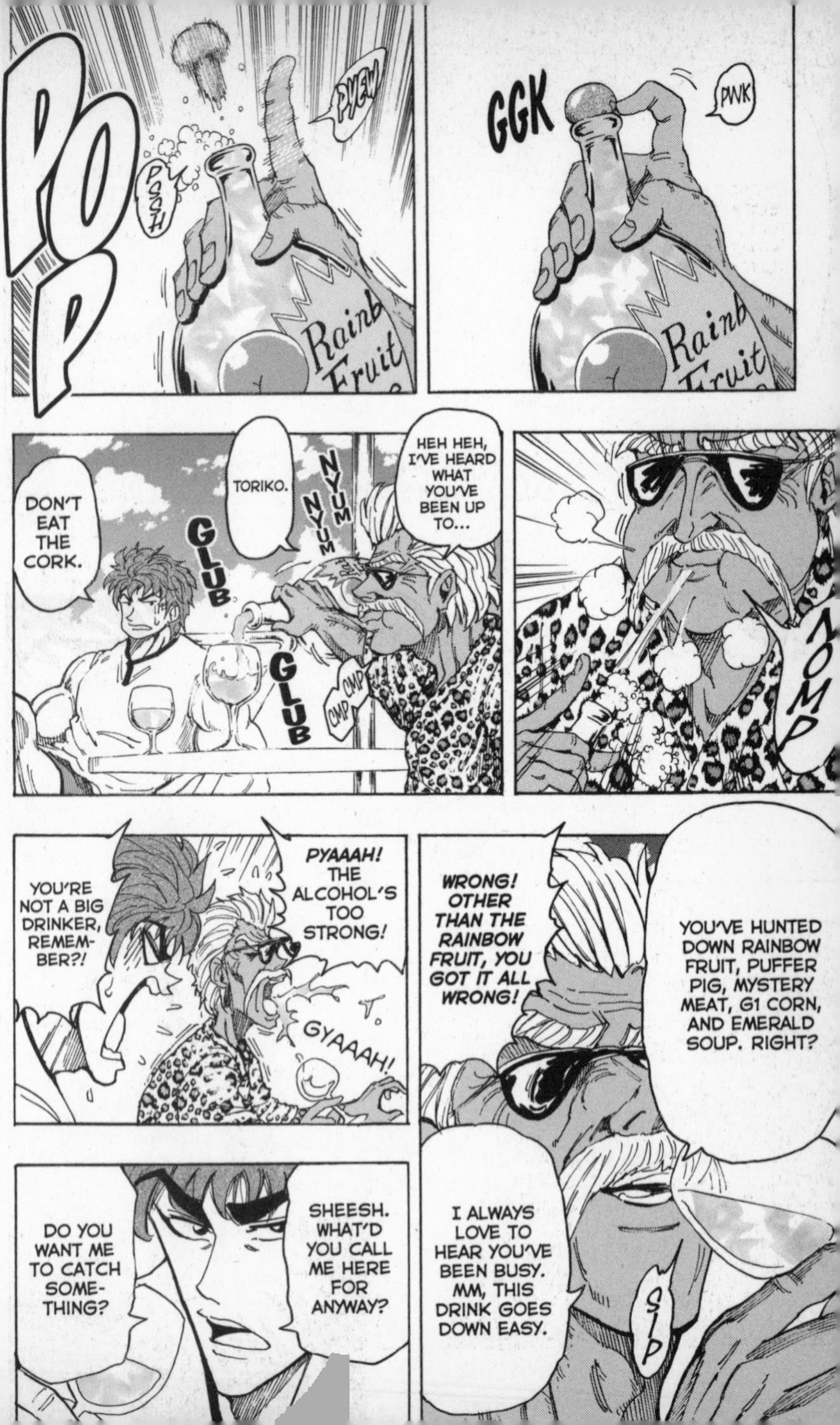
PWK
GGK
PYEW
PSSH
POP
NOMP
HEH HEH, I'VE HEARD WHAT YOU'VE BEEN UP TO...
NYUM NYUM NYUM
TORIKO.
GLUB
DON'T EAT THE CORK.
CMP CMP
GLUB
YOU'VE HUNTED DOWN RAINBOW FRUIT, PUFFER PIG, MYSTERY MEAT, G1 CORN, AND EMERALD SOUP. RIGHT?
WRONG! OTHER THAN THE RAINBOW FRUIT, YOU GOT IT ALL WRONG!
I ALWAYS LOVE TO HEAR YOU'VE BEEN BUSY. MM, THIS DRINK GOES DOWN EASY.
SIP
PYAAAH! THE ALCOHOL'S TOO STRONG!
YOU'RE NOT A BIG DRINKER, REMEMBER?!
GYAAAH!
SHEESH. WHAT'D YOU CALL ME HERE FOR ANYWAY?
DO YOU WANT ME TO CATCH SOMETHING?

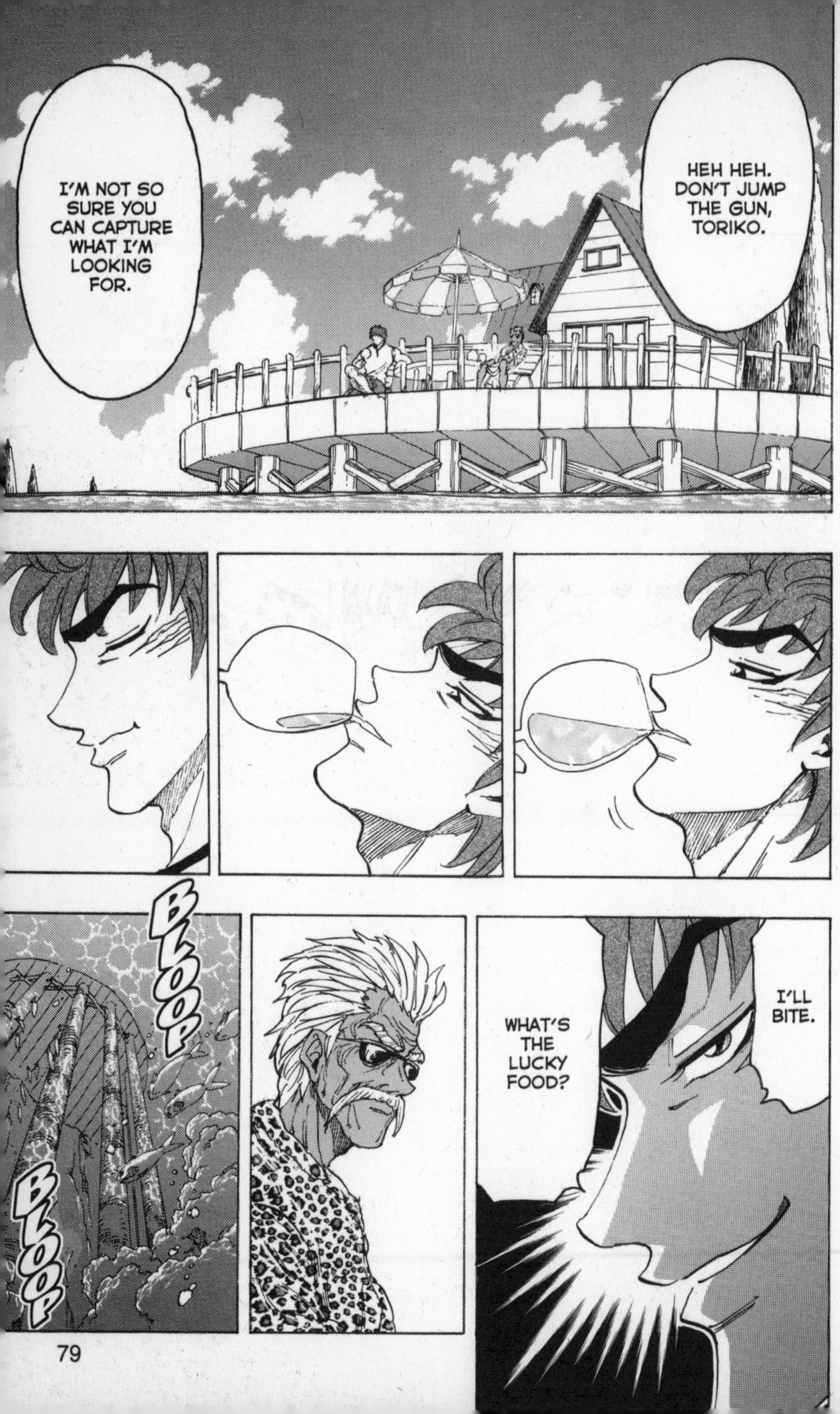
HEH HEH. DON'T JUMP THE GUN, TORIKO.
I'M NOT SO SURE YOU CAN CAPTURE WHAT I'M LOOKING FOR.
I'LL BITE.
WHAT'S THE LUCKY FOOD?
BLOOP
BLOOP

SPLOO

SH

HE

GOD!

MORE OR LESS.

NH

SPLOSH

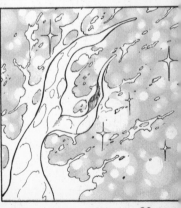

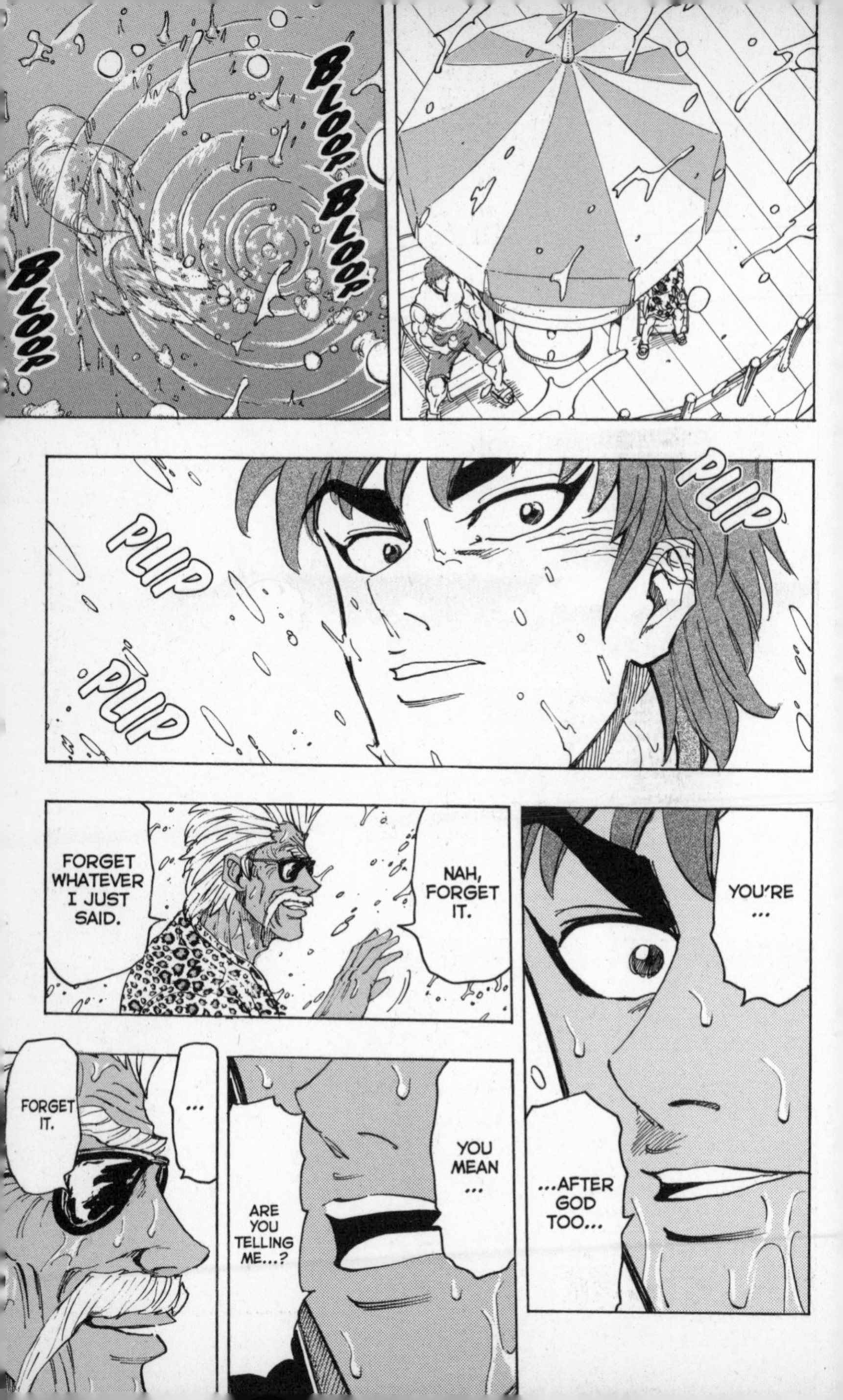
BLOOP
BLOOP
BLOOP
PLIP
PLIP
PLIP
YOU'RE ...
...AFTER GOD TOO...
NAH, FORGET IT.
FORGET WHATEVER I JUST SAID.
YOU MEAN ...
ARE YOU TELLING ME...?
...
FORGET IT.

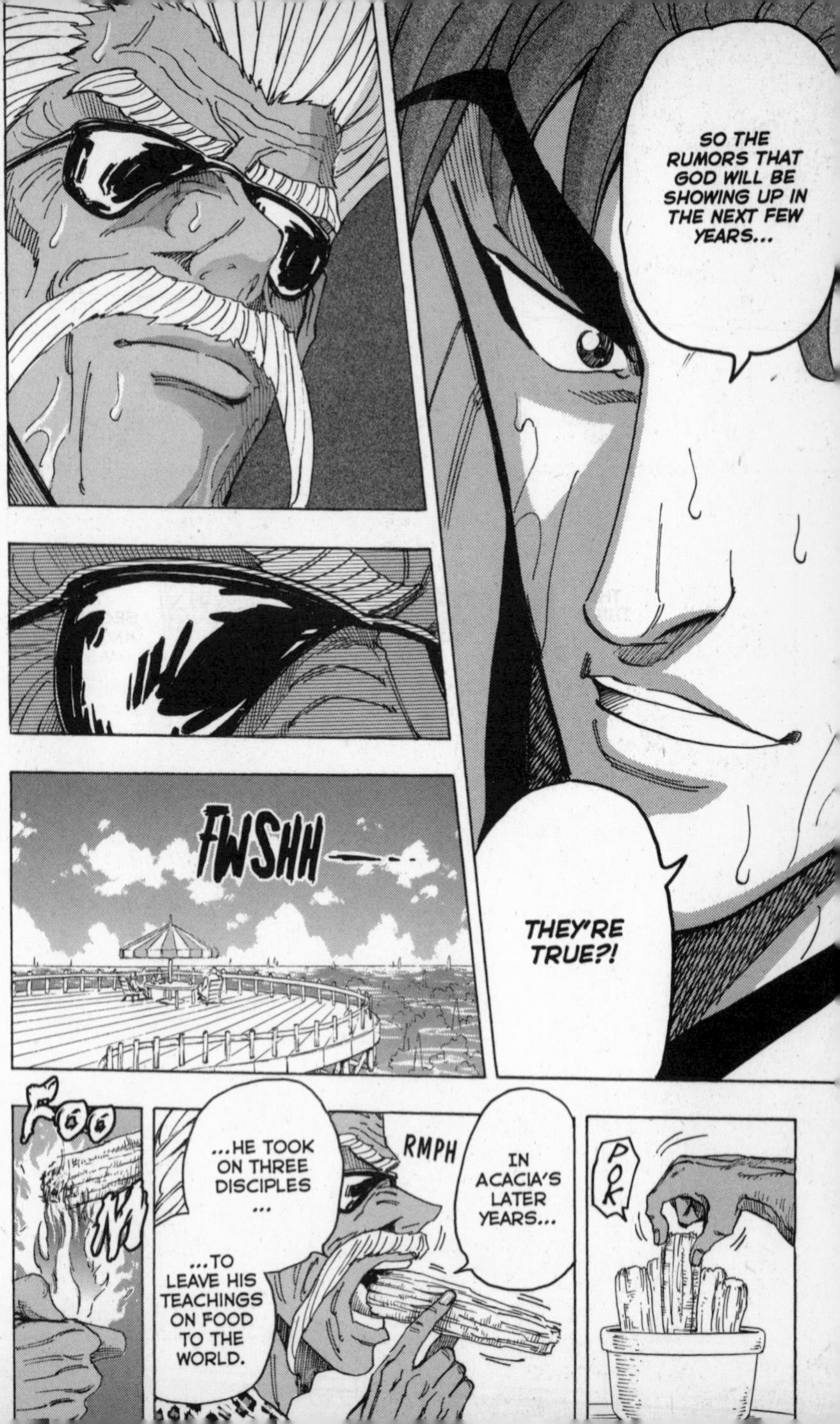
SO THE RUMORS THAT GOD WILL BE SHOWING UP IN THE NEXT FEW YEARS...
THEY'RE TRUE?!
FWSHH
POK
IN ACACIA'S LATER YEARS...
RMPH
...HE TOOK ON THREE DISCIPLES...
...TO LEAVE HIS TEACHINGS ON FOOD TO THE WORLD.

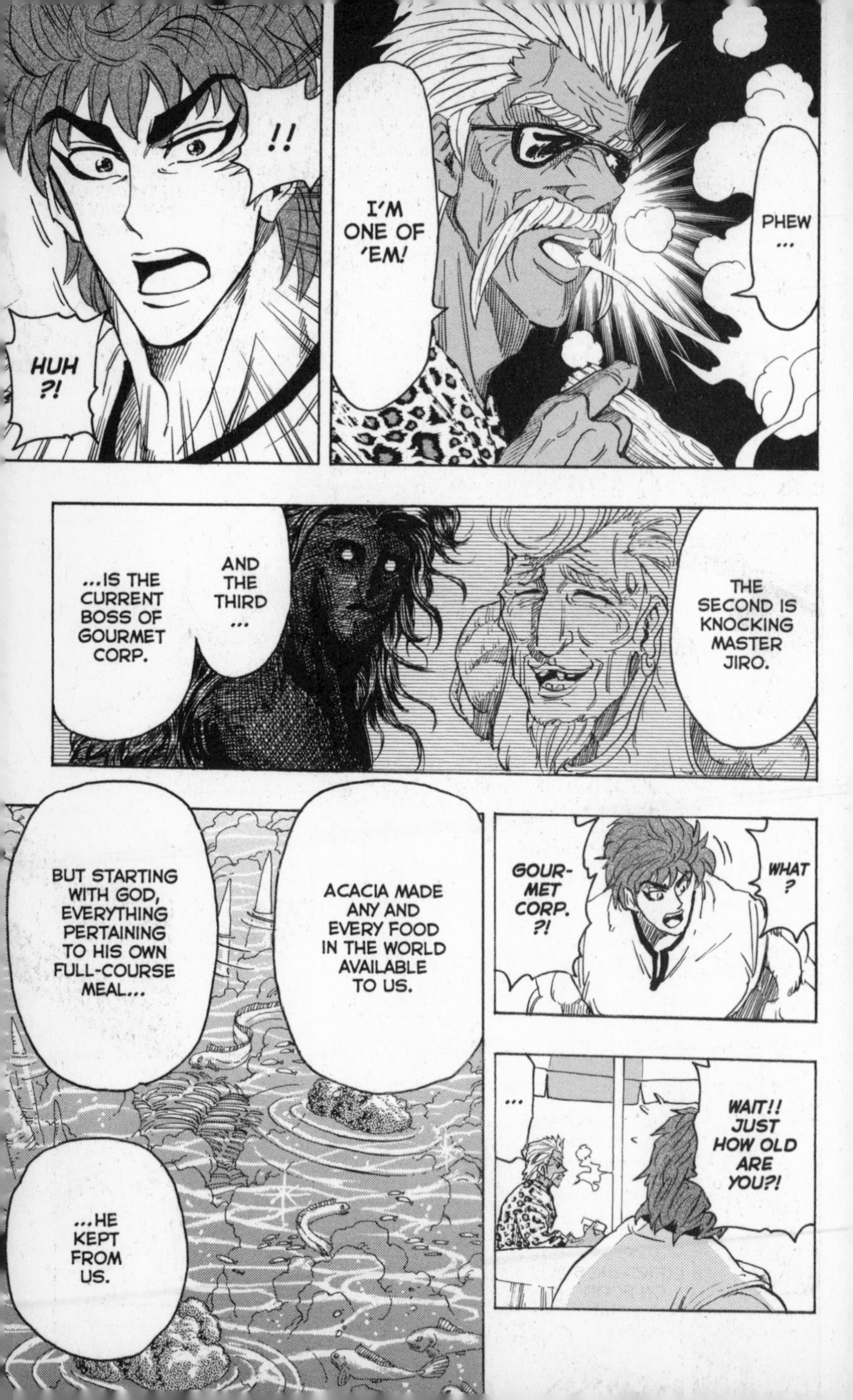
PHEW...
I'M ONE OF 'EM!
!!
HUH?!
THE SECOND IS KNOCKING MASTER JIRO.
AND THE THIRD...
...IS THE CURRENT BOSS OF GOURMET CORP.
WHAT?
GOURMET CORP.?!
WAIT!! JUST HOW OLD ARE YOU?!
...
ACACIA MADE ANY AND EVERY FOOD IN THE WORLD AVAILABLE TO US.
BUT STARTING WITH GOD, EVERYTHING PERTAINING TO HIS OWN FULL-COURSE MEAL...
...HE KEPT FROM US.

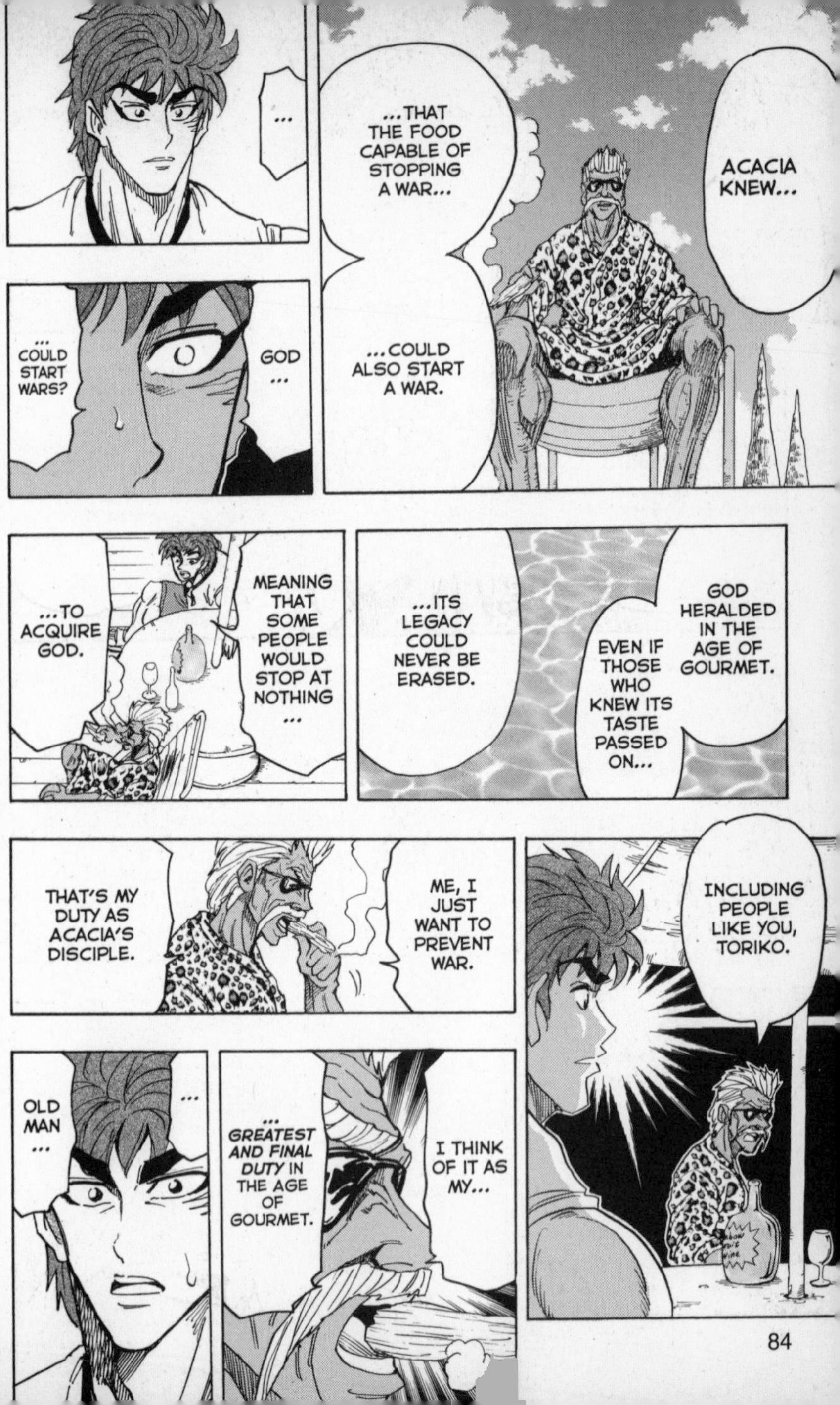
ACACIA KNEW...
...THAT THE FOOD CAPABLE OF STOPPING A WAR...
...COULD ALSO START A WAR.
...
GOD ...
... COULD START WARS?
GOD HERALDED IN THE AGE OF GOURMET.
EVEN IF THOSE WHO KNEW ITS TASTE PASSED ON...
...ITS LEGACY COULD NEVER BE ERASED.
MEANING THAT SOME PEOPLE WOULD STOP AT NOTHING ...
...TO ACQUIRE GOD.
INCLUDING PEOPLE LIKE YOU, TORIKO.
ME, I JUST WANT TO PREVENT WAR.
THAT'S MY DUTY AS ACACIA'S DISCIPLE.
I THINK OF IT AS MY...
... *GREATEST AND FINAL DUTY* IN THE AGE OF GOURMET.
...
OLD MAN ...

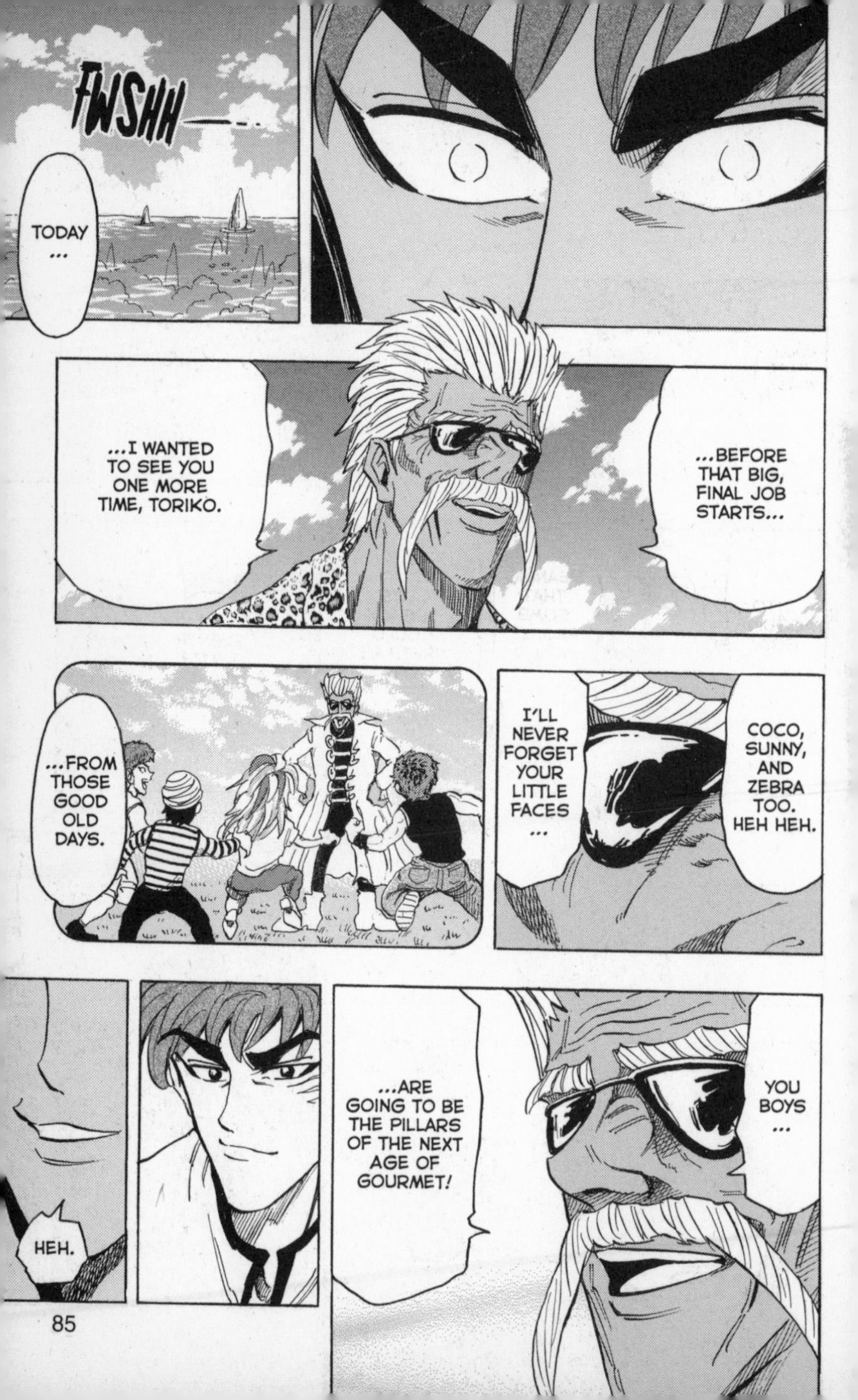
FWSHH
TODAY...
...BEFORE THAT BIG, FINAL JOB STARTS...
...I WANTED TO SEE YOU ONE MORE TIME, TORIKO.
COCO, SUNNY, AND ZEBRA TOO. HEH HEH.
I'LL NEVER FORGET YOUR LITTLE FACES...
...FROM THOSE GOOD OLD DAYS.
YOU BOYS...
...ARE GOING TO BE THE PILLARS OF THE NEXT AGE OF GOURMET!
HEH.

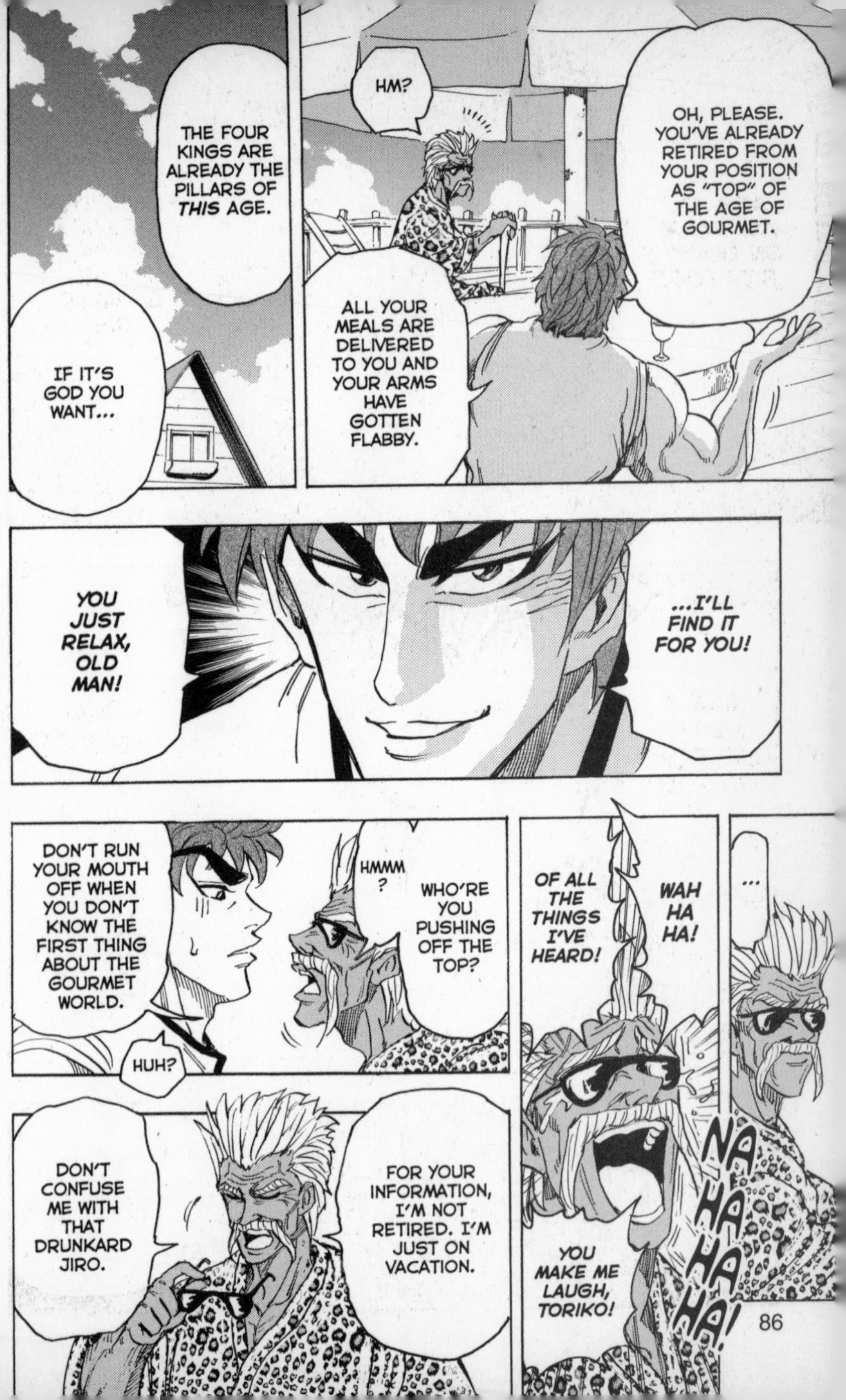

OH, PLEASE. YOU'VE ALREADY RETIRED FROM YOUR POSITION AS "TOP" OF THE AGE OF GOURMET.
HM?
ALL YOUR MEALS ARE DELIVERED TO YOU AND YOUR ARMS HAVE GOTTEN FLABBY.
THE FOUR KINGS ARE ALREADY THE PILLARS OF *THIS* AGE.
IF IT'S GOD YOU WANT...
...I'LL FIND IT FOR YOU!
YOU JUST RELAX, OLD MAN!
...
WAH HA HA!
OF ALL THE THINGS I'VE HEARD!
NA HA HA HA HA!
YOU MAKE ME LAUGH, TORIKO!
HMMM?
WHO'RE YOU PUSHING OFF THE TOP?
DON'T RUN YOUR MOUTH OFF WHEN YOU DON'T KNOW THE FIRST THING ABOUT THE GOURMET WORLD.
HUH?
FOR YOUR INFORMATION, I'M NOT RETIRED. I'M JUST ON VACATION.
DON'T CONFUSE ME WITH THAT DRUNKARD JIRO.

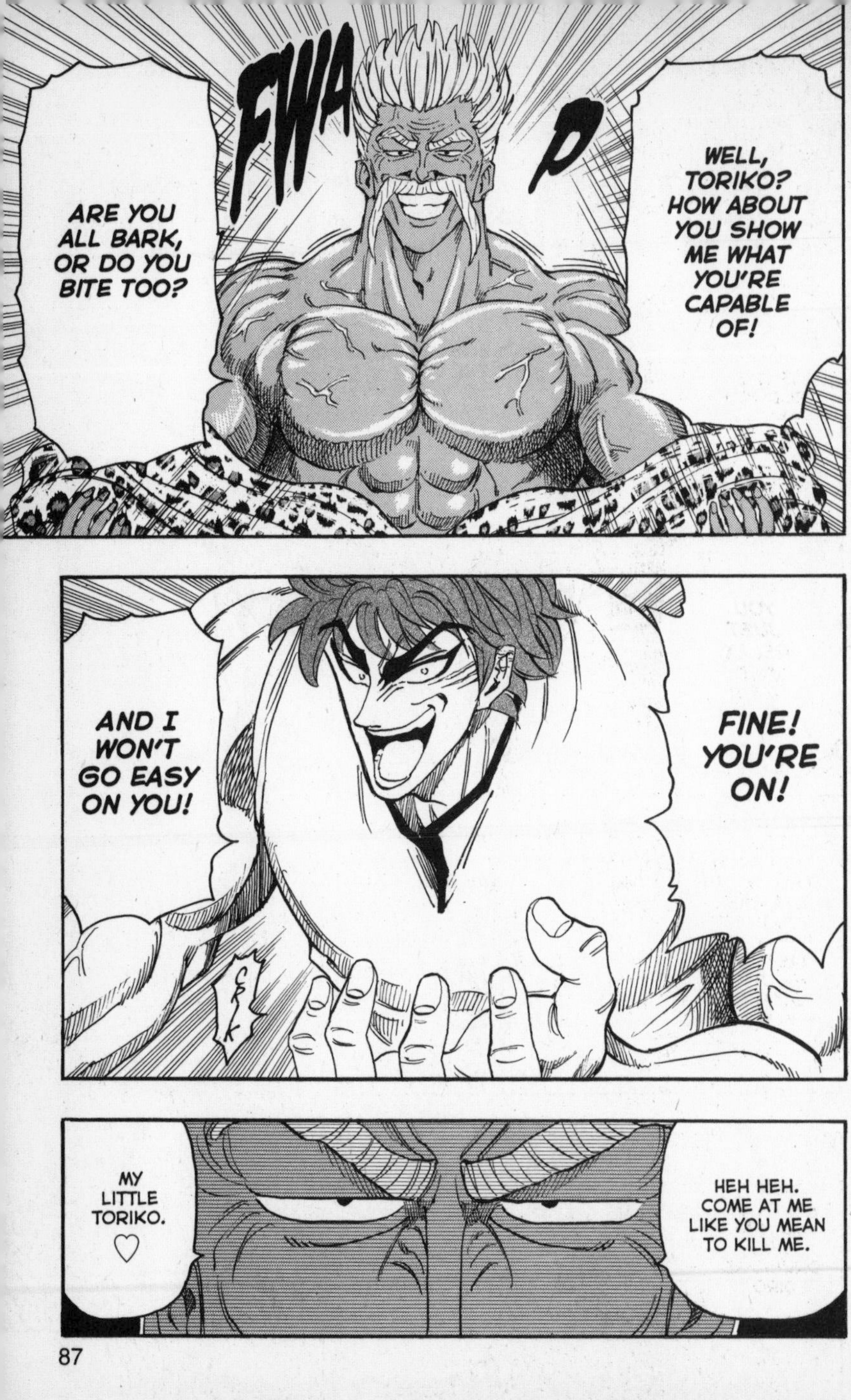
WELL, TORIKO? HOW ABOUT YOU SHOW ME WHAT YOU'RE CAPABLE OF!
FWAP
ARE YOU ALL BARK, OR DO YOU BITE TOO?
FINE! YOU'RE ON!
AND I WON'T GO EASY ON YOU!
CRK
HEH HEH. COME AT ME LIKE YOU MEAN TO KILL ME.
MY LITTLE TORIKO. ♡

TORIKO

GOURMET CHECKLIST

Vol. 111

DORMANCY EXTRACT
(SYNTHETIC SOLUTION)

CAPTURE LEVEL: ---
HABITAT: PROPERTY OF TEPPEI (DETAILS UNKNOWN)
LENGTH: ---
HEIGHT: ---
WEIGHT: ---
PRICE: 15,000,000 YEN PER DROP

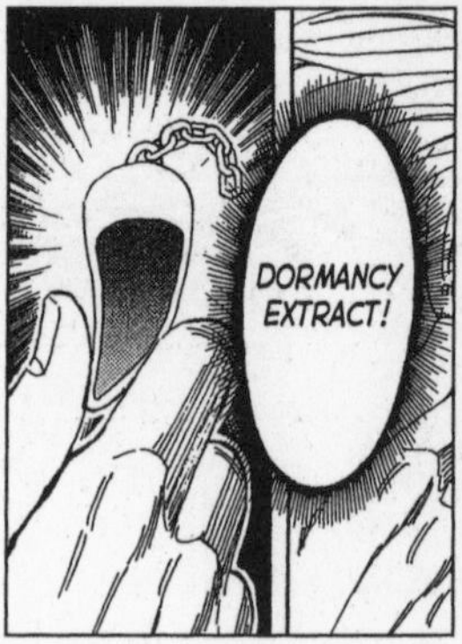
DORMANCY EXTRACT!

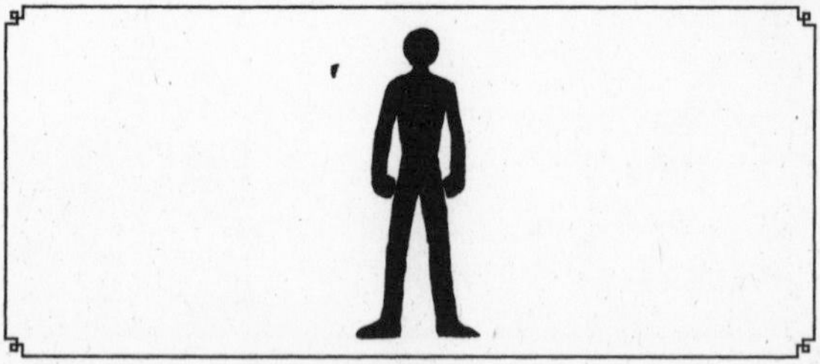

SCALE

TEPPEI THE REVIVER CREATED THIS SOLUTION BY COMBINING VARIOUS PLANT EXTRACTS. USED AS A SEDATIVE, IT TEMPORARILY KNOCKS OUT A TARGET PLANT, SHRINKING ITS CELLS AND SOMETIMES EVEN KILLING IT ALTOGETHER. IF MISHANDLED, IT'S A DEADLY POISON, SO THIS SPECIAL TOOL HAS ONLY BEEN MASTERED BY A SELECT FEW GOURMET REVIVERS. NATURALLY, ITS USE IS RESTRICTED UNDER GOURMET LAW.

GOURMET 102: FIGHTING TIME!!

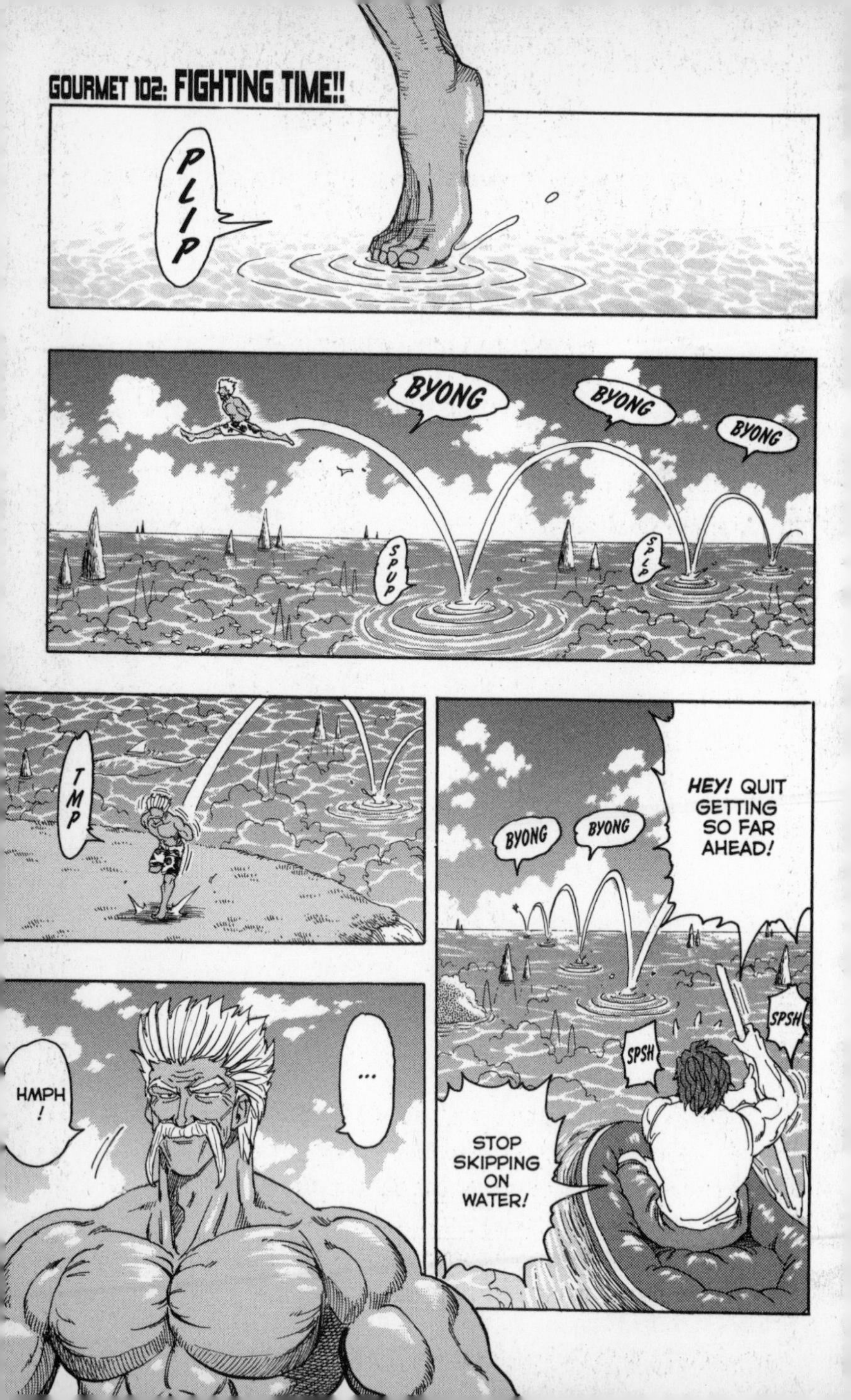
PLIP
BYONG
BYONG
BYONG
SPLP
SPUP
HEY! QUIT GETTING SO FAR AHEAD!
BYONG
BYONG
SPSH
SPSH
STOP SKIPPING ON WATER!
TMP
...
HMPH!

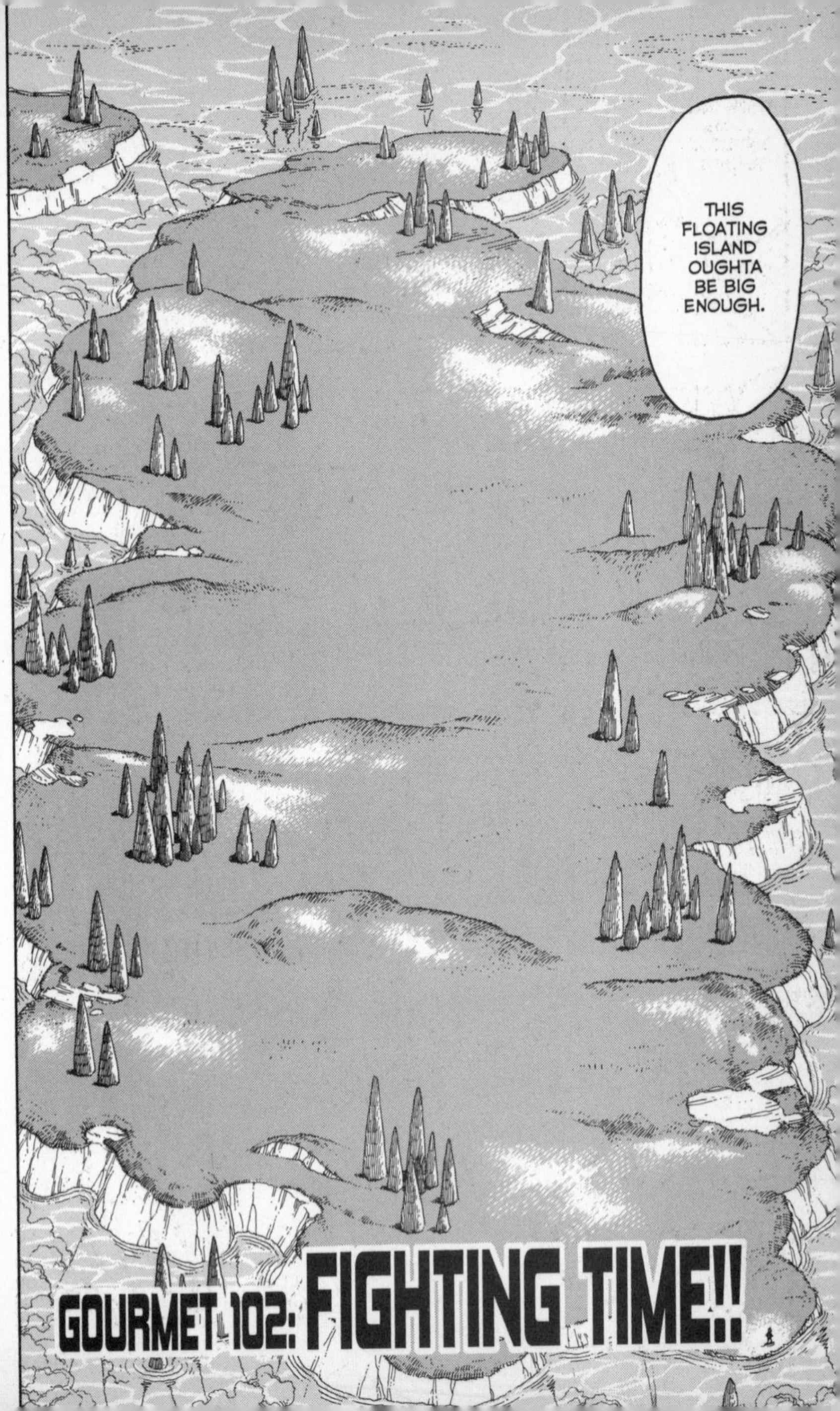
THIS FLOATING ISLAND OUGHTA BE BIG ENOUGH.
GOURMET 102: FIGHTING TIME!!

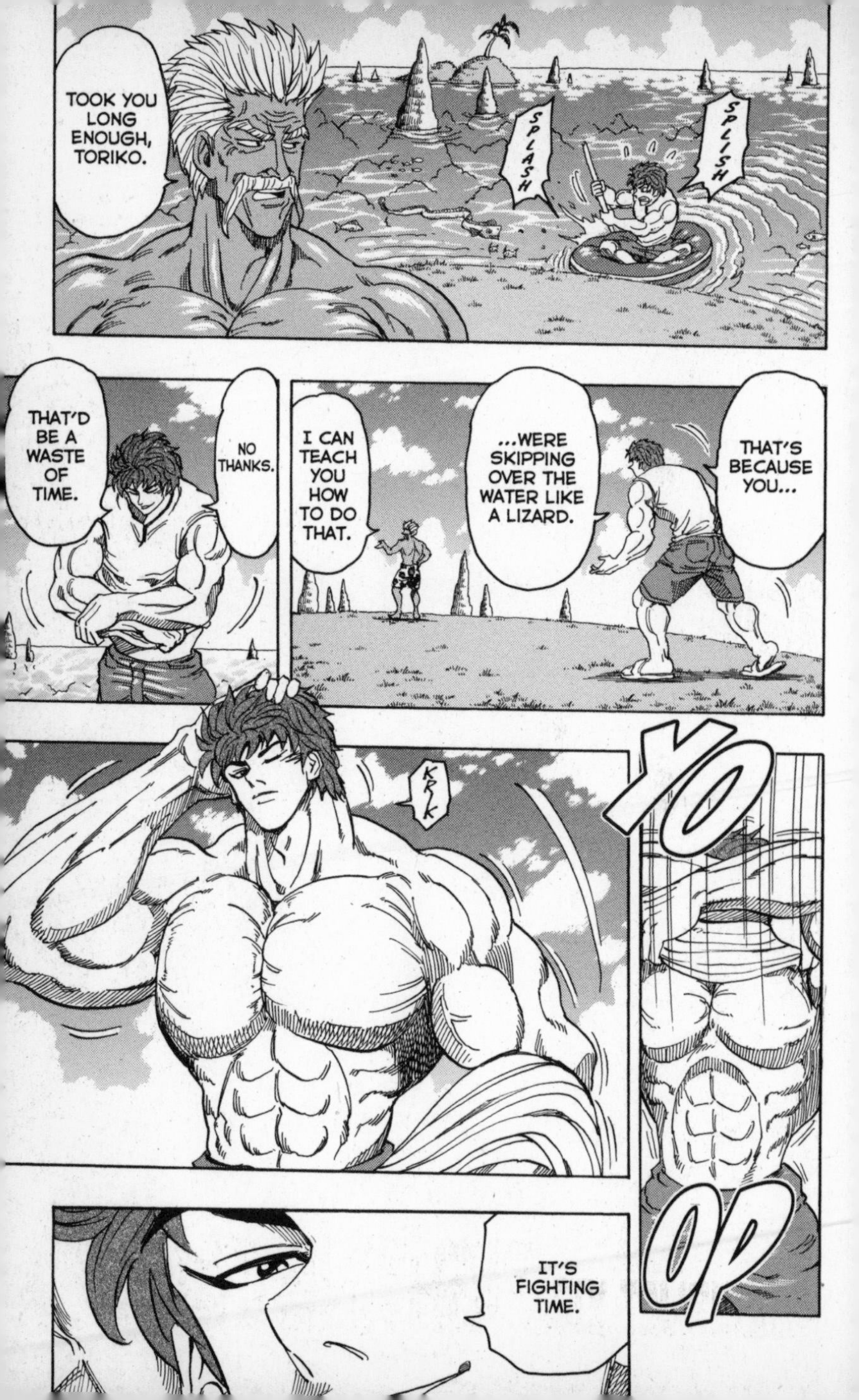

SPLISH
SPLASH
TOOK YOU LONG ENOUGH, TORIKO.
THAT'S BECAUSE YOU...
...WERE SKIPPING OVER THE WATER LIKE A LIZARD.
I CAN TEACH YOU HOW TO DO THAT.
NO THANKS.
THAT'D BE A WASTE OF TIME.
YOOP
KRIK
IT'S FIGHTING TIME.

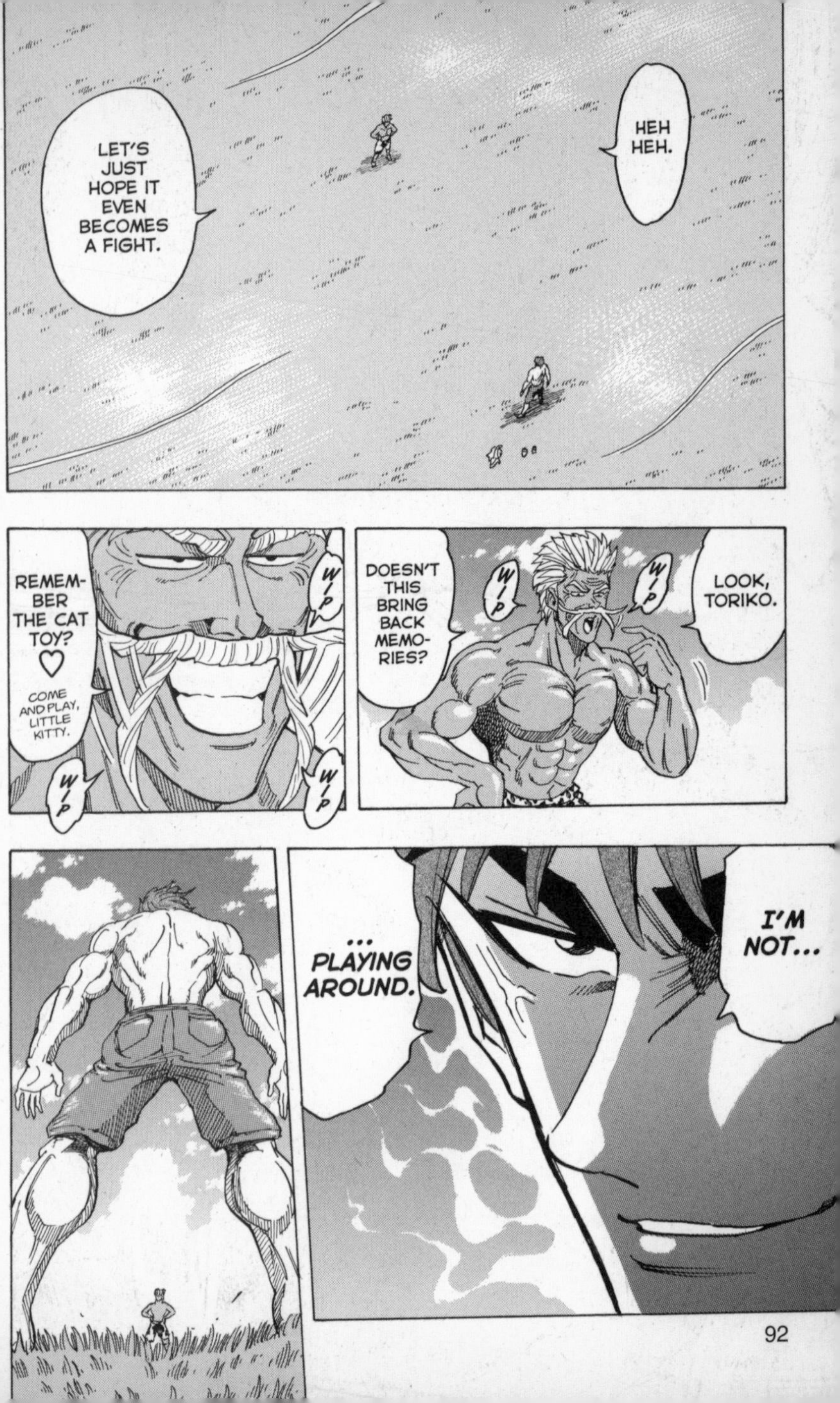
HEH HEH.
LET'S JUST HOPE IT EVEN BECOMES A FIGHT.
LOOK, TORIKO.
WIP
DOESN'T THIS BRING BACK MEMO-RIES?
WIP
WIP
REMEM-BER THE CAT TOY? ♡
COME AND PLAY, LITTLE KITTY.
WIP
WIP
I'M NOT...
... PLAYING AROUND.

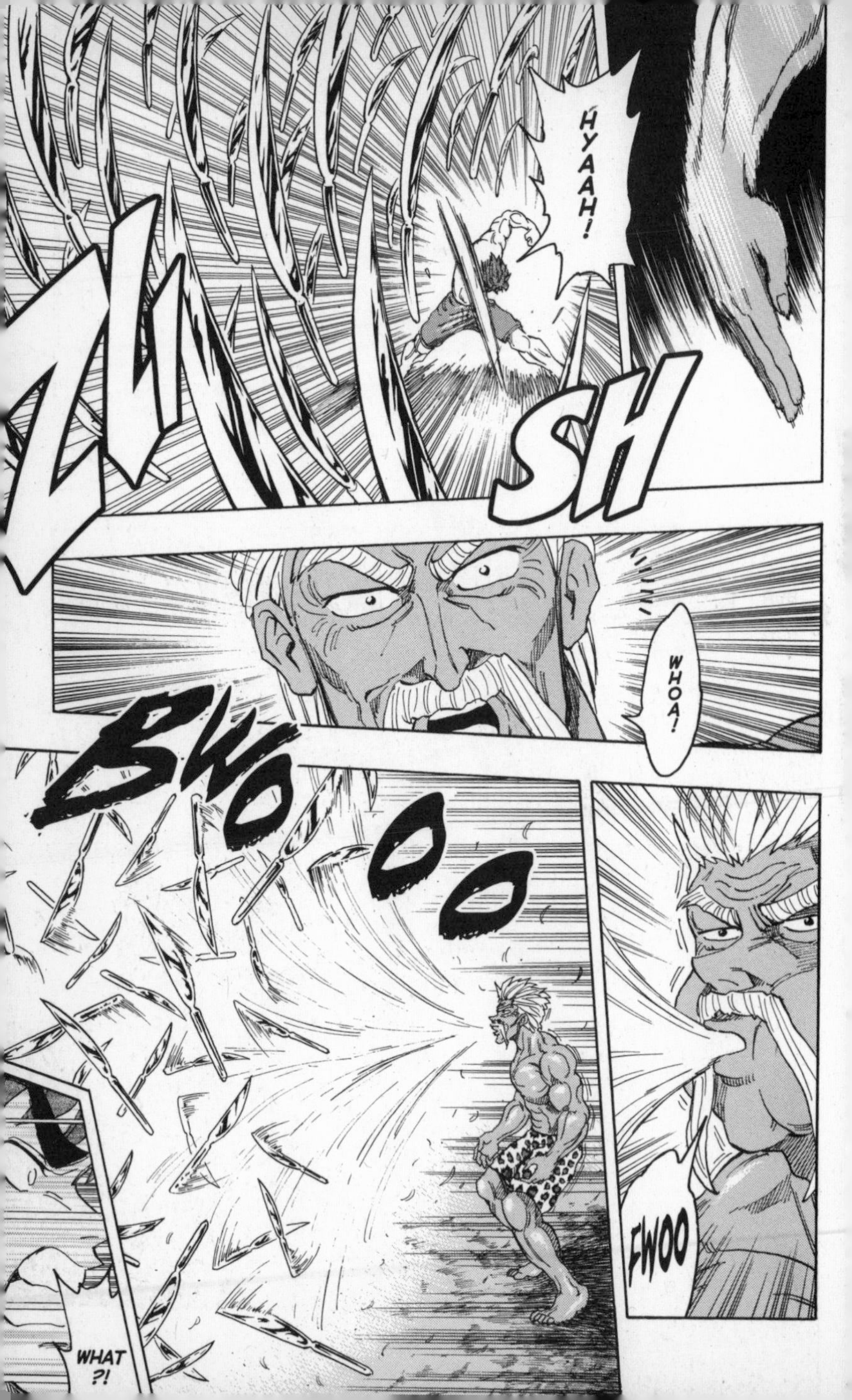
HYAAAH!
ZUSH
WHOA!
FWOO
BWOOOO
WHAT?!

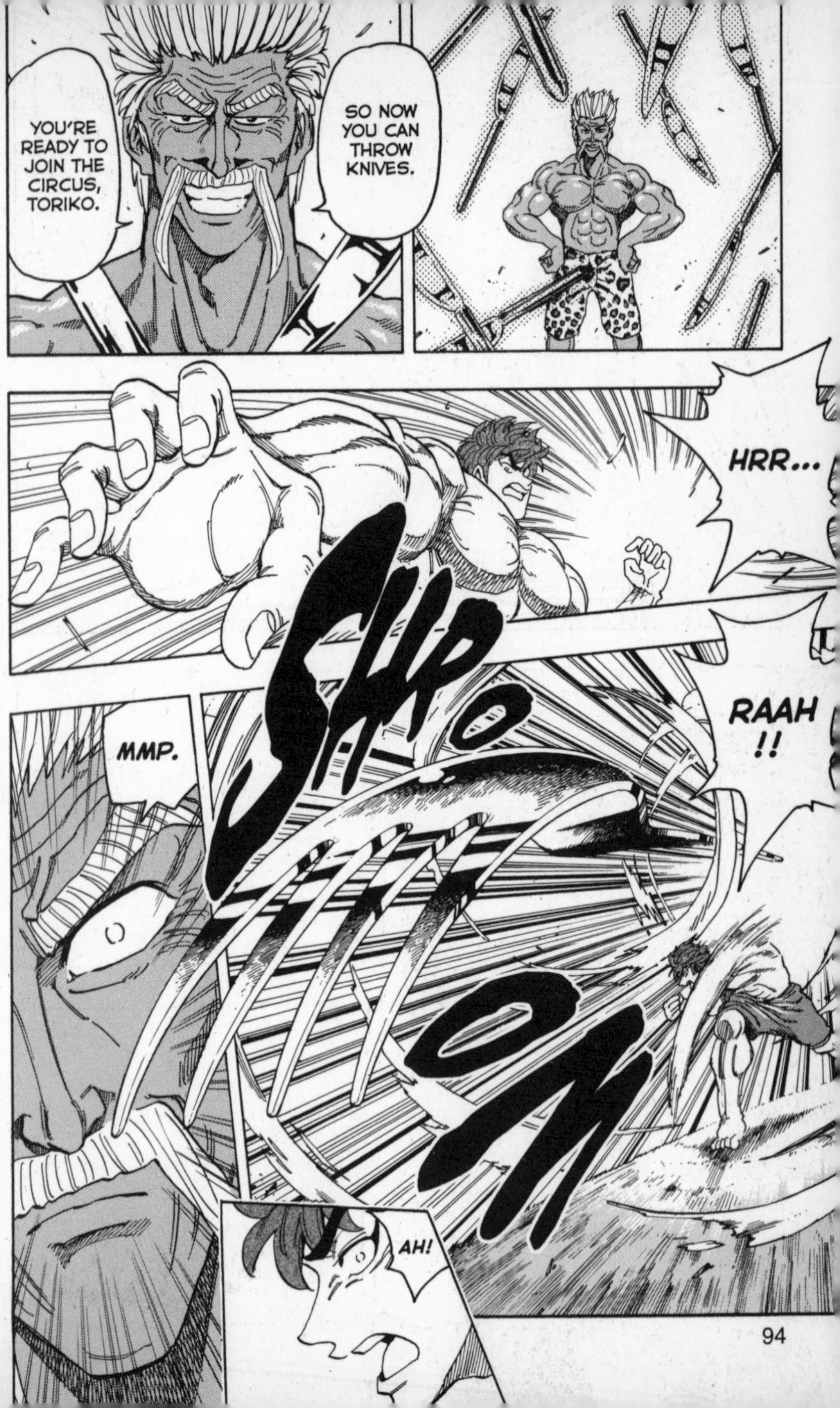
SO NOW YOU CAN THROW KNIVES.
YOU'RE READY TO JOIN THE CIRCUS, TORIKO.
HRR...
RAAH!!
SHROOM
MMP.
AH!

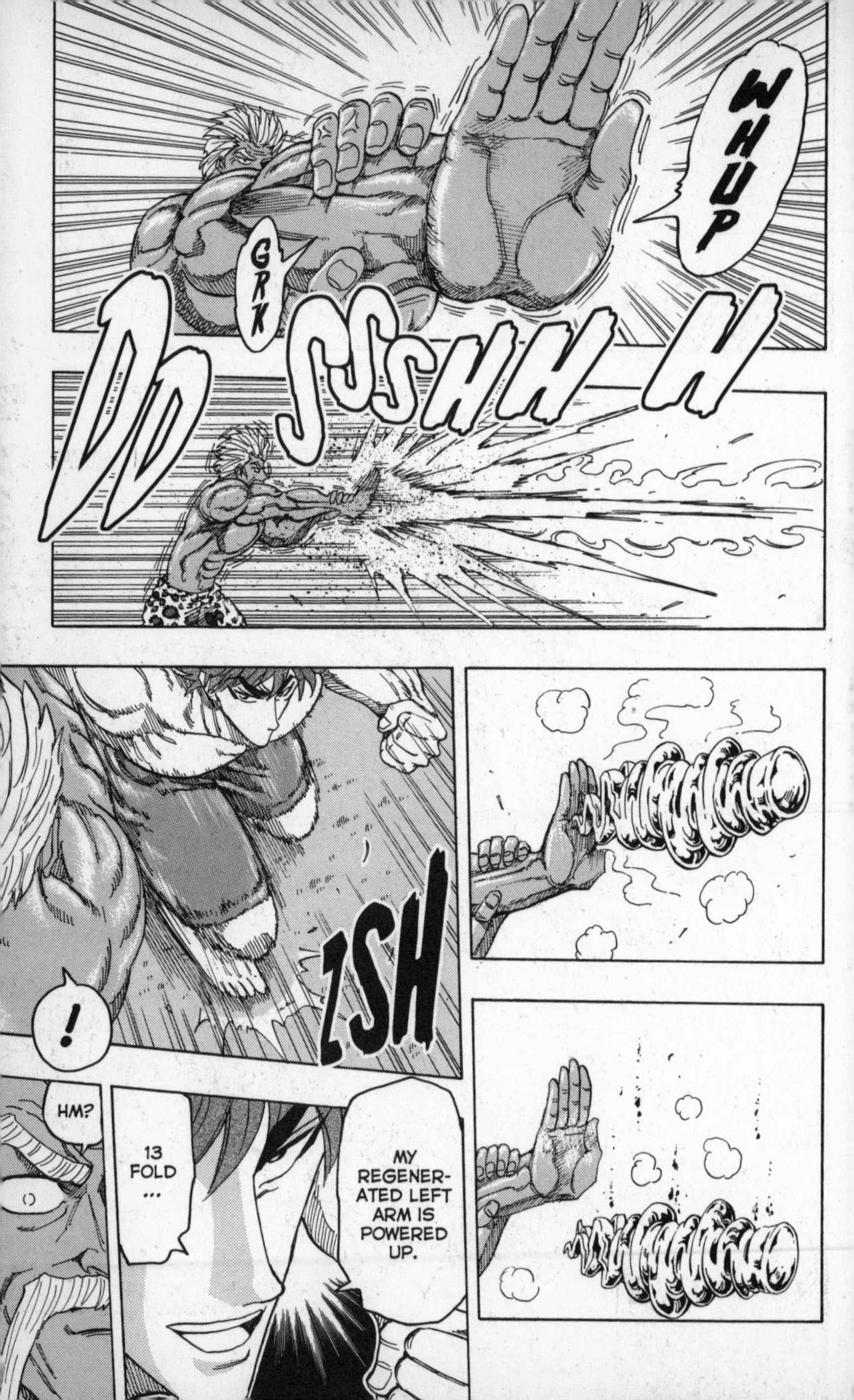
WHUP
GRK
DOSSHHH
ZSH
!
MY REGENER-ATED LEFT ARM IS POWERED UP.
13 FOLD ...
HM?

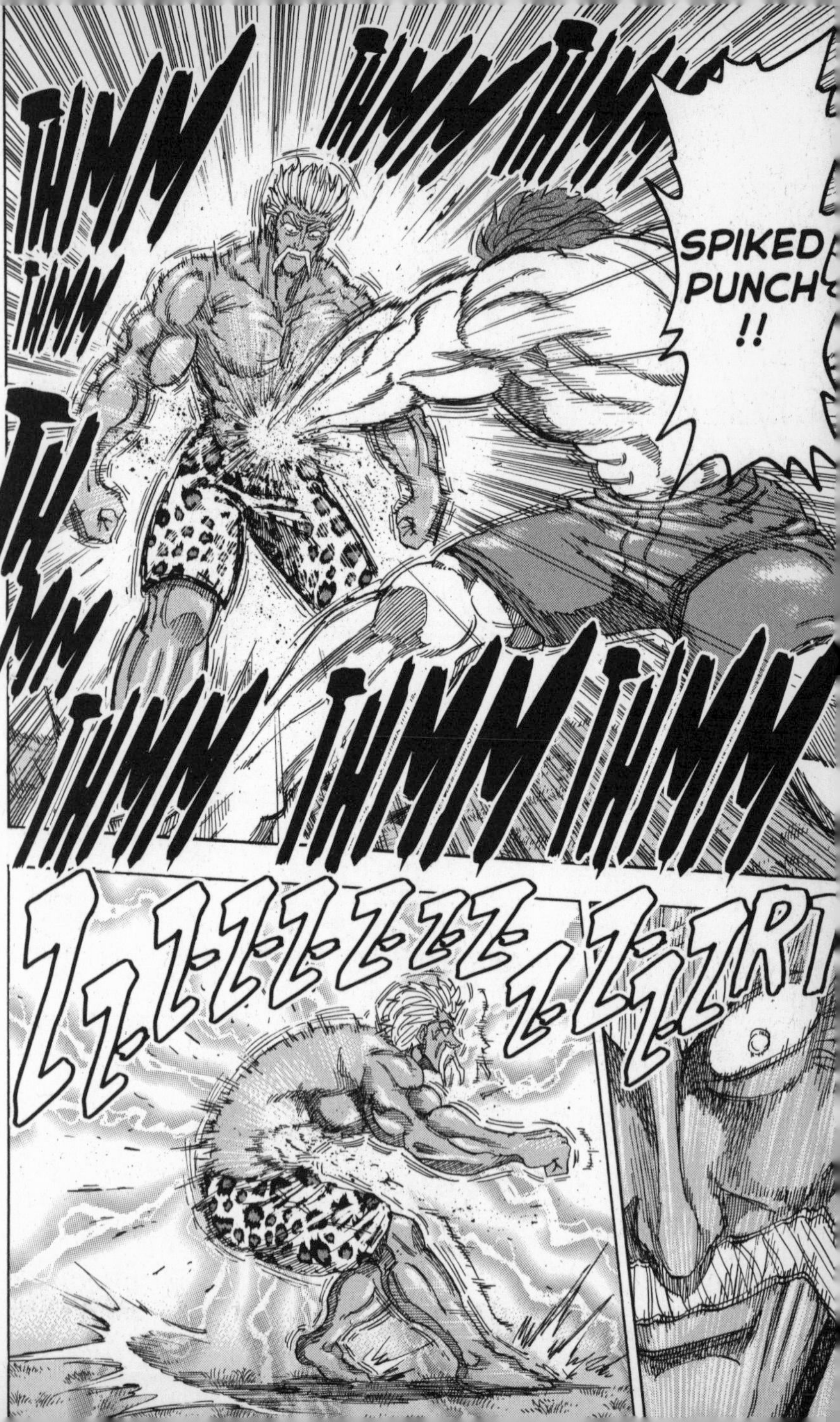

SPIKED PUNCH !!
THMM THMM
THMM
THMM
THMM
THMM THMM THMM
ZZZZZZZZZZZZRT

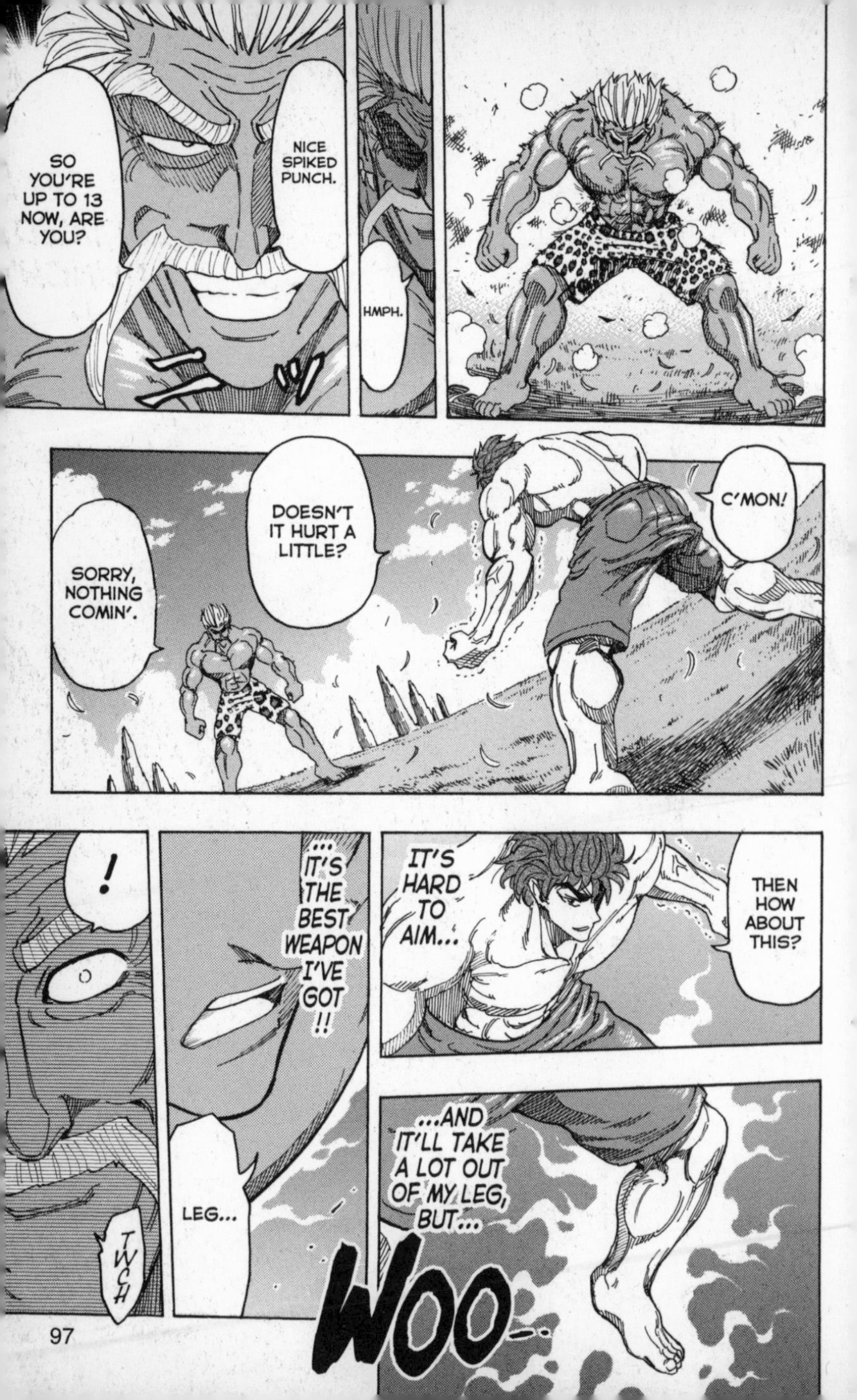
NICE SPIKED PUNCH.
HMPH.
SO YOU'RE UP TO 13 NOW, ARE YOU?
C'MON!
DOESN'T IT HURT A LITTLE?
SORRY, NOTHING COMIN'.
THEN HOW ABOUT THIS?
IT'S HARD TO AIM...
...AND IT'LL TAKE A LOT OUT OF MY LEG, BUT...
WOO-
...IT'S THE BEST WEAPON I'VE GOT!!
LEG...
!
TWCH

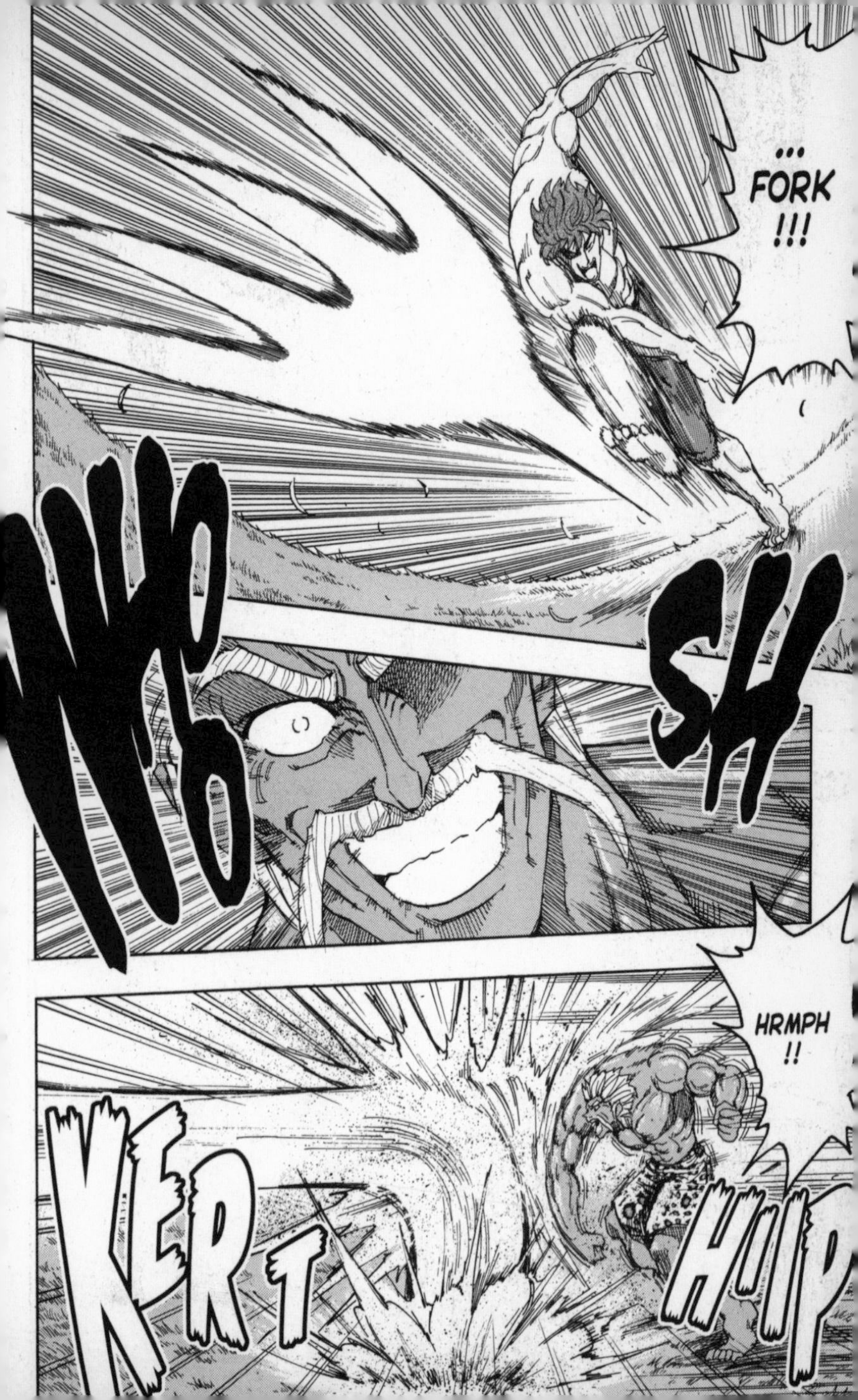
...FORK !!!
WHOOSH
HRMPH !!
KERTHIP

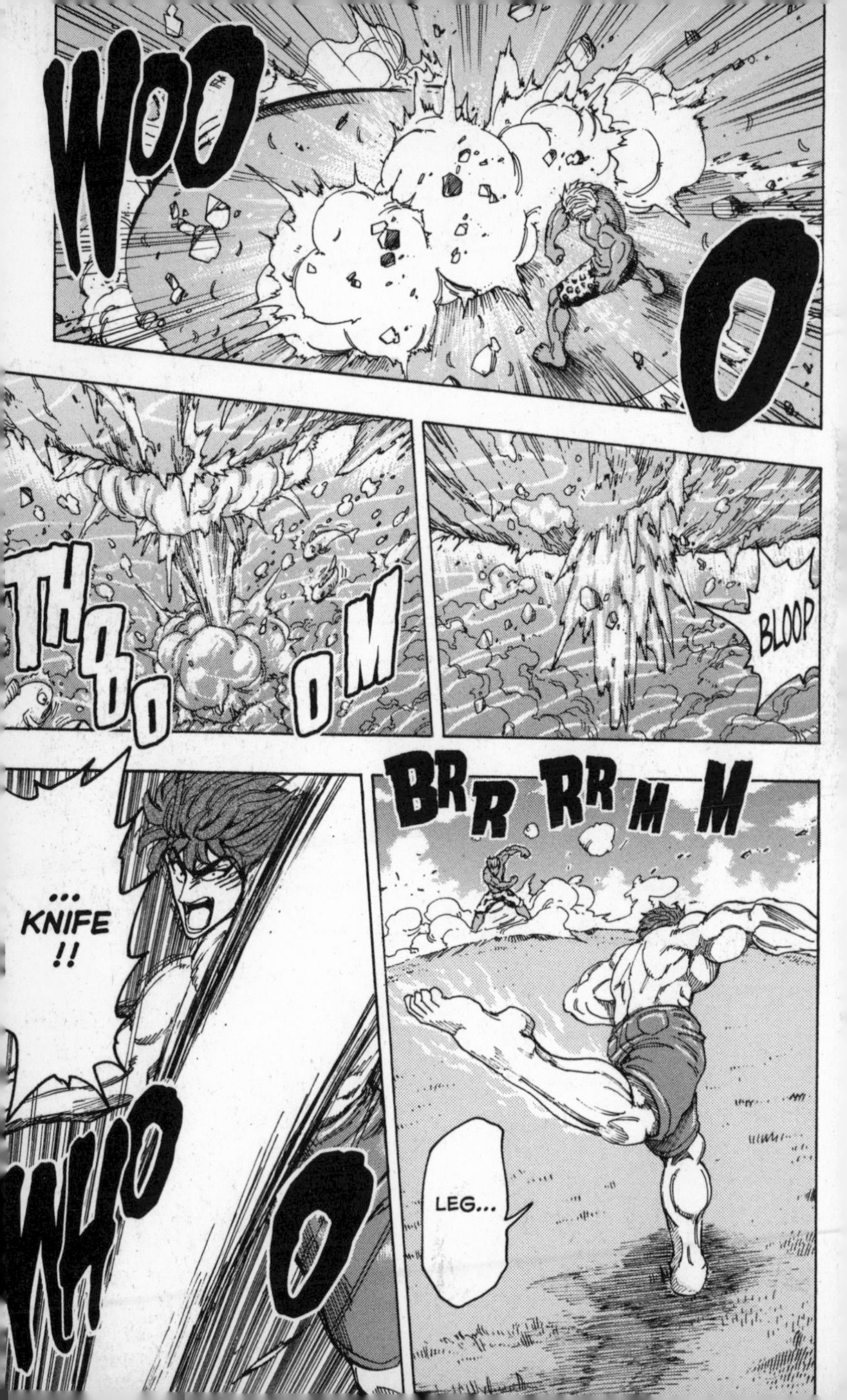
WOOO
BLOOP
THOOOM
BRRRRRMM
LEG...
... KNIFE !!
WHOOO

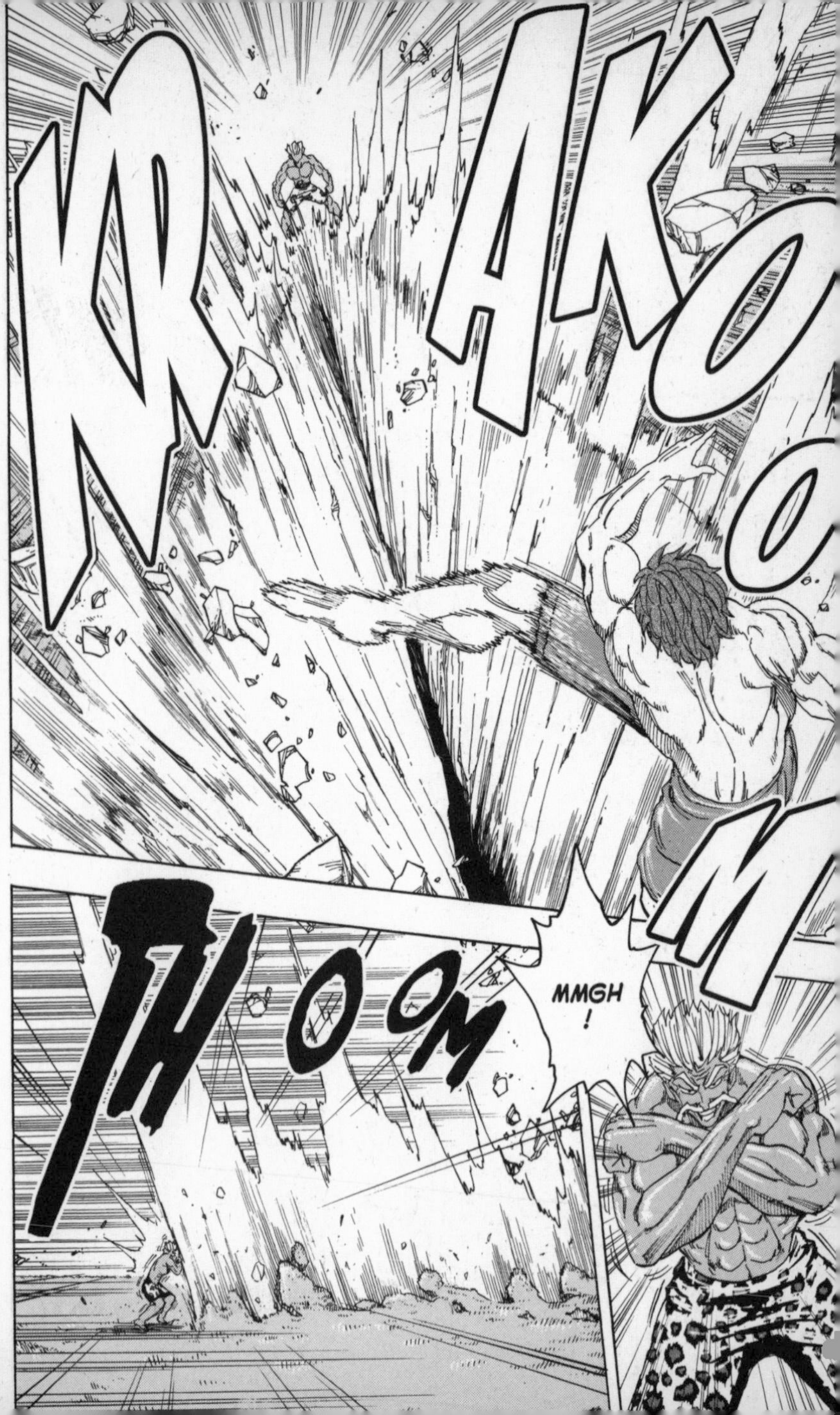
KRAKOOM
MMGH!
THOOM

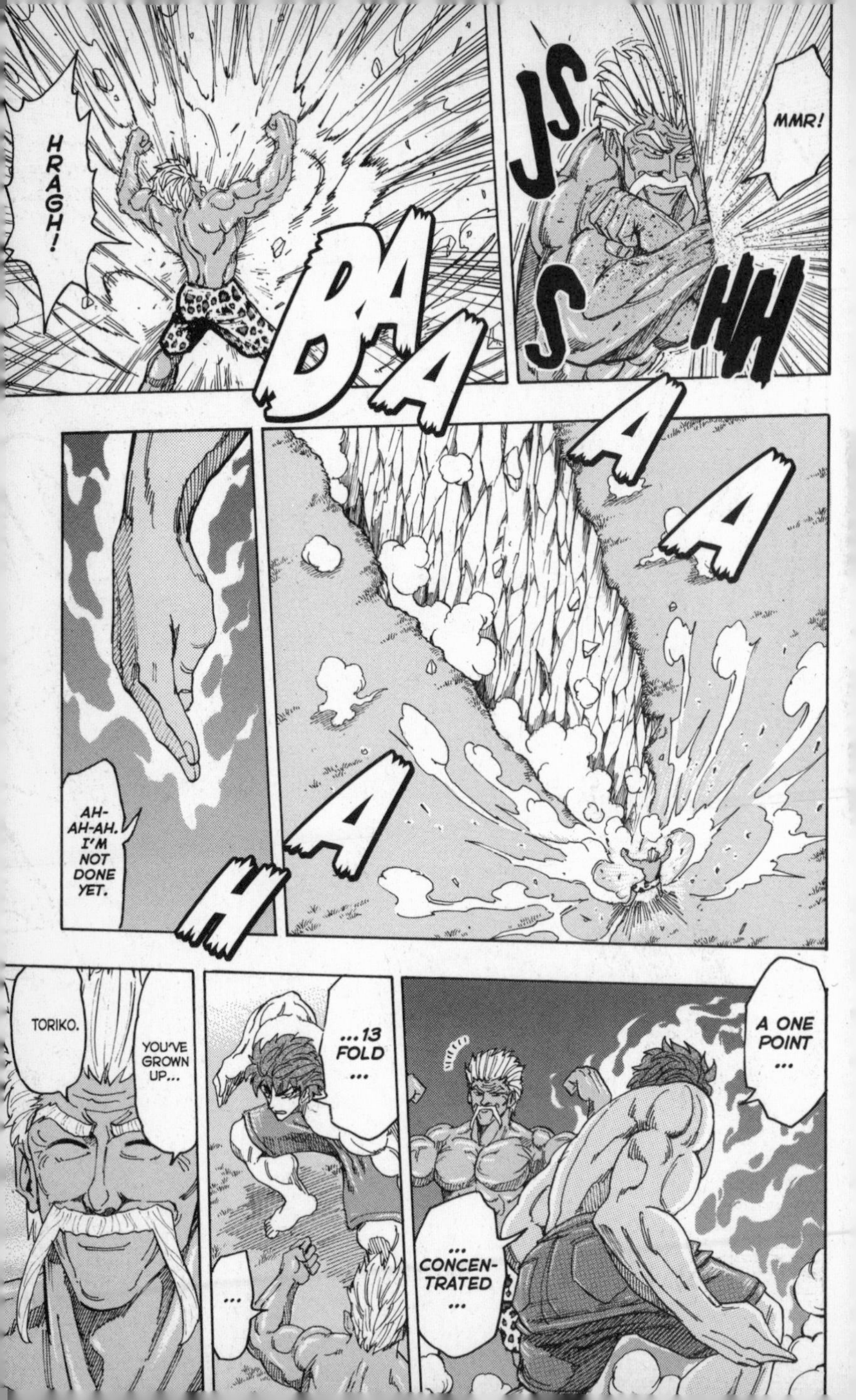
MMR!
JSSHH
HRAGH!
BADAAAAAH
AH-AH-AH. I'M NOT DONE YET.
A ONE POINT...
...CONCENTRATED...
...13 FOLD...
...
TORIKO.
YOU'VE GROWN UP...

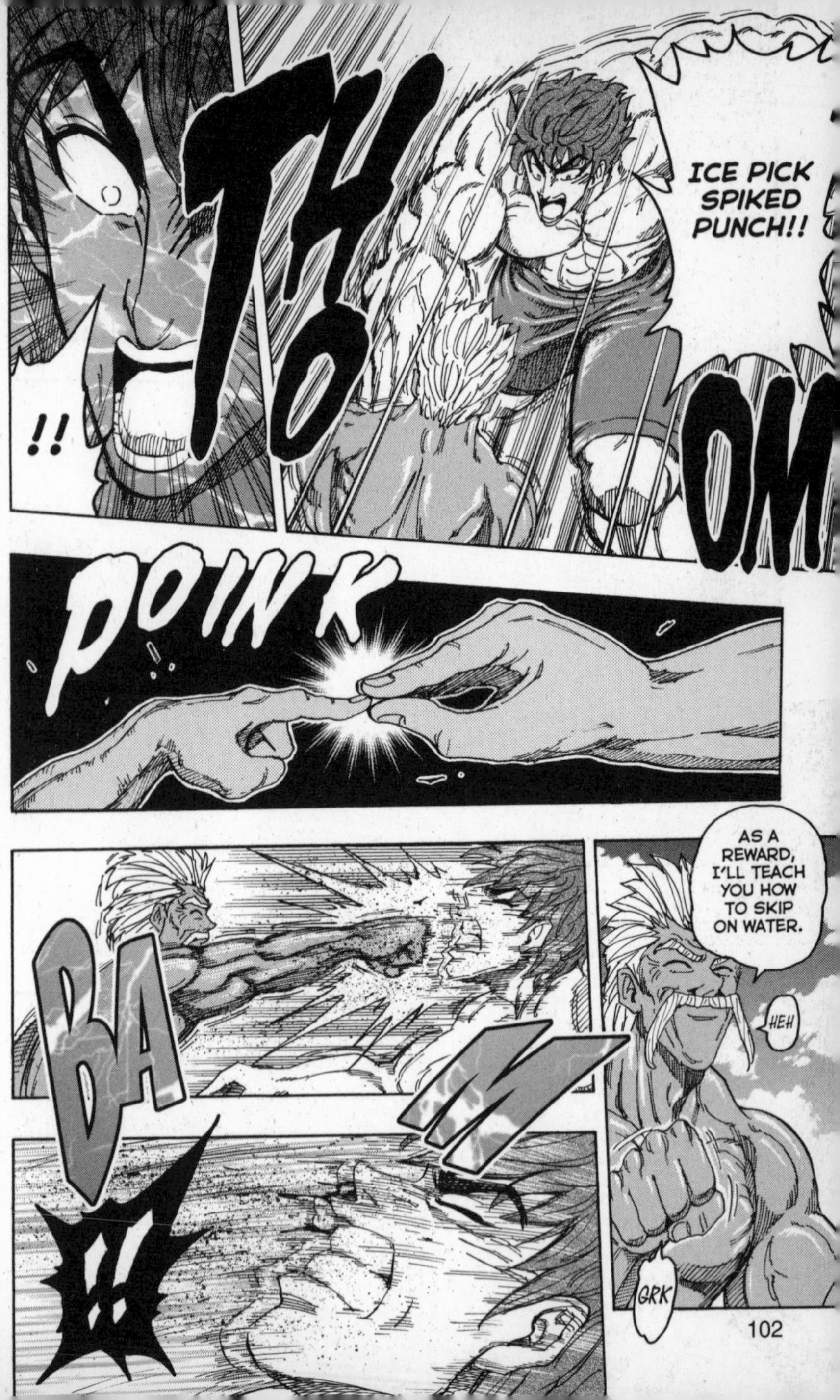
ICE PICK SPIKED PUNCH!!
THO
OM
!!
POINK
AS A REWARD, I'LL TEACH YOU HOW TO SKIP ON WATER.
HEH
GRK
BAM
!!

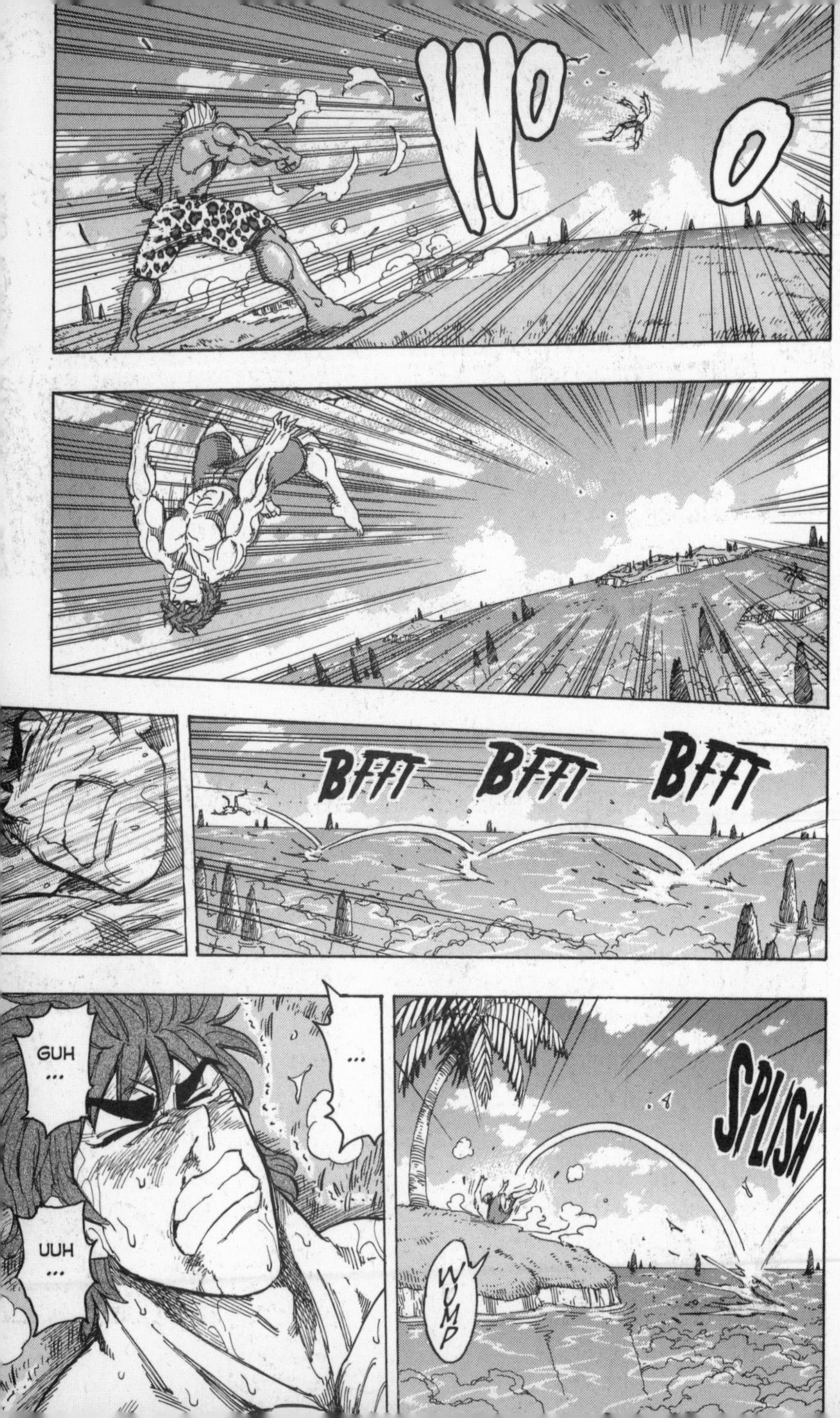
WO
O
BFFT
BFFT
BFFT
SPLISH
WUMP
...
GUH ...
UUH ...

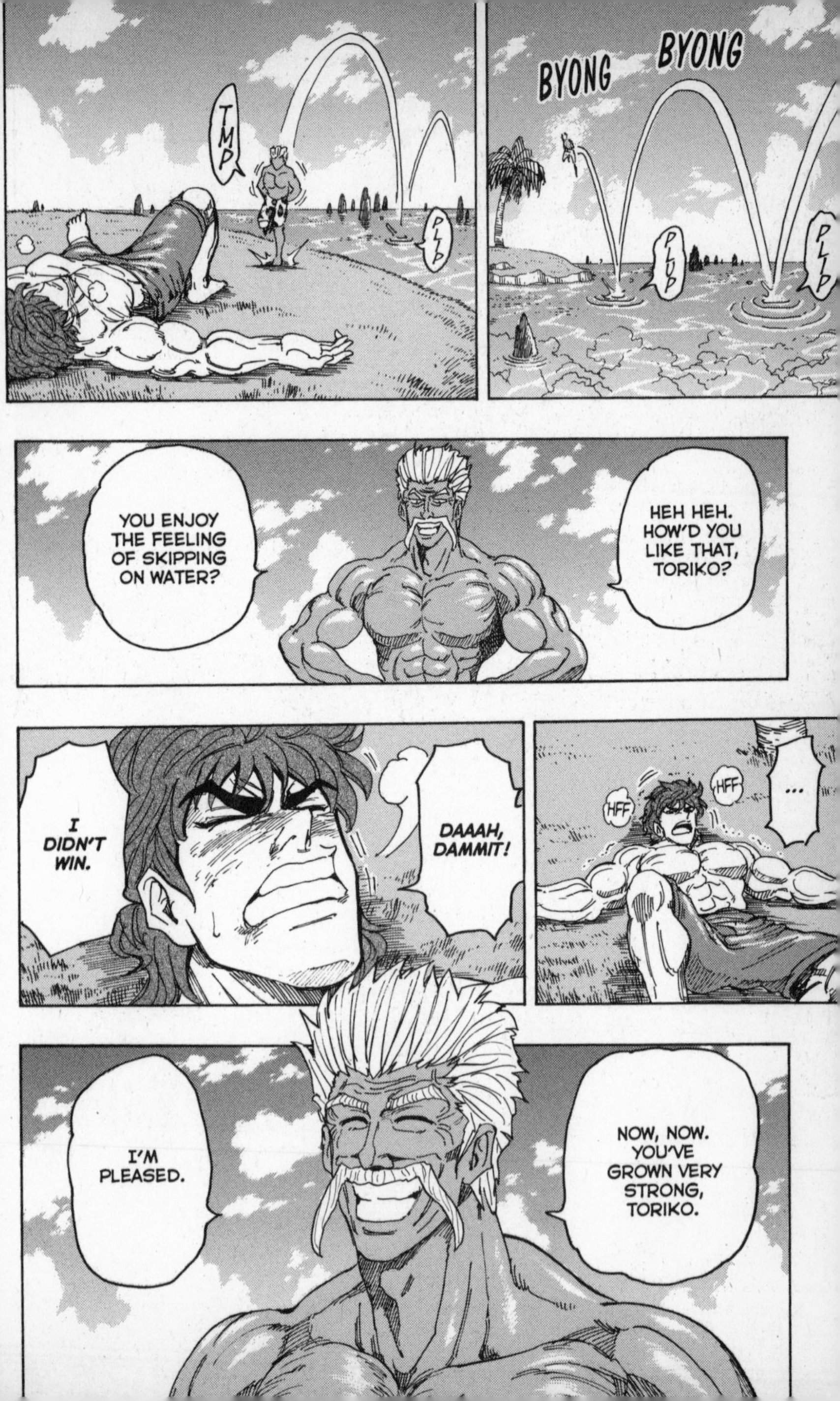
BYONG
BYONG
PLIP
PLUP
PLIP
TMP
HEH HEH. HOW'D YOU LIKE THAT, TORIKO?
YOU ENJOY THE FEELING OF SKIPPING ON WATER?
...
HFF
HFF
DAAAH, DAMMIT!
I DIDN'T WIN.
NOW, NOW. YOU'VE GROWN VERY STRONG, TORIKO.
I'M PLEASED.

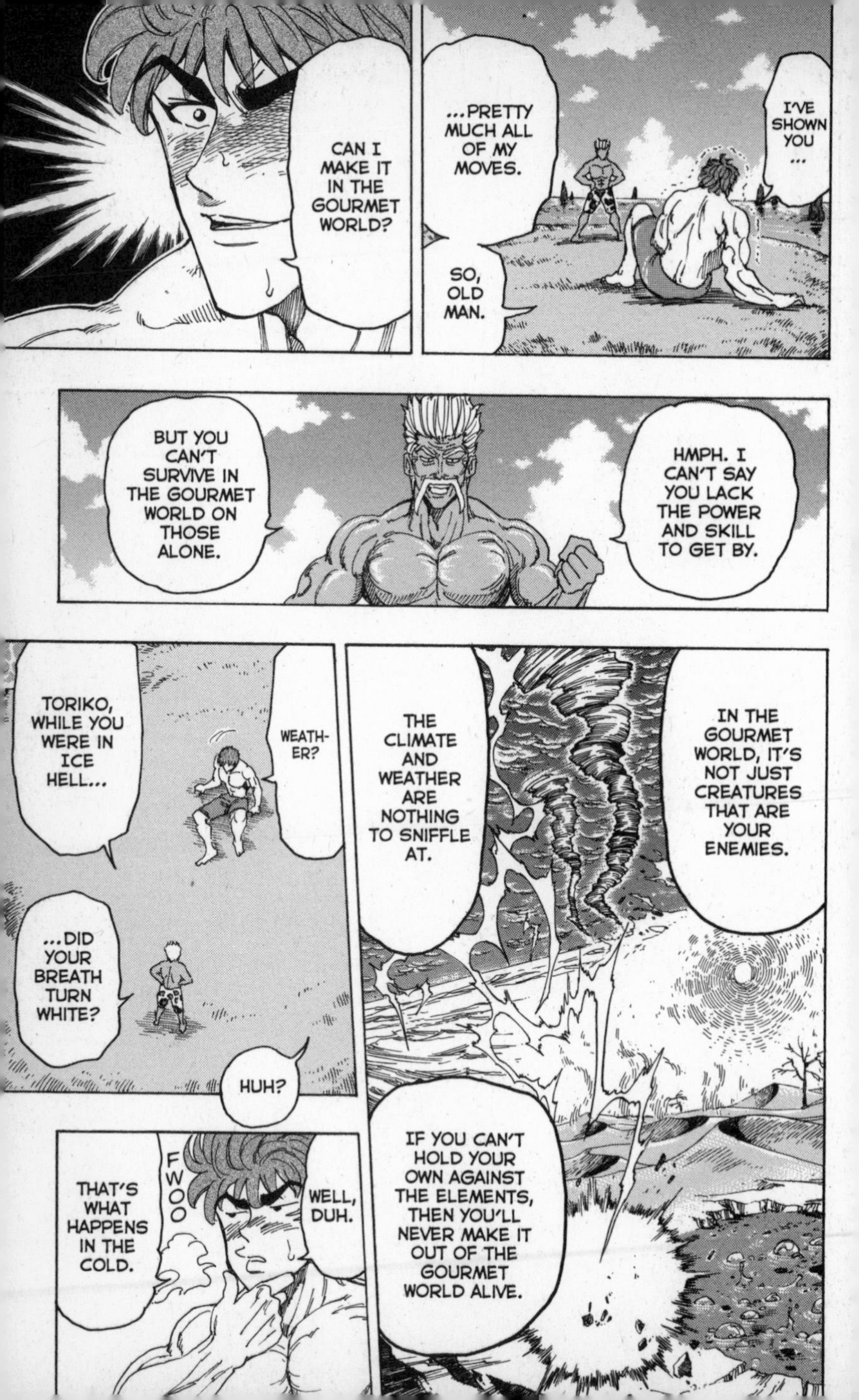
I'VE SHOWN YOU ...
...PRETTY MUCH ALL OF MY MOVES.
SO, OLD MAN.
CAN I MAKE IT IN THE GOURMET WORLD?
HMPH. I CAN'T SAY YOU LACK THE POWER AND SKILL TO GET BY.
BUT YOU CAN'T SURVIVE IN THE GOURMET WORLD ON THOSE ALONE.
IN THE GOURMET WORLD, IT'S NOT JUST CREATURES THAT ARE YOUR ENEMIES.
THE CLIMATE AND WEATHER ARE NOTHING TO SNIFFLE AT.
IF YOU CAN'T HOLD YOUR OWN AGAINST THE ELEMENTS, THEN YOU'LL NEVER MAKE IT OUT OF THE GOURMET WORLD ALIVE.
WEATH-ER?
TORIKO, WHILE YOU WERE IN ICE HELL...
...DID YOUR BREATH TURN WHITE?
HUH?
WELL, DUH.
FWOO
THAT'S WHAT HAPPENS IN THE COLD.

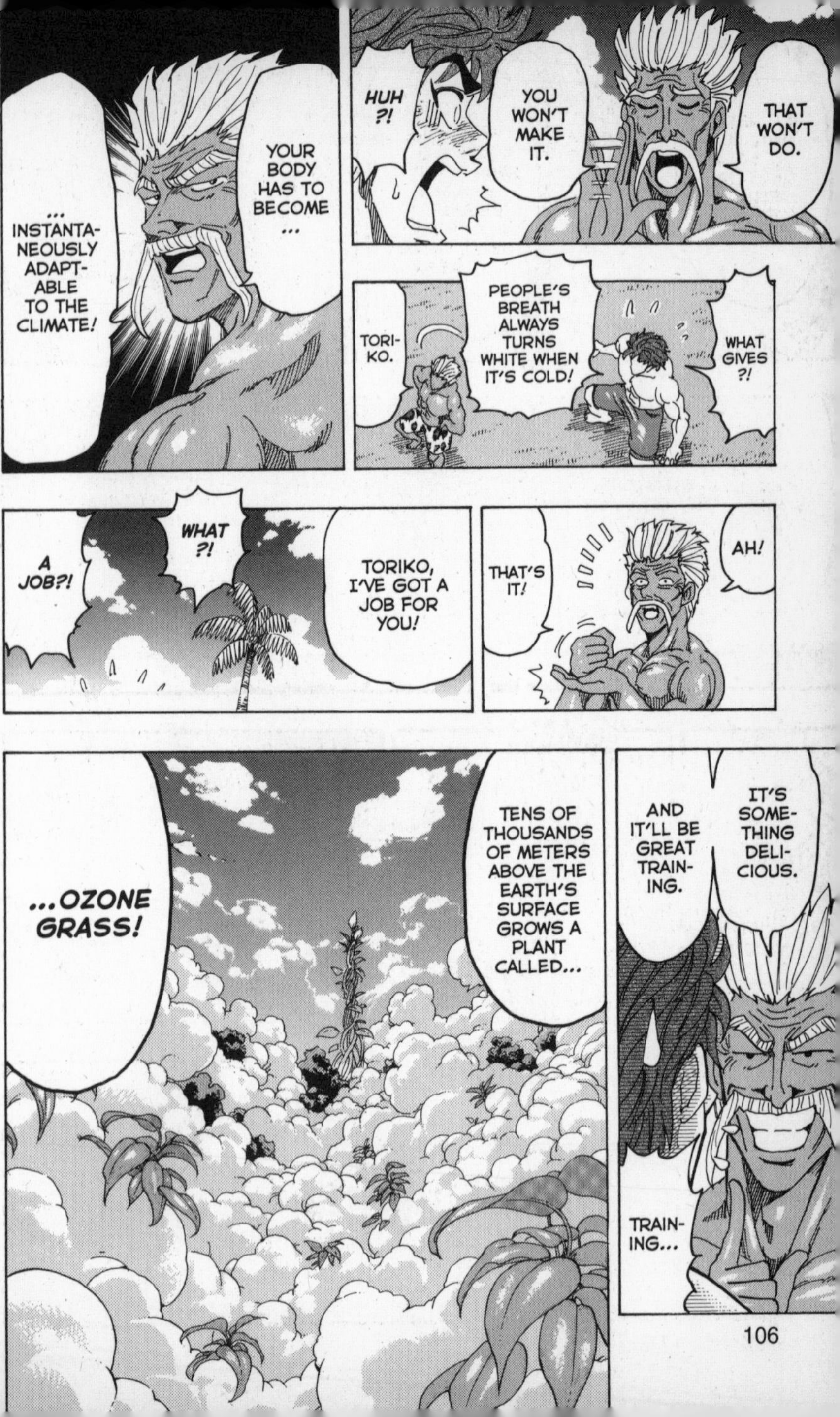
THAT WON'T DO.
YOU WON'T MAKE IT.
HUH?!
WHAT GIVES?!
PEOPLE'S BREATH ALWAYS TURNS WHITE WHEN IT'S COLD!
TORIKO.
YOUR BODY HAS TO BECOME ...
... INSTANTANEOUSLY ADAPTABLE TO THE CLIMATE!
AH!
THAT'S IT!
TORIKO, I'VE GOT A JOB FOR YOU!
WHAT?!
A JOB?!
IT'S SOMETHING DELICIOUS.
AND IT'LL BE GREAT TRAINING.
TRAINING...
TENS OF THOUSANDS OF METERS ABOVE THE EARTH'S SURFACE GROWS A PLANT CALLED...
...OZONE GRASS!

OZONE GAS?!
NO, OZONE GRASS!
SINCE ONE BITE WILL SEND YOU INTO HEAVENLY BLISS, IT'S ALSO KNOWN AS HEAVENLY GRASS.
HOW ABOUT MAKING IT THE SALAD IN YOUR FULL-COURSE MEAL?
OH.
GULP
I'LL EXPLAIN THE DETAILS ONCE WE GET BACK.
THERE'S MORE I WANT TO TELL YOU.
FOLLOW ME, TORIKO!
BYONG BYONG
HEY! I CAN'T SKIP MY WAY HOME!!
ARGH! I'LL JUST SWIM!
SWFF
HAAAAA!!
SPLASH SPLASH
OZONE GRASS, HUH?
NICE!

Menu 7.

OZONE GRASS

TORIKO

GOURMET CHECKLIST

Vol. 112

LIMOUSINE JELLYFISH
(UNCLASSIFIED)

CAPTURE LEVEL: ---

HABITAT: UNKNOWN

LENGTH: 25 METERS (GRANNY SETSU'S PET)

HEIGHT: ---

WEIGHT: UNKNOWN

PRICE: ---

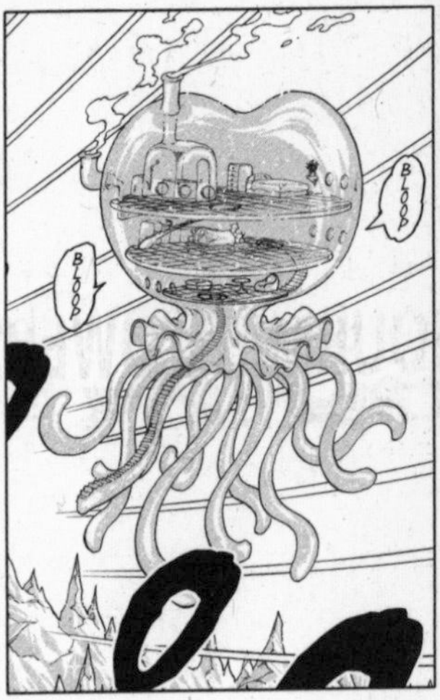
BLOOP
BLOOP

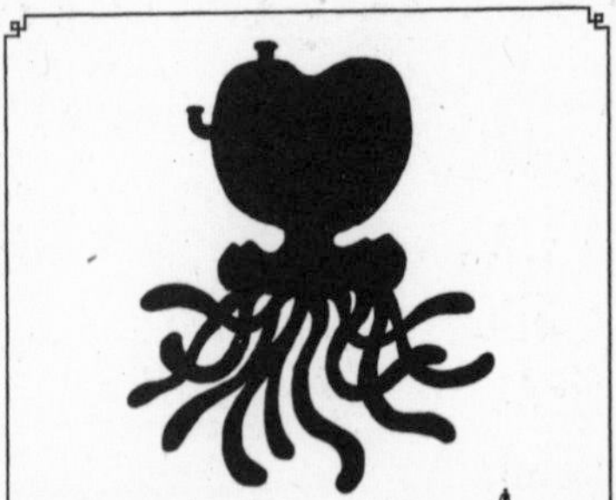

SCALE

GOURMET LIVING LEGEND GRANNY SETSU'S PET. WHETHER OVER LAND OR SEA, THE LIMOUSINE JELLYFISH IS A PREMIER TRAVELING EXPERIENCE. ITS INTERIOR IS ELASTIC AND CAN BE SHAPED INTO FURNITURE, COOKWARE, AND OTHER STAPLES OF A RUDIMENTARY LIVING SPACE. AS FAR AS ITS BIOLOGY, THE LIMOUSINE JELLYFISH'S NATURAL HABITAT IS A COMPLETE MYSTERY AND IT IS UNKNOWN WHETHER IT EVEN ORIGINATED IN THE HUMAN WORLD. LIMOUSINE JELLYFISH RARELY MAKE AN APPEARANCE ON THE MARKET, SO IT IS HARD TO DETERMINE A PRICE, BUT THEY ARE ESTIMATED TO EXCEED THE COST OF SEVERAL HUNDRED LUXURY AUTOMOBILES.

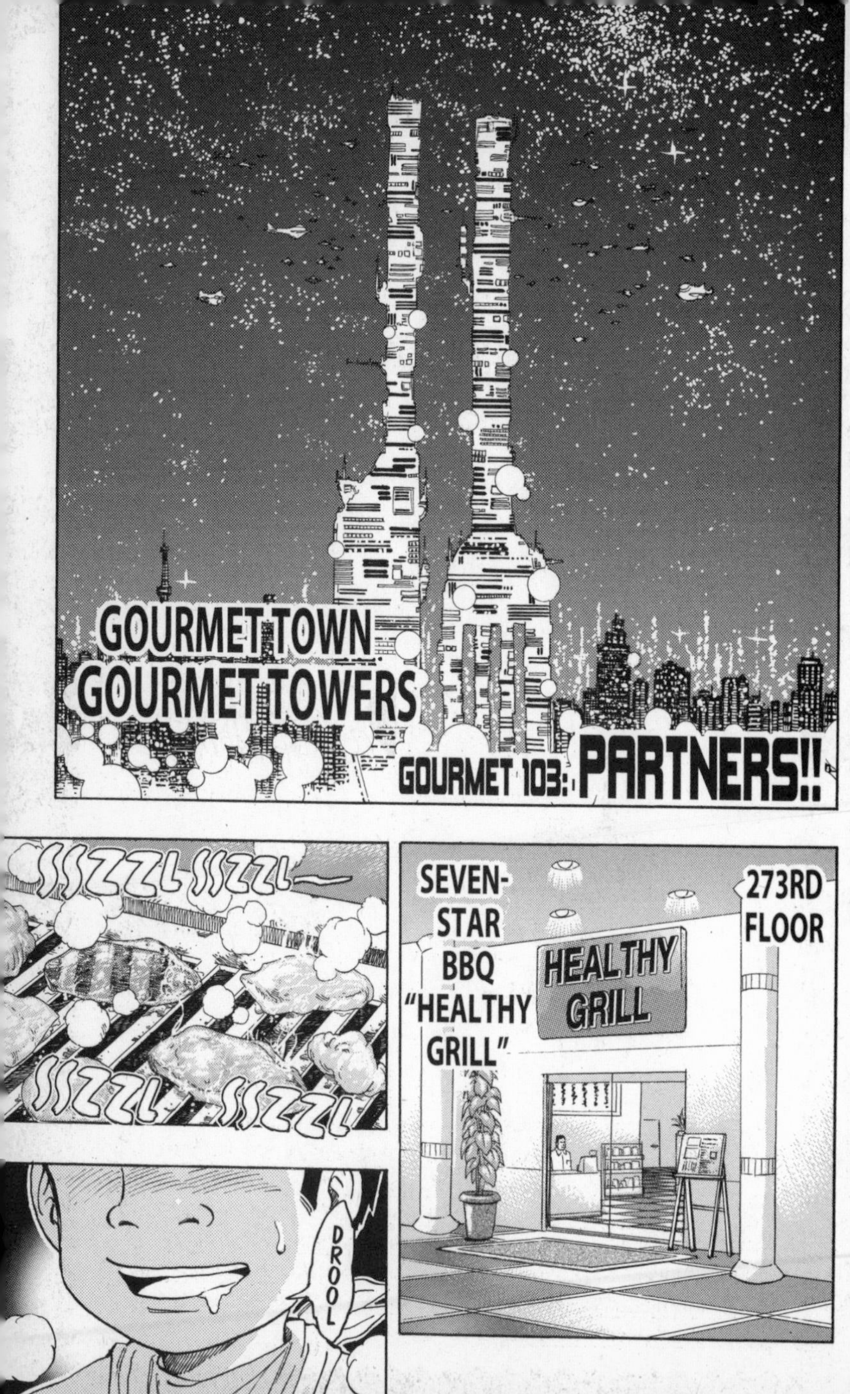

GOURMET TOWN
GOURMET TOWERS
GOURMET 103: PARTNERS!!
273RD FLOOR
SEVEN-STAR BBQ "HEALTHY GRILL"
HEALTHY GRILL
SSZZL SSZZL
SSZZL SSZZL
DROOL

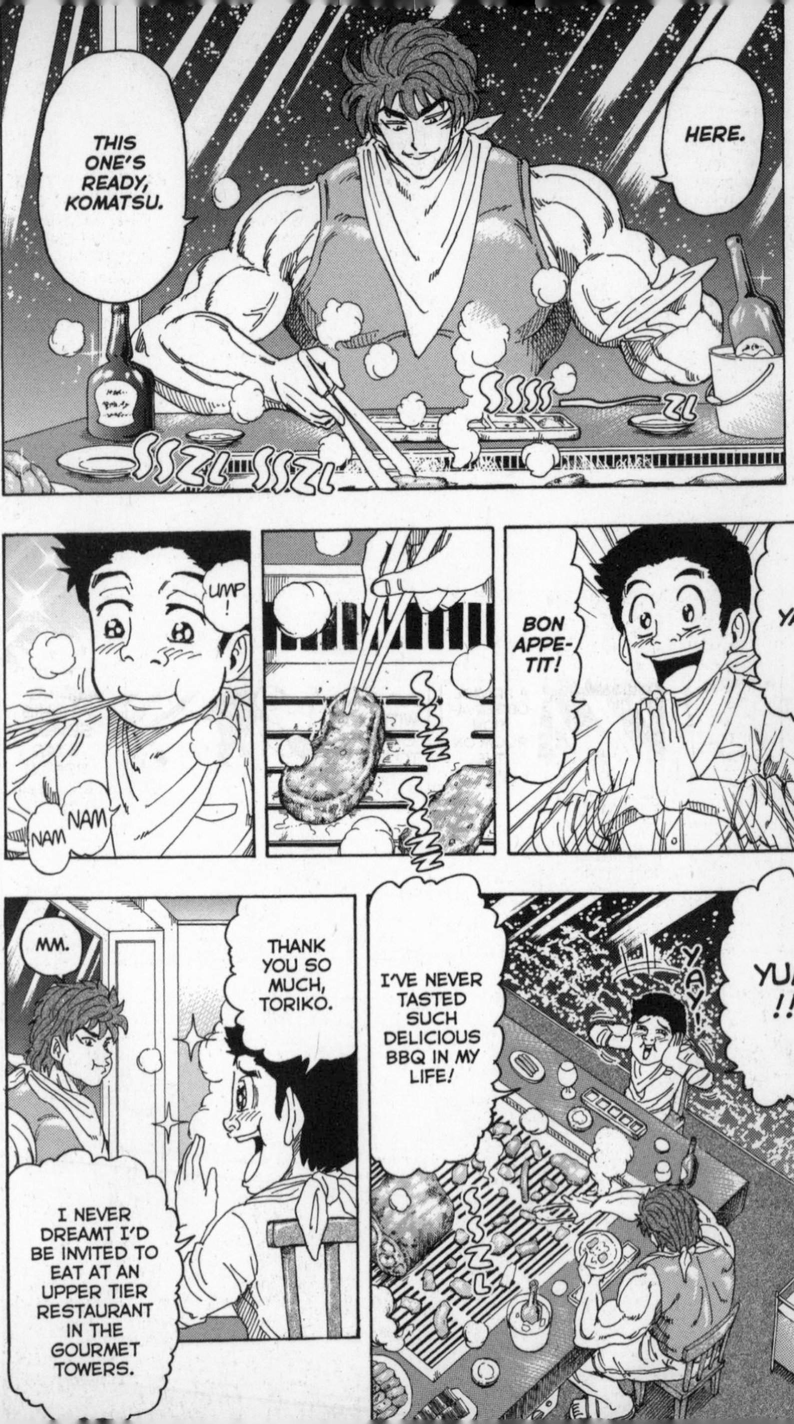
HERE.
THIS ONE'S READY, KOMATSU.
SSSS
ZL
SSZL SSZL
YAY!
BON APPE-TIT!
UMP!
NAM NAM
YUM!!
YAY!
I'VE NEVER TASTED SUCH DELICIOUS BBQ IN MY LIFE!
THANK YOU SO MUCH, TORIKO.
MM.
I NEVER DREAMT I'D BE INVITED TO EAT AT AN UPPER TIER RESTAURANT IN THE GOURMET TOWERS.

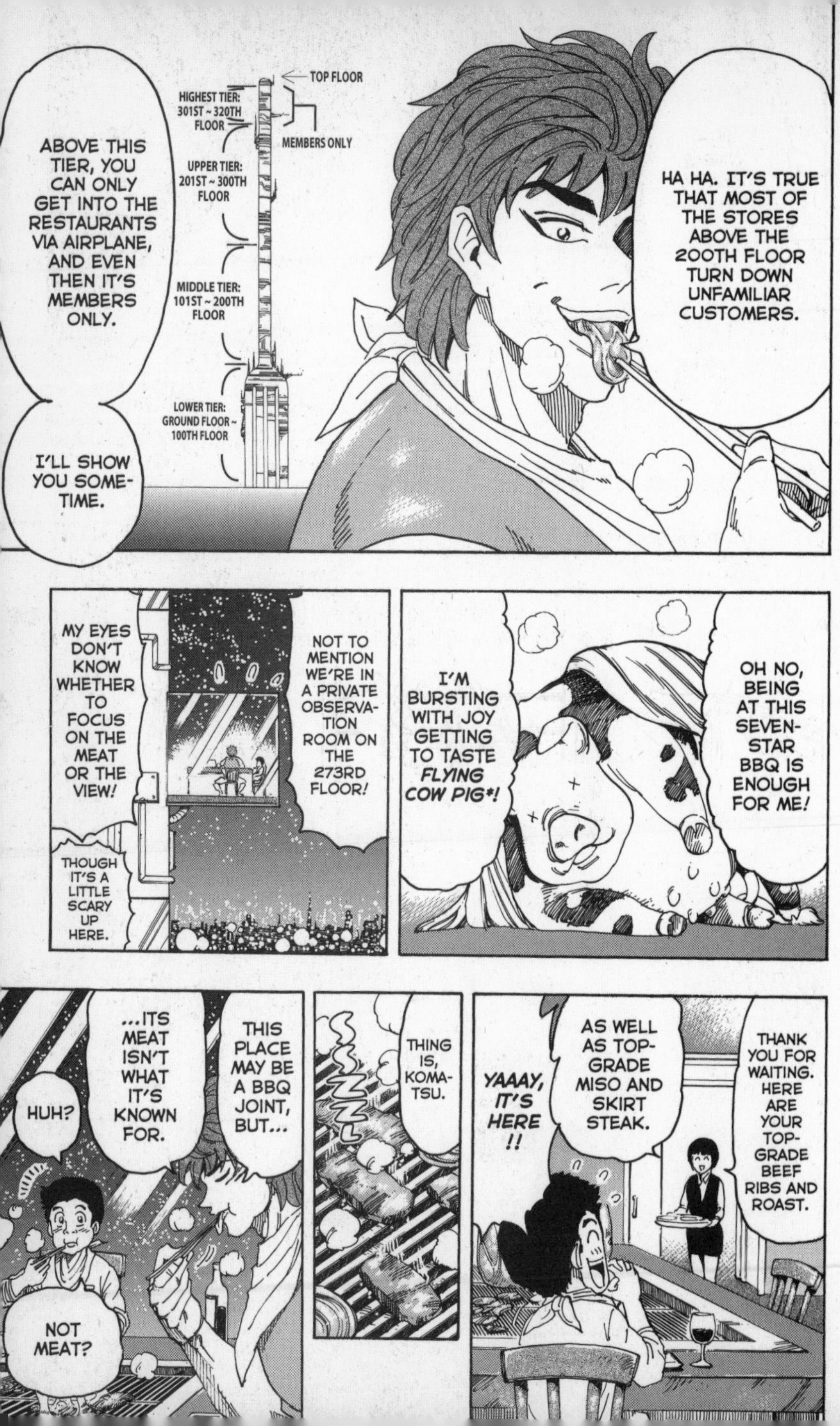
HA HA. IT'S TRUE THAT MOST OF THE STORES ABOVE THE 200TH FLOOR TURN DOWN UNFAMILIAR CUSTOMERS.
TOP FLOOR
HIGHEST TIER: 301ST ~ 320TH FLOOR
MEMBERS ONLY
UPPER TIER: 201ST ~ 300TH FLOOR
MIDDLE TIER: 101ST ~ 200TH FLOOR
LOWER TIER: GROUND FLOOR ~ 100TH FLOOR
ABOVE THIS TIER, YOU CAN ONLY GET INTO THE RESTAURANTS VIA AIRPLANE, AND EVEN THEN IT'S MEMBERS ONLY.
I'LL SHOW YOU SOME-TIME.
OH NO, BEING AT THIS SEVEN-STAR BBQ IS ENOUGH FOR ME!
I'M BURSTING WITH JOY GETTING TO TASTE FLYING COW PIG*!
NOT TO MENTION WE'RE IN A PRIVATE OBSERVATION ROOM ON THE 273RD FLOOR!
MY EYES DON'T KNOW WHETHER TO FOCUS ON THE MEAT OR THE VIEW!
THOUGH IT'S A LITTLE SCARY UP HERE.
THANK YOU FOR WAITING. HERE ARE YOUR TOP-GRADE BEEF RIBS AND ROAST.
AS WELL AS TOP-GRADE MISO AND SKIRT STEAK.
YAAAY, IT'S HERE!!
THING IS, KOMA-TSU.
THIS PLACE MAY BE A BBQ JOINT, BUT...
...ITS MEAT ISN'T WHAT IT'S KNOWN FOR.
HUH?
NOT MEAT?

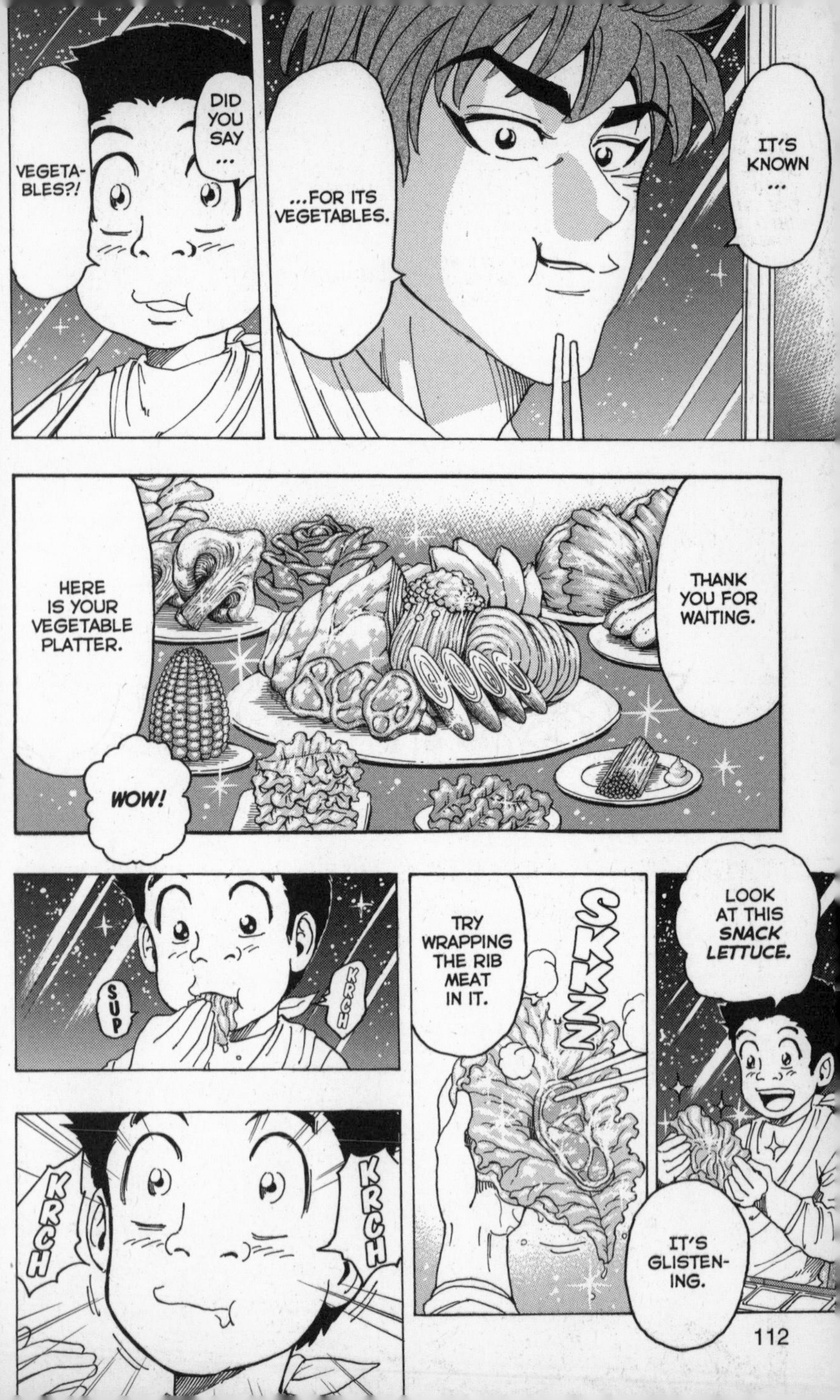
IT'S KNOWN ...
...FOR ITS VEGETABLES.
DID YOU SAY ...
VEGETA-BLES?!
THANK YOU FOR WAITING.
HERE IS YOUR VEGETABLE PLATTER.
WOW!
LOOK AT THIS *SNACK LETTUCE.*
IT'S GLISTEN-ING.
SKKZZ
TRY WRAPPING THE RIB MEAT IN IT.
KRCH
SUP
KRCH
KRCH

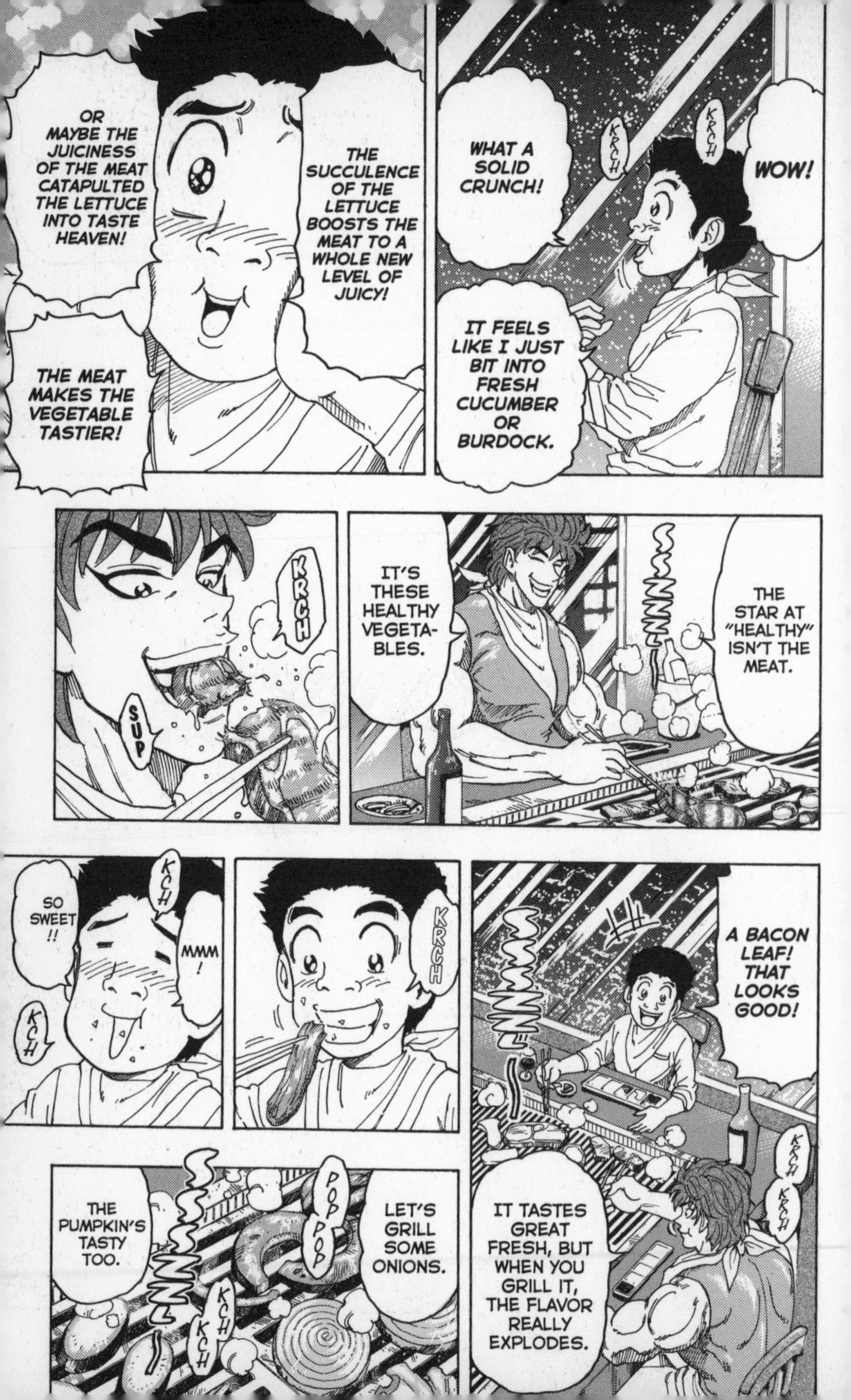
WOW!
KRCH
KRCH
WHAT A SOLID CRUNCH!
IT FEELS LIKE I JUST BIT INTO FRESH CUCUMBER OR BURDOCK.
THE SUCCULENCE OF THE LETTUCE BOOSTS THE MEAT TO A WHOLE NEW LEVEL OF JUICY!
OR MAYBE THE JUICINESS OF THE MEAT CATAPULTED THE LETTUCE INTO TASTE HEAVEN!
THE MEAT MAKES THE VEGETABLE TASTIER!
THE STAR AT "HEALTHY" ISN'T THE MEAT.
IT'S THESE HEALTHY VEGETABLES.
KRCH
SUP
A BACON LEAF! THAT LOOKS GOOD!
KRCH
KCH
SO SWEET!!
MMM!
KCH
KRCH KRCH
IT TASTES GREAT FRESH, BUT WHEN YOU GRILL IT, THE FLAVOR REALLY EXPLODES.
LET'S GRILL SOME ONIONS.
POP POP
THE PUMPKIN'S TASTY TOO.
KCH KCH

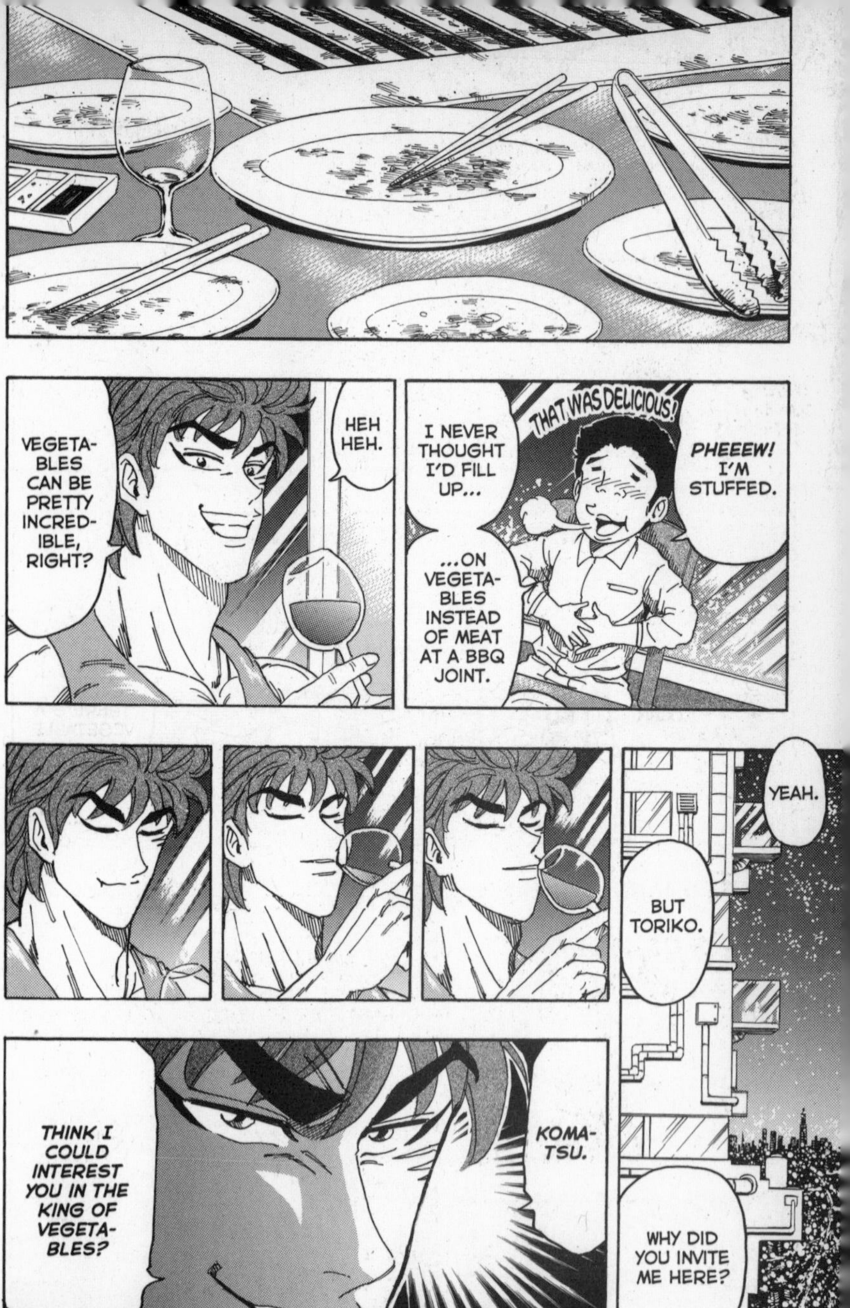
PHEEEW! I'M STUFFED.
THAT WAS DELICIOUS!
I NEVER THOUGHT I'D FILL UP...
...ON VEGETA-BLES INSTEAD OF MEAT AT A BBQ JOINT.
HEH HEH.
VEGETA-BLES CAN BE PRETTY INCRED-IBLE, RIGHT?
YEAH.
BUT TORIKO.
WHY DID YOU INVITE ME HERE?
KOMA-TSU.
THINK I COULD INTEREST YOU IN THE KING OF VEGETA-BLES?

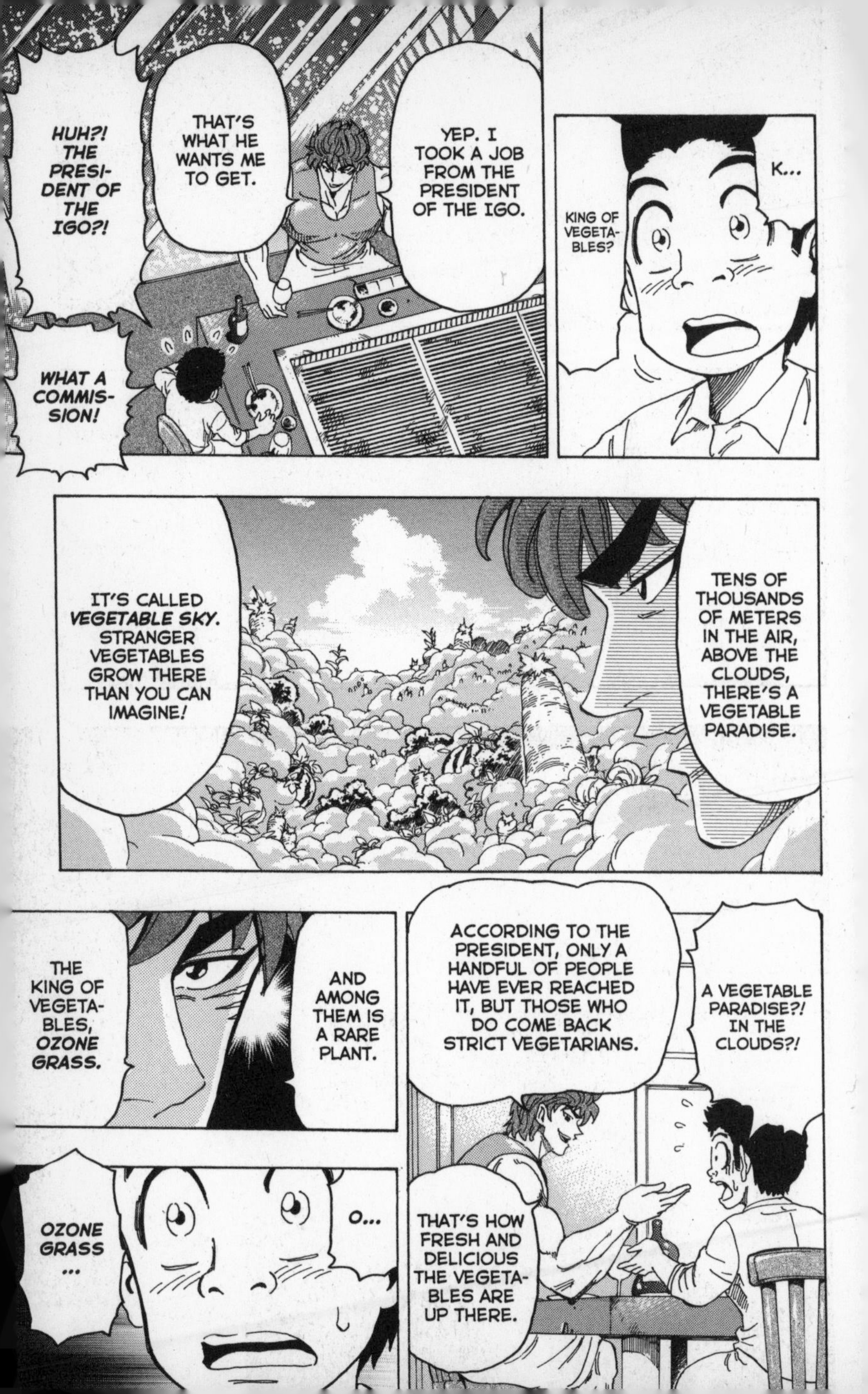
K...
KING OF VEGETABLES?
YEP. I TOOK A JOB FROM THE PRESIDENT OF THE IGO.
THAT'S WHAT HE WANTS ME TO GET.
HUH?! THE PRESIDENT OF THE IGO?!
WHAT A COMMISSION!
TENS OF THOUSANDS OF METERS IN THE AIR, ABOVE THE CLOUDS, THERE'S A VEGETABLE PARADISE.
IT'S CALLED *VEGETABLE SKY*. STRANGER VEGETABLES GROW THERE THAN YOU CAN IMAGINE!
A VEGETABLE PARADISE?! IN THE CLOUDS?!
ACCORDING TO THE PRESIDENT, ONLY A HANDFUL OF PEOPLE HAVE EVER REACHED IT, BUT THOSE WHO DO COME BACK STRICT VEGETARIANS.
THAT'S HOW FRESH AND DELICIOUS THE VEGETABLES ARE UP THERE.
AND AMONG THEM IS A RARE PLANT.
THE KING OF VEGETABLES, OZONE GRASS.
O...
OZONE GRASS ...

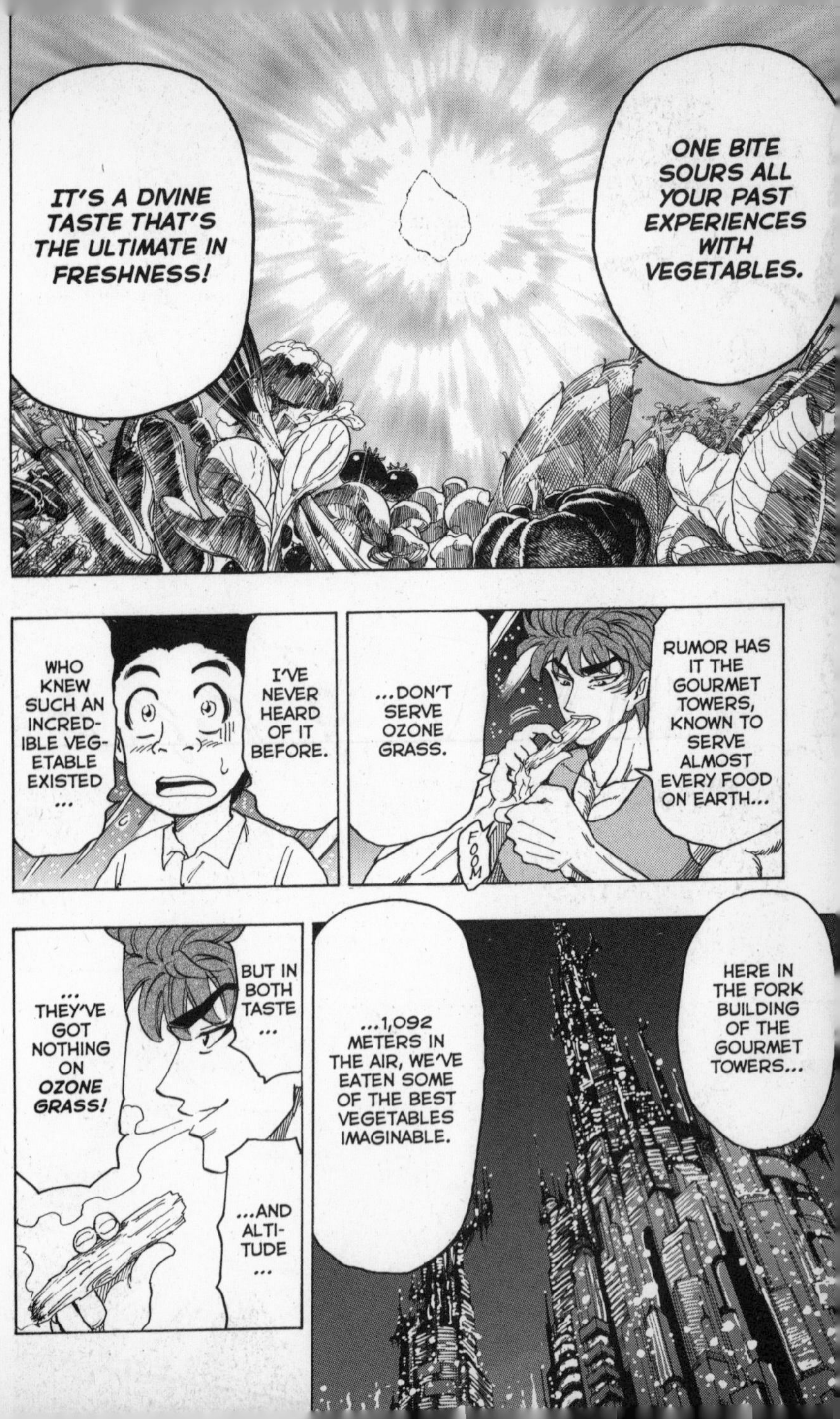
ONE BITE SOURS ALL YOUR PAST EXPERIENCES WITH VEGETABLES.
IT'S A DIVINE TASTE THAT'S THE ULTIMATE IN FRESHNESS!
RUMOR HAS IT THE GOURMET TOWERS, KNOWN TO SERVE ALMOST EVERY FOOD ON EARTH...
...DON'T SERVE OZONE GRASS.
FOOM
I'VE NEVER HEARD OF IT BEFORE.
WHO KNEW SUCH AN INCRED-IBLE VEG-ETABLE EXISTED ...
HERE IN THE FORK BUILDING OF THE GOURMET TOWERS...
...1,092 METERS IN THE AIR, WE'VE EATEN SOME OF THE BEST VEGETABLES IMAGINABLE.
BUT IN BOTH TASTE ...
...AND ALTI-TUDE ...
... THEY'VE GOT NOTHING ON OZONE GRASS!

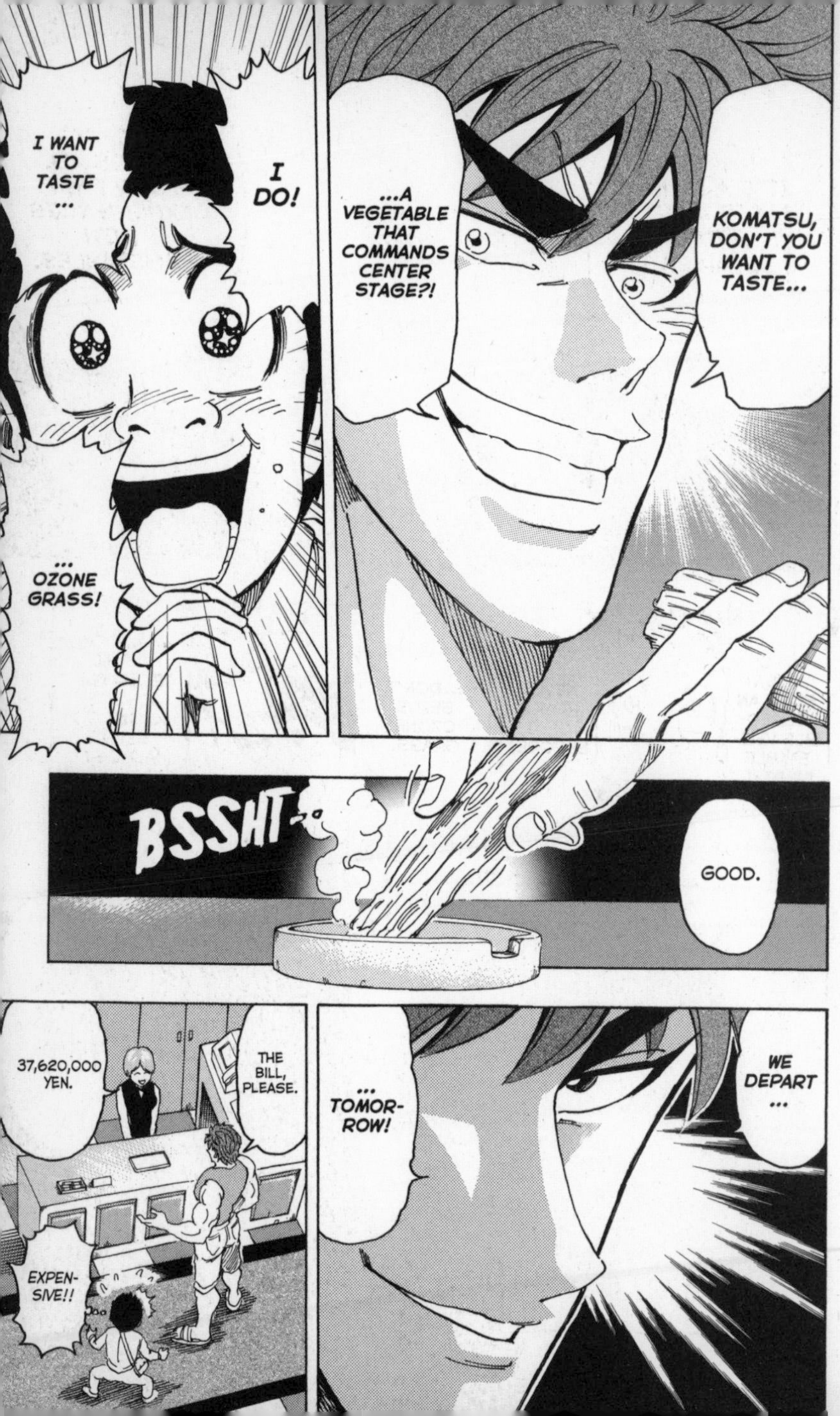
KOMATSU, DON'T YOU WANT TO TASTE...
...A VEGETABLE THAT COMMANDS CENTER STAGE?!
I DO!
I WANT TO TASTE...
...OZONE GRASS!
GOOD.
BSSHT
WE DEPART...
...TOMOR-ROW!
THE BILL, PLEASE.
37,620,000 YEN.
EXPEN-SIVE!!

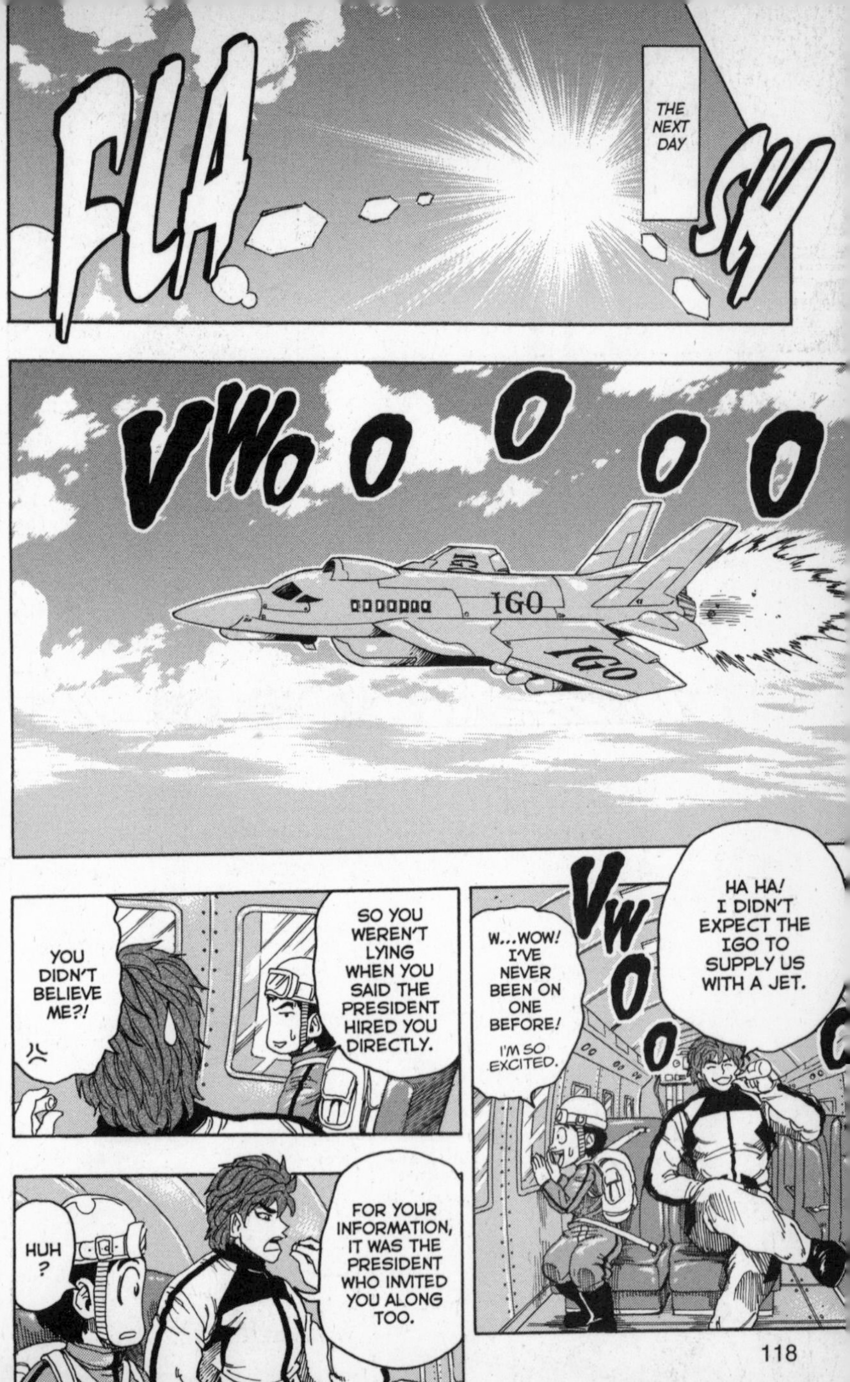
THE NEXT DAY
FLASH
VWOOOOO
VWOOO
HA HA! I DIDN'T EXPECT THE IGO TO SUPPLY US WITH A JET.
W...WOW! I'VE NEVER BEEN ON ONE BEFORE!
I'M SO EXCITED.
SO YOU WEREN'T LYING WHEN YOU SAID THE PRESIDENT HIRED YOU DIRECTLY.
YOU DIDN'T BELIEVE ME?!
FOR YOUR INFORMATION, IT WAS THE PRESIDENT WHO INVITED YOU ALONG TOO.
HUH?

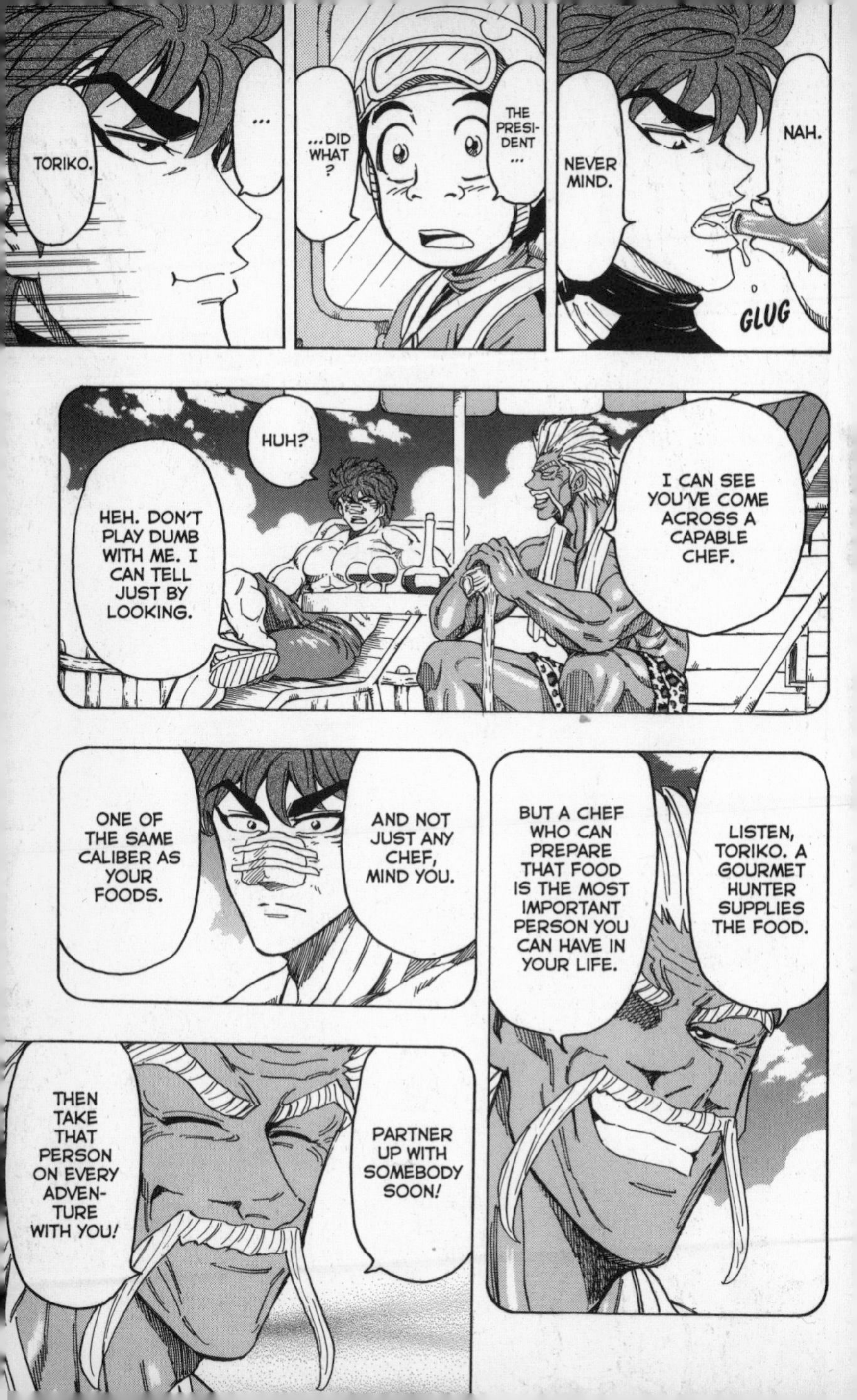
NAH.
NEVER MIND.
GLUG
THE PRESI-DENT ...
...DID WHAT?
...
TORIKO.
I CAN SEE YOU'VE COME ACROSS A CAPABLE CHEF.
HUH?
HEH. DON'T PLAY DUMB WITH ME. I CAN TELL JUST BY LOOKING.
LISTEN, TORIKO. A GOURMET HUNTER SUPPLIES THE FOOD.
BUT A CHEF WHO CAN PREPARE THAT FOOD IS THE MOST IMPORTANT PERSON YOU CAN HAVE IN YOUR LIFE.
AND NOT JUST ANY CHEF, MIND YOU.
ONE OF THE SAME CALIBER AS YOUR FOODS.
PARTNER UP WITH SOMEBODY SOON!
THEN TAKE THAT PERSON ON EVERY ADVEN-TURE WITH YOU!

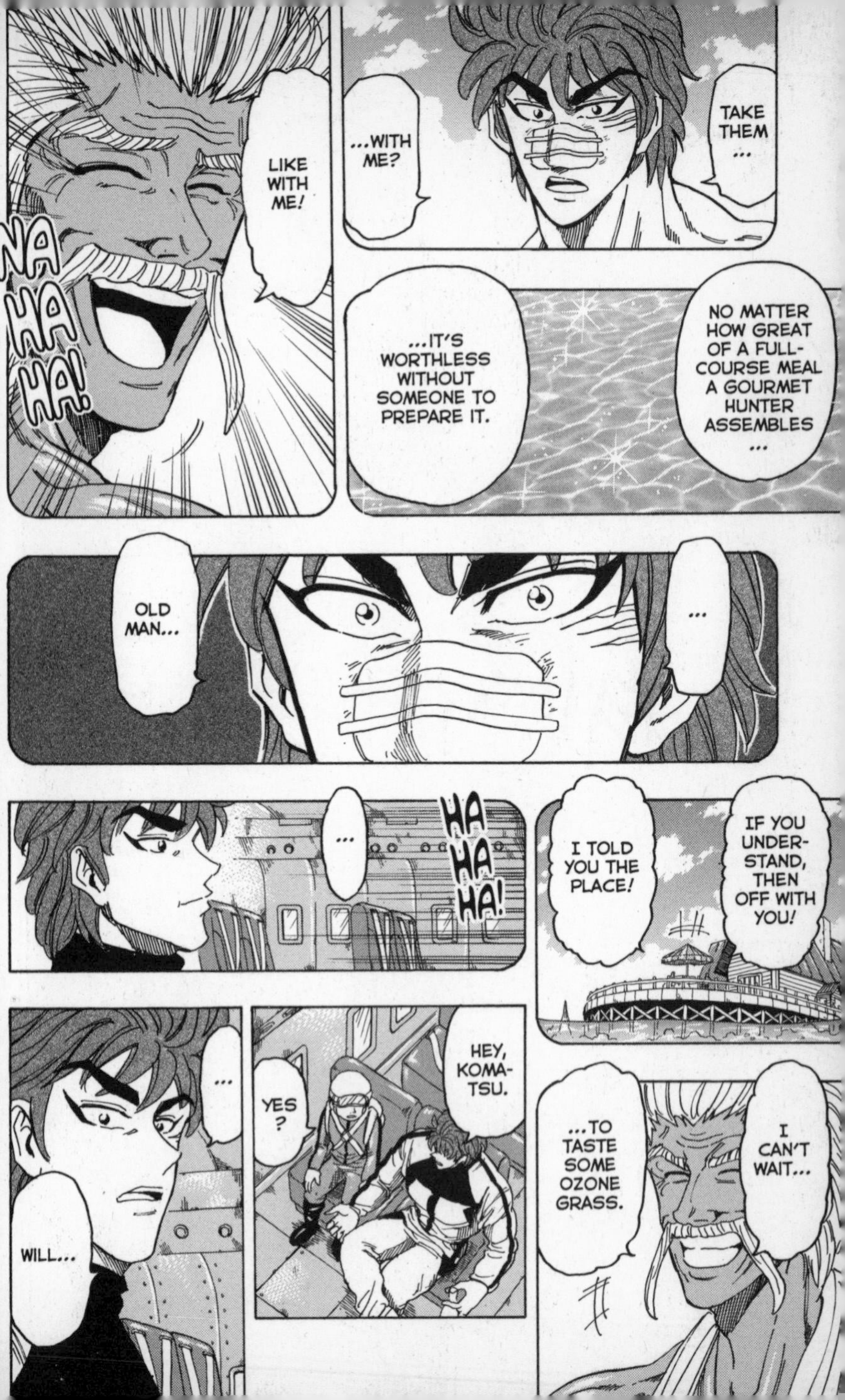
TAKE THEM...
...WITH ME?
NO MATTER HOW GREAT OF A FULL-COURSE MEAL A GOURMET HUNTER ASSEMBLES...
...IT'S WORTHLESS WITHOUT SOMEONE TO PREPARE IT.
LIKE WITH ME!
NA HA HA HA!
...
OLD MAN...
IF YOU UNDERSTAND, THEN OFF WITH YOU!
I TOLD YOU THE PLACE!
HA HA HA!
...
I CAN'T WAIT...
...TO TASTE SOME OZONE GRASS.
HEY, KOMATSU.
YES?
...
WILL...

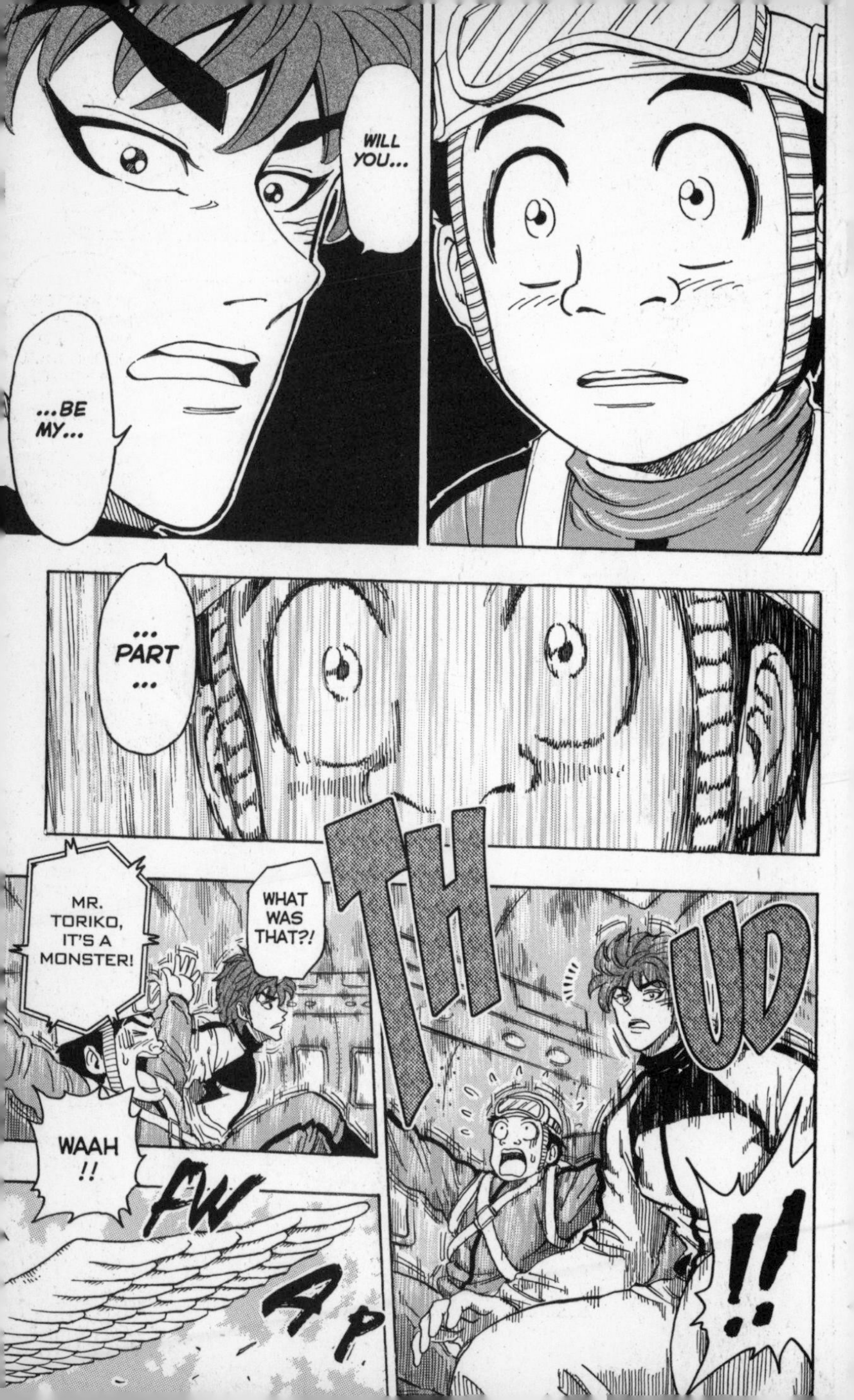

WILL YOU...
...BE MY...
... PART ...
THUD
!!
WHAT WAS THAT?!
MR. TORIKO, IT'S A MONSTER!
WAAH !!
FWAP

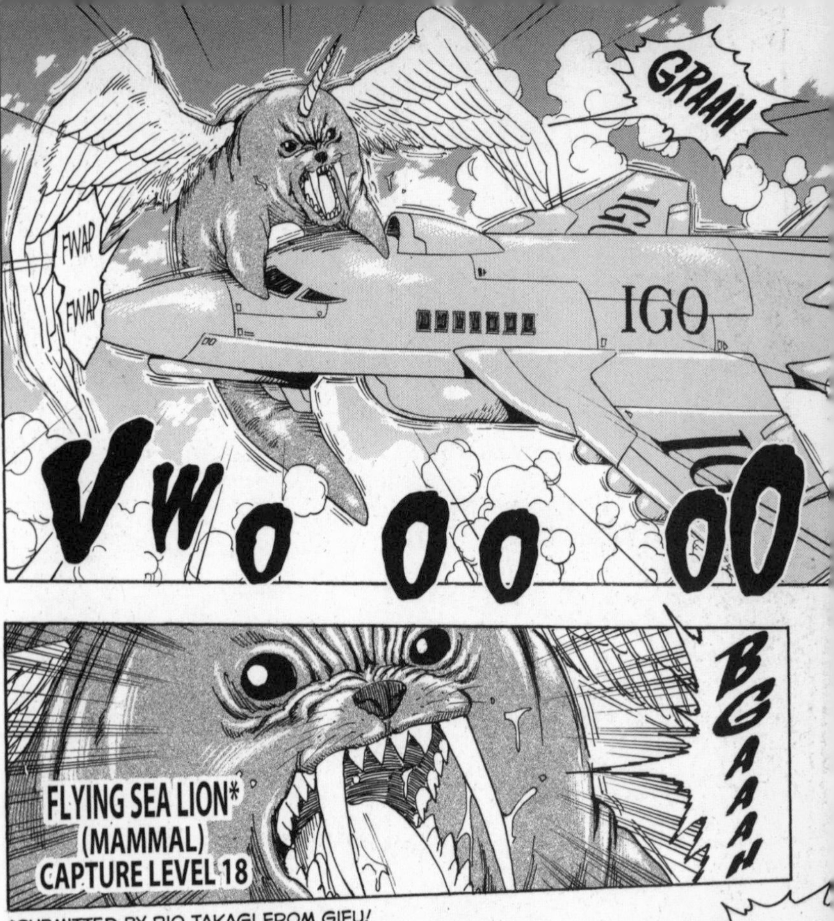
GRAAH
FWAP FWAP
VWOOOOOO
BGAAAAAH
FLYING SEA LION*
(MAMMAL)
CAPTURE LEVEL 18

*SUBMITTED BY RIO TAKAGI FROM GIFU!

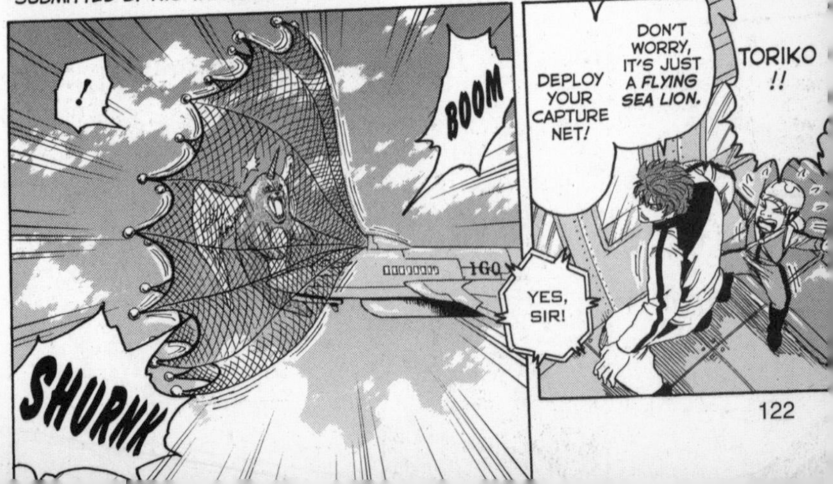
TORIKO!!
DON'T WORRY, IT'S JUST A *FLYING SEA LION.*
DEPLOY YOUR CAPTURE NET!
YES, SIR!
BOOM
!
SHURNK

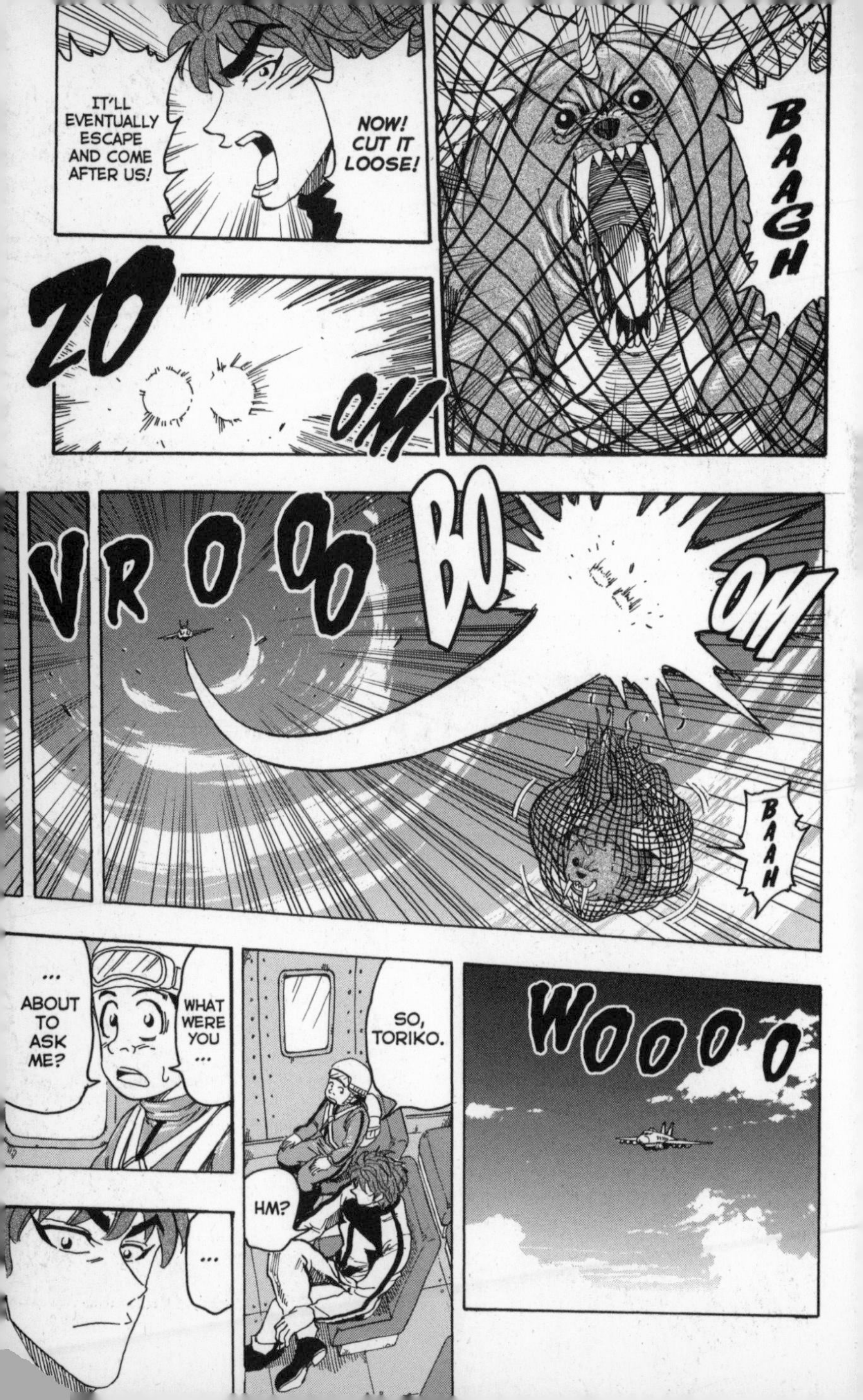
BAAAGH
NOW! CUT IT LOOSE!
IT'LL EVENTUALLY ESCAPE AND COME AFTER US!
ZOOM
VROOO
BOOM
BAAAH
WOOOO
SO, TORIKO.
HM?
WHAT WERE YOU ...
... ABOUT TO ASK ME?
...

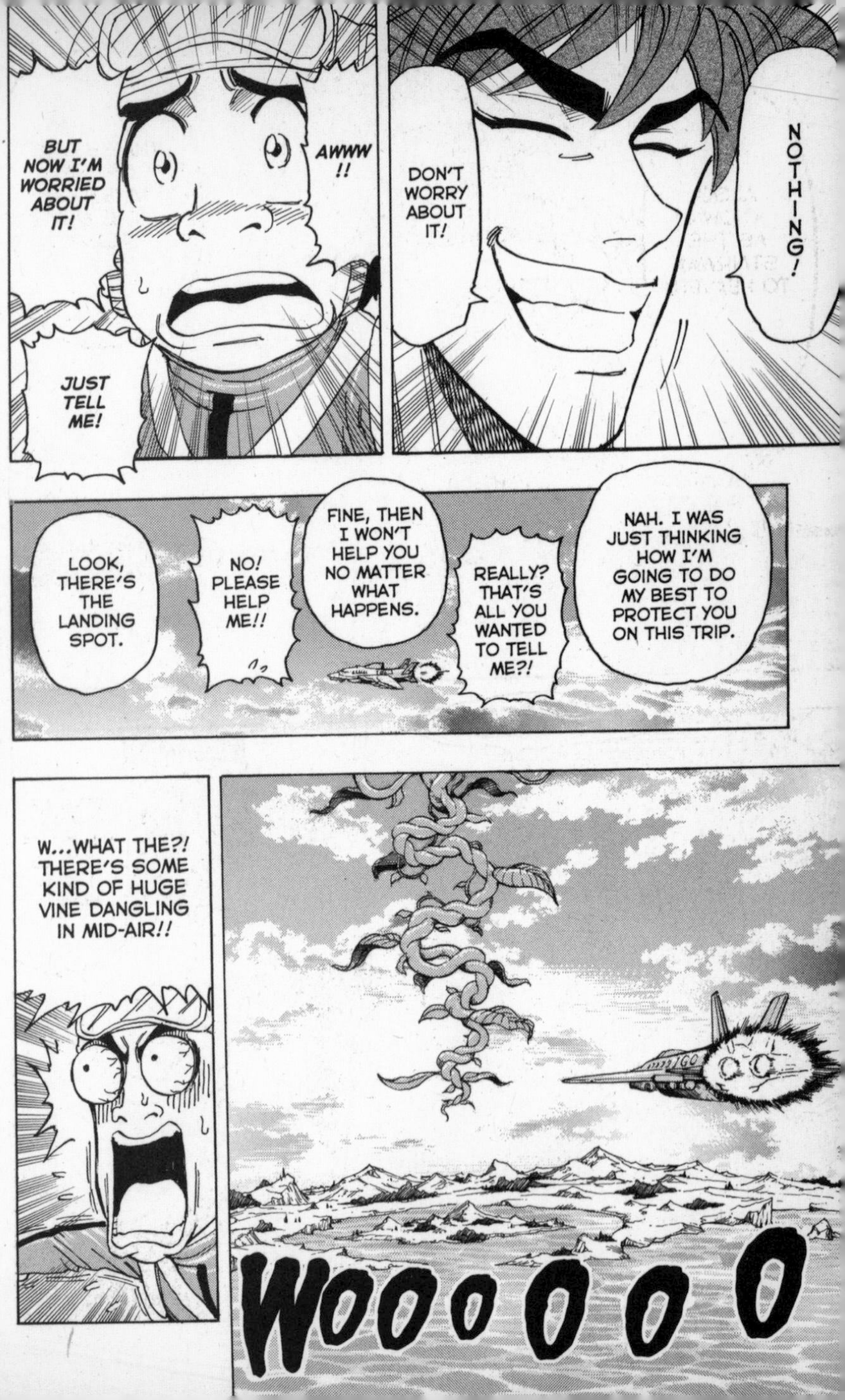
NOTHING!
DON'T WORRY ABOUT IT!
AWWW!!
BUT NOW I'M WORRIED ABOUT IT!
JUST TELL ME!
NAH. I WAS JUST THINKING HOW I'M GOING TO DO MY BEST TO PROTECT YOU ON THIS TRIP.
REALLY? THAT'S ALL YOU WANTED TO TELL ME?!
FINE, THEN I WON'T HELP YOU NO MATTER WHAT HAPPENS.
NO! PLEASE HELP ME!!
LOOK, THERE'S THE LANDING SPOT.
WOOOOOOO
W...WHAT THE?! THERE'S SOME KIND OF HUGE VINE DANGLING IN MID-AIR!!

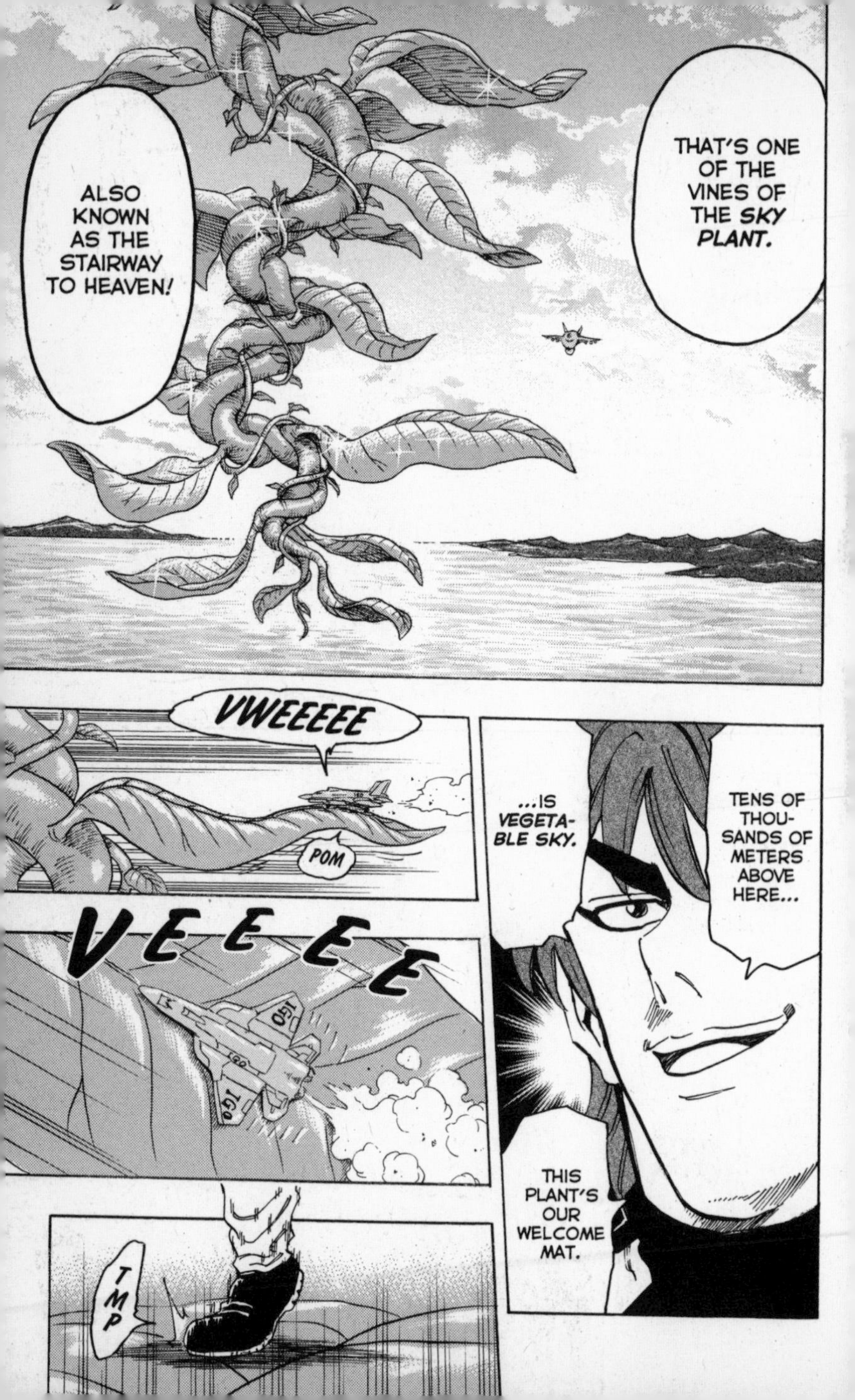
THAT'S ONE OF THE VINES OF THE *SKY PLANT.*
ALSO KNOWN AS THE STAIRWAY TO HEAVEN!
TENS OF THOU-SANDS OF METERS ABOVE HERE...
...IS *VEGETA-BLE SKY.*
THIS PLANT'S OUR WELCOME MAT.
VWEEEEE
POM
VEEEE
TMP

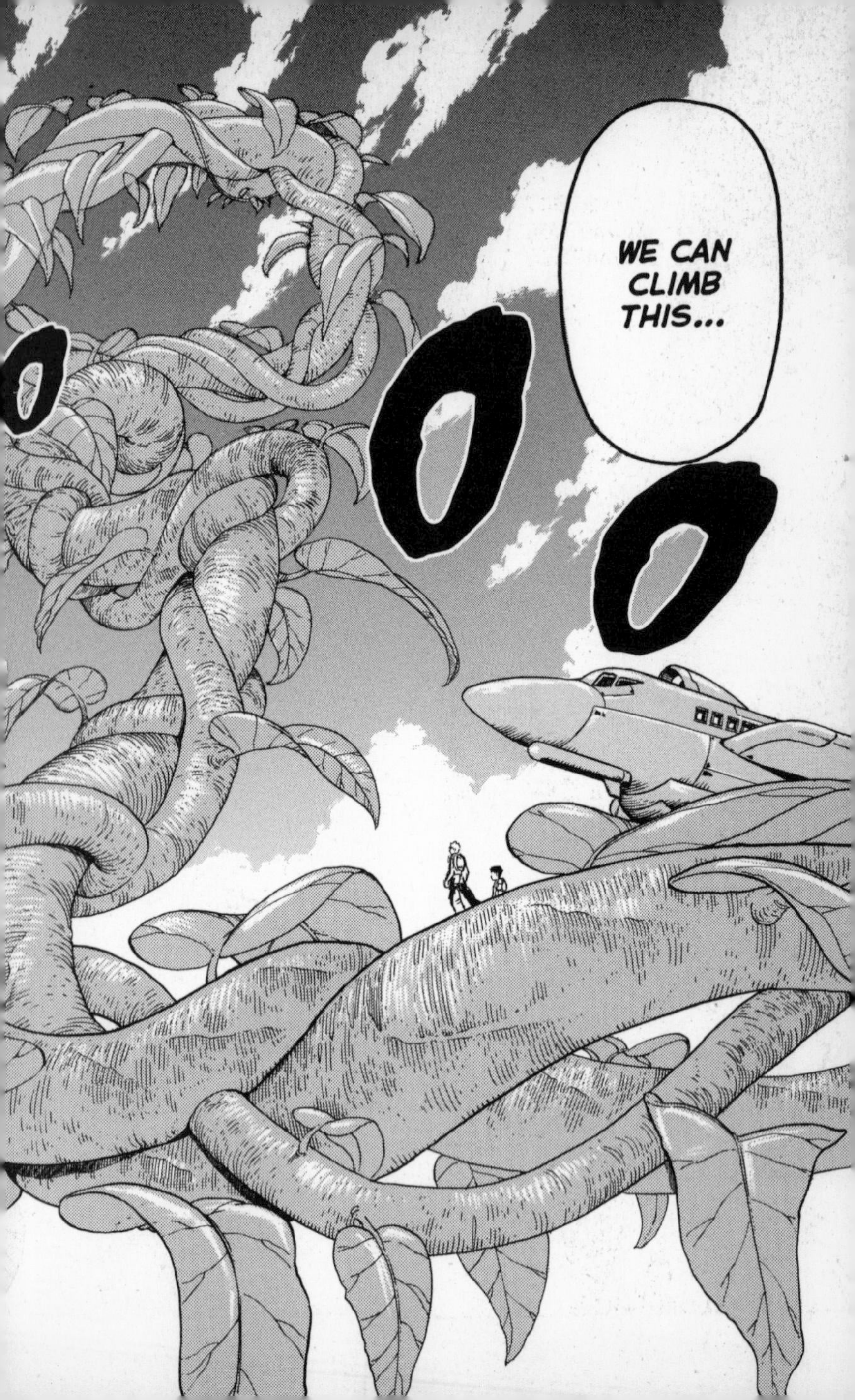
WE CAN CLIMB THIS...

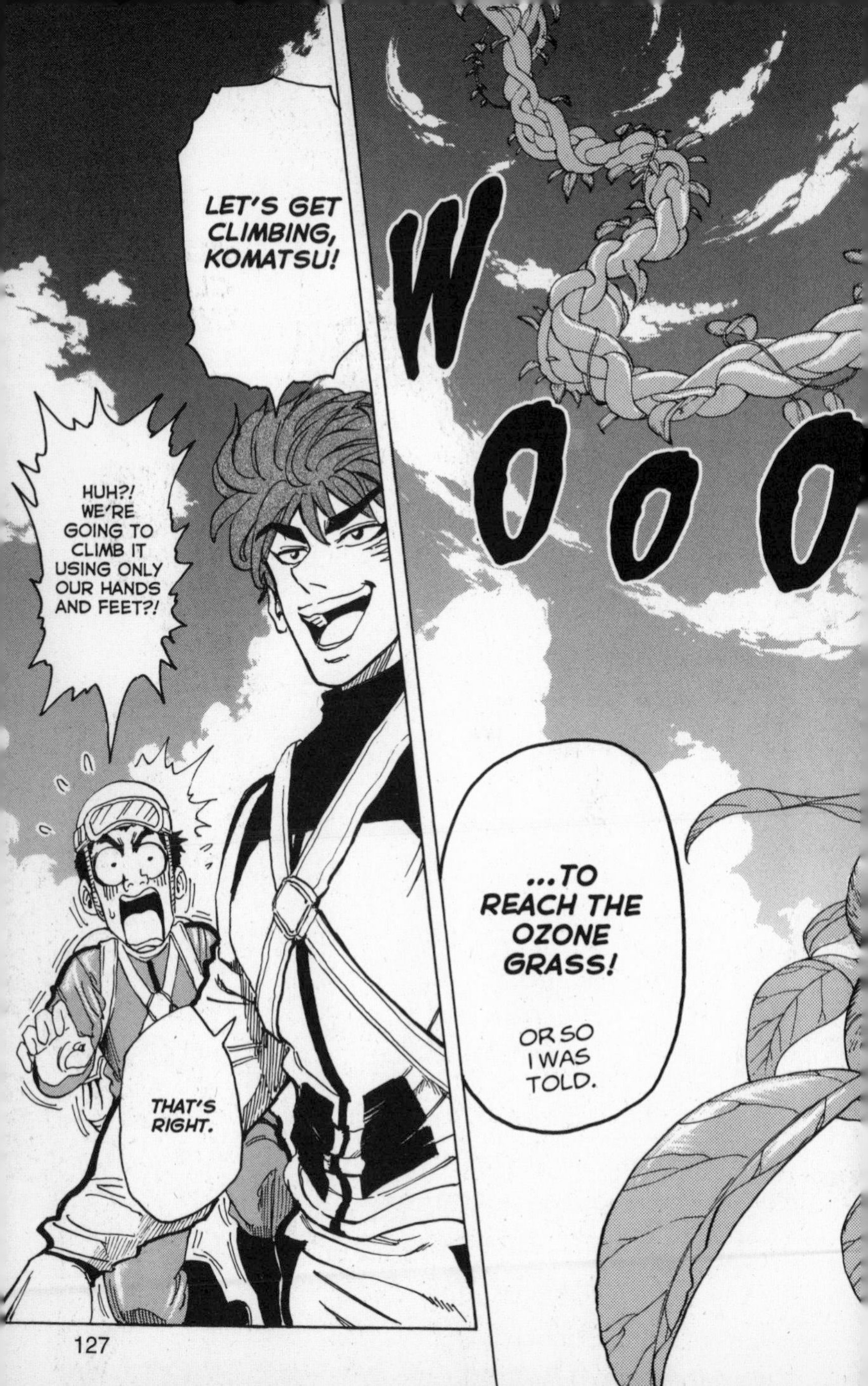
WOOO
...TO REACH THE OZONE GRASS!
OR SO I WAS TOLD.
LET'S GET CLIMBING, KOMATSU!
HUH?! WE'RE GOING TO CLIMB IT USING ONLY OUR HANDS AND FEET?!
THAT'S RIGHT.

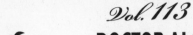

TORIKO

GOURMET CHECKLIST

Vol. 113

DOCTOR ALOE
(PLANT)

CAPTURE LEVEL: 62

HABITAT: WASTELANDS

LENGTH: ---

HEIGHT: GROWS TO NEARLY 10 METERS

WEIGHT: 300 GRAMS PER METER

PRICE: 60–900,000 YEN PER METER

(EFFECTIVENESS DEPENDS ON CROP)

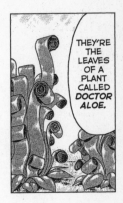

THEY'RE THE LEAVES OF A PLANT CALLED *DOCTOR ALOE*.

SCALE

NATURE'S OWN BANDAGE! IT HEALS SCRAPES, BURNS, FROSTBITE, AND OTHER AFFLICTIONS. WITH JUST ONE METER COSTING UPWARDS OF 60,000,000 YEN, IT'S A COSTLY BUT WORTHWHILE INVESTMENT, CONSIDERING NEARLY ANY INJURY CAN BE HEALED BY THE CURATIVE PROPERTIES OF DOCTOR ALOE. THIS IS ONE ITEM A REVIVER NEVER GOES WITHOUT.

GOURMET 104: STAIRWAY TO HEAVEN!!

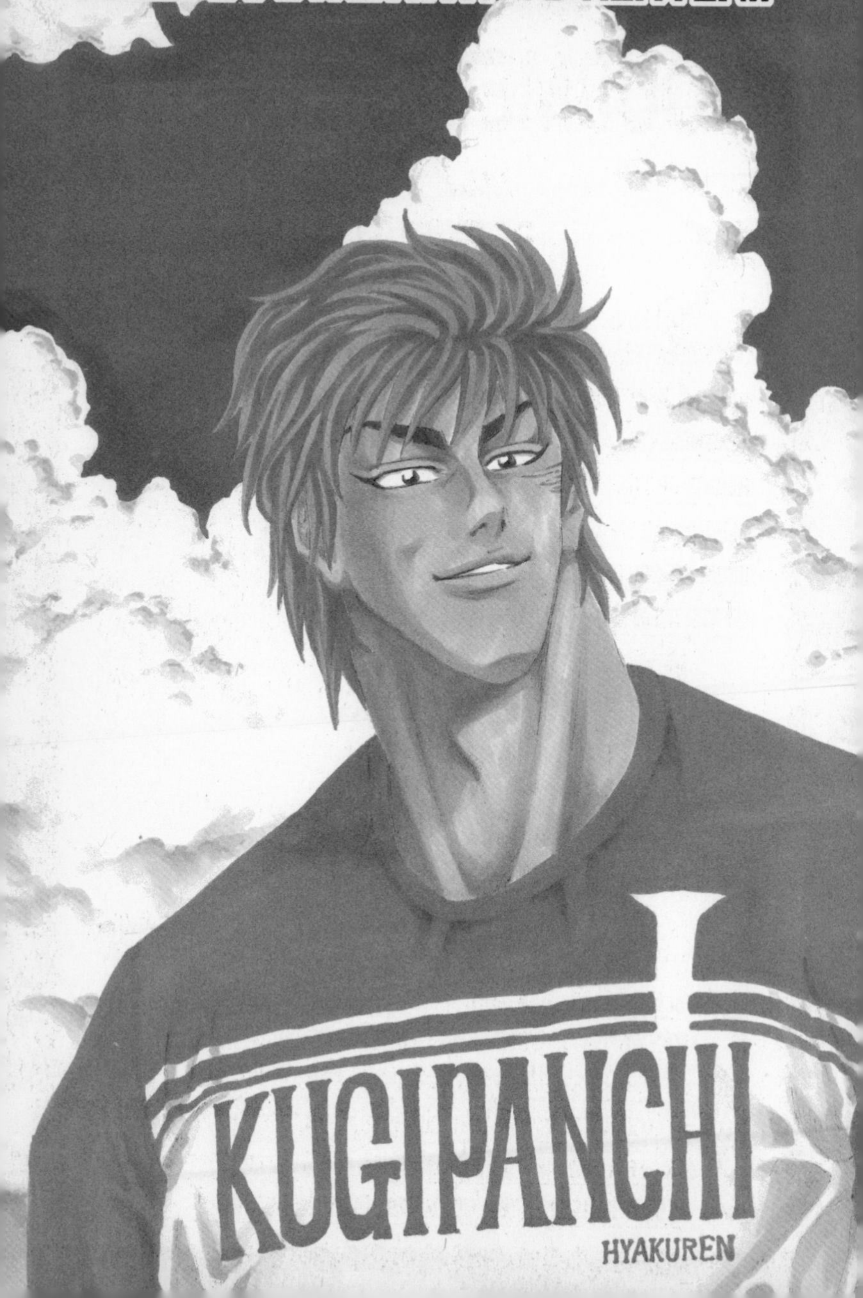
KUGIPANCHI
HYAKUREN

TORIKO

GOURMET CHECKLIST

Vol. 114
THERAPY BUTTERFLY
(INSECT)

CAPTURE LEVEL: LESS THAN 1

HABITAT: LIFE

LENGTH: 15 CM

HEIGHT: ---

WEIGHT: 10 G

PRICE: 700 YEN (BLUE), 800 YEN (RED)

THERAPY BUTTERFLY
(INSECT)
CAPTURE LEVEL: LESS THAN 1

SCALE

A BUTTERFLY WITH AN AFFINITY FOR THE SICK OR WEAK AREAS OF OTHER LIVING CREATURES. THERE ARE TWO VARIETIES, RED ONES AND BLUE ONES. THE BLUE ONES WILL ALIGHT ON RELATIVELY LIGHT INJURIES, WHILE THE RED ONES WILL GRAVITATE TO MORE SEVERE AFFLICTIONS. THOSE WITH MORTAL WOUNDS WILL FIND BOTH KINDS DRAWN TO THEM. THERAPY BUTTERFLIES HAVE BEEN USED IN RESCUE EFFORTS AFTER EARTHQUAKES AND NATURAL DISASTERS, WHERE THEY'VE EARNED THE NICKNAME "NATURE'S RESCUE SQUAD."

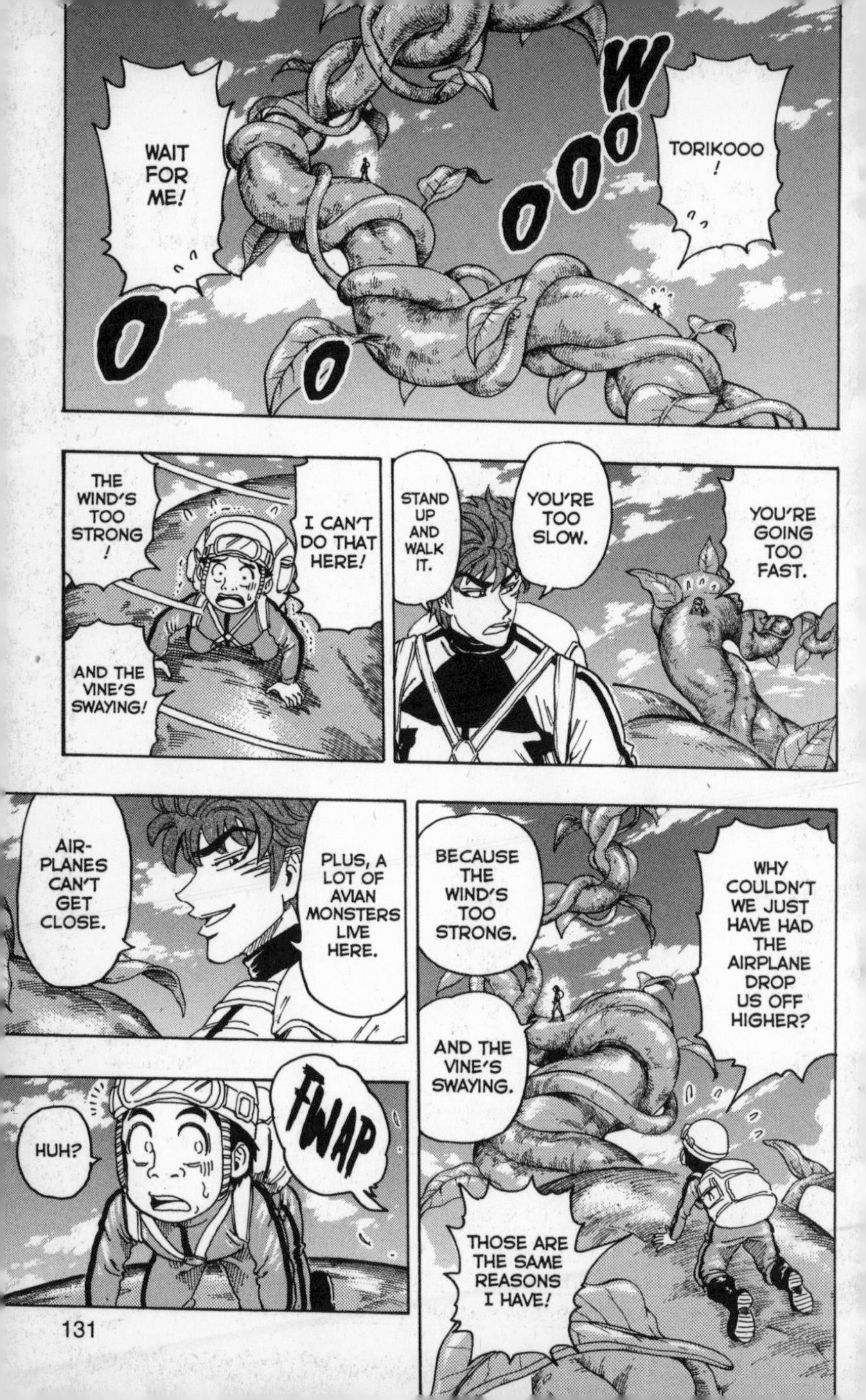
TORIKOOO!
WOOOOOO
WAIT FOR ME!
YOU'RE GOING TOO FAST.
YOU'RE TOO SLOW.
STAND UP AND WALK IT.
I CAN'T DO THAT HERE!
THE WIND'S TOO STRONG!
AND THE VINE'S SWAYING!
WHY COULDN'T WE JUST HAVE HAD THE AIRPLANE DROP US OFF HIGHER?
BECAUSE THE WIND'S TOO STRONG.
AND THE VINE'S SWAYING.
THOSE ARE THE SAME REASONS I HAVE!
PLUS, A LOT OF AVIAN MONSTERS LIVE HERE.
AIR-PLANES CAN'T GET CLOSE.
FWAP
HUH?

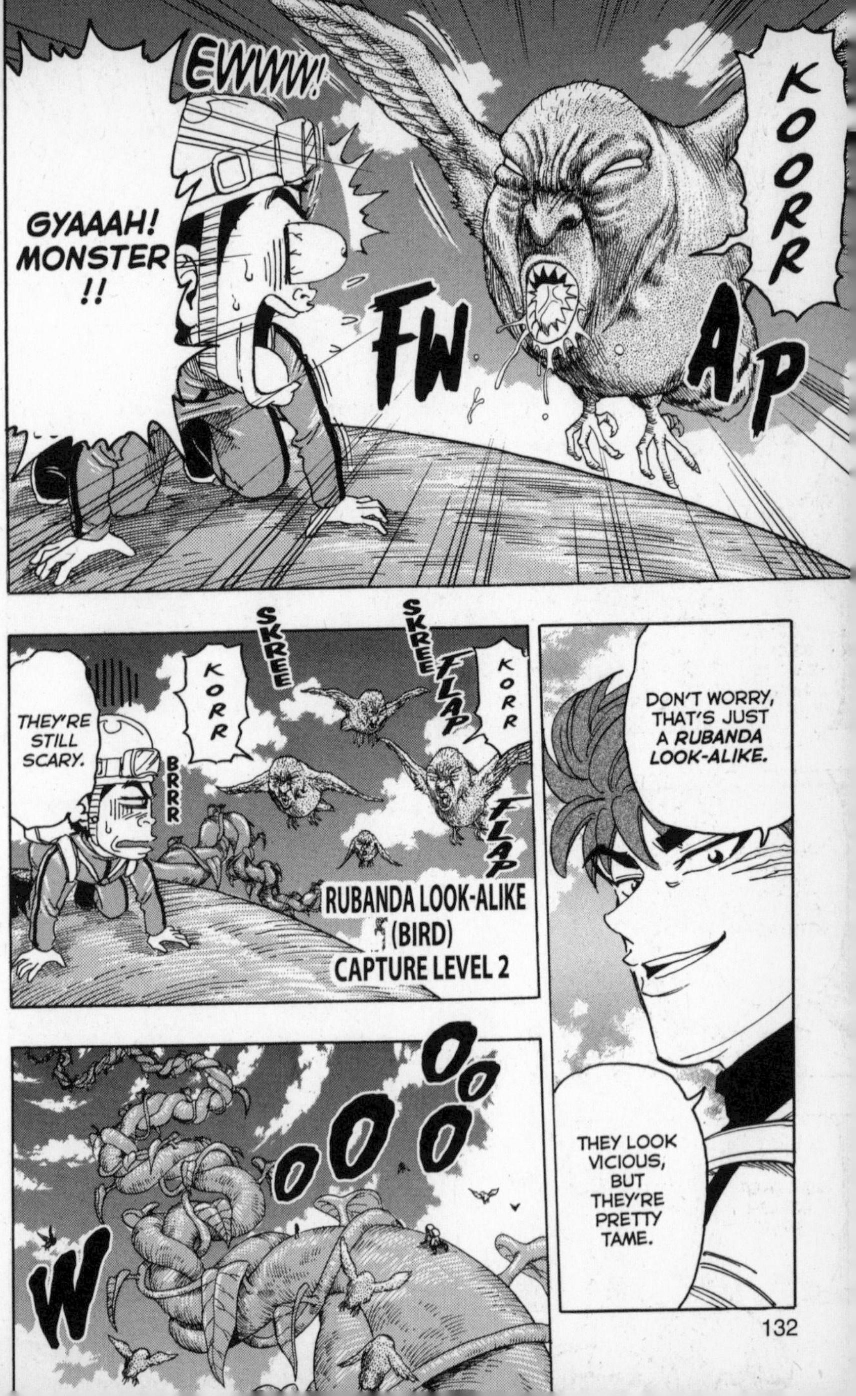
KOORR
EWWWW!
FWAP
GYAAAH! MONSTER!!
DON'T WORRY, THAT'S JUST A RUBANDA LOOK-ALIKE.
THEY LOOK VICIOUS, BUT THEY'RE PRETTY TAME.
KORR
SKREE
FLAP FLAP
SKREE
KORR
THEY'RE STILL SCARY.
BRRR
RUBANDA LOOK-ALIKE (BIRD) CAPTURE LEVEL 2
WOOOOO

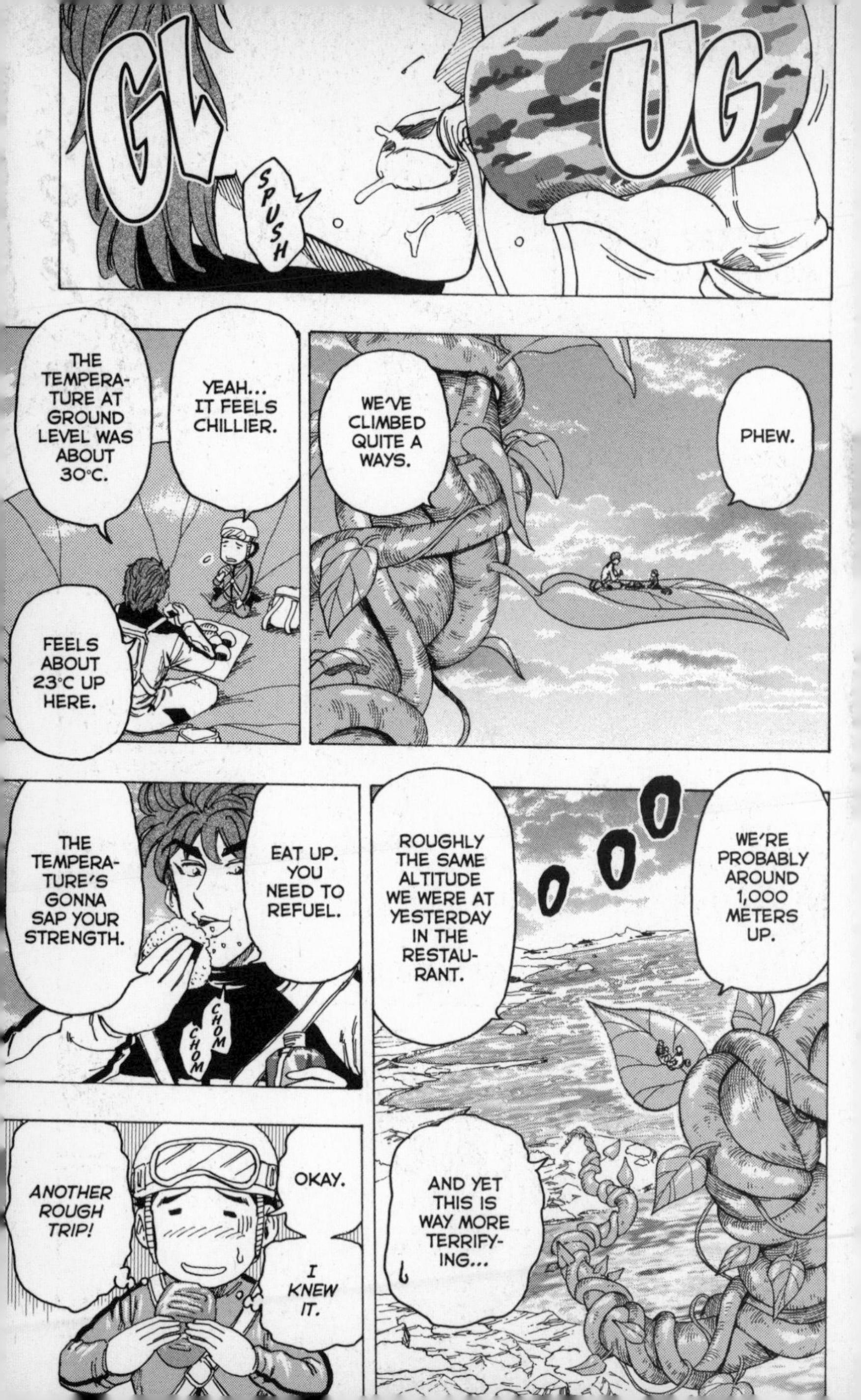
GL UG
SPUSH
PHEW.
WE'VE CLIMBED QUITE A WAYS.
YEAH... IT FEELS CHILLIER.
THE TEMPERATURE AT GROUND LEVEL WAS ABOUT 30°C.
FEELS ABOUT 23°C UP HERE.
WE'RE PROBABLY AROUND 1,000 METERS UP.
ROUGHLY THE SAME ALTITUDE WE WERE AT YESTERDAY IN THE RESTAURANT.
AND YET THIS IS WAY MORE TERRIFYING...
EAT UP. YOU NEED TO REFUEL.
THE TEMPERATURE'S GONNA SAP YOUR STRENGTH.
CHOM CHOM
OKAY.
I KNEW IT.
ANOTHER ROUGH TRIP!

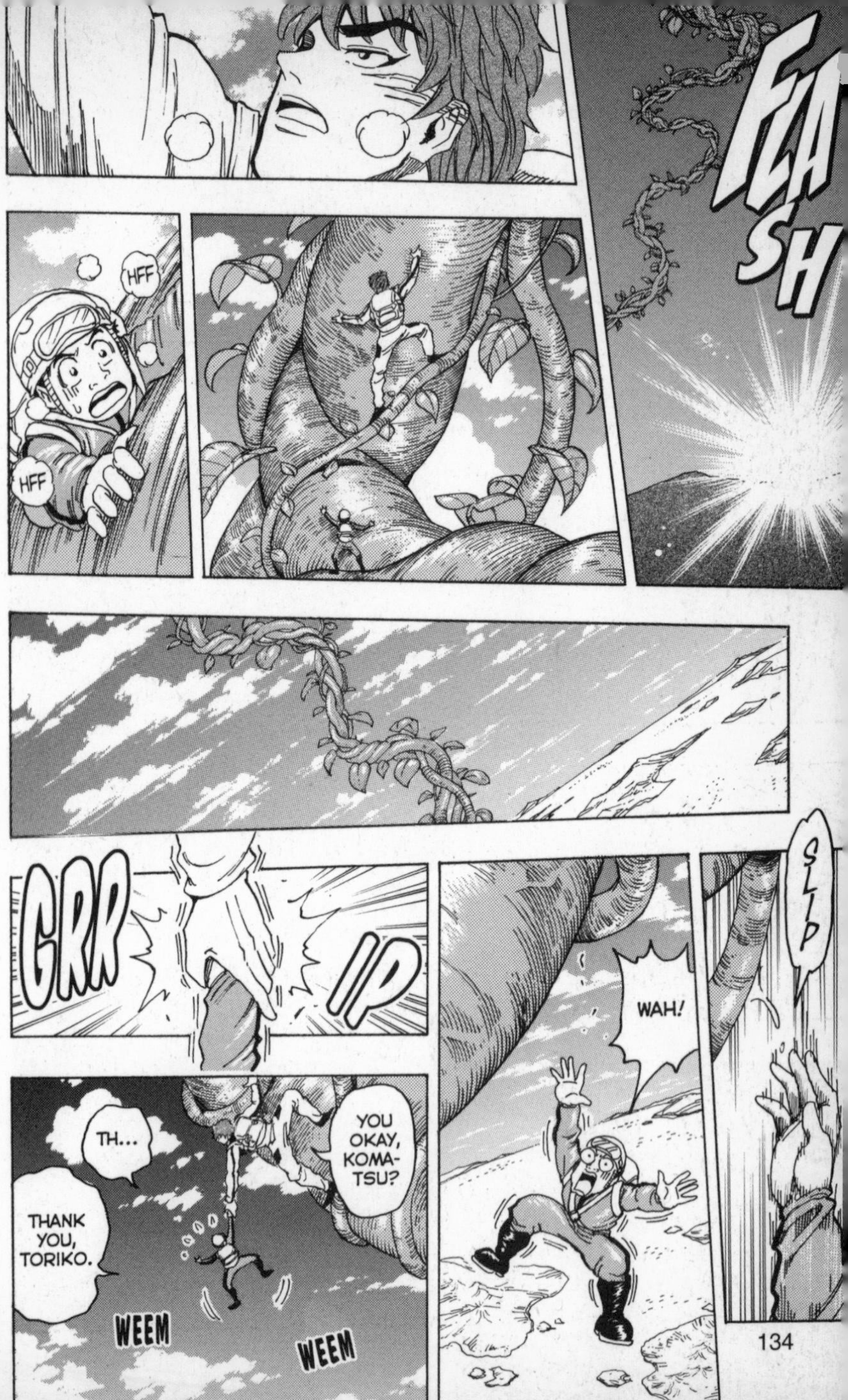
FLASH
HFF
HFF
SLIP
WAH!
GRRIP
YOU OKAY, KOMATSU?
TH...
THANK YOU, TORIKO.
WEEM
WEEM

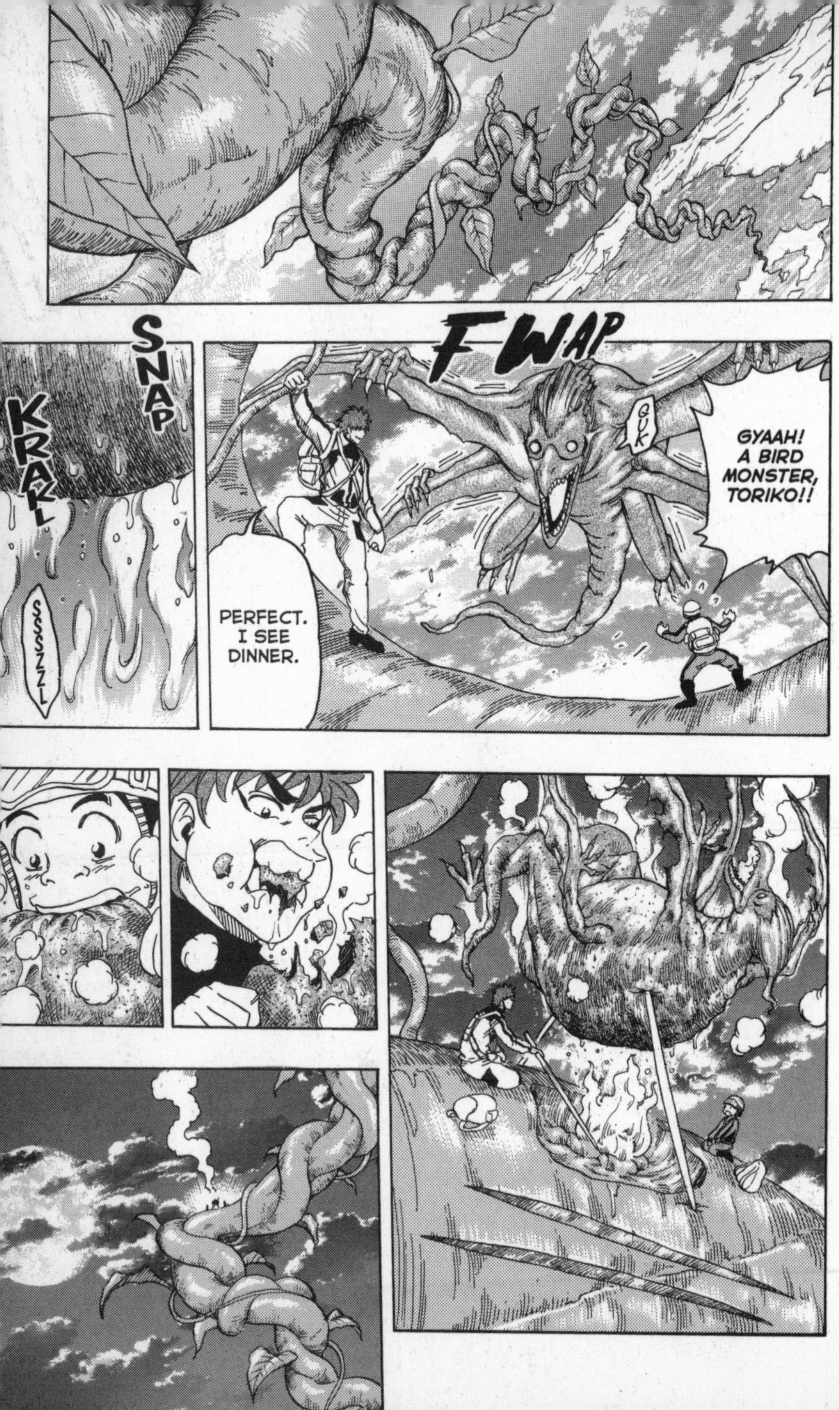
FWAP
GUK
GYAAH! A BIRD MONSTER, TORIKO!!
PERFECT. I SEE DINNER.
SNAP
KRAKL
SSSZZL

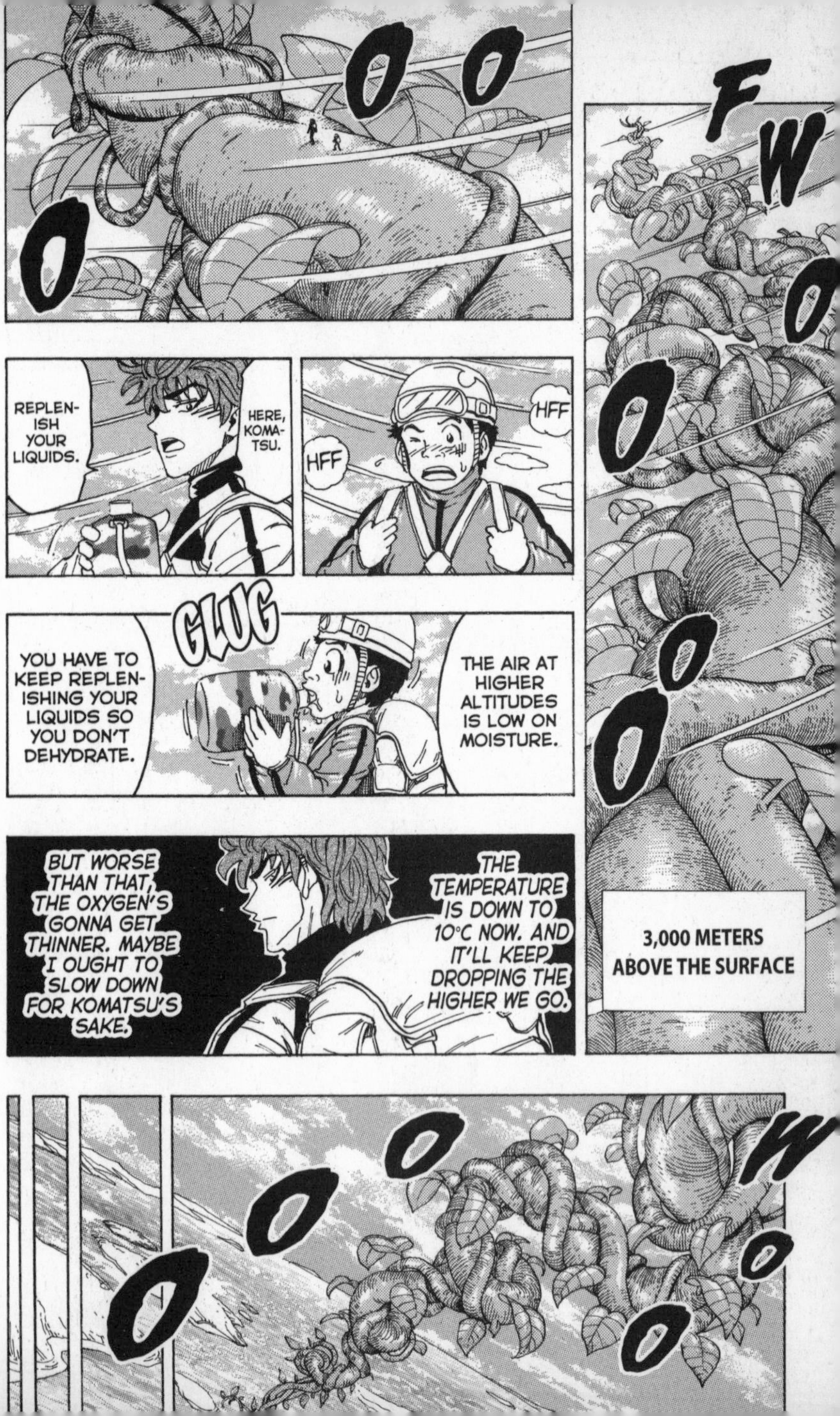
FWOOOOO
3,000 METERS ABOVE THE SURFACE
OOOO
HFF
HFF
HERE, KOMATSU.
REPLENISH YOUR LIQUIDS.
GLUG
THE AIR AT HIGHER ALTITUDES IS LOW ON MOISTURE.
YOU HAVE TO KEEP REPLENISHING YOUR LIQUIDS SO YOU DON'T DEHYDRATE.
THE TEMPERATURE IS DOWN TO 10°C NOW. AND IT'LL KEEP DROPPING THE HIGHER WE GO.
BUT WORSE THAN THAT, THE OXYGEN'S GONNA GET THINNER. MAYBE I OUGHT TO SLOW DOWN FOR KOMATSU'S SAKE.
FWOOOOOO

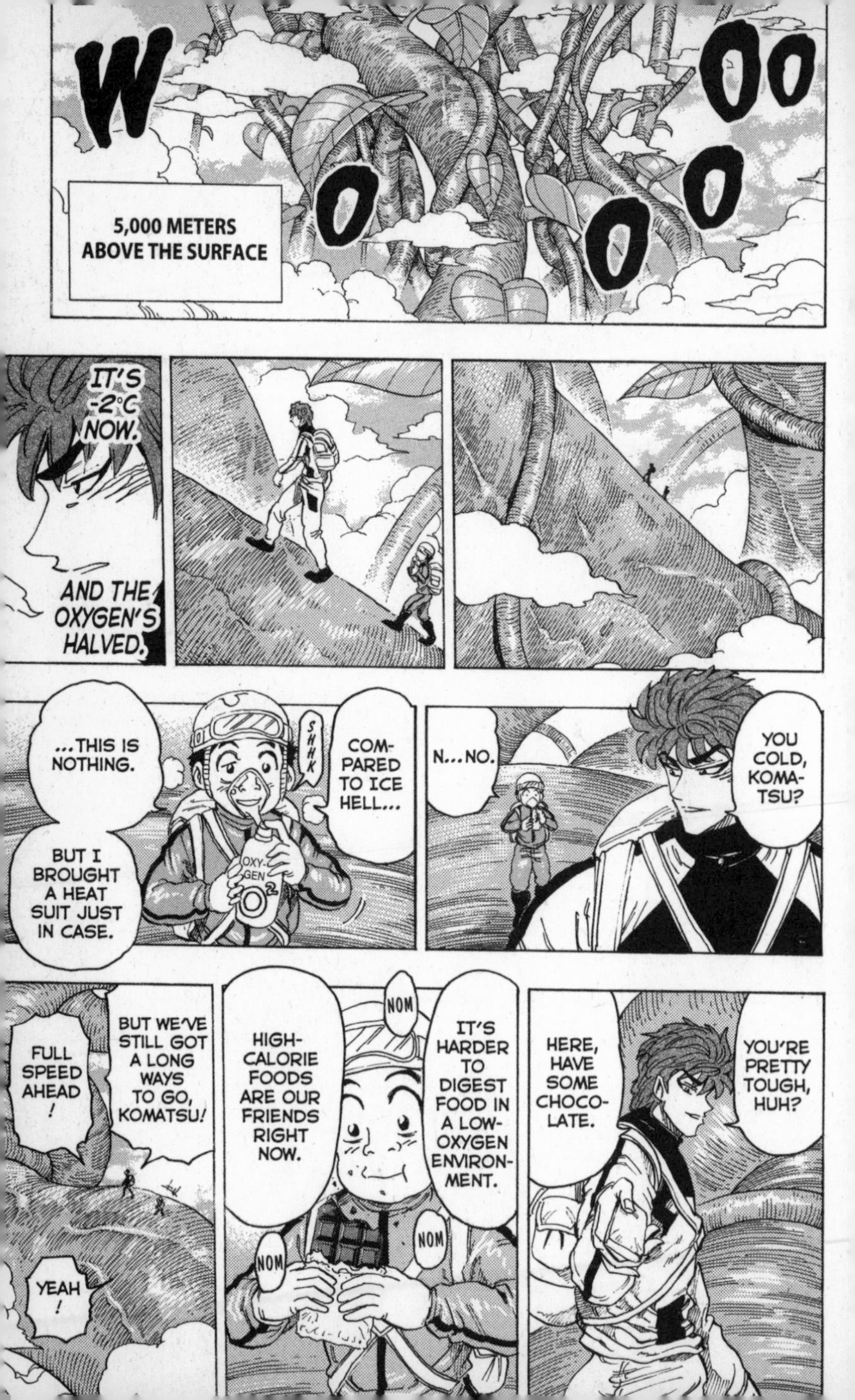
WOOOOOO
5,000 METERS ABOVE THE SURFACE
IT'S -2°C NOW.
AND THE OXYGEN'S HALVED.
YOU COLD, KOMATSU?
N...NO.
COMPARED TO ICE HELL...
SHHK
...THIS IS NOTHING.
OXYGEN O2
BUT I BROUGHT A HEAT SUIT JUST IN CASE.
YOU'RE PRETTY TOUGH, HUH?
HERE, HAVE SOME CHOCOLATE.
IT'S HARDER TO DIGEST FOOD IN A LOW-OXYGEN ENVIRONMENT.
NOM
HIGH-CALORIE FOODS ARE OUR FRIENDS RIGHT NOW.
NOM
NOM
BUT WE'VE STILL GOT A LONG WAYS TO GO, KOMATSU!
FULL SPEED AHEAD!
YEAH!

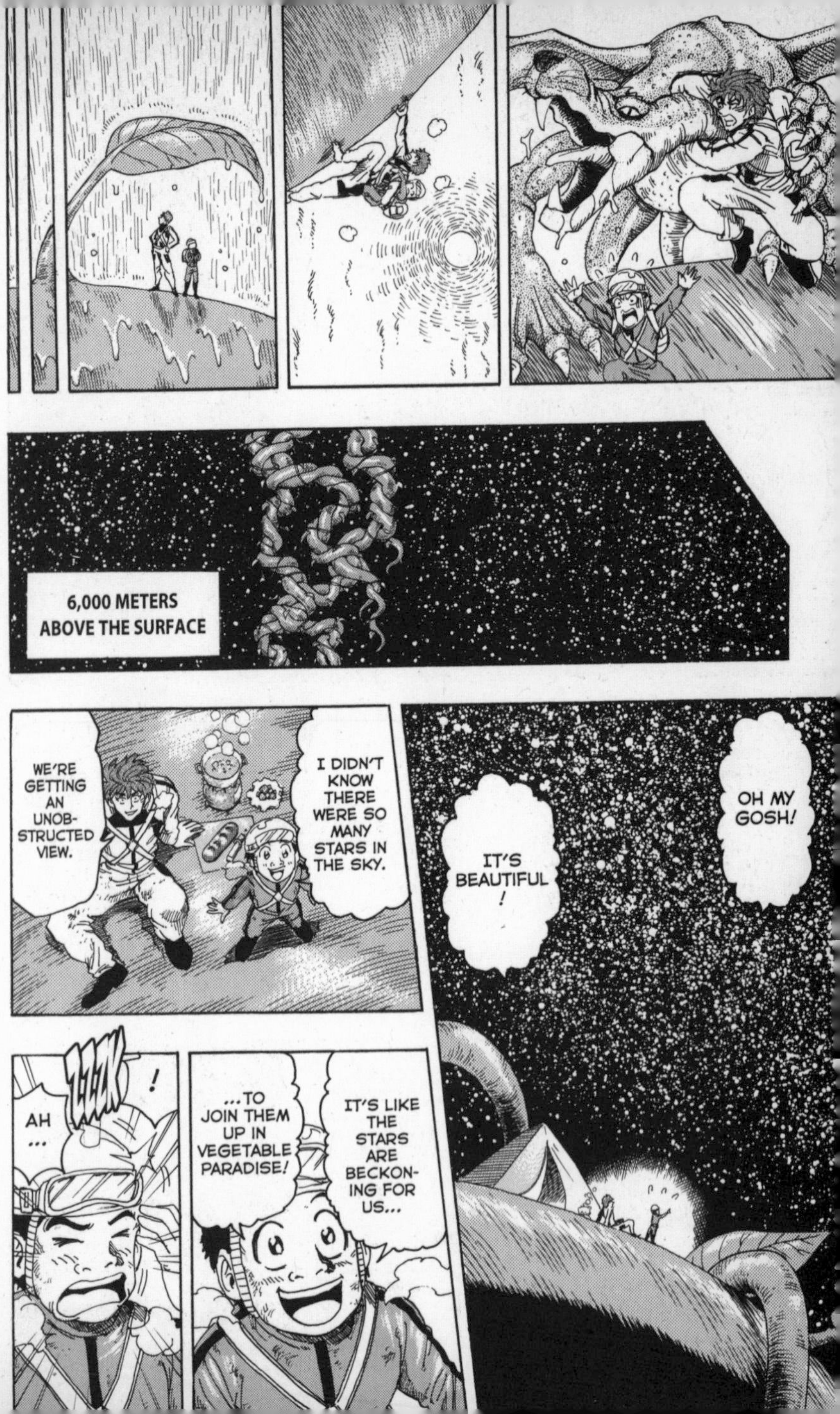
6,000 METERS ABOVE THE SURFACE
OH MY GOSH!
IT'S BEAUTIFUL!
I DIDN'T KNOW THERE WERE SO MANY STARS IN THE SKY.
WE'RE GETTING AN UNOB-STRUCTED VIEW.
IT'S LIKE THE STARS ARE BECKON-ING FOR US...
...TO JOIN THEM UP IN VEGETABLE PARADISE!
!
AH ...

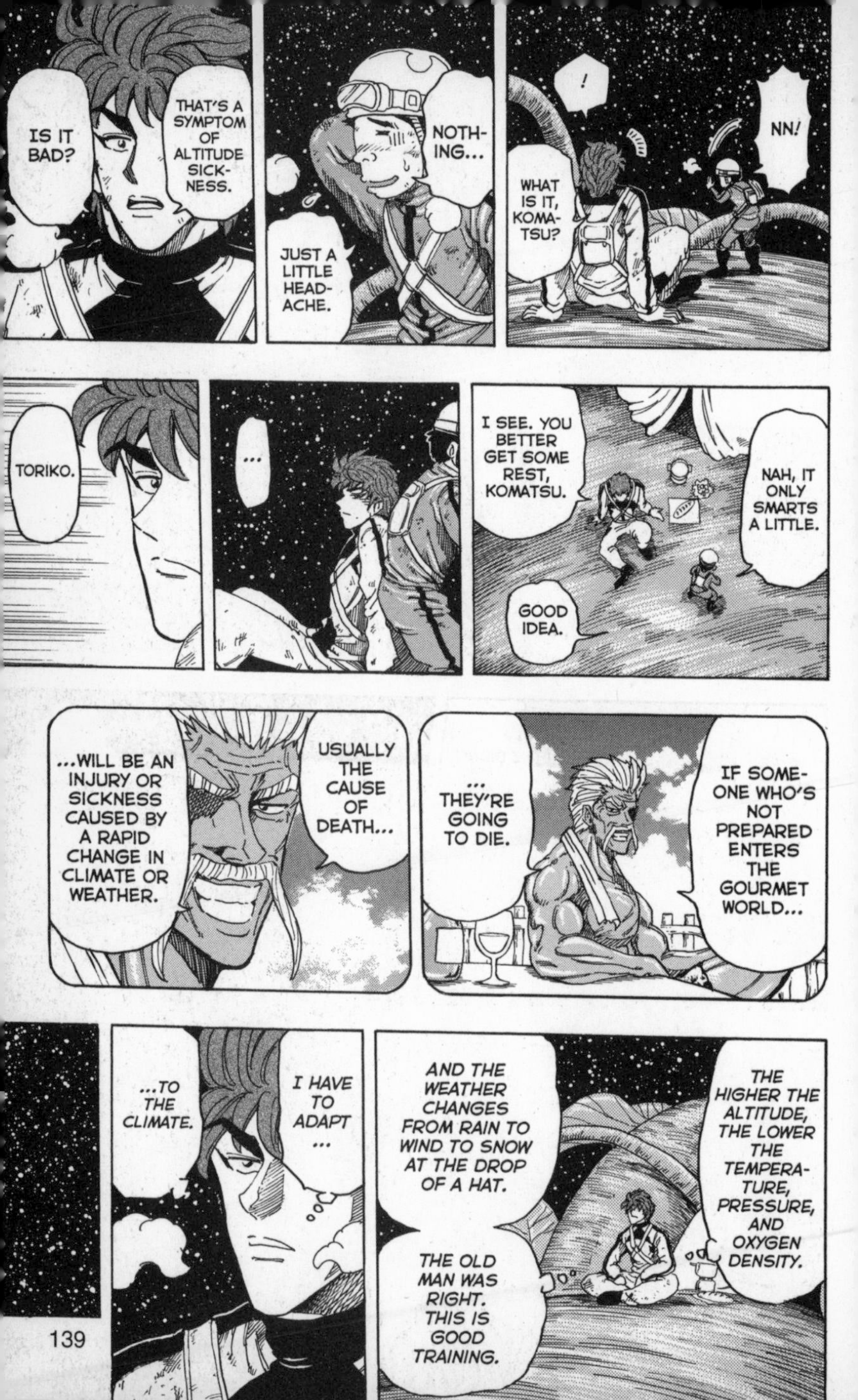
NN!
!
WHAT IS IT, KOMA-TSU?
NOTH-ING...
JUST A LITTLE HEAD-ACHE.
THAT'S A SYMPTOM OF ALTITUDE SICK-NESS.
IS IT BAD?
NAH, IT ONLY SMARTS A LITTLE.
I SEE. YOU BETTER GET SOME REST, KOMATSU.
GOOD IDEA.
...
TORIKO.
IF SOME-ONE WHO'S NOT PREPARED ENTERS THE GOURMET WORLD...
... THEY'RE GOING TO DIE.
USUALLY THE CAUSE OF DEATH...
...WILL BE AN INJURY OR SICKNESS CAUSED BY A RAPID CHANGE IN CLIMATE OR WEATHER.
THE HIGHER THE ALTITUDE, THE LOWER THE TEMPERA-TURE, PRESSURE, AND OXYGEN DENSITY.
AND THE WEATHER CHANGES FROM RAIN TO WIND TO SNOW AT THE DROP OF A HAT.
THE OLD MAN WAS RIGHT. THIS IS GOOD TRAINING.
I HAVE TO ADAPT ...
...TO THE CLIMATE.

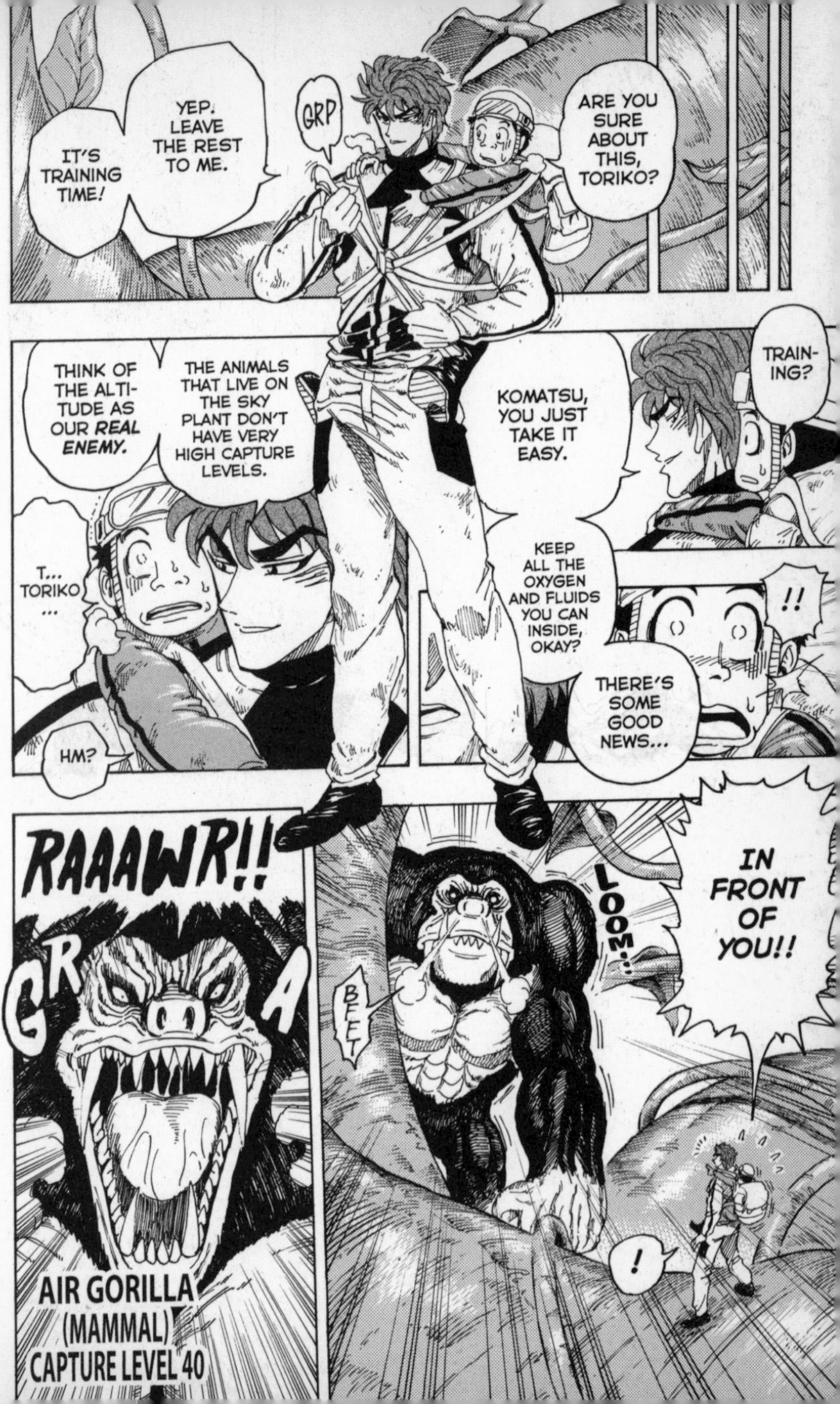
ARE YOU SURE ABOUT THIS, TORIKO?
GRP
YEP. LEAVE THE REST TO ME.
IT'S TRAINING TIME!
TRAINING?
KOMATSU, YOU JUST TAKE IT EASY.
!!
KEEP ALL THE OXYGEN AND FLUIDS YOU CAN INSIDE, OKAY?
THERE'S SOME GOOD NEWS...
THE ANIMALS THAT LIVE ON THE SKY PLANT DON'T HAVE VERY HIGH CAPTURE LEVELS.
THINK OF THE ALTITUDE AS OUR *REAL ENEMY.*
T... TORIKO ...
HM?
IN FRONT OF YOU!!
LOOM!!
BEFT
!
RAAAWR!!
GRA
AIR GORILLA (MAMMAL) CAPTURE LEVEL 40

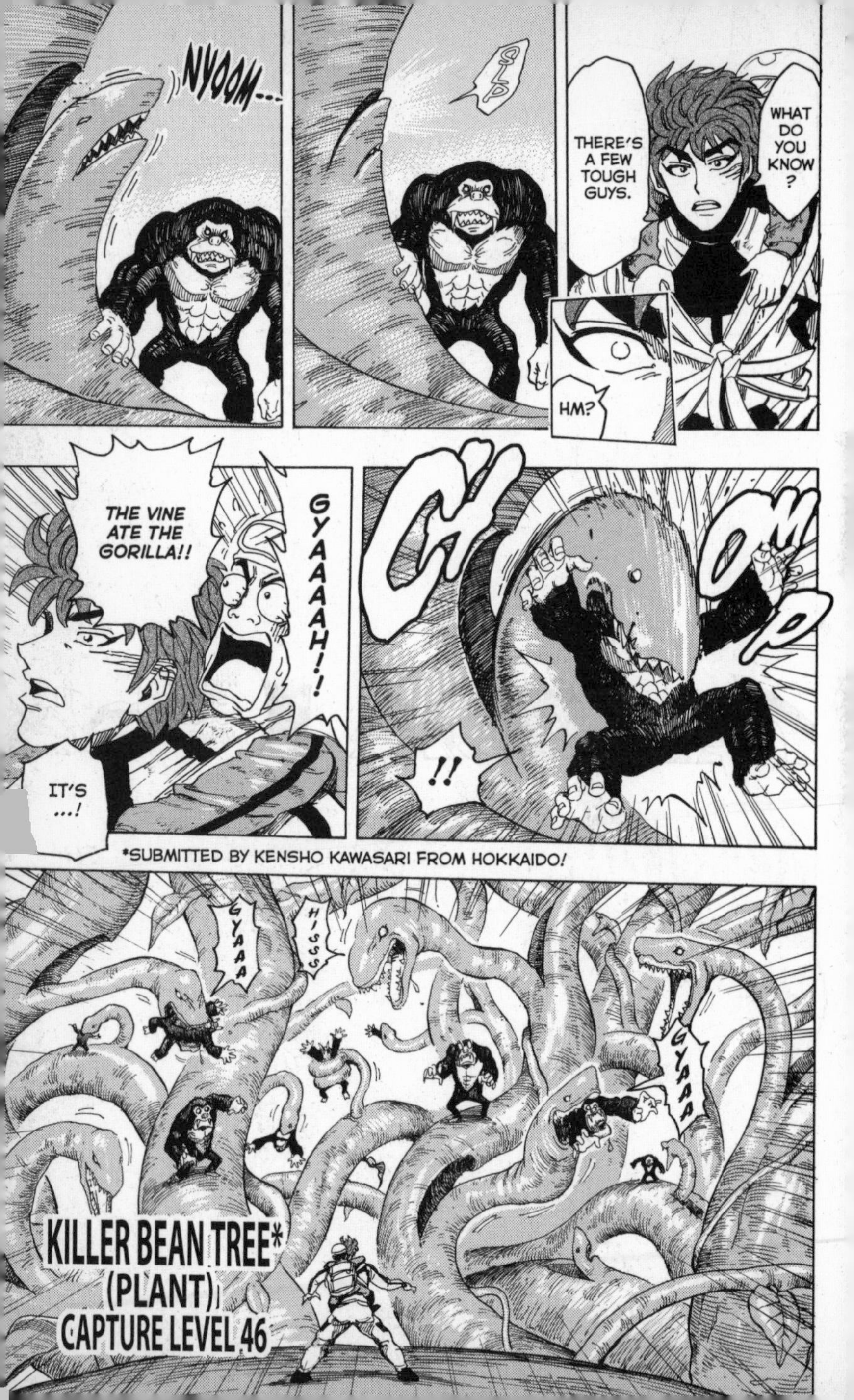
WHAT DO YOU KNOW?
THERE'S A FEW TOUGH GUYS.
HM?
GLP
NYOOM...
CHOMP
!!
GYAAAAAH!!
THE VINE ATE THE GORILLA!!
IT'S ...!
*SUBMITTED BY KENSHO KAWASARI FROM HOKKAIDO!
GYAAA
HISSS
GYAAA
KILLER BEAN TREE* (PLANT) CAPTURE LEVEL 46

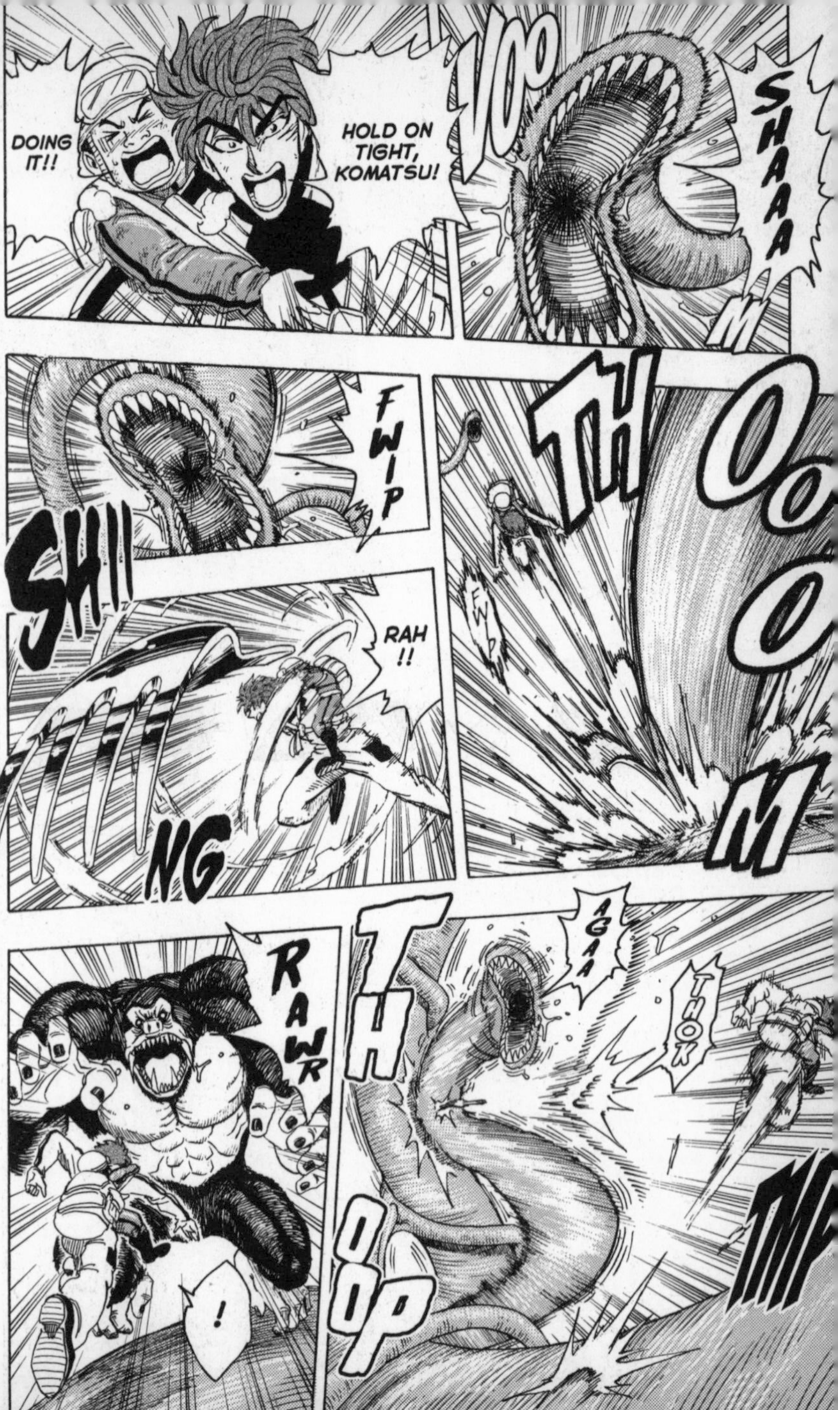
SHAAAM
VOOO
HOLD ON TIGHT, KOMATSU!
DOING IT!!
THOOOM
FWP
FWIP
SHIING
RAH!!
THOK
AGAA
THOOP
RAWR
!

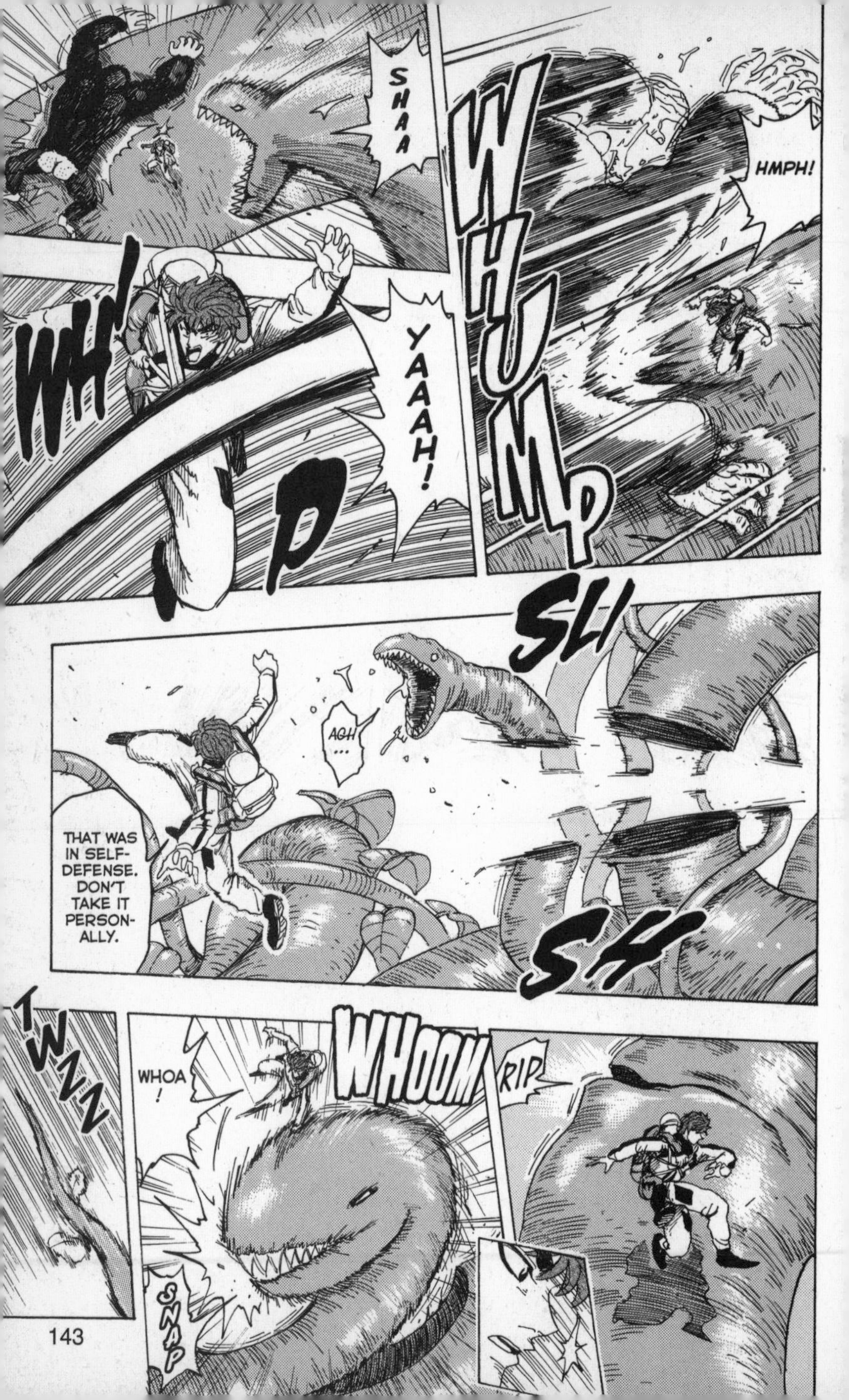
WHUMP
HMPH!
SHAA
YAAAAH!
WHUP
SLISH
AGH...
THAT WAS IN SELF-DEFENSE. DON'T TAKE IT PERSONALLY.
RIP
WHOOM
WHOA!
SNAP
TWZZ

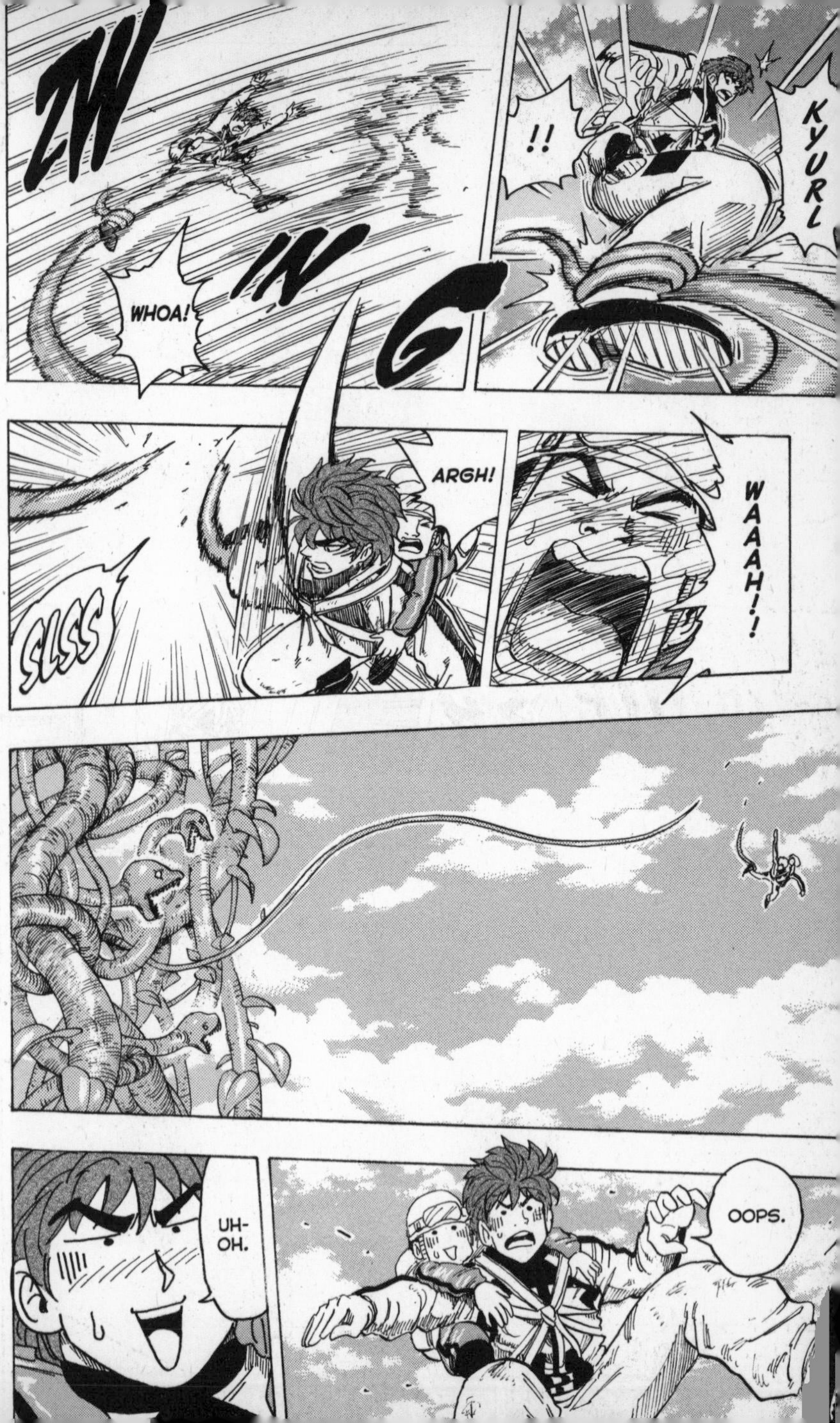
KYURL
!!
ZWING
WHOA!
WAAAAH!!
ARGH!
SLSS
OOPS.
UH-OH.

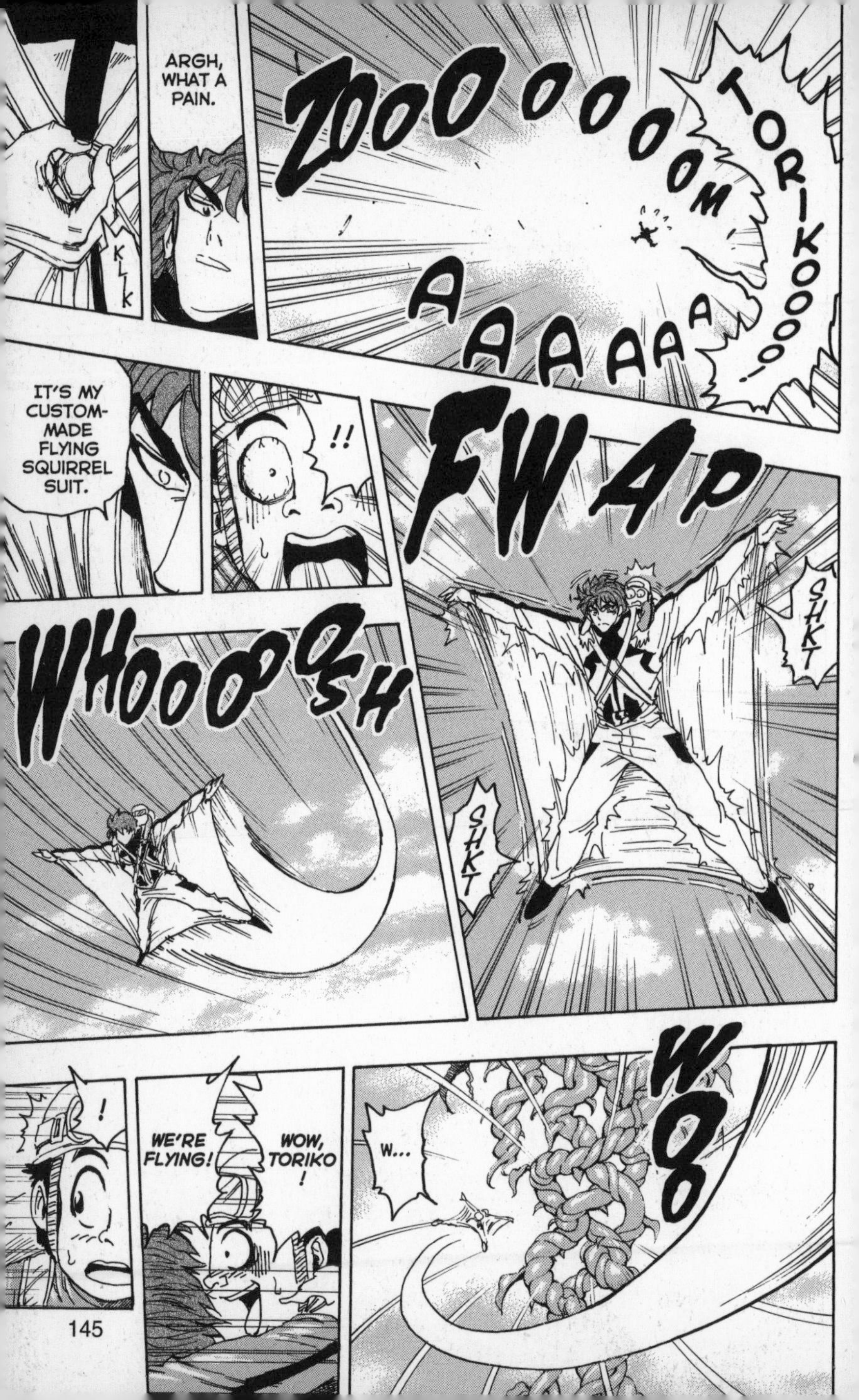
TORIKOOOOO...!
ZOOOOOOOOM
AAAAAAA
ARGH, WHAT A PAIN.
KLIK
FWAP
SHKT
SHKT
!!
IT'S MY CUSTOM-MADE FLYING SQUIRREL SUIT.
WHOOOOOSH
WOO
W...
WOW, TORIKO!
WE'RE FLYING!
!

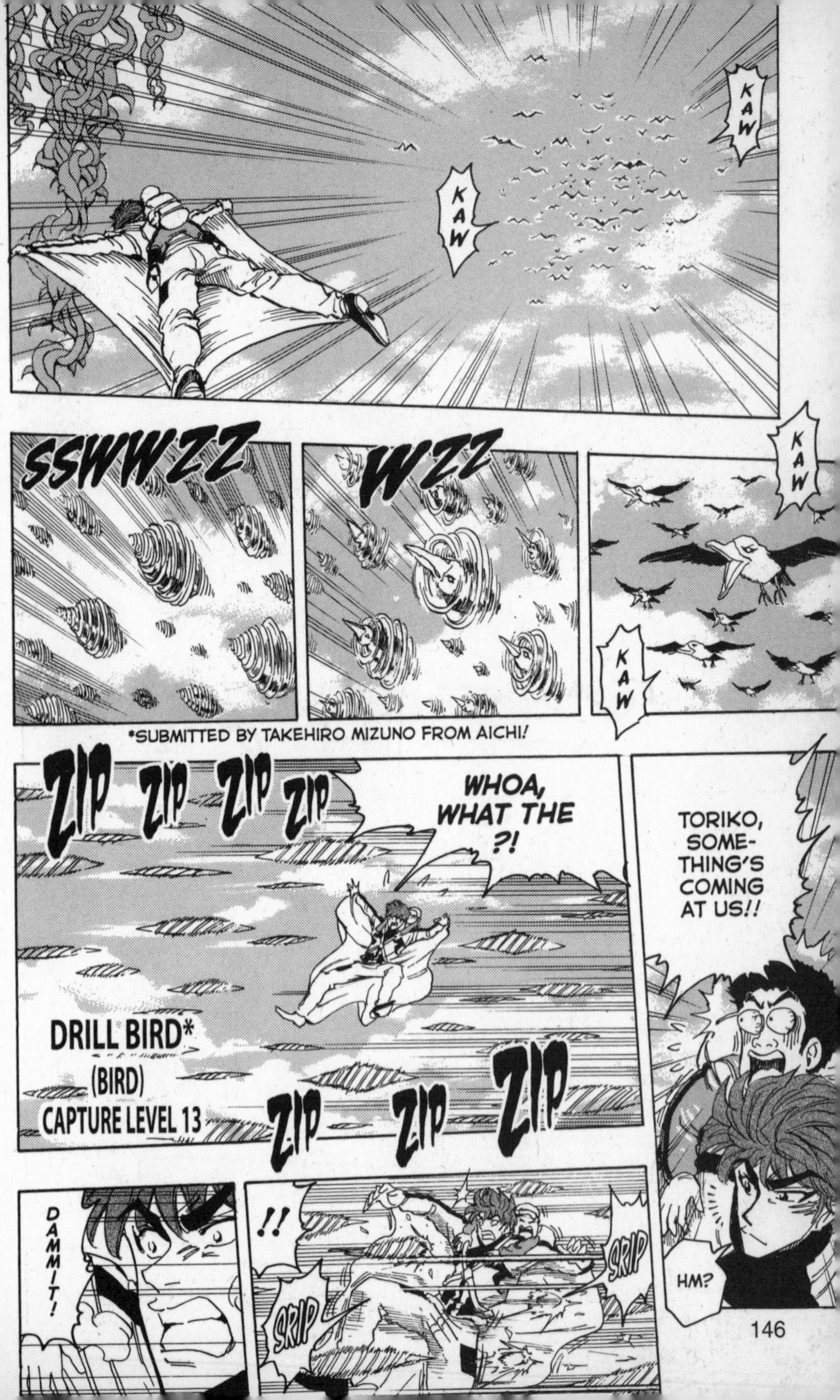
KAW
KAW
KAW
KAW
WZZ
SSWWZZ
*SUBMITTED BY TAKEHIRO MIZUNO FROM AICHI!
TORIKO, SOME-THING'S COMING AT US!!
HM?
ZIP ZIP ZIP ZIP
WHOA, WHAT THE ?!
DRILL BIRD*
(BIRD)
CAPTURE LEVEL 13
ZIP ZIP ZIP
!!
SRIP
SRIP
DAMMIT!

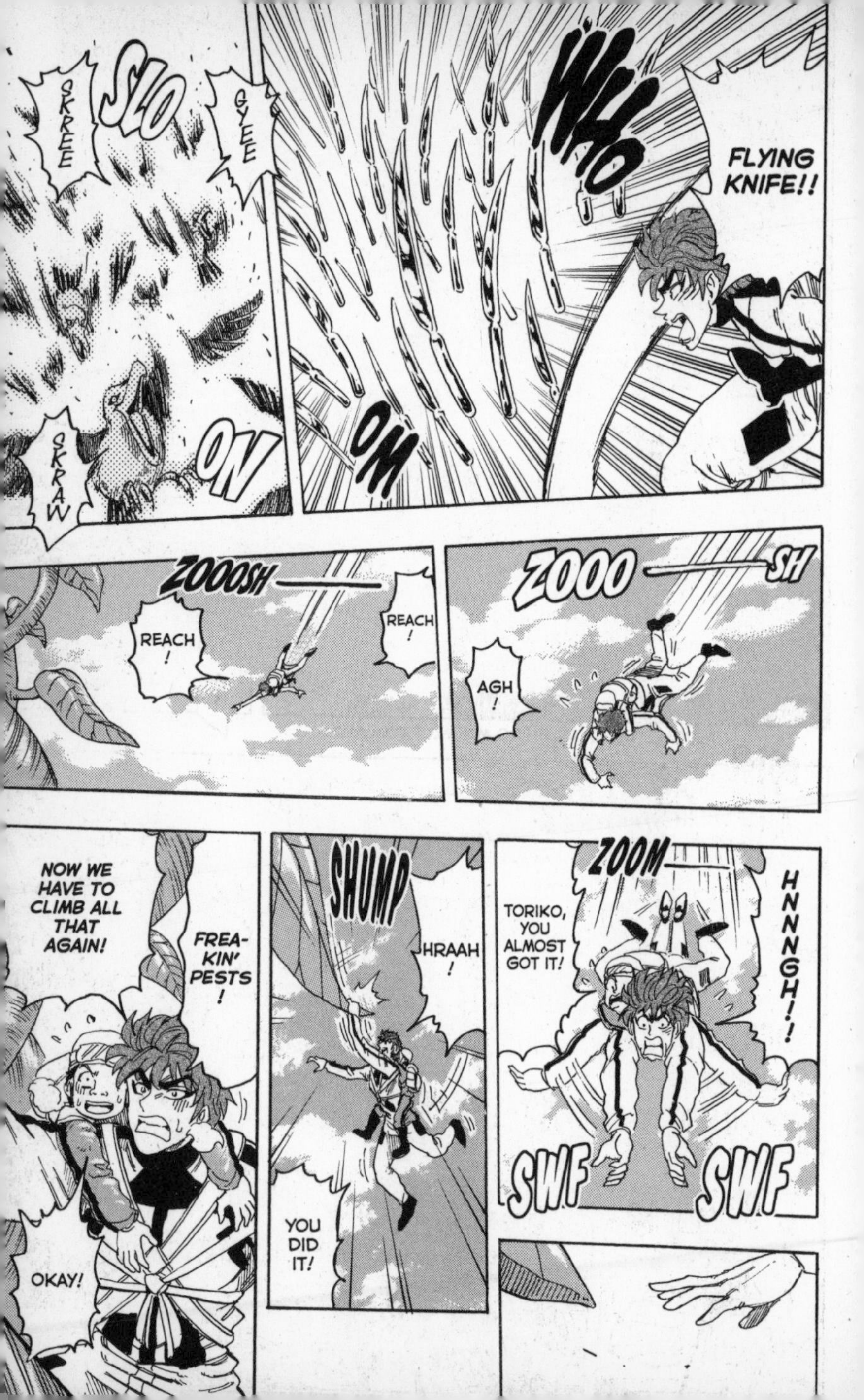
WHO
OM
FLYING KNIFE!!
SLO
GYEE
SKREE
ON
SKRAW
ZOOO——SH
AGH!
ZOOOSH——
REACH!
REACH!
ZOOM——
HNNNGH!!
TORIKO, YOU ALMOST GOT IT!
SWF
SWF
SHUMP
HRAAH!
YOU DID IT!
FREA-KIN' PESTS!
NOW WE HAVE TO CLIMB ALL THAT AGAIN!
OKAY!

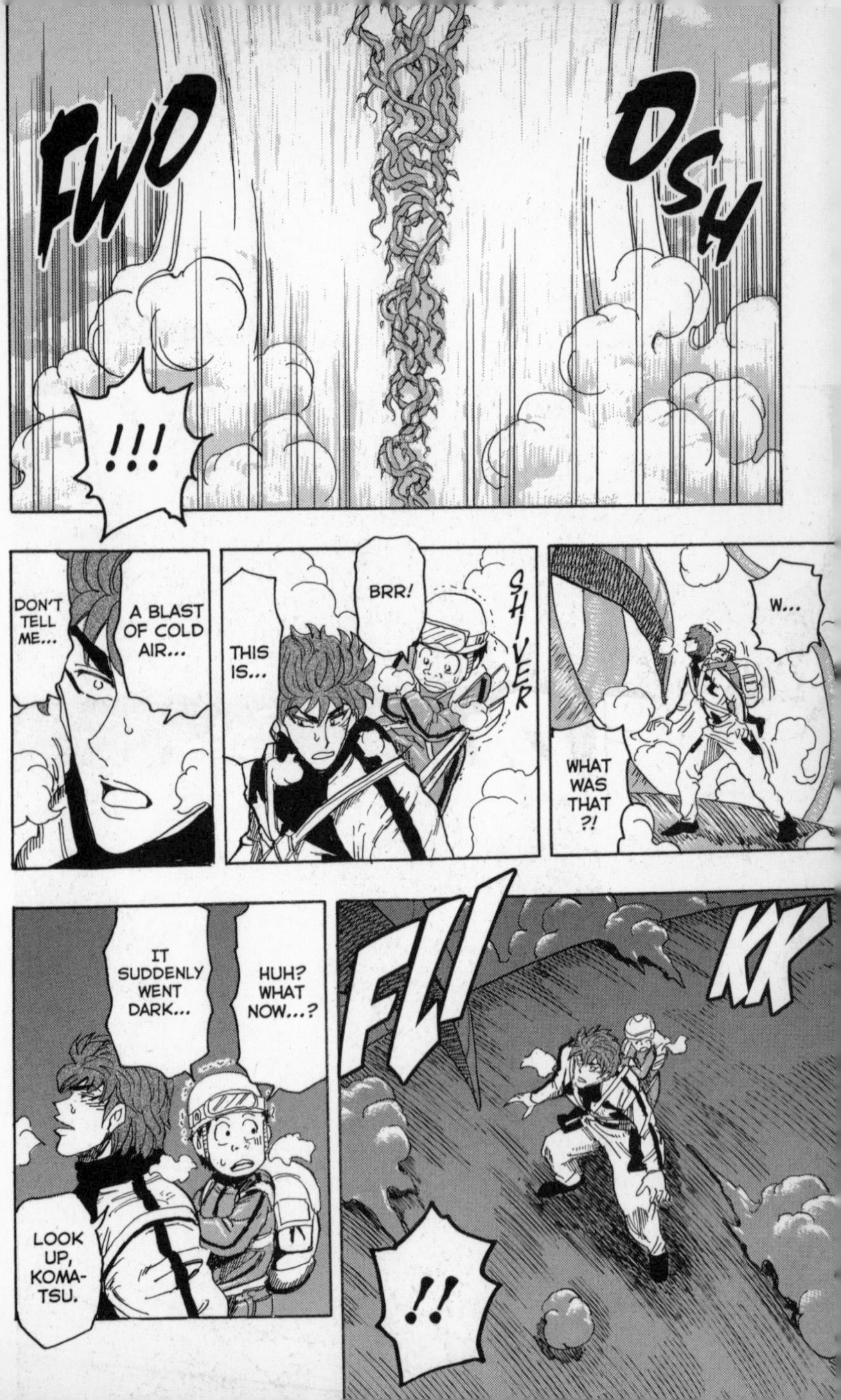
FWO
OSH
!!!
W...
WHAT WAS THAT?!
BRR!
SHIVER
THIS IS...
A BLAST OF COLD AIR...
DON'T TELL ME...
FLI
KK
!!
HUH? WHAT NOW...?
IT SUDDENLY WENT DARK...
LOOK UP, KOMATSU.

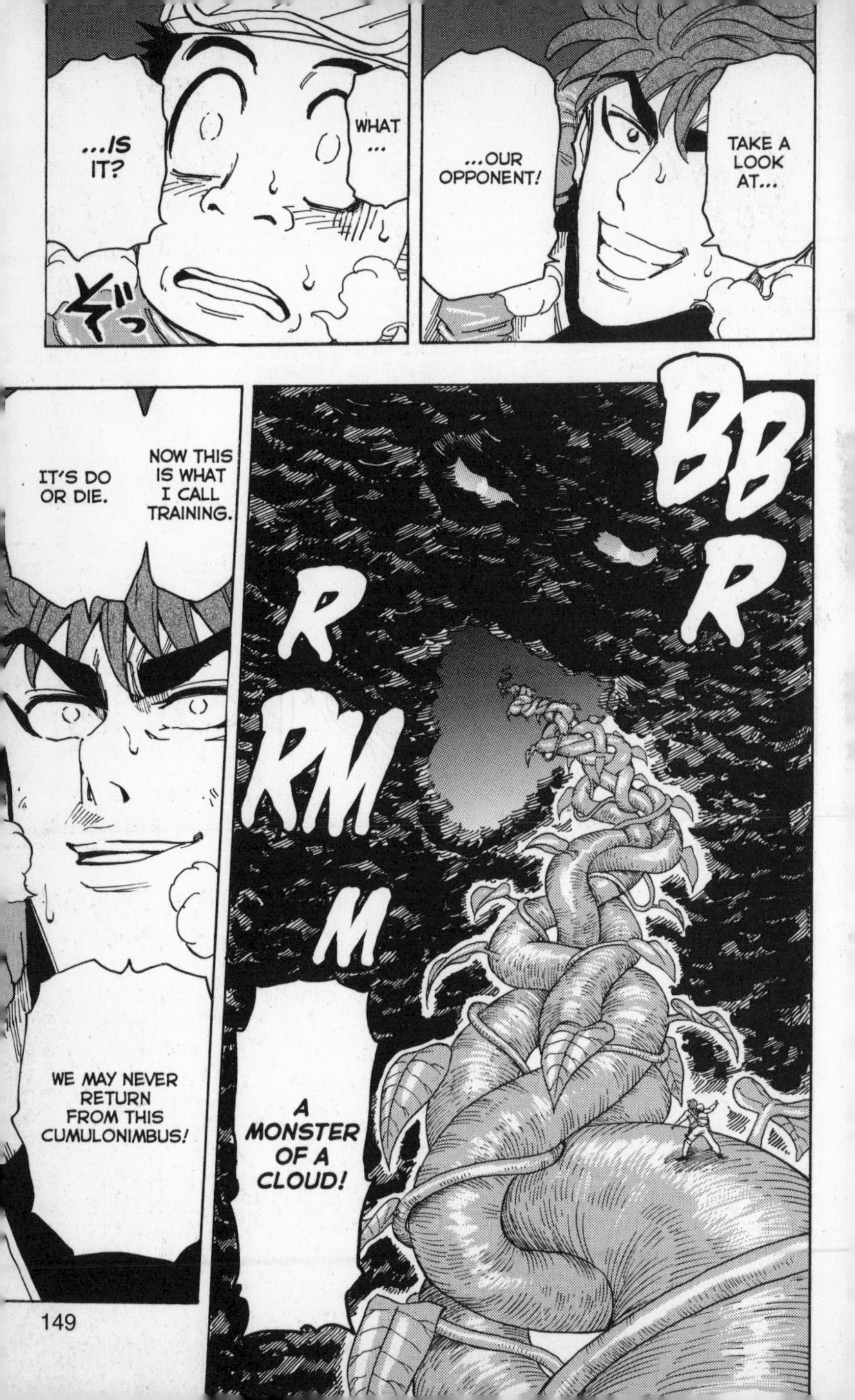
TAKE A LOOK AT...
...OUR OPPONENT!
WHAT...
...IS IT?
BBRRRMM
A MONSTER OF A CLOUD!
NOW THIS IS WHAT I CALL TRAINING.
IT'S DO OR DIE.
WE MAY NEVER RETURN FROM THIS CUMULONIMBUS!

TORIKO

GOURMET CHECKLIST

Vol. 115

DOCTOR CACTUS
(PLANT)

CAPTURE LEVEL: LESS THAN 1
HABITAT: LIFE AND OTHER MILD CLIMATES
LENGTH: 1–3 METERS
HEIGHT: ---
WEIGHT: 60 KG
PRICE: 1,500,000 YEN PER PLANT

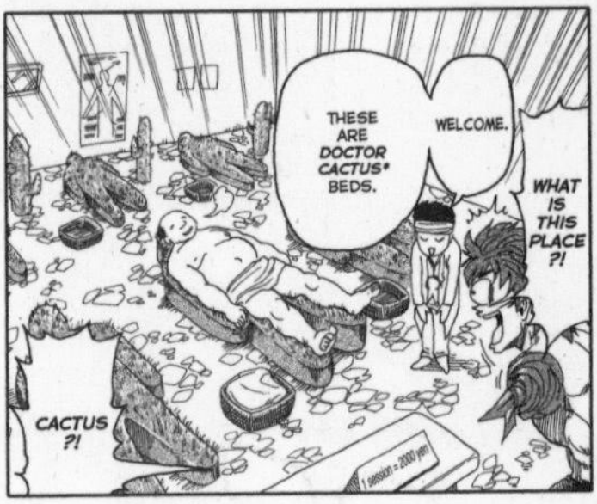
WHAT IS THIS PLACE?!
WELCOME.
THESE ARE DOCTOR CACTUS' BEDS.
1 session = 2000 yen
CACTUS?!

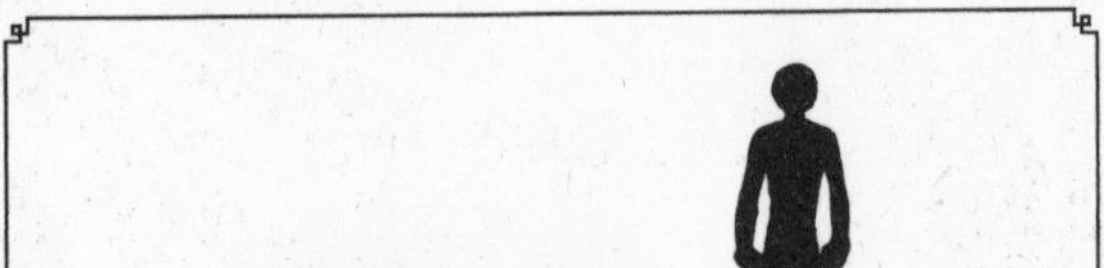

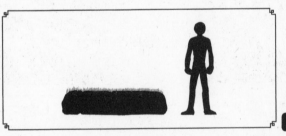

SCALE

THIS PRICKLY HUMAN-SHAPED CACTUS IS A NATURAL ACUPUNCTURE BED. ITS MANY NEEDLES PIERCE EVERY PRESSURE POINT, ADJUSTING BLOOD AND CHI FLOW, AS WELL AS WORKING OUT KNOTS IN YOUR MUSCLES. ALSO, WHEN THE SKIN OF THE CACTUS IS PEELED OFF, THE PULP INSIDE CAN BE APPLIED TO BURNS AND CUTS TO EXPEDITE HEALING. IT'S GREAT FOR PHYSICAL THERAPY AND PROMOTING GOOD HEALTH.

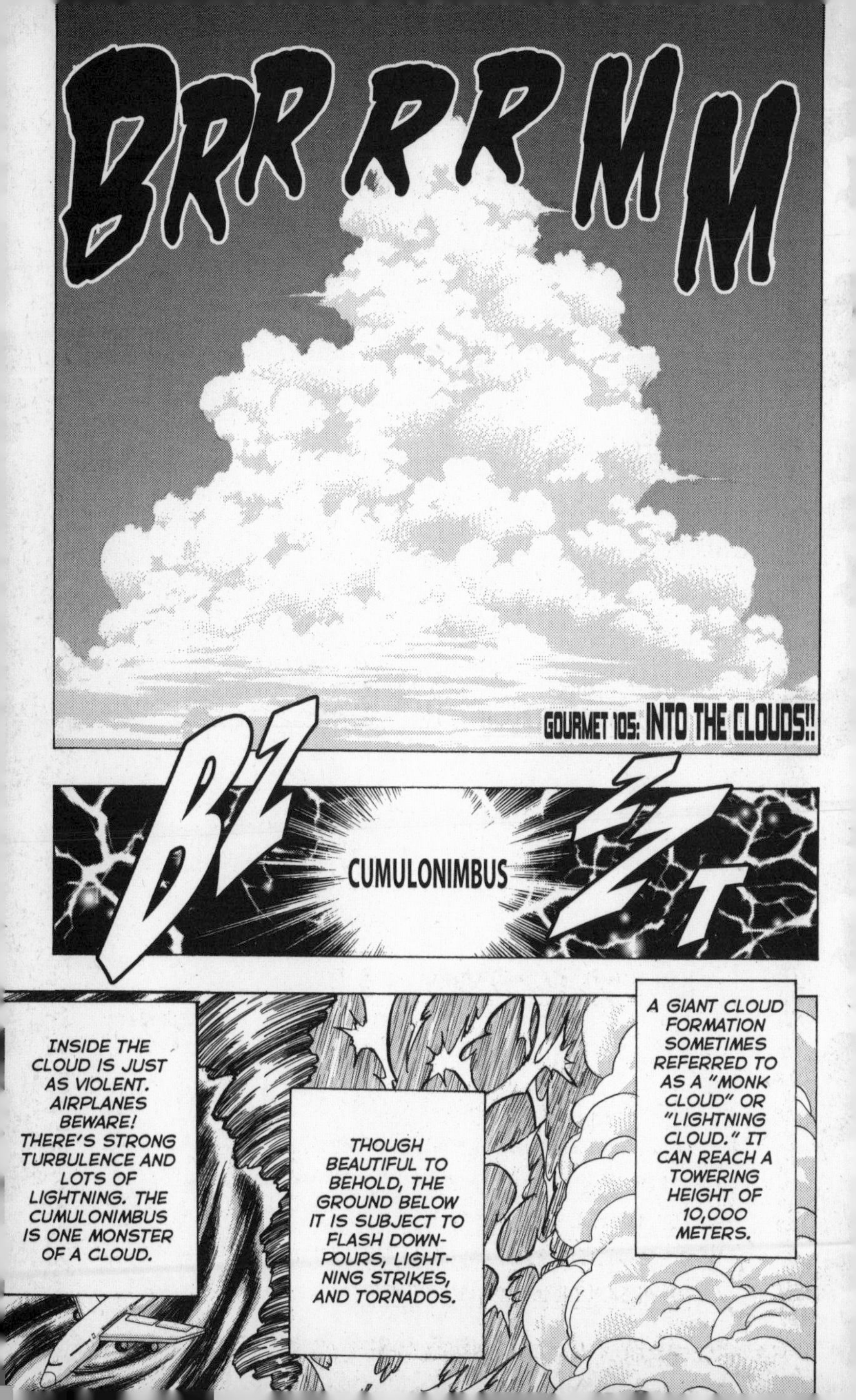
BRRRRMMM
GOURMET 105: INTO THE CLOUDS!!
BZZZT
CUMULONIMBUS
A GIANT CLOUD FORMATION SOMETIMES REFERRED TO AS A "MONK CLOUD" OR "LIGHTNING CLOUD." IT CAN REACH A TOWERING HEIGHT OF 10,000 METERS.
THOUGH BEAUTIFUL TO BEHOLD, THE GROUND BELOW IT IS SUBJECT TO FLASH DOWN-POURS, LIGHT-NING STRIKES, AND TORNADOS.
INSIDE THE CLOUD IS JUST AS VIOLENT. AIRPLANES BEWARE! THERE'S STRONG TURBULENCE AND LOTS OF LIGHTNING. THE CUMULONIMBUS IS ONE MONSTER OF A CLOUD.

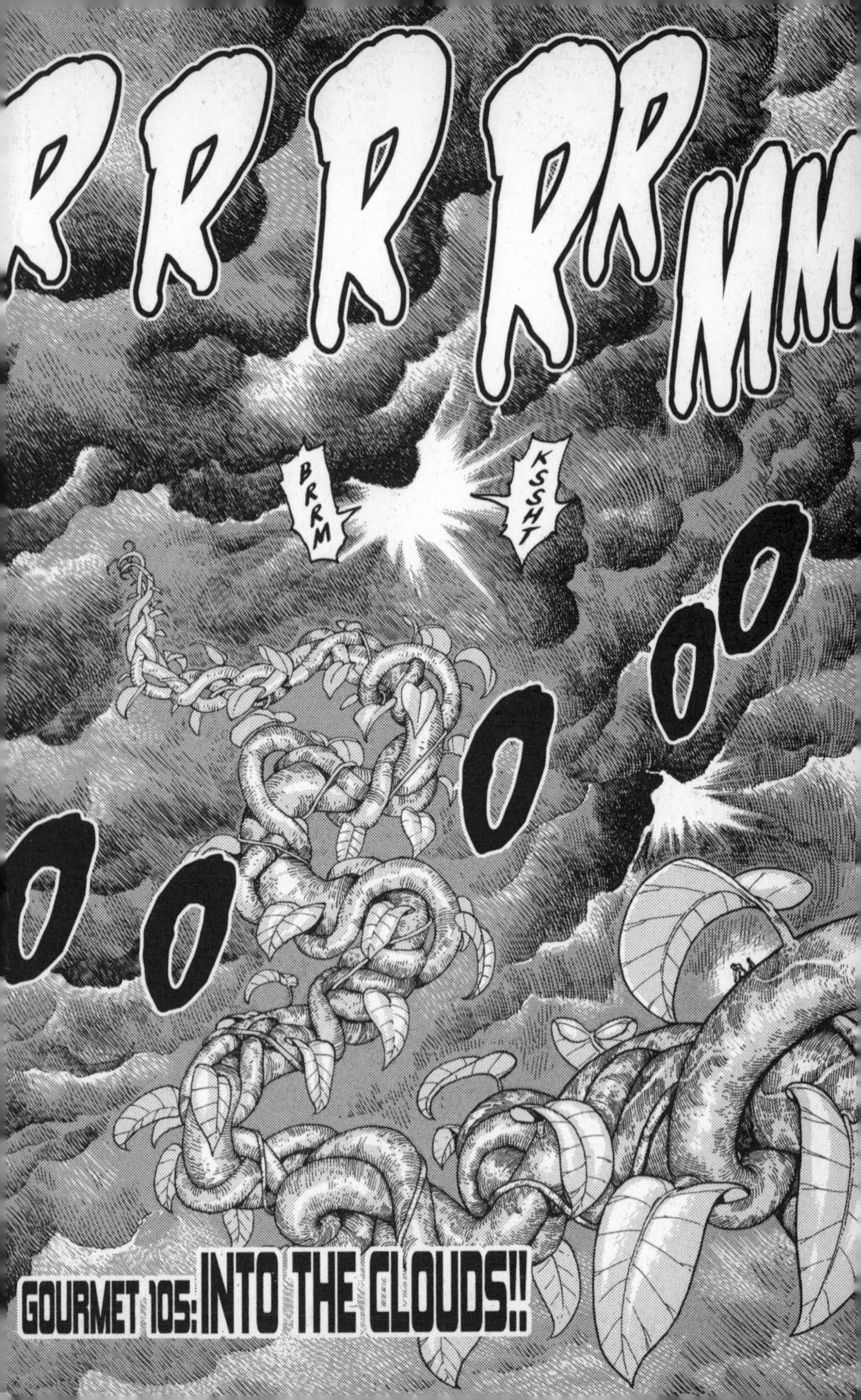
RRRRRMM
OOOOOOO
KSSHT
BRRM
GOURMET 105: INTO THE CLOUDS!!

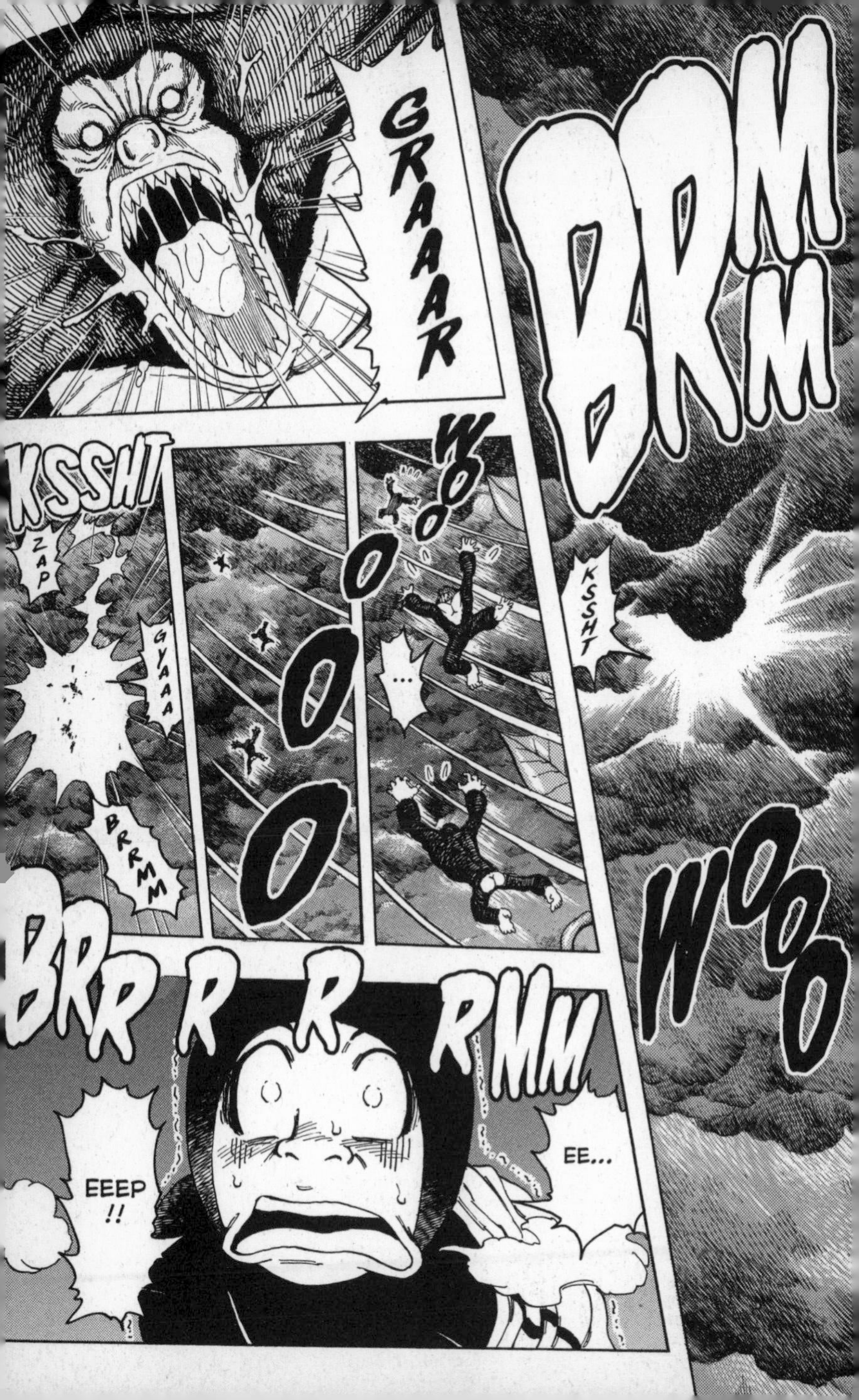
BRMM
KSSHT
WOOO
GRAAAAR
WOOOOOO
...
KSSHT
ZAP
GYAAA
BRRMM
BRRRRMM
EE...
EEEP !!

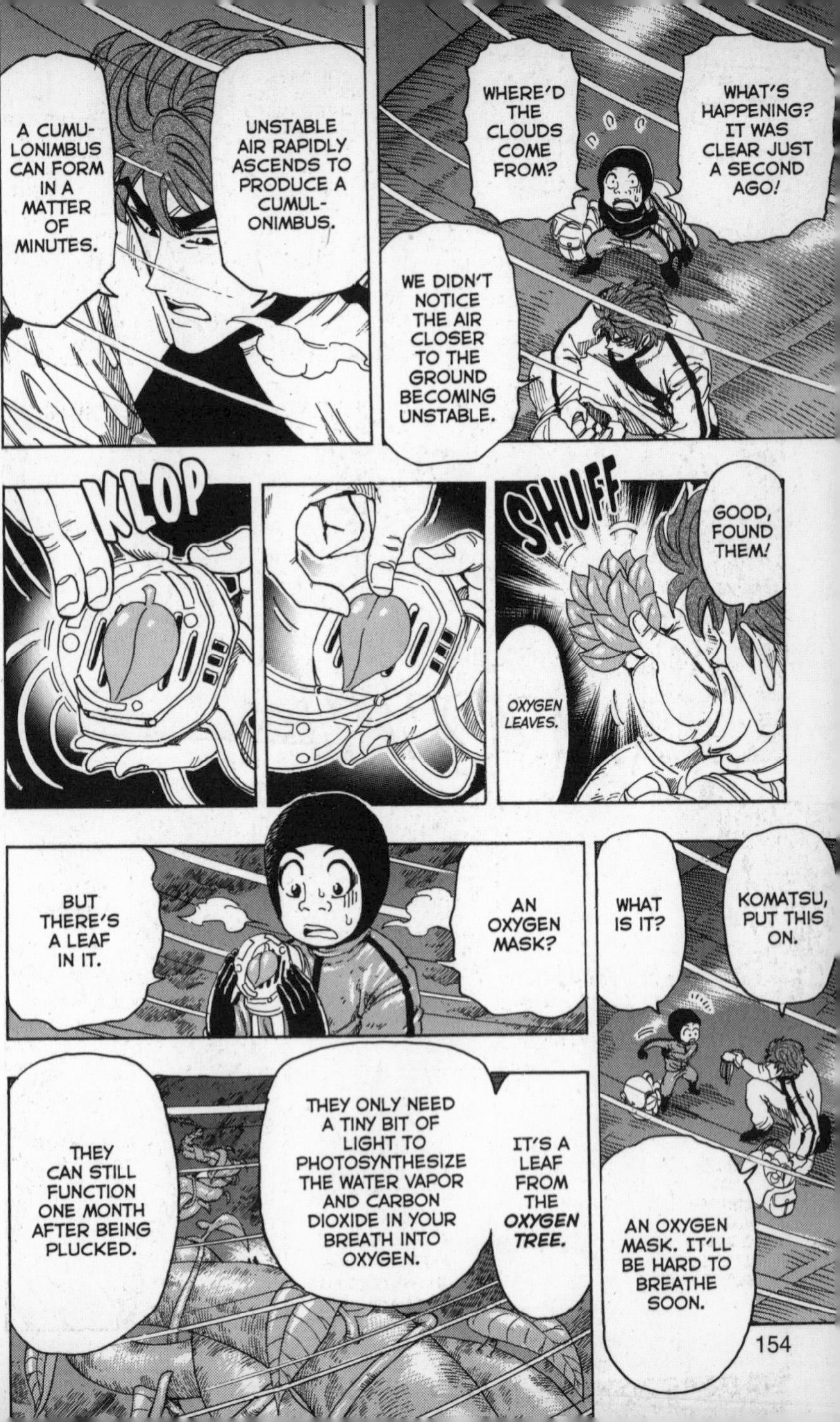

WHAT'S HAPPENING? IT WAS CLEAR JUST A SECOND AGO!
WHERE'D THE CLOUDS COME FROM?
WE DIDN'T NOTICE THE AIR CLOSER TO THE GROUND BECOMING UNSTABLE.
UNSTABLE AIR RAPIDLY ASCENDS TO PRODUCE A CUMUL-ONIMBUS.
A CUMU-LONIMBUS CAN FORM IN A MATTER OF MINUTES.
SHUFF
GOOD, FOUND THEM!
OXYGEN LEAVES.
KLOP
KOMATSU, PUT THIS ON.
WHAT IS IT?
AN OXYGEN MASK. IT'LL BE HARD TO BREATHE SOON.
AN OXYGEN MASK?
BUT THERE'S A LEAF IN IT.
IT'S A LEAF FROM THE *OXYGEN TREE.*
THEY ONLY NEED A TINY BIT OF LIGHT TO PHOTOSYNTHESIZE THE WATER VAPOR AND CARBON DIOXIDE IN YOUR BREATH INTO OXYGEN.
THEY CAN STILL FUNCTION ONE MONTH AFTER BEING PLUCKED.

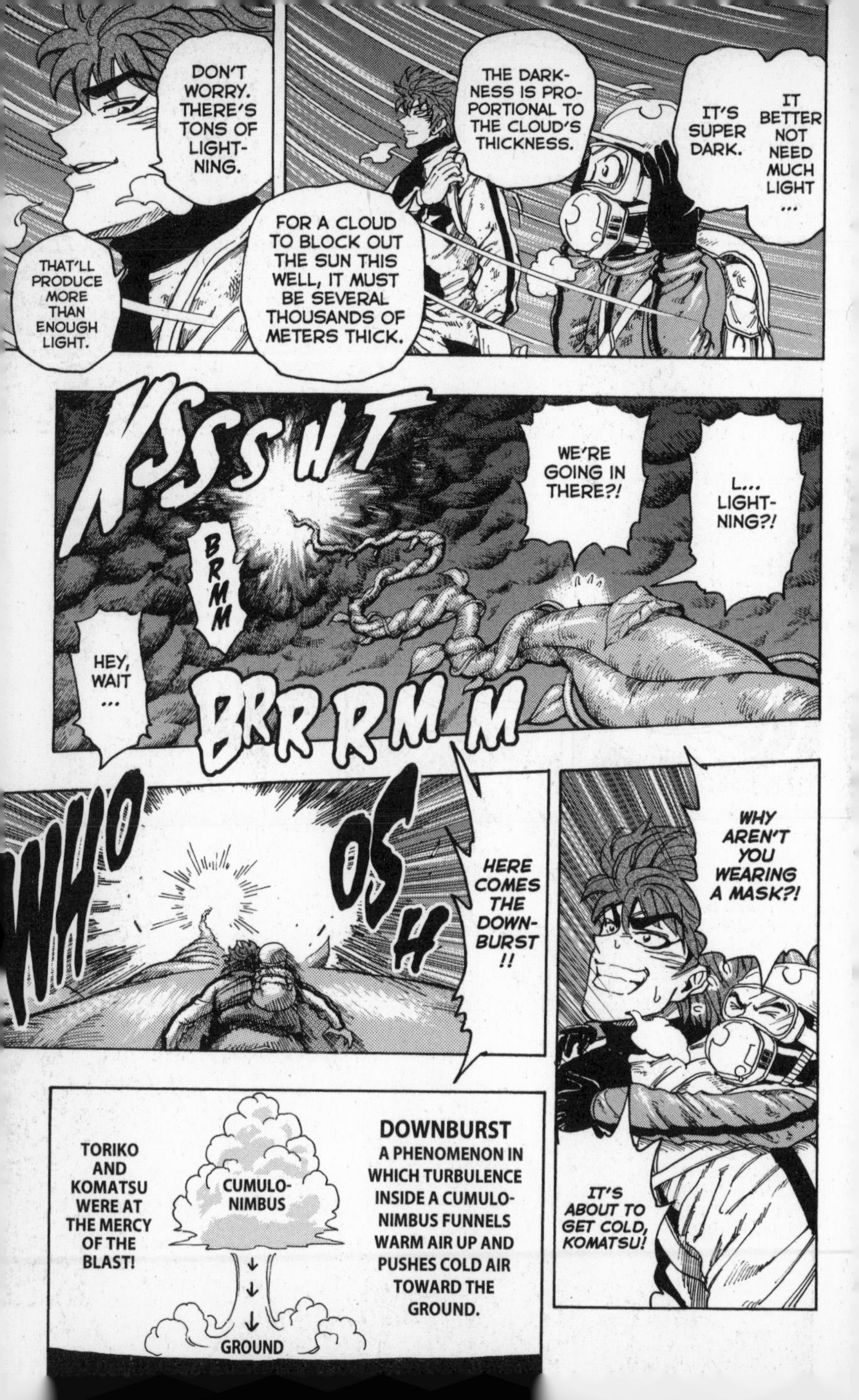
IT BETTER NOT NEED MUCH LIGHT...
IT'S SUPER DARK.
THE DARKNESS IS PROPORTIONAL TO THE CLOUD'S THICKNESS.
FOR A CLOUD TO BLOCK OUT THE SUN THIS WELL, IT MUST BE SEVERAL THOUSANDS OF METERS THICK.
DON'T WORRY. THERE'S TONS OF LIGHTNING.
THAT'LL PRODUCE MORE THAN ENOUGH LIGHT.
KSSSHT
L... LIGHTNING?!
WE'RE GOING IN THERE?!
BRMM
HEY, WAIT...
BRRRMM
WHY AREN'T YOU WEARING A MASK?!
IT'S ABOUT TO GET COLD, KOMATSU!
HERE COMES THE DOWNBURST!!
WHOOSH
DOWNBURST
A PHENOMENON IN WHICH TURBULENCE INSIDE A CUMULONIMBUS FUNNELS WARM AIR UP AND PUSHES COLD AIR TOWARD THE GROUND.
CUMULONIMBUS
GROUND
TORIKO AND KOMATSU WERE AT THE MERCY OF THE BLAST!

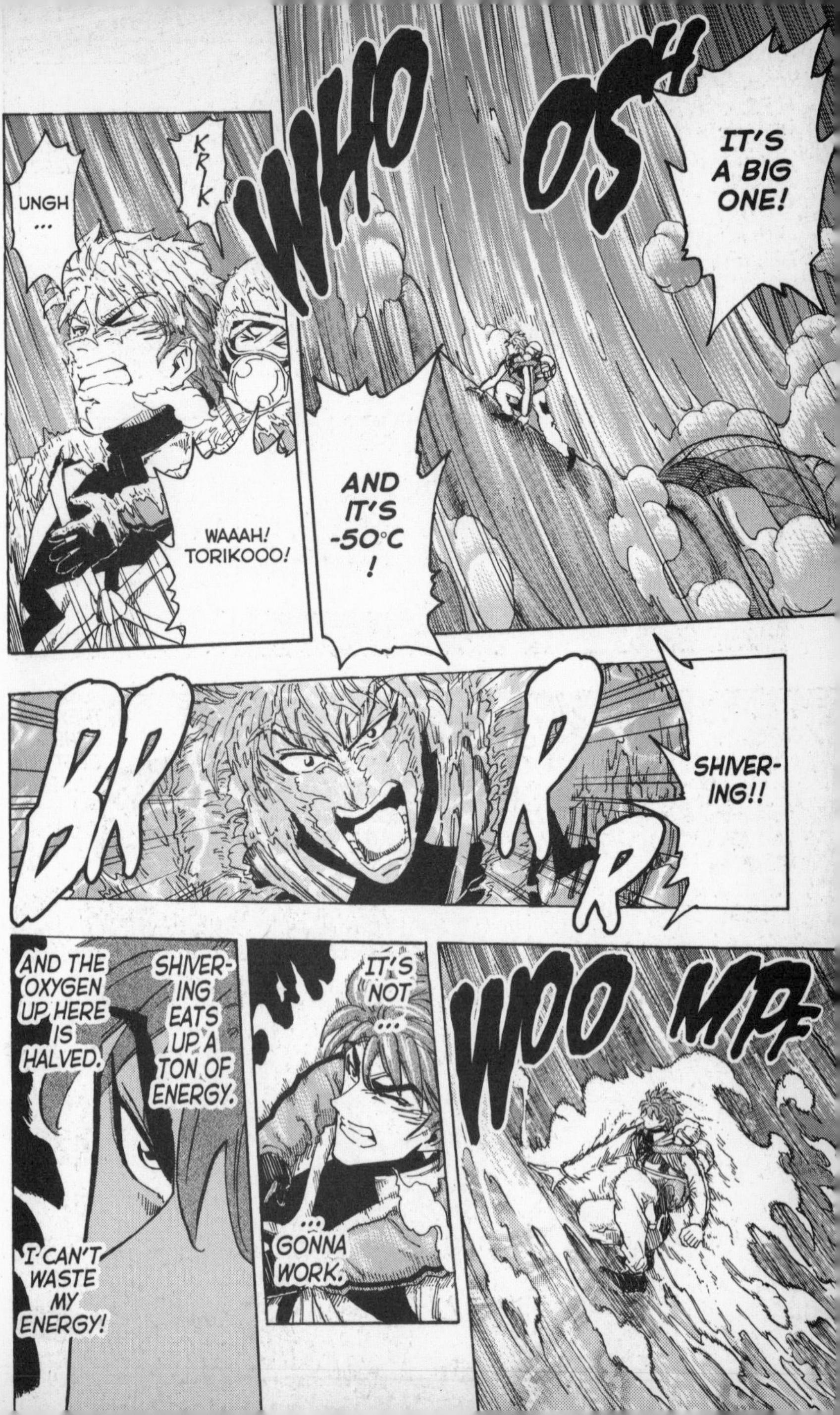
WHOOSH
IT'S A BIG ONE!
AND IT'S -50°C!
KRIK
UNGH...
WAAAH! TORIKOOO!
SHIVERING!!
BRRR
WOOMPF
IT'S NOT...
...GONNA WORK.
SHIVERING EATS UP A TON OF ENERGY.
AND THE OXYGEN UP HERE IS HALVED.
I CAN'T WASTE MY ENERGY!

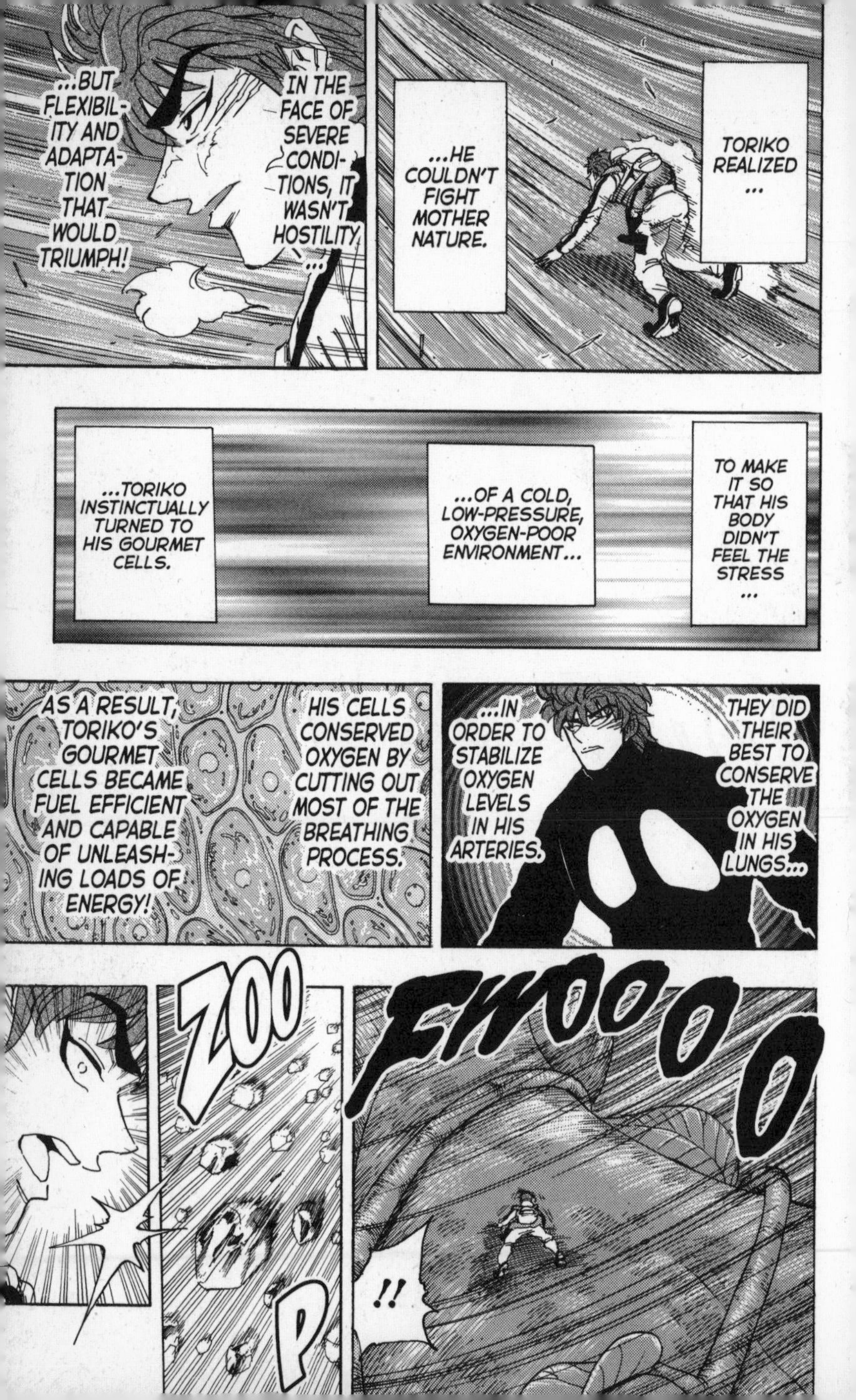
TORIKO REALIZED ...
...HE COULDN'T FIGHT MOTHER NATURE.
IN THE FACE OF SEVERE CONDI-TIONS, IT WASN'T HOSTILITY...
...BUT FLEXIBIL-ITY AND ADAPTA-TION THAT WOULD TRIUMPH!
TO MAKE IT SO THAT HIS BODY DIDN'T FEEL THE STRESS...
...OF A COLD, LOW-PRESSURE, OXYGEN-POOR ENVIRONMENT...
...TORIKO INSTINCTUALLY TURNED TO HIS GOURMET CELLS.
THEY DID THEIR BEST TO CONSERVE THE OXYGEN IN HIS LUNGS...
...IN ORDER TO STABILIZE OXYGEN LEVELS IN HIS ARTERIES.
HIS CELLS CONSERVED OXYGEN BY CUTTING OUT MOST OF THE BREATHING PROCESS.
AS A RESULT, TORIKO'S GOURMET CELLS BECAME FUEL EFFICIENT AND CAPABLE OF UNLEASH-ING LOADS OF ENERGY!
FWOOOO
!!
ZOO
P

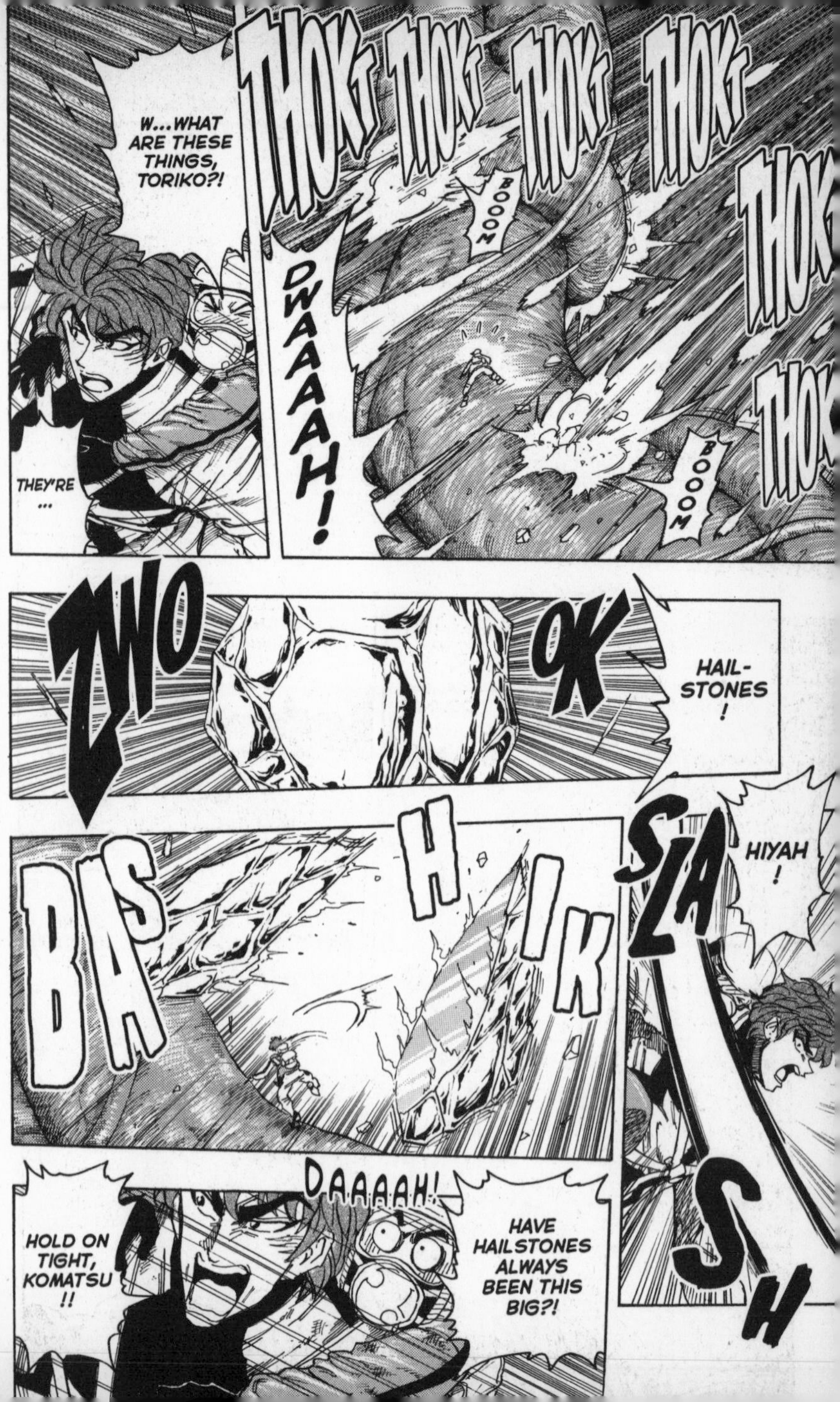
THOK THOK THOK THOK THOK THOK
BOOOM
DWAAAAAH!
BOOOM
W...WHAT ARE THESE THINGS, TORIKO?!
THEY'RE ...
HAIL-STONES !
ZWOOK
HIYAH !
SLASH
BASHIK
DAAAAH!
HAVE HAILSTONES ALWAYS BEEN THIS BIG?!
HOLD ON TIGHT, KOMATSU !!

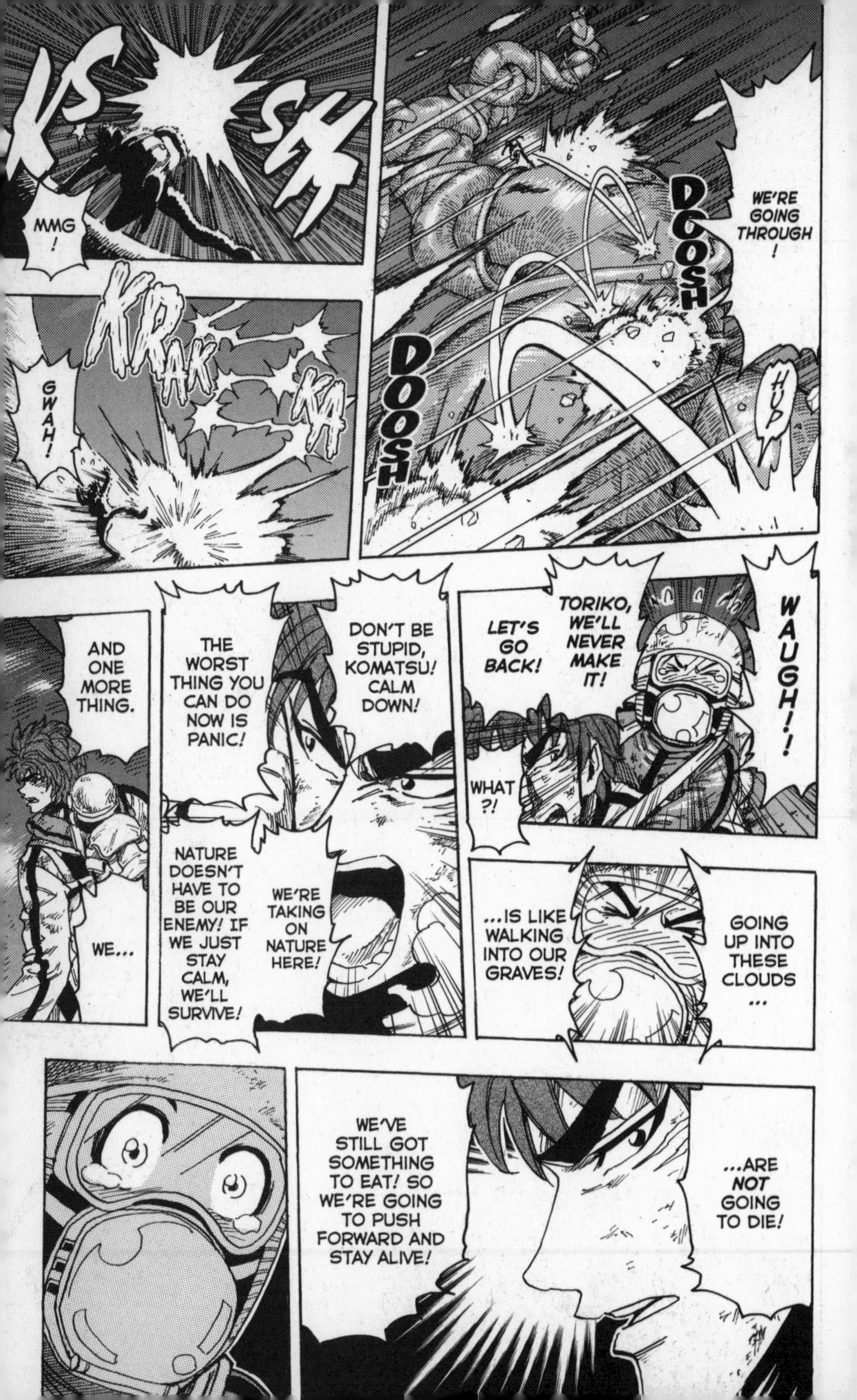
WE'RE GOING THROUGH!
DOOSH
HUP
DOOSH
KSSH
MMG!
KRAKKA
GWAH!
WAUGH!!
TORIKO, WE'LL NEVER MAKE IT!
LET'S GO BACK!
WHAT?!
GOING UP INTO THESE CLOUDS...
...IS LIKE WALKING INTO OUR GRAVES!
DON'T BE STUPID, KOMATSU! CALM DOWN!
THE WORST THING YOU CAN DO NOW IS PANIC!
WE'RE TAKING ON NATURE HERE!
NATURE DOESN'T HAVE TO BE OUR ENEMY! IF WE JUST STAY CALM, WE'LL SURVIVE!
AND ONE MORE THING.
WE...
...ARE NOT GOING TO DIE!
WE'VE STILL GOT SOMETHING TO EAT! SO WE'RE GOING TO PUSH FORWARD AND STAY ALIVE!

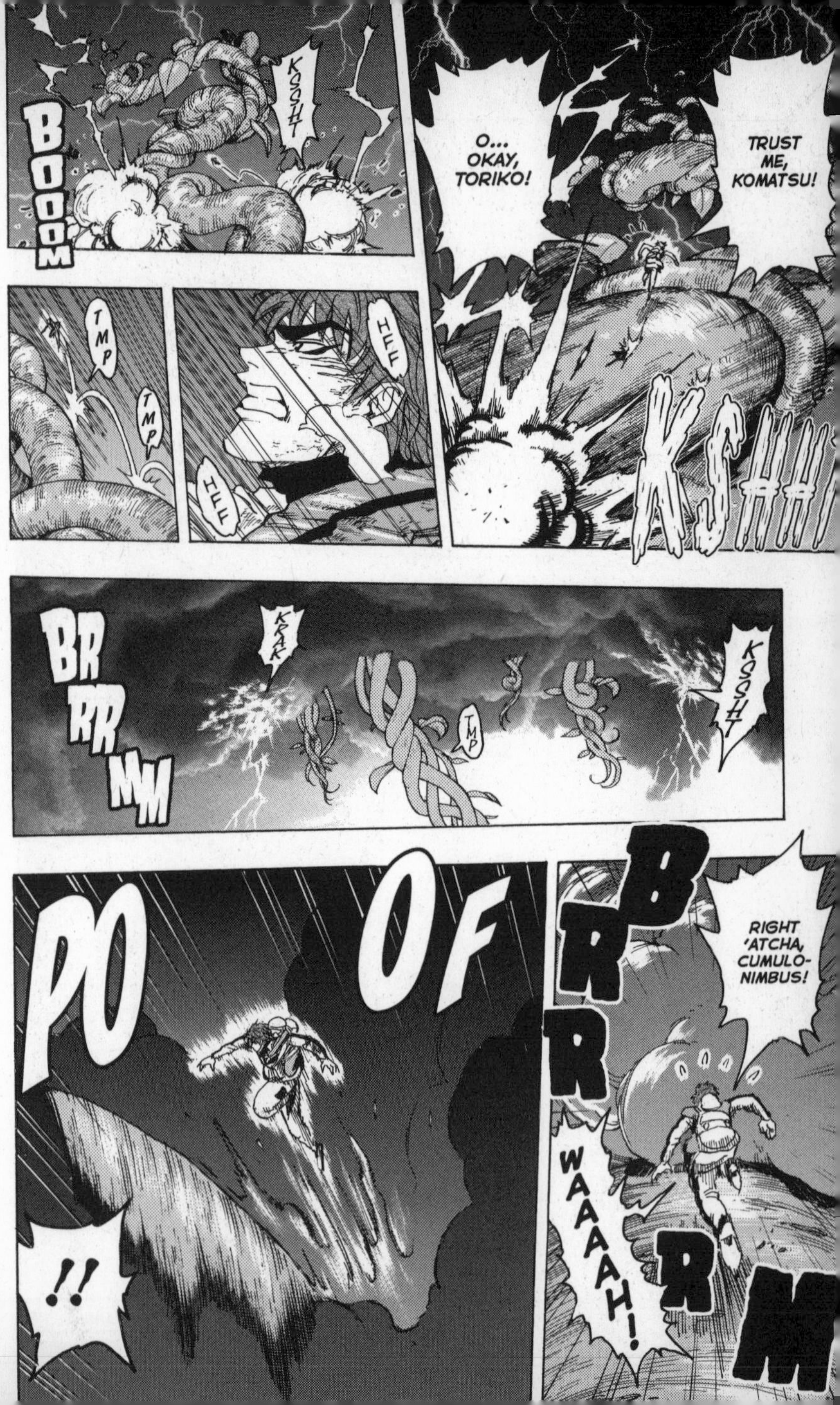
TRUST ME, KOMATSU!
O... OKAY, TORIKO!
KSHHH
KSSHT
BOOOOM
HFF
HFF
TMP
TMP
KSSHT
TMP
KRAK
BRRRMM
RIGHT 'ATCHA, CUMULONIMBUS!
WAAAAH!
BRRRRM
POOF
!!

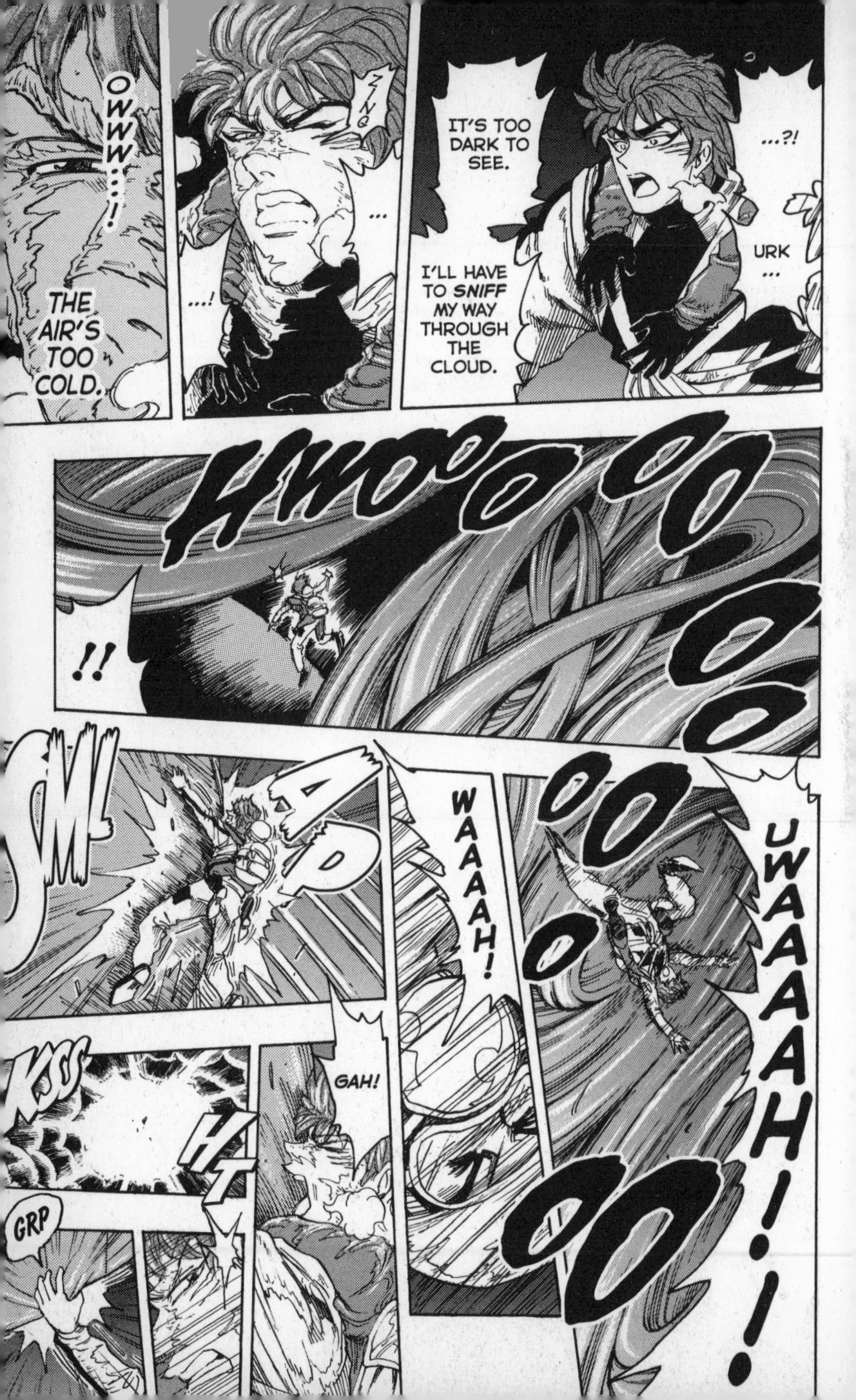
...?!
URK ...
IT'S TOO DARK TO SEE.
I'LL HAVE TO SNIFF MY WAY THROUGH THE CLOUD.
ZING
...
...!
OWWW...!
THE AIR'S TOO COLD.
HWOOOOOOOOOOOOOOO
!!
UWAAAAAAH!!
WAAAAH!
SMAP
GAH!
KSSHT
GRP

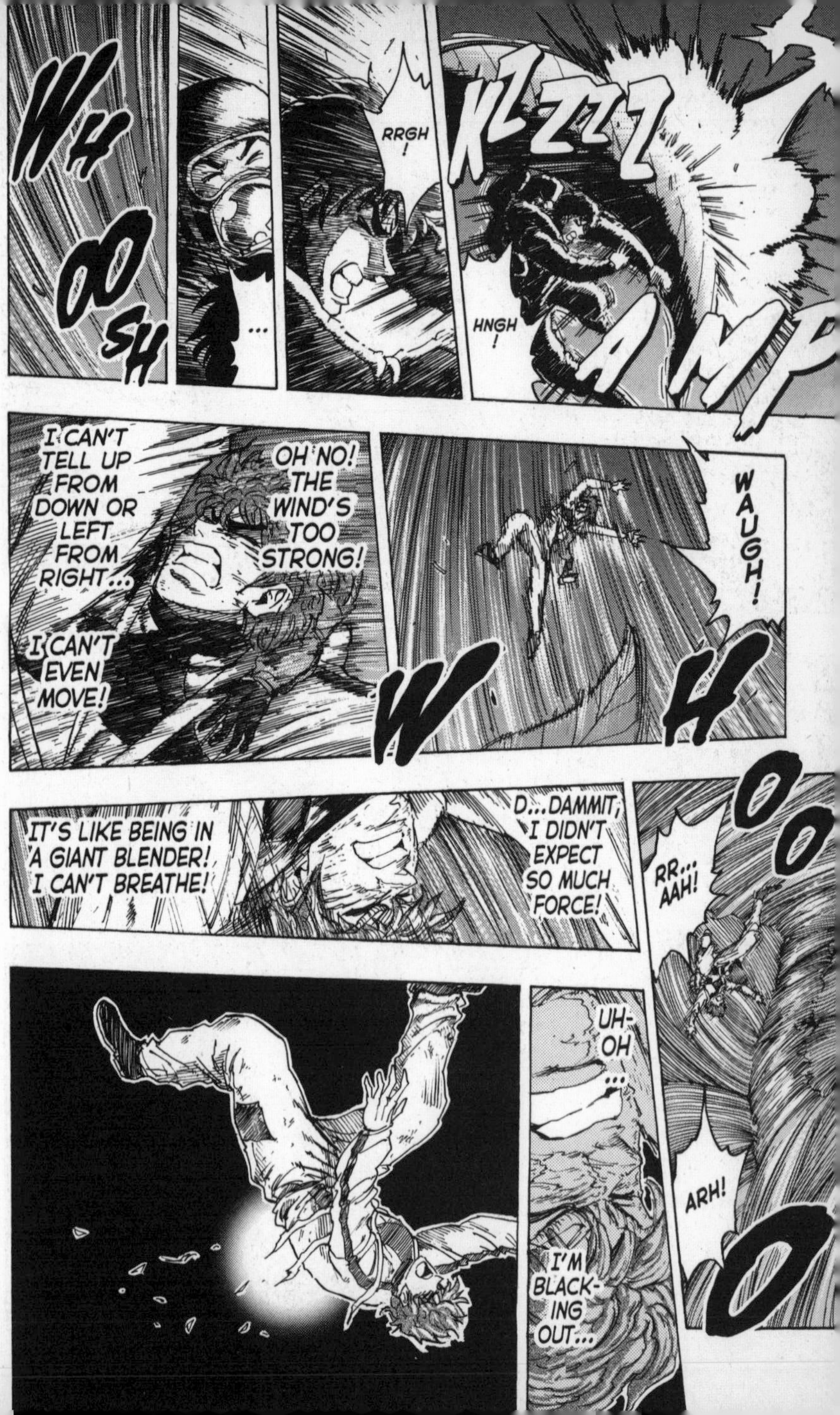
KZZZZZ
HNGH!
AMP
RRGH!
...
WHOOSH
WAUGH!
OH NO! THE WIND'S TOO STRONG!
I CAN'T TELL UP FROM DOWN OR LEFT FROM RIGHT...
I CAN'T EVEN MOVE!
WHOOO
RR... AAH!
ARH!
D...DAMMIT, I DIDN'T EXPECT SO MUCH FORCE!
IT'S LIKE BEING IN A GIANT BLENDER! I CAN'T BREATHE!
UH-OH...
I'M BLACKING OUT...

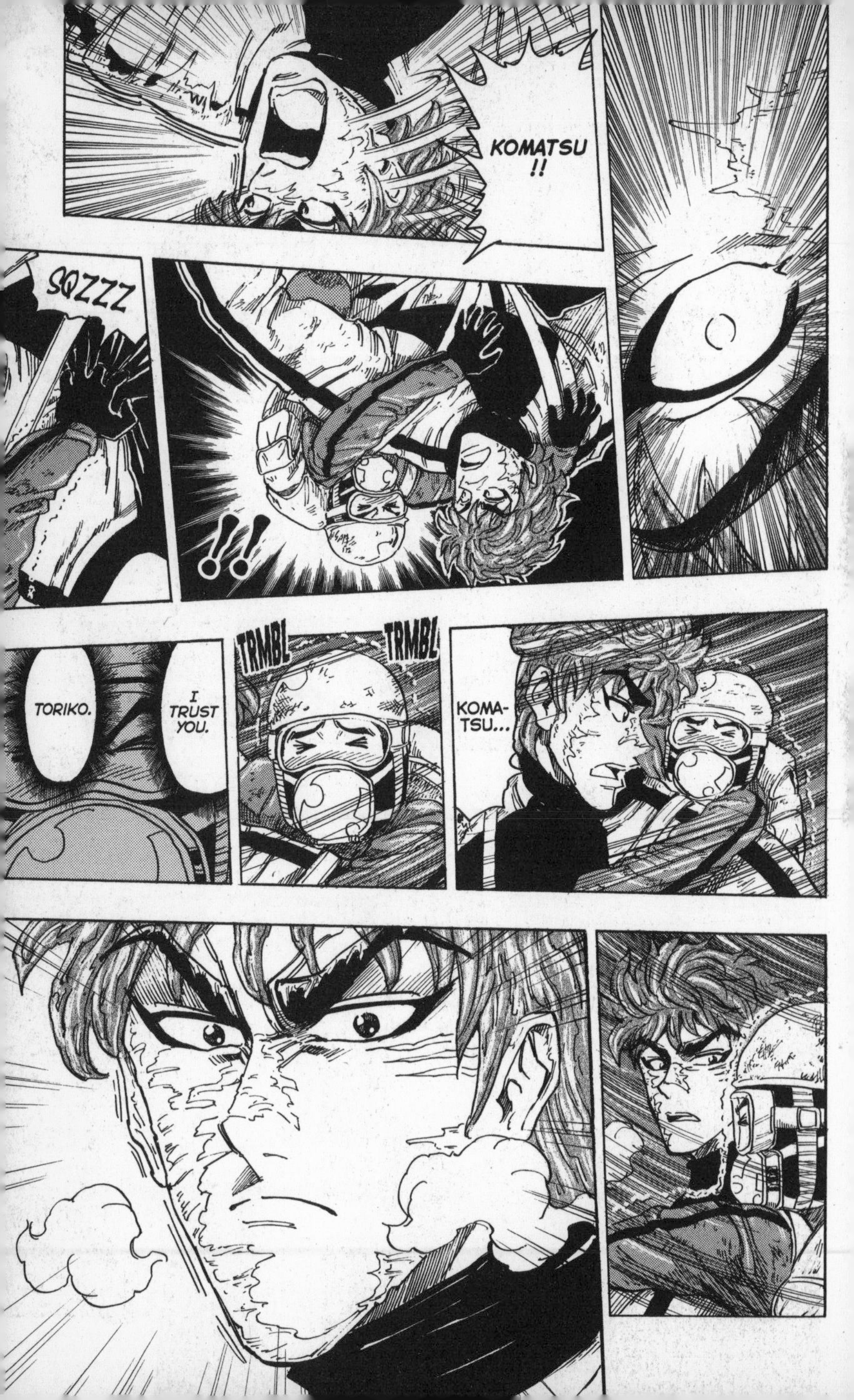
KOMATSU !!
!!
SQZZZ
KOMA-TSU...
TRMBL
TRMBL
I TRUST YOU.
TORIKO.

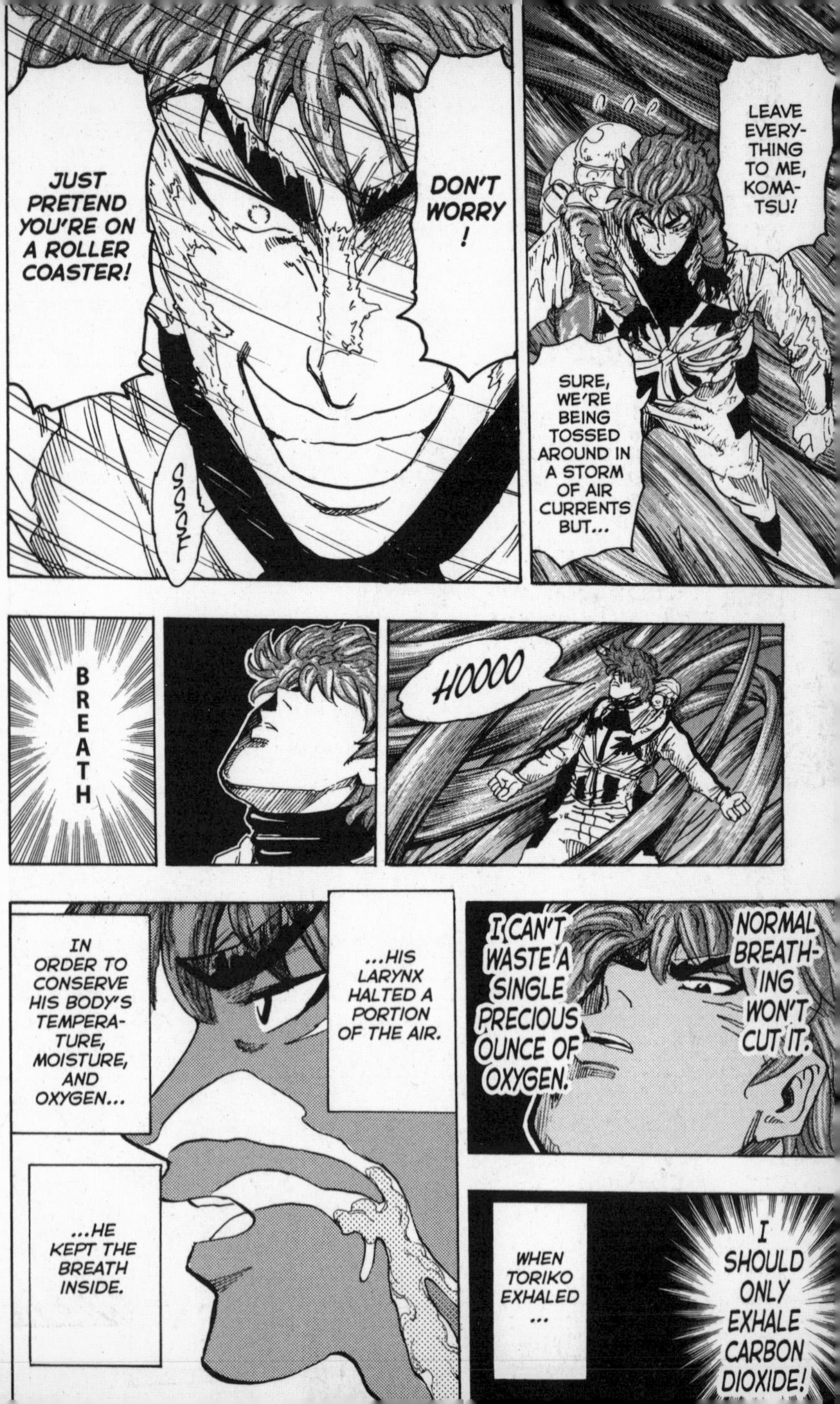
LEAVE EVERYTHING TO ME, KOMATSU!
SURE, WE'RE BEING TOSSED AROUND IN A STORM OF AIR CURRENTS BUT...
DON'T WORRY!
JUST PRETEND YOU'RE ON A ROLLER COASTER!
SSSF
HOOOO
BREATH
NORMAL BREATHING WON'T CUT IT.
I CAN'T WASTE A SINGLE PRECIOUS OUNCE OF OXYGEN.
I SHOULD ONLY EXHALE CARBON DIOXIDE!
WHEN TORIKO EXHALED...
...HIS LARYNX HALTED A PORTION OF THE AIR.
IN ORDER TO CONSERVE HIS BODY'S TEMPERATURE, MOISTURE, AND OXYGEN...
...HE KEPT THE BREATH INSIDE.

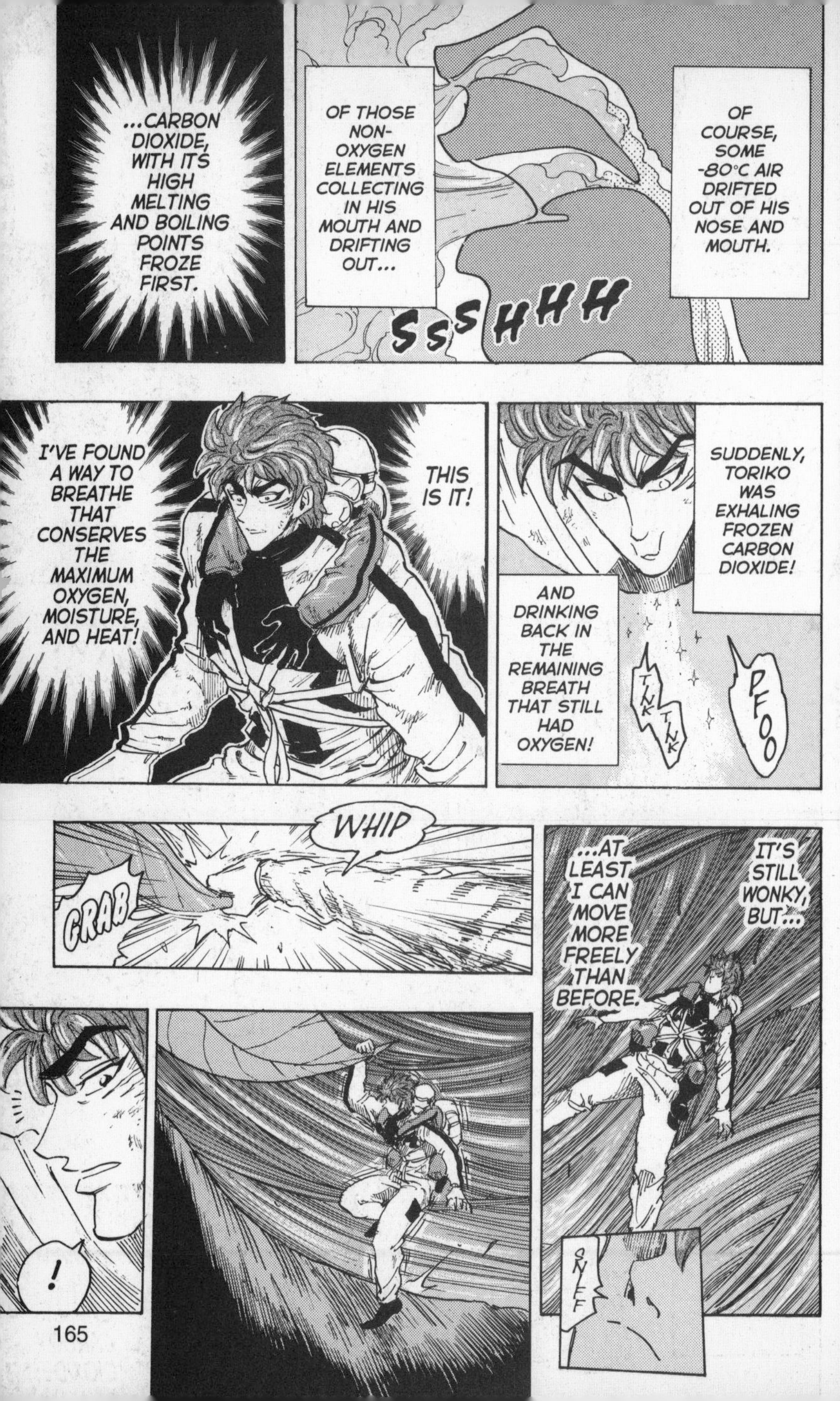
OF COURSE, SOME -80°C AIR DRIFTED OUT OF HIS NOSE AND MOUTH.
OF THOSE NON-OXYGEN ELEMENTS COLLECTING IN HIS MOUTH AND DRIFTING OUT...
SSSHHH
...CARBON DIOXIDE, WITH ITS HIGH MELTING AND BOILING POINTS FROZE FIRST.
SUDDENLY, TORIKO WAS EXHALING FROZEN CARBON DIOXIDE!
AND DRINKING BACK IN THE REMAINING BREATH THAT STILL HAD OXYGEN!
PFOO
TINK TINK
THIS IS IT!
I'VE FOUND A WAY TO BREATHE THAT CONSERVES THE MAXIMUM OXYGEN, MOISTURE, AND HEAT!
IT'S STILL WONKY, BUT...
...AT LEAST I CAN MOVE MORE FREELY THAN BEFORE.
SNIFF
WHIP
CRAB
!

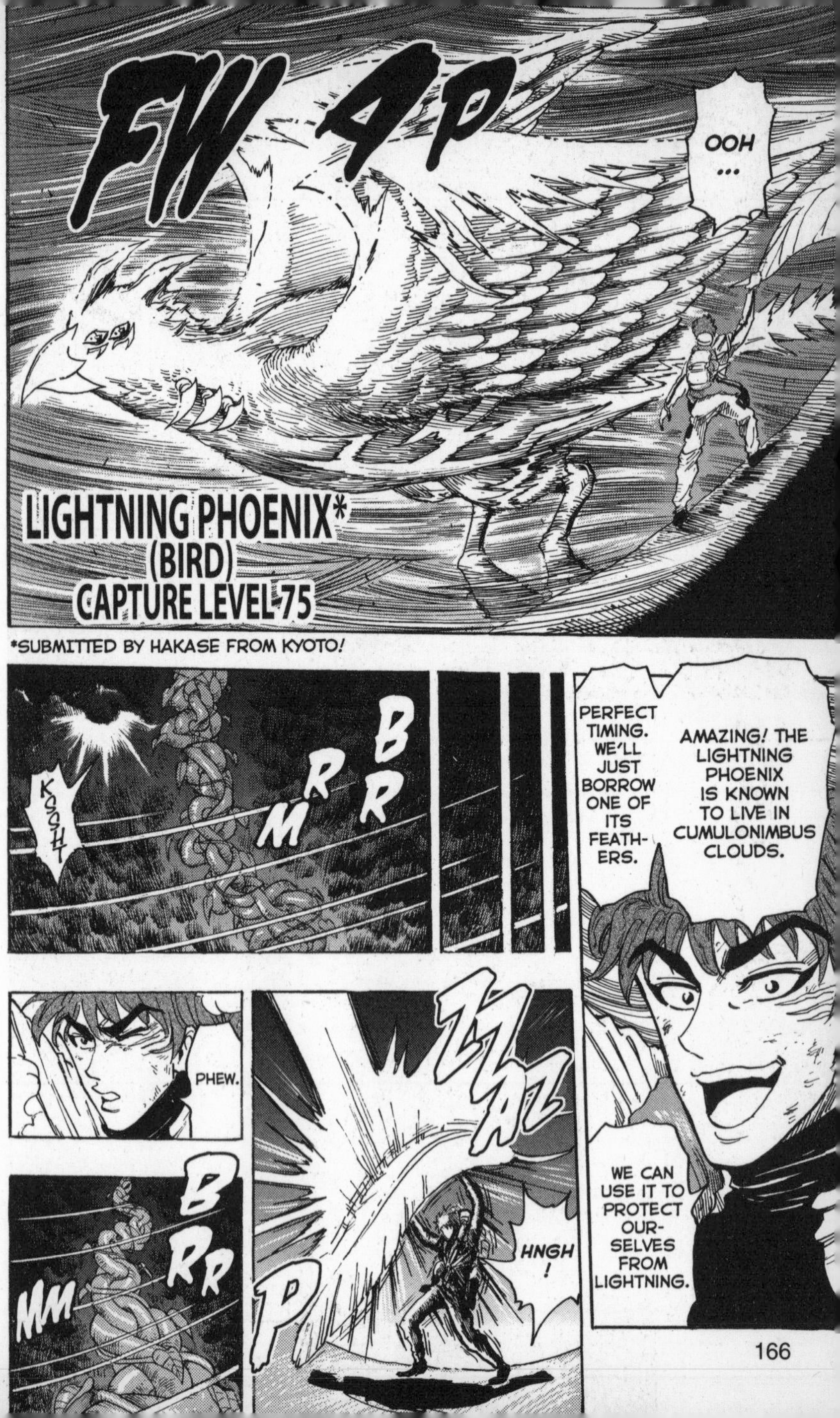
FWAP
OOH ...
LIGHTNING PHOENIX*
(BIRD)
CAPTURE LEVEL 75
AMAZING! THE LIGHTNING PHOENIX IS KNOWN TO LIVE IN CUMULONIMBUS CLOUDS.
PERFECT TIMING. WE'LL JUST BORROW ONE OF ITS FEATH-ERS.
WE CAN USE IT TO PROTECT OUR-SELVES FROM LIGHTNING.
BRRMM
KSSHT
ZZAAP
HNGH!
PHEW.
BRRMM

*SUBMITTED BY HAKASE FROM KYOTO!

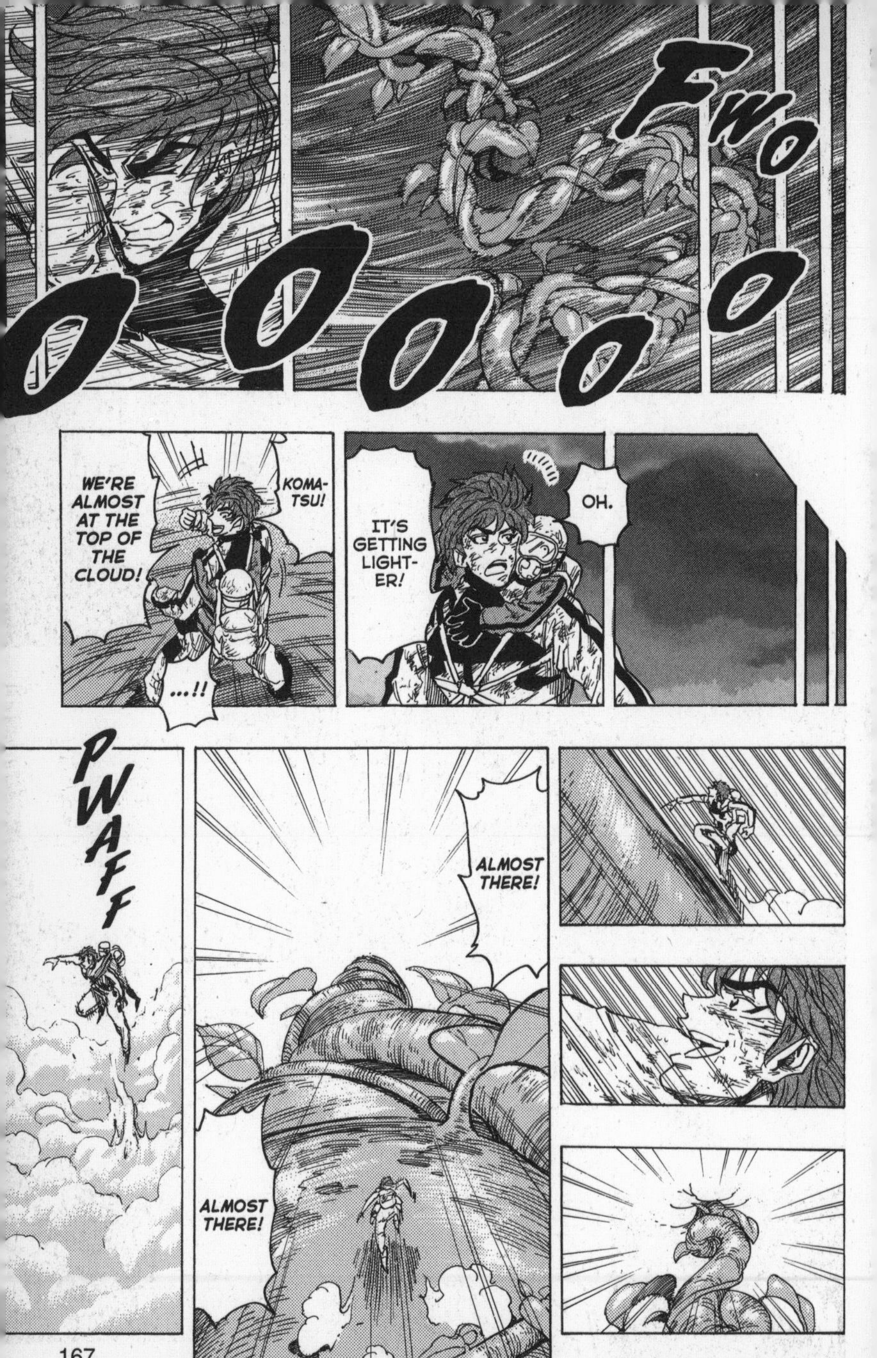
FWOOOOOO
OH.
IT'S GETTING LIGHTER!
KOMA-TSU!
WE'RE ALMOST AT THE TOP OF THE CLOUD!
...!!
ALMOST THERE!
ALMOST THERE!
PWAFF

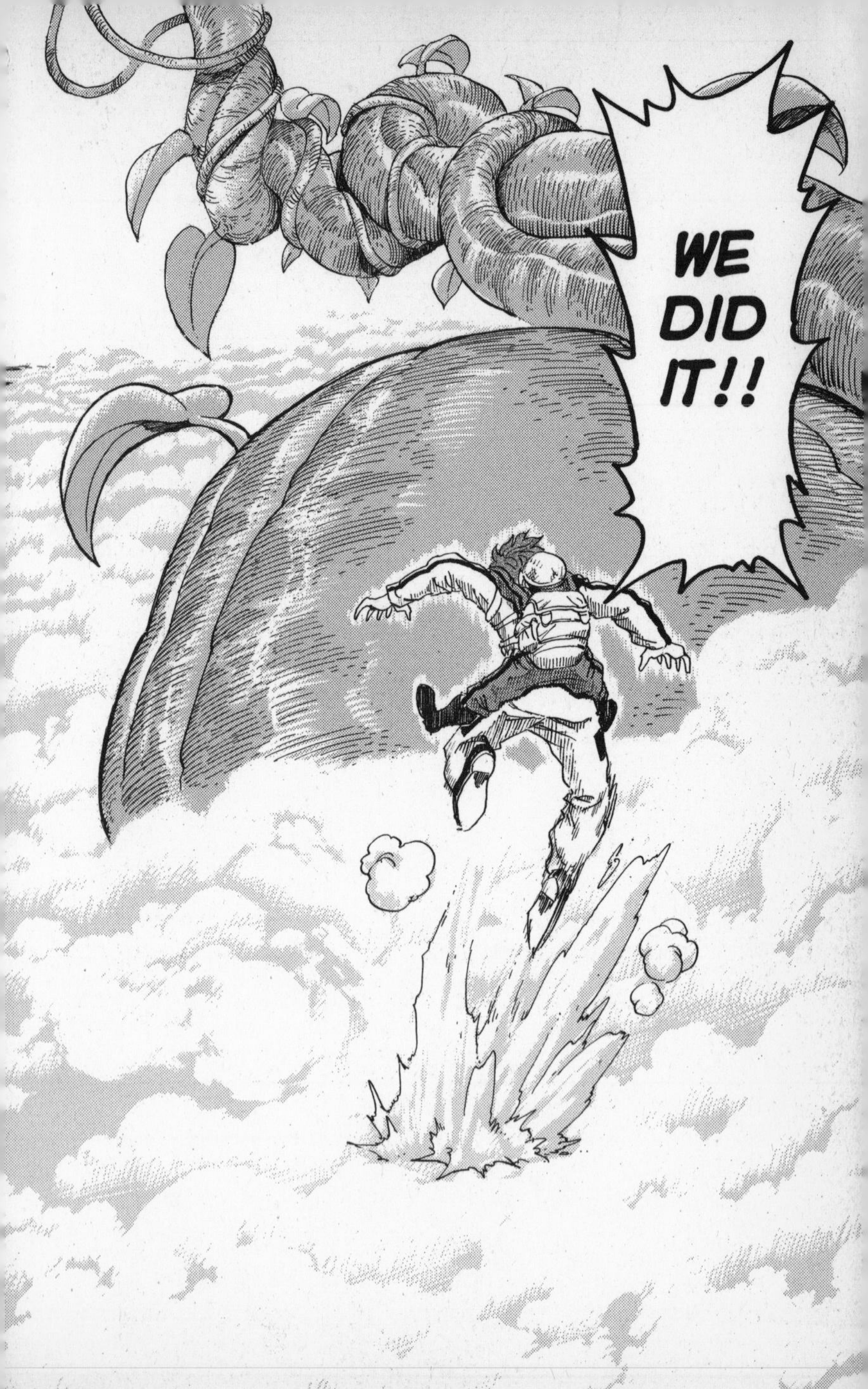
WE DID IT!!

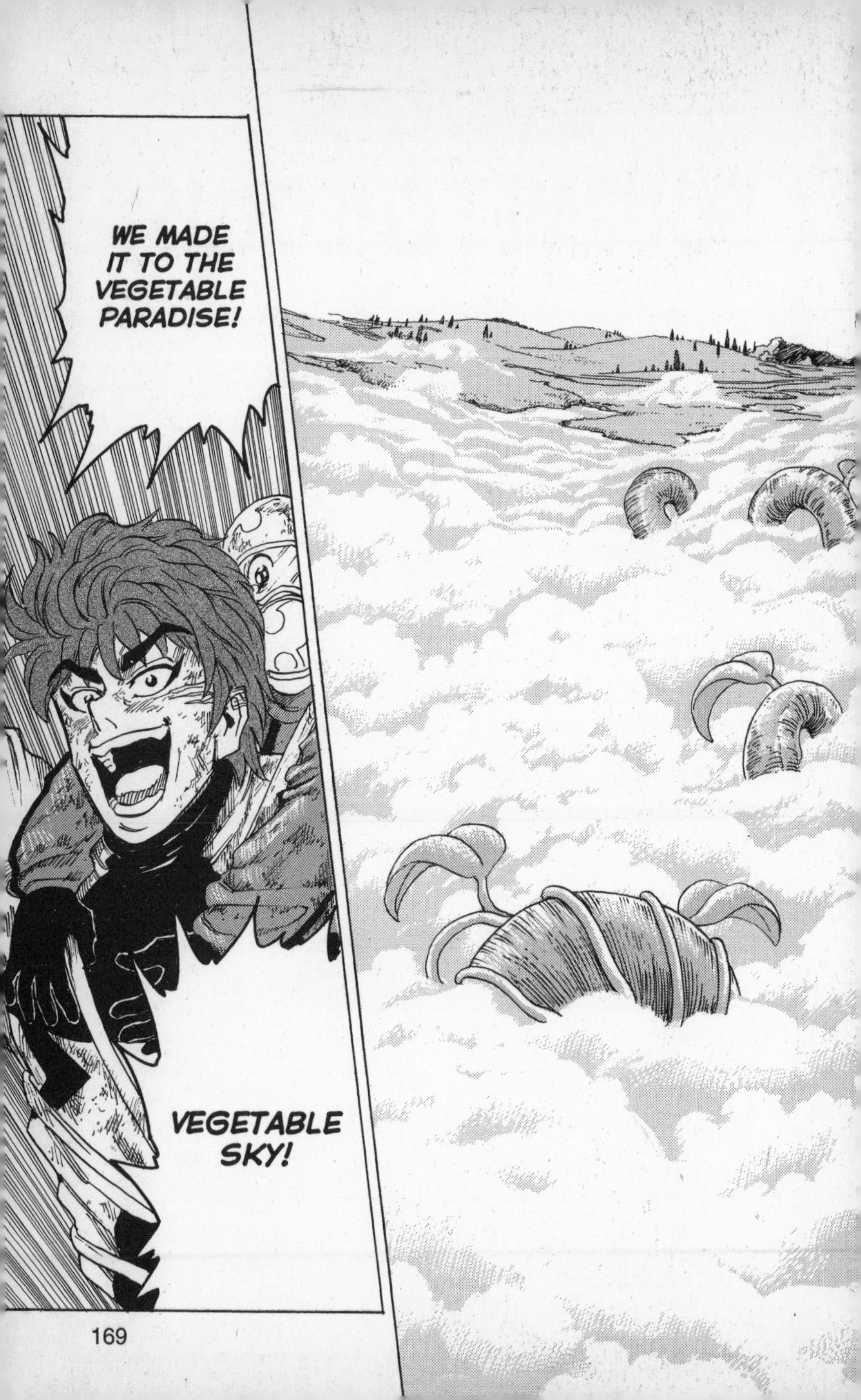
WE MADE IT TO THE VEGETABLE PARADISE!
VEGETABLE SKY!

TORIKO

GOURMET CHECKLIST

Vol. 116

HOT SPRING SHARK
(FISH)

CAPTURE LEVEL: 20

HABITAT: CALM OCEANS

LENGTH: 10–50 METERS

HEIGHT: ---

WEIGHT: 10–200 TONS

PRICE: 20,000,000 YEN (AS A NATURAL BATHTUB, NOT FOR EATING). ONE GALLON OF THE HOT SPRING SHARK'S SPRING WATER IS 800 YEN.

HOT SPRING SHARK*
(FISH)
CAPTURE LEVEL 20

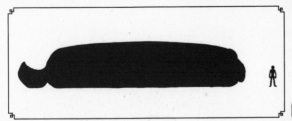

SCALE

A STRANGE SHARK THAT SPOUTS HOT WATER FROM A BLOWHOLE IN ITS CONCAVE BACK. BATHING IN THE SHARK'S WATERS WILL TRANSFORM EVEN THE DRIEST HIDE INTO SMOOTH, GLEAMING SKIN. ALSO, SINCE VARIOUS SPECIES OF DOCTOR FISH MAKE HOT SPRING SHARKS THEIR HOME, BATHERS CAN HEAL WHILE THEY BEAUTIFY. THAT MAKES HOT SPRING SHARKS SOME OF THE MOST POPULAR ATTRACTIONS IN LIFE.

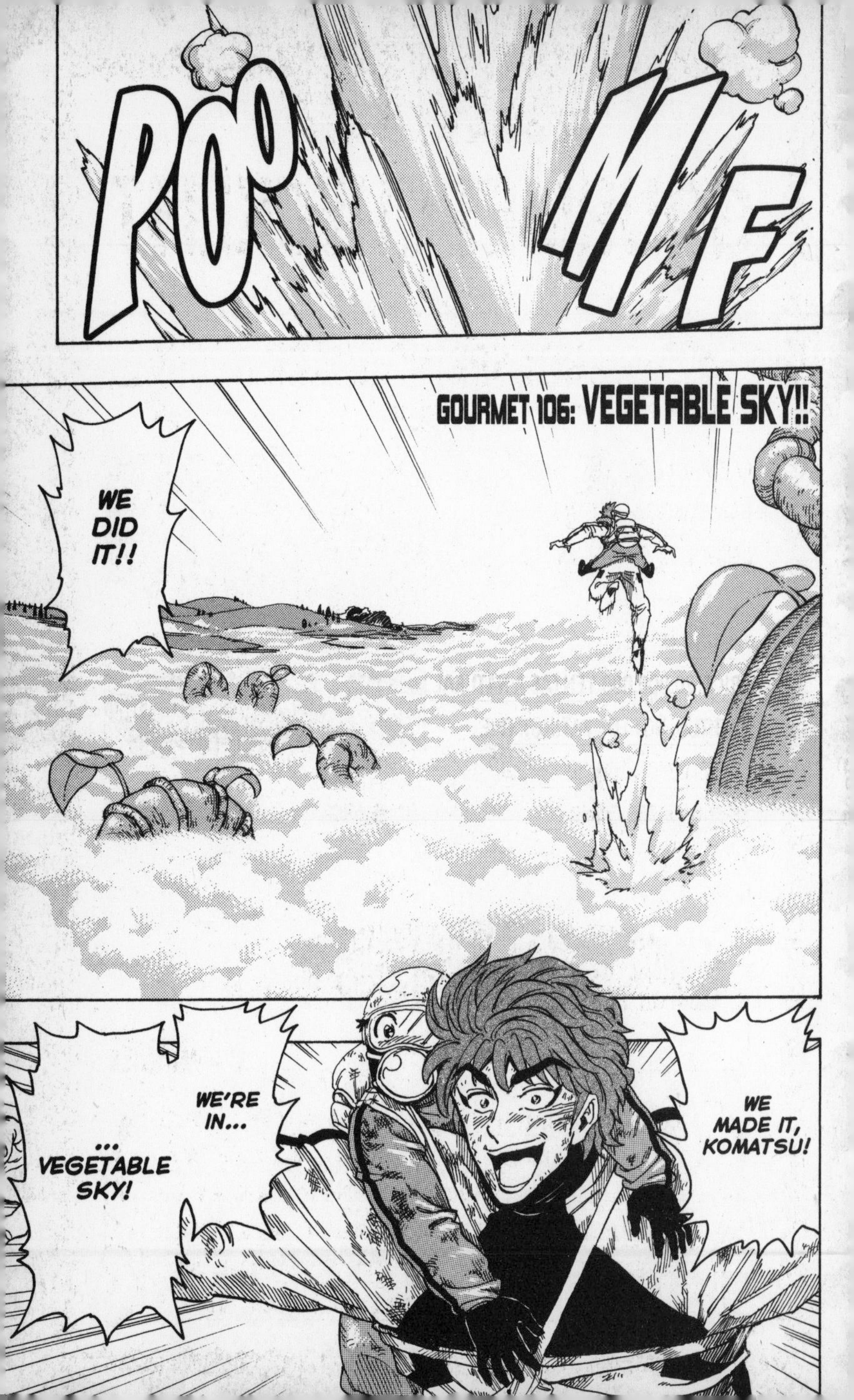
POOMF
GOURMET 106: VEGETABLE SKY!!
WE DID IT!!
WE MADE IT, KOMATSU!
WE'RE IN...
...VEGETABLE SKY!

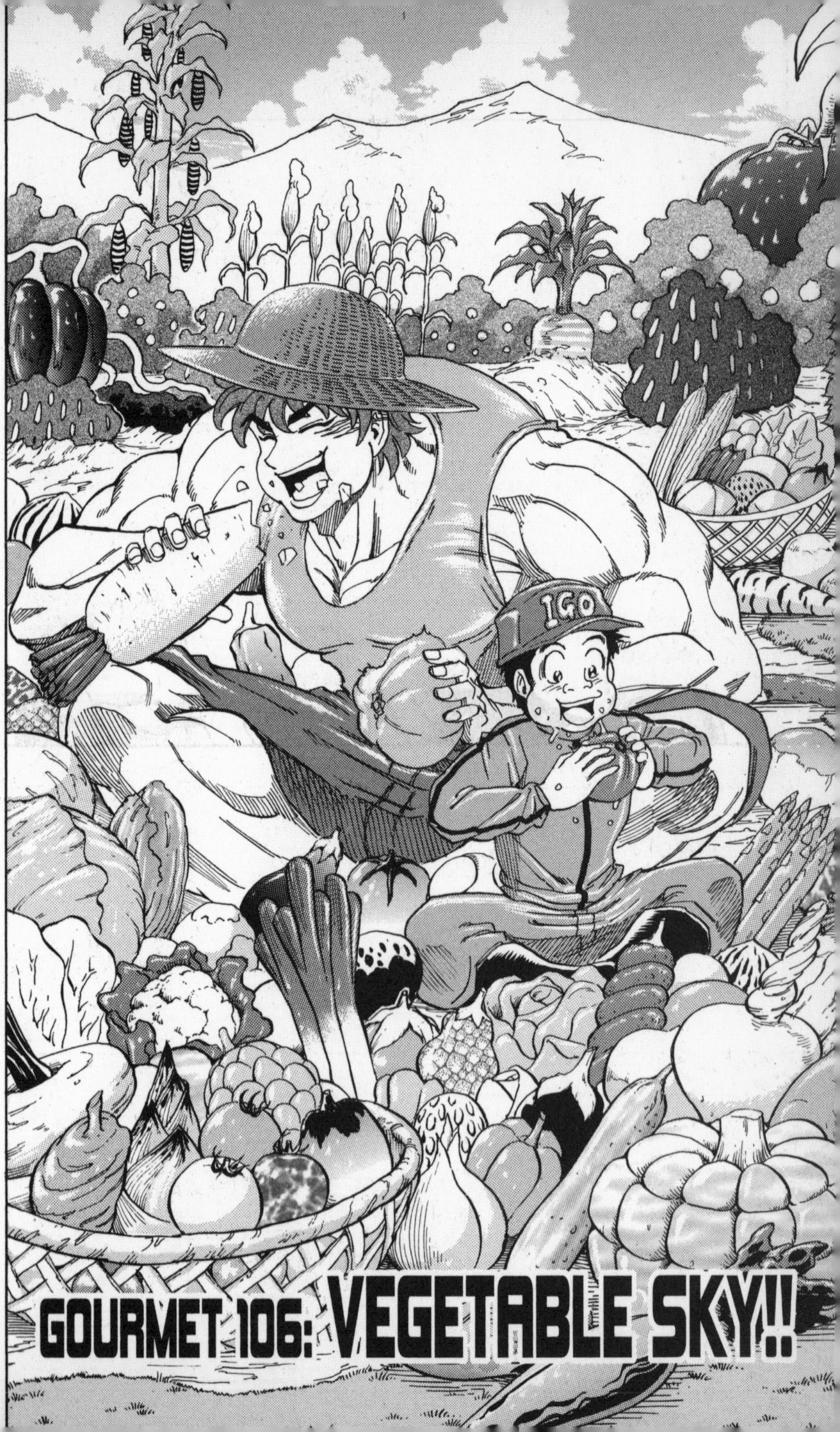
IGO

GOURMET 106: VEGETABLE SKY!!

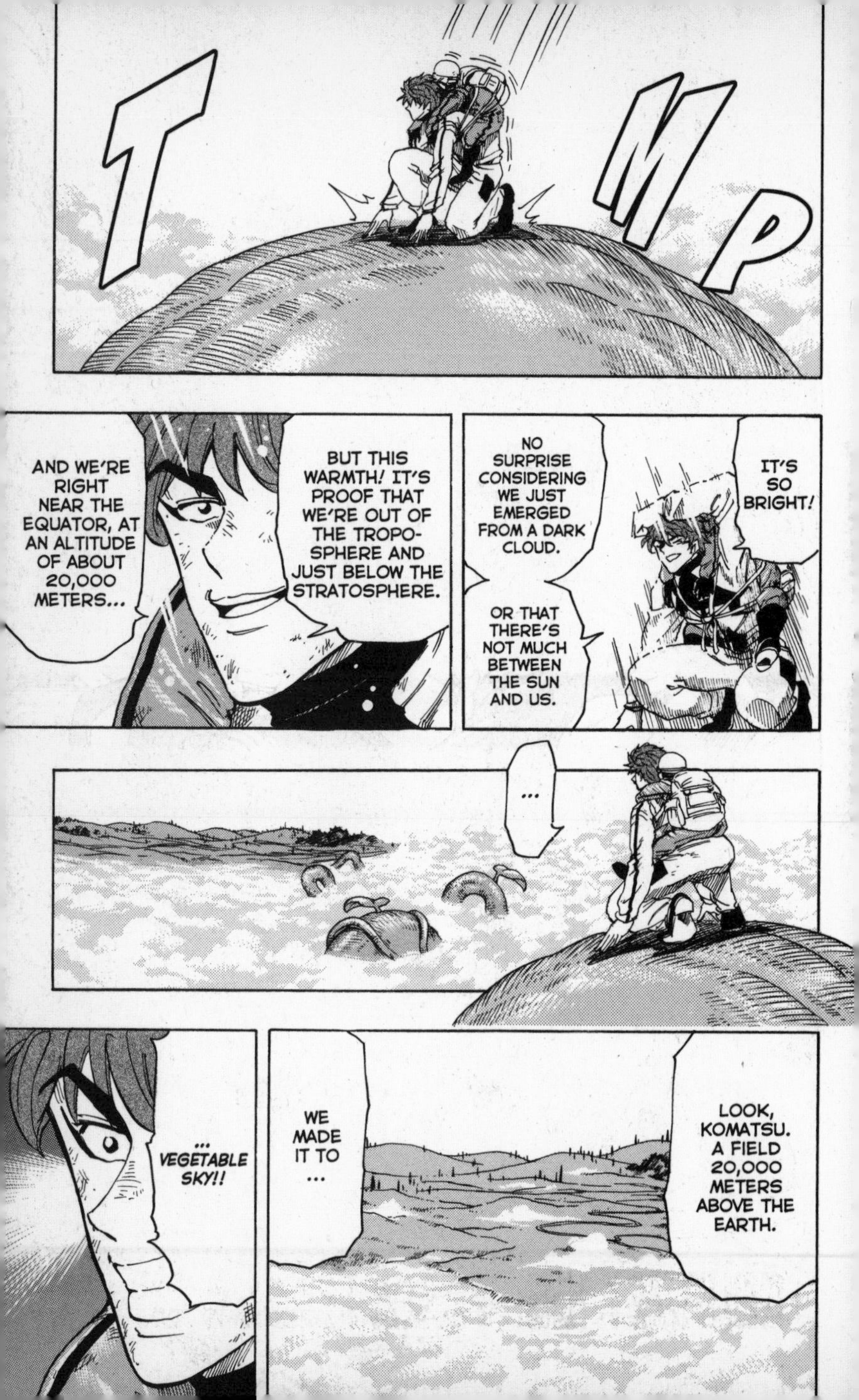
TMP
IT'S SO BRIGHT!
NO SURPRISE CONSIDERING WE JUST EMERGED FROM A DARK CLOUD.
OR THAT THERE'S NOT MUCH BETWEEN THE SUN AND US.
BUT THIS WARMTH! IT'S PROOF THAT WE'RE OUT OF THE TROPO-SPHERE AND JUST BELOW THE STRATOSPHERE.
AND WE'RE RIGHT NEAR THE EQUATOR, AT AN ALTITUDE OF ABOUT 20,000 METERS...
...
LOOK, KOMATSU. A FIELD 20,000 METERS ABOVE THE EARTH.
WE MADE IT TO ...
... VEGETABLE SKY!!

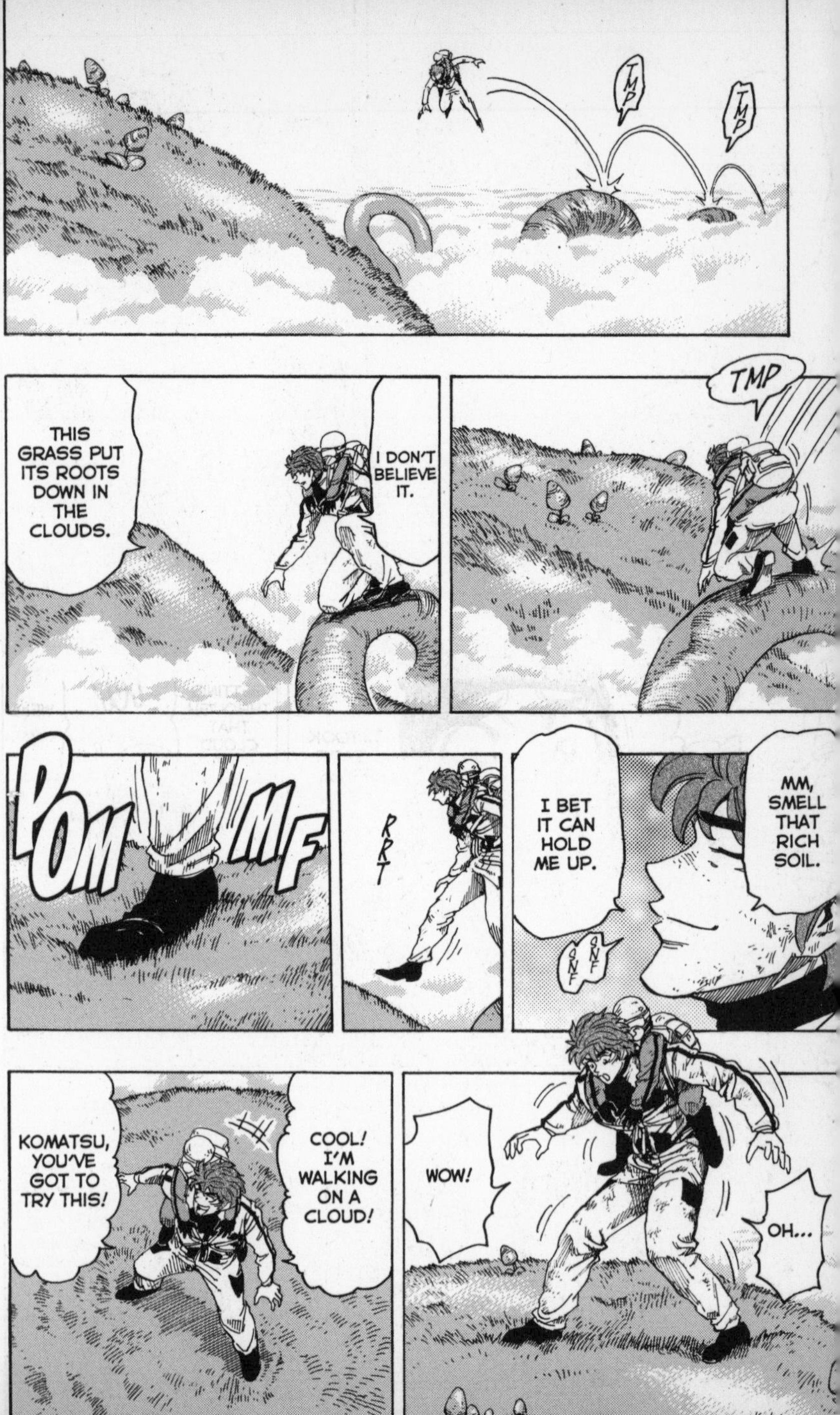

TMP
TMP
TMP
I DON'T BELIEVE IT.
THIS GRASS PUT ITS ROOTS DOWN IN THE CLOUDS.
MM, SMELL THAT RICH SOIL.
SNF SNF
I BET IT CAN HOLD ME UP.
RRT
POMMF
OH...
WOW!
COOL! I'M WALKING ON A CLOUD!
KOMATSU, YOU'VE GOT TO TRY THIS!

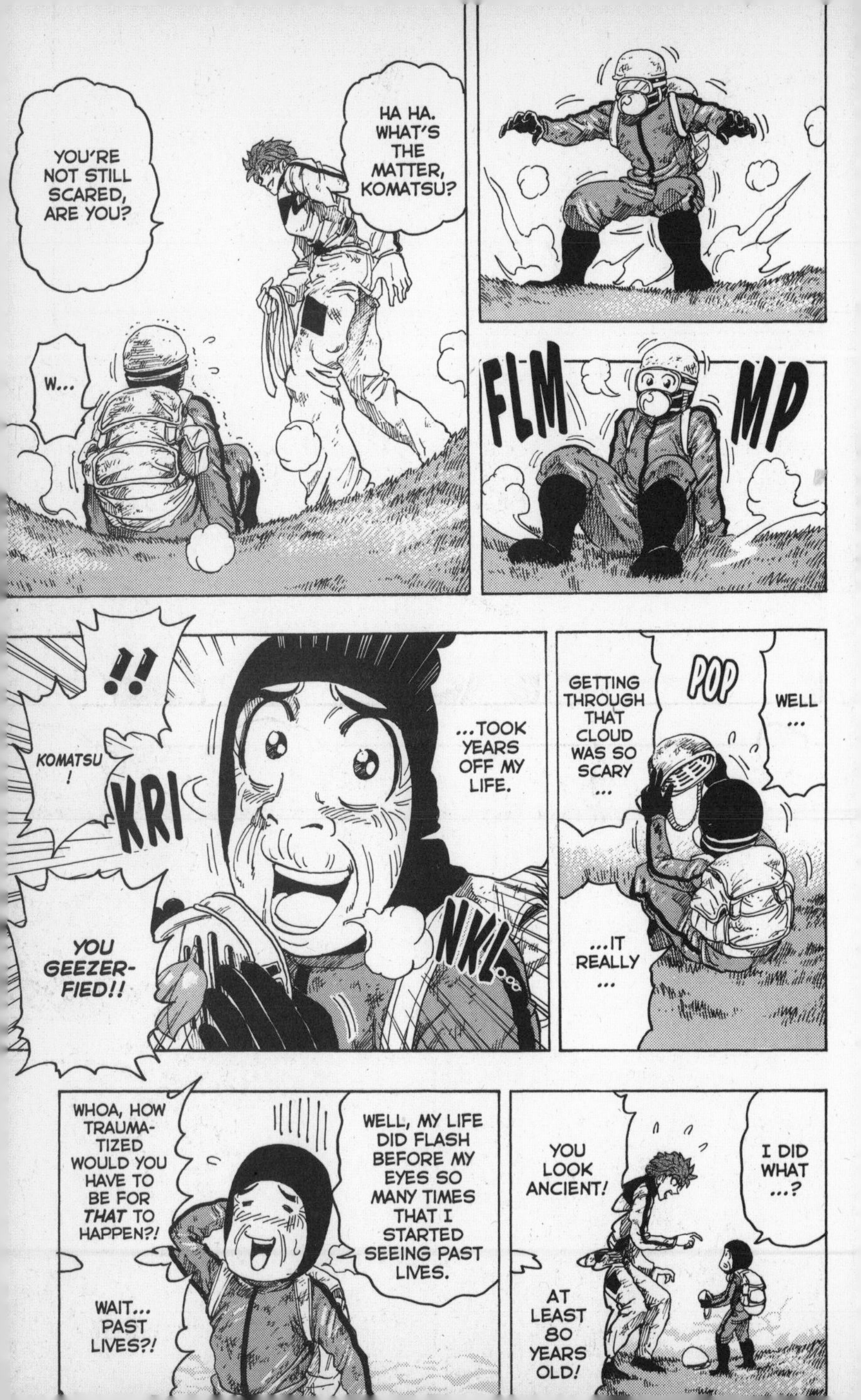
FLM MP
HA HA. WHAT'S THE MATTER, KOMATSU?
YOU'RE NOT STILL SCARED, ARE YOU?
W...
WELL...
POP
GETTING THROUGH THAT CLOUD WAS SO SCARY...
...IT REALLY...
...TOOK YEARS OFF MY LIFE.
!!
KOMATSU!
KRI NKL
YOU GEEZER-FIED!!
I DID WHAT...?
YOU LOOK ANCIENT!
AT LEAST 80 YEARS OLD!
WELL, MY LIFE DID FLASH BEFORE MY EYES SO MANY TIMES THAT I STARTED SEEING PAST LIVES.
WHOA, HOW TRAUMATIZED WOULD YOU HAVE TO BE FOR *THAT* TO HAPPEN?!
WAIT... PAST LIVES?!

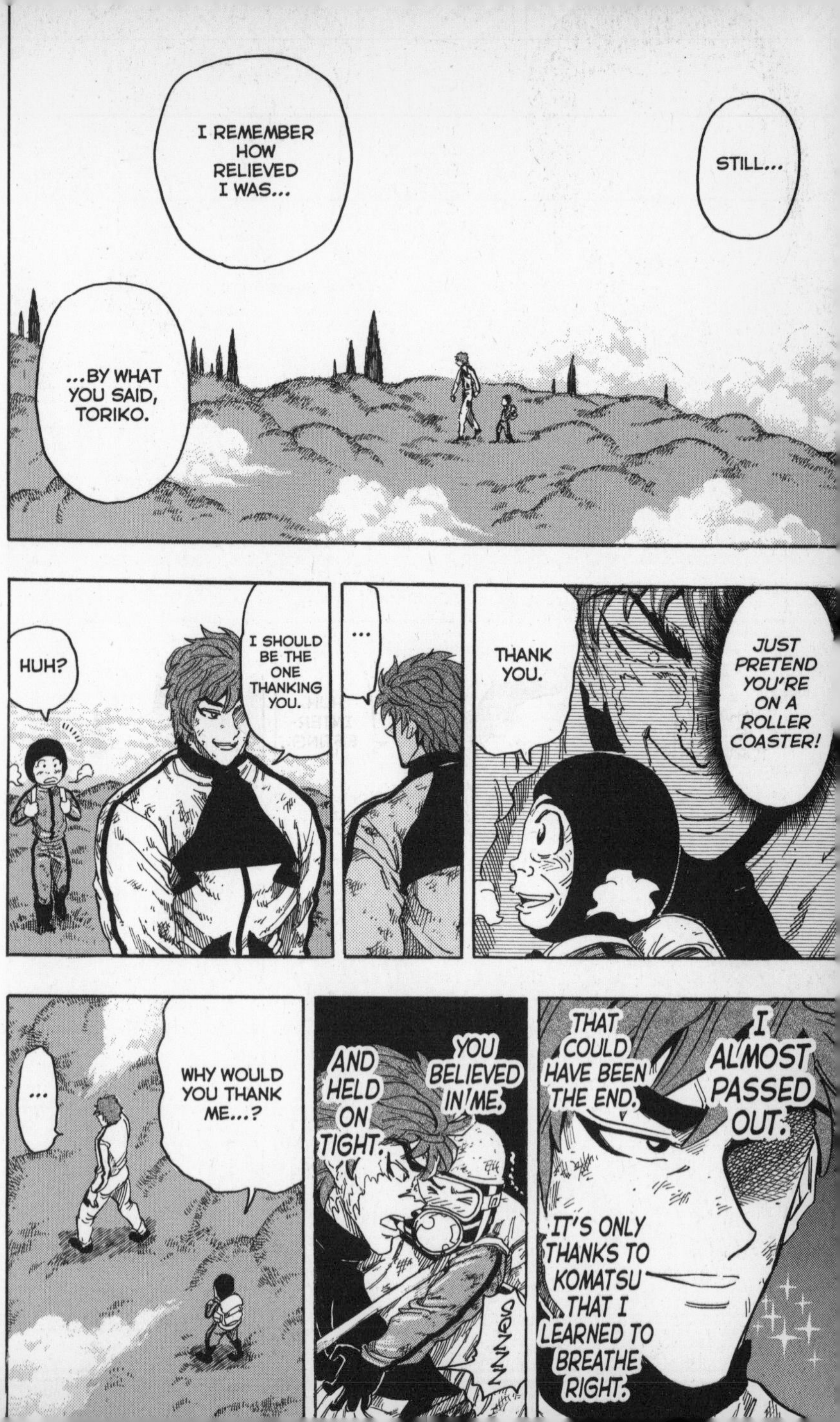
STILL...
I REMEMBER HOW RELIEVED I WAS...
...BY WHAT YOU SAID, TORIKO.
JUST PRETEND YOU'RE ON A ROLLER COASTER!
THANK YOU.
...
I SHOULD BE THE ONE THANKING YOU.
HUH?
I ALMOST PASSED OUT.
THAT COULD HAVE BEEN THE END.
IT'S ONLY THANKS TO KOMATSU THAT I LEARNED TO BREATHE RIGHT.
YOU BELIEVED IN ME.
AND HELD ON TIGHT.
WHY WOULD YOU THANK ME...?
...

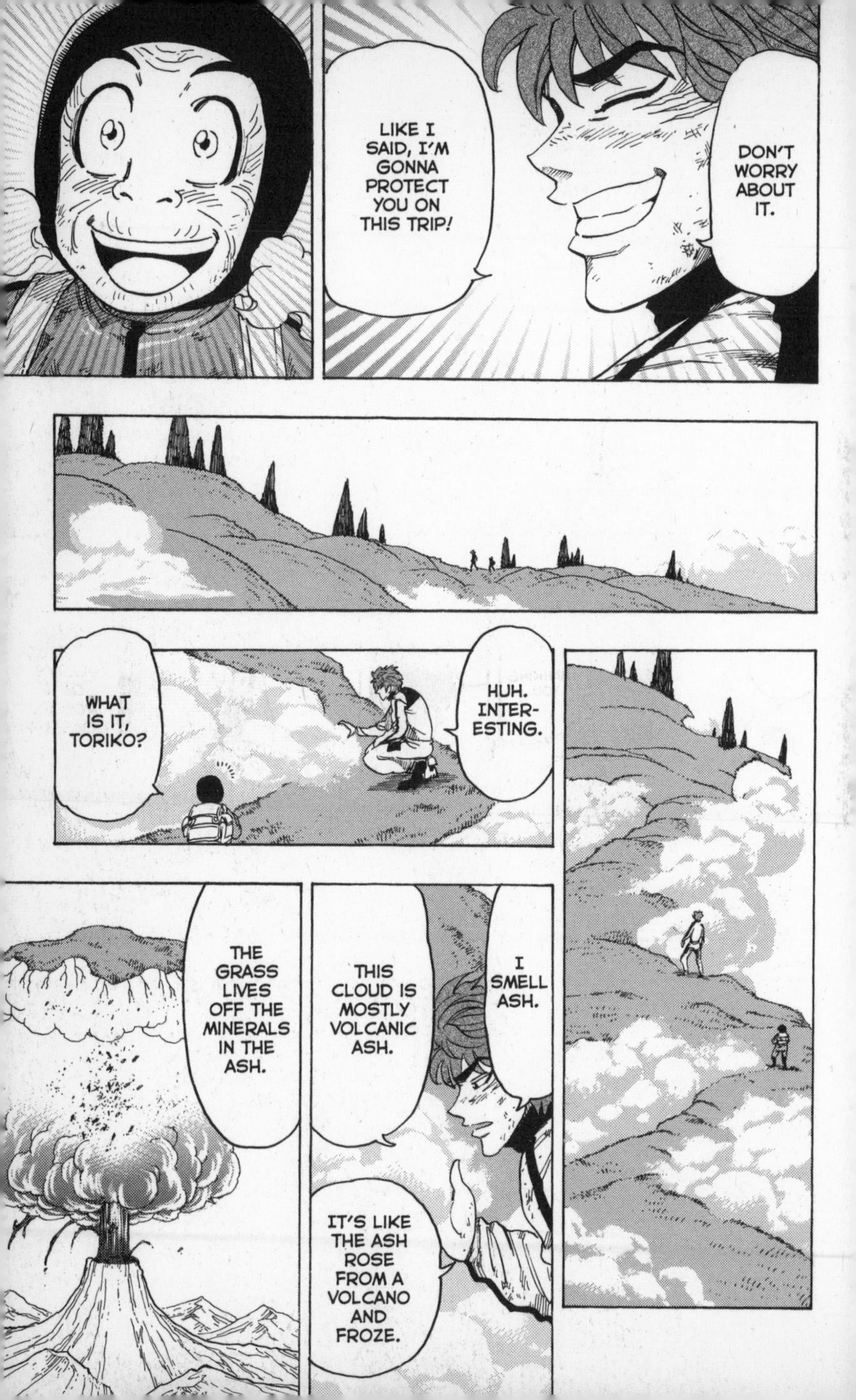
DON'T WORRY ABOUT IT.
LIKE I SAID, I'M GONNA PROTECT YOU ON THIS TRIP!
HUH. INTER-ESTING.
WHAT IS IT, TORIKO?
I SMELL ASH.
THIS CLOUD IS MOSTLY VOLCANIC ASH.
IT'S LIKE THE ASH ROSE FROM A VOLCANO AND FROZE.
THE GRASS LIVES OFF THE MINERALS IN THE ASH.

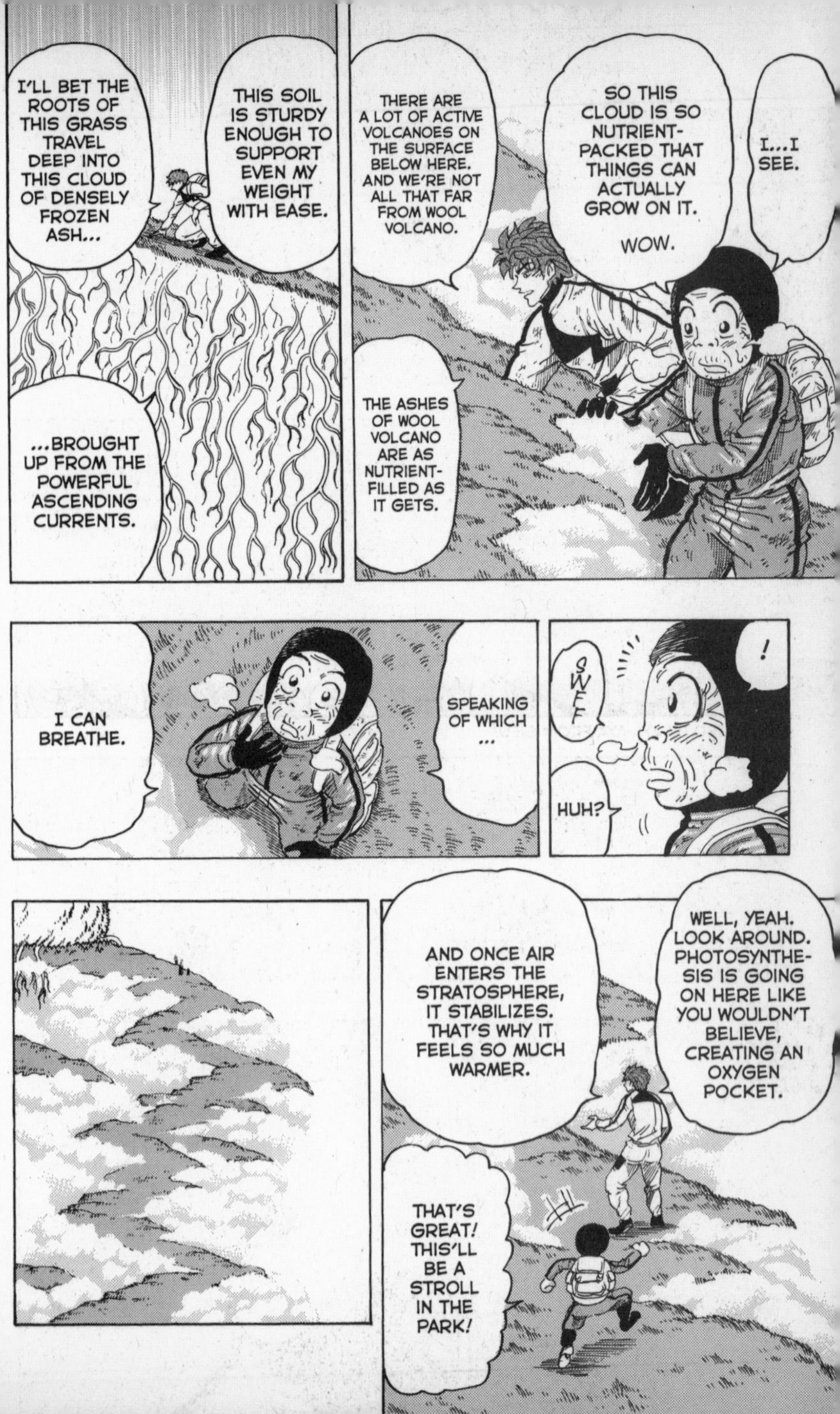
I...I SEE.
SO THIS CLOUD IS SO NUTRIENT-PACKED THAT THINGS CAN ACTUALLY GROW ON IT.
WOW.
THERE ARE A LOT OF ACTIVE VOLCANOES ON THE SURFACE BELOW HERE. AND WE'RE NOT ALL THAT FAR FROM WOOL VOLCANO.
THE ASHES OF WOOL VOLCANO ARE AS NUTRIENT-FILLED AS IT GETS.
THIS SOIL IS STURDY ENOUGH TO SUPPORT EVEN MY WEIGHT WITH EASE.
I'LL BET THE ROOTS OF THIS GRASS TRAVEL DEEP INTO THIS CLOUD OF DENSELY FROZEN ASH...
...BROUGHT UP FROM THE POWERFUL ASCENDING CURRENTS.
!
SWFF
HUH?
SPEAKING OF WHICH ...
I CAN BREATHE.
WELL, YEAH. LOOK AROUND. PHOTOSYNTHESIS IS GOING ON HERE LIKE YOU WOULDN'T BELIEVE, CREATING AN OXYGEN POCKET.
AND ONCE AIR ENTERS THE STRATOSPHERE, IT STABILIZES. THAT'S WHY IT FEELS SO MUCH WARMER.
THAT'S GREAT! THIS'LL BE A STROLL IN THE PARK!

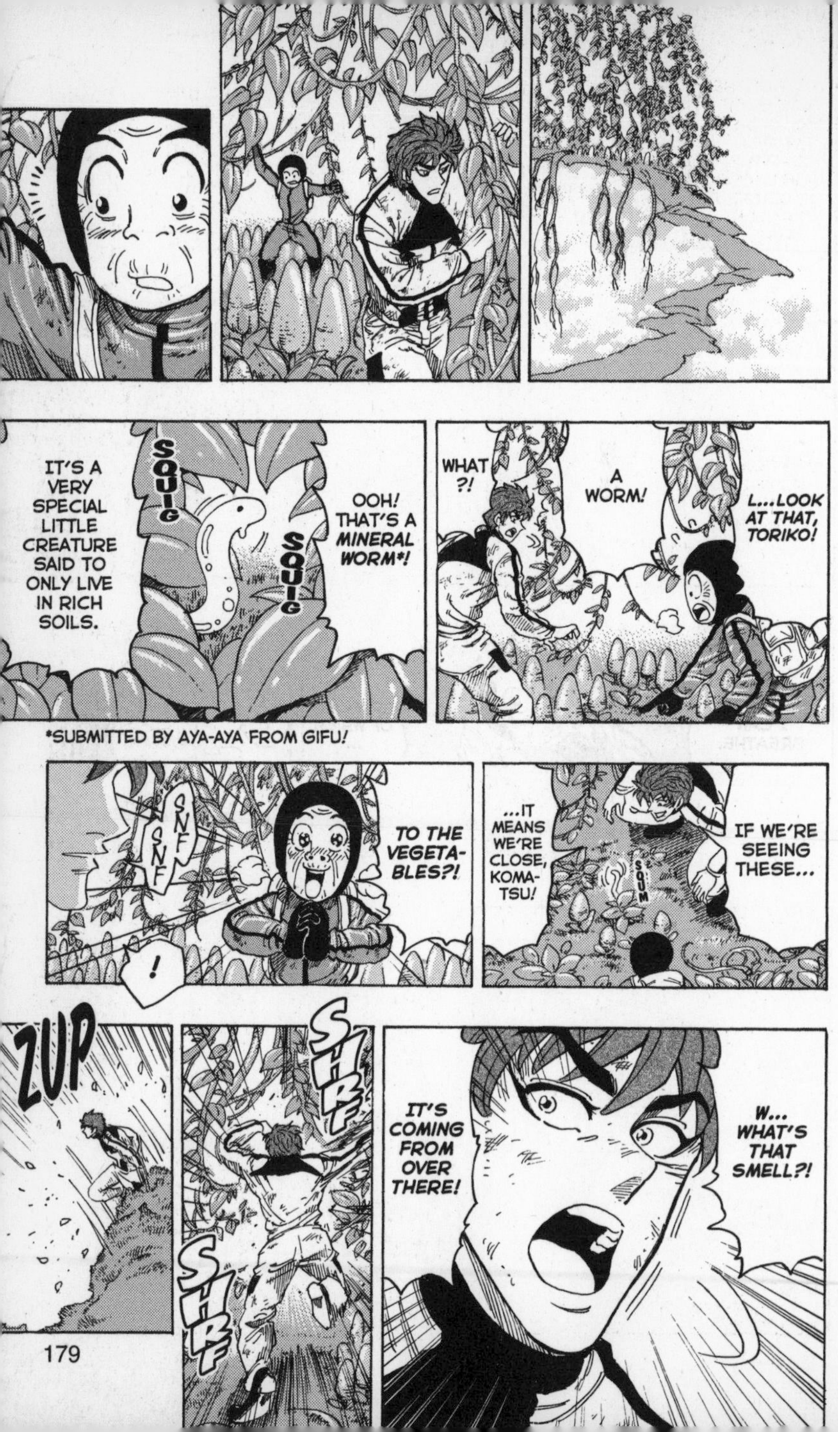
L...LOOK AT THAT, TORIKO!
A WORM!
WHAT?!
OOH! THAT'S A MINERAL WORM*!
SQUIG
SQUIG
IT'S A VERY SPECIAL LITTLE CREATURE SAID TO ONLY LIVE IN RICH SOILS.
IF WE'RE SEEING THESE...
SQUM
...IT MEANS WE'RE CLOSE, KOMATSU!
TO THE VEGETABLES?!
SNF
SNF
!
W... WHAT'S THAT SMELL?!
IT'S COMING FROM OVER THERE!
SHRF
SHRF
ZUP

*SUBMITTED BY AYA-AYA FROM GIFU!

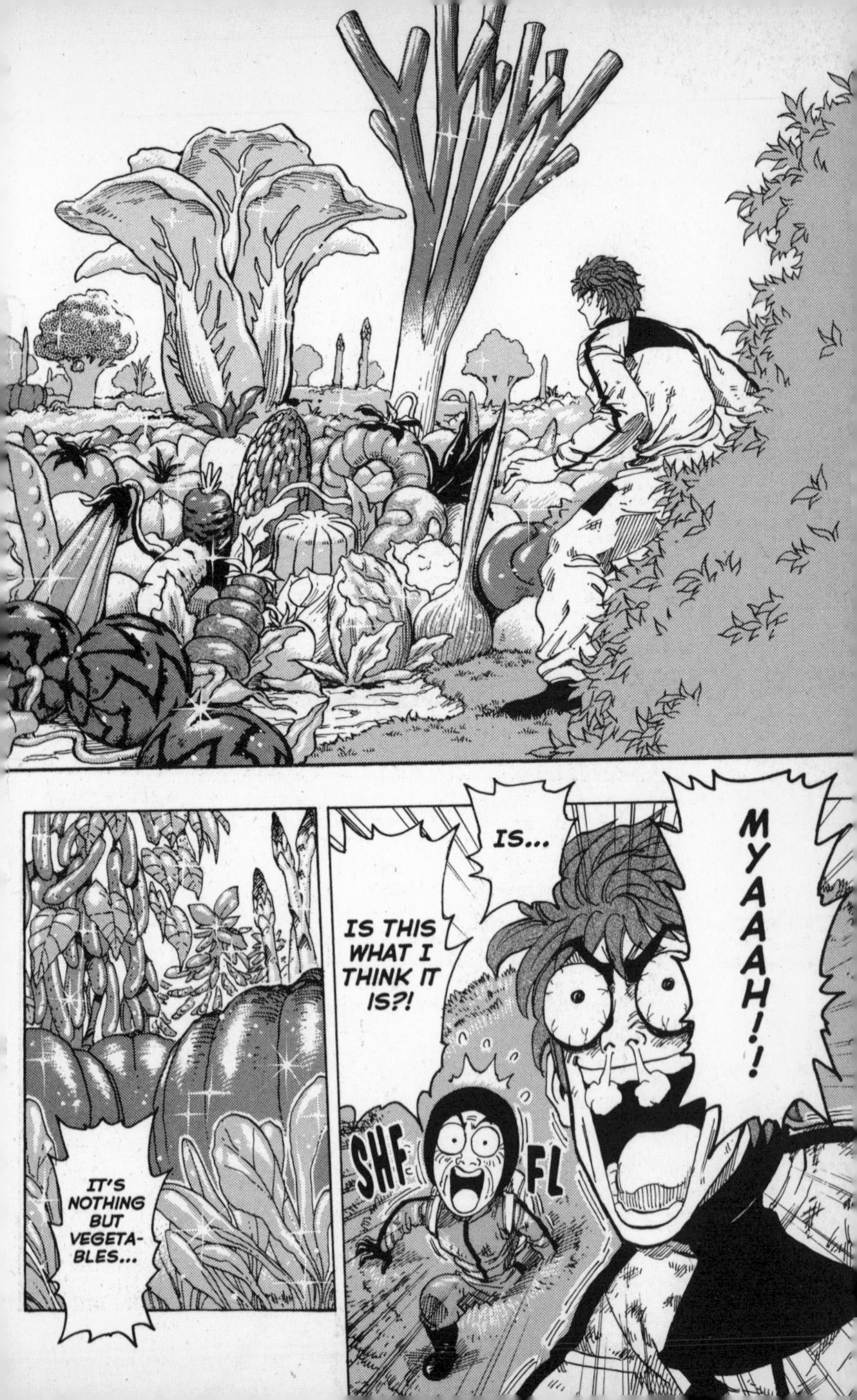
MYAAAH!!!
IS...
IS THIS WHAT I THINK IT IS?!
SHF FL
IT'S NOTHING BUT VEGETA-BLES...

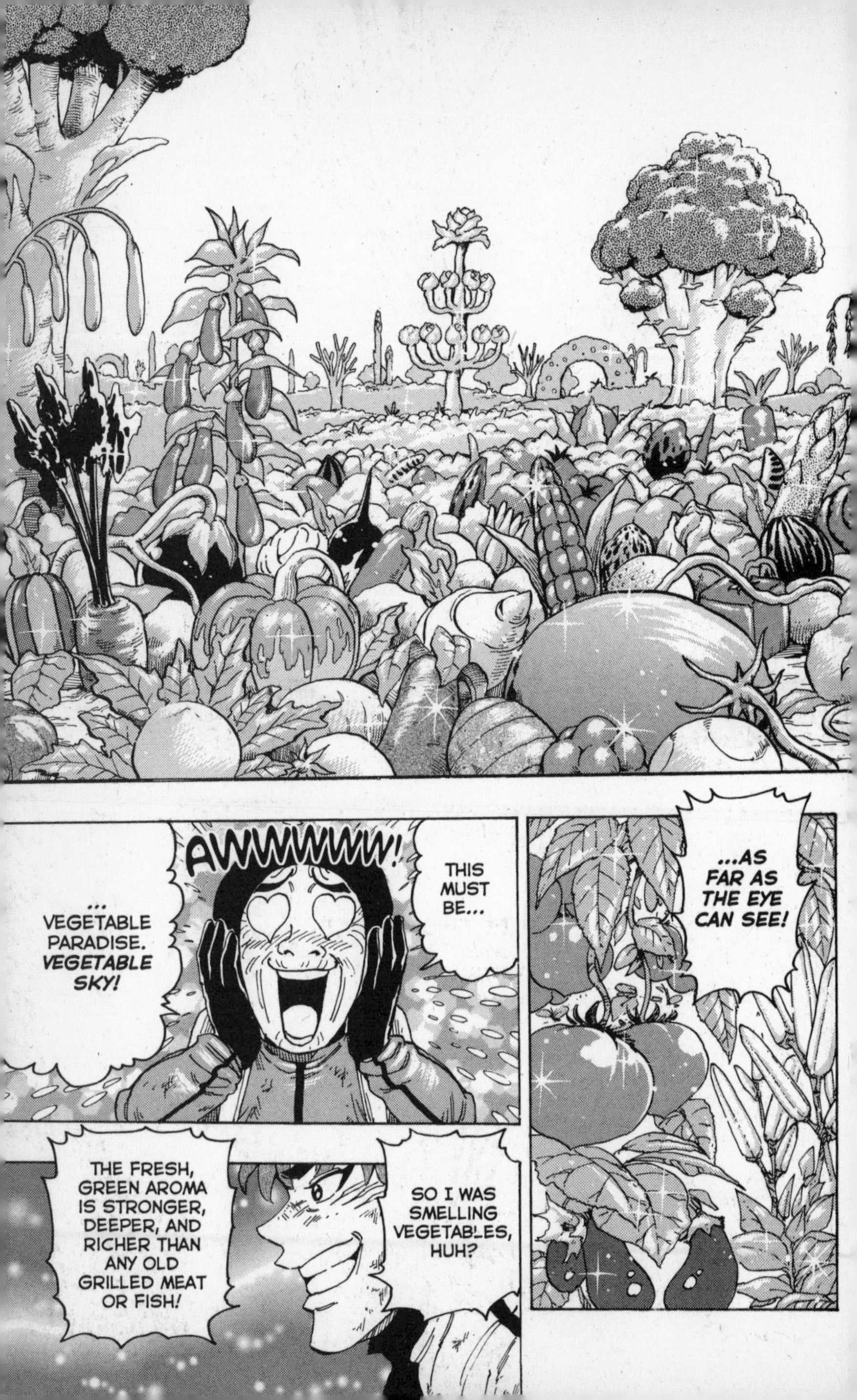
...AS FAR AS THE EYE CAN SEE!
THIS MUST BE...
AWWWWWW!
...VEGETABLE PARADISE. VEGETABLE SKY!
SO I WAS SMELLING VEGETABLES, HUH?
THE FRESH, GREEN AROMA IS STRONGER, DEEPER, AND RICHER THAN ANY OLD GRILLED MEAT OR FISH!

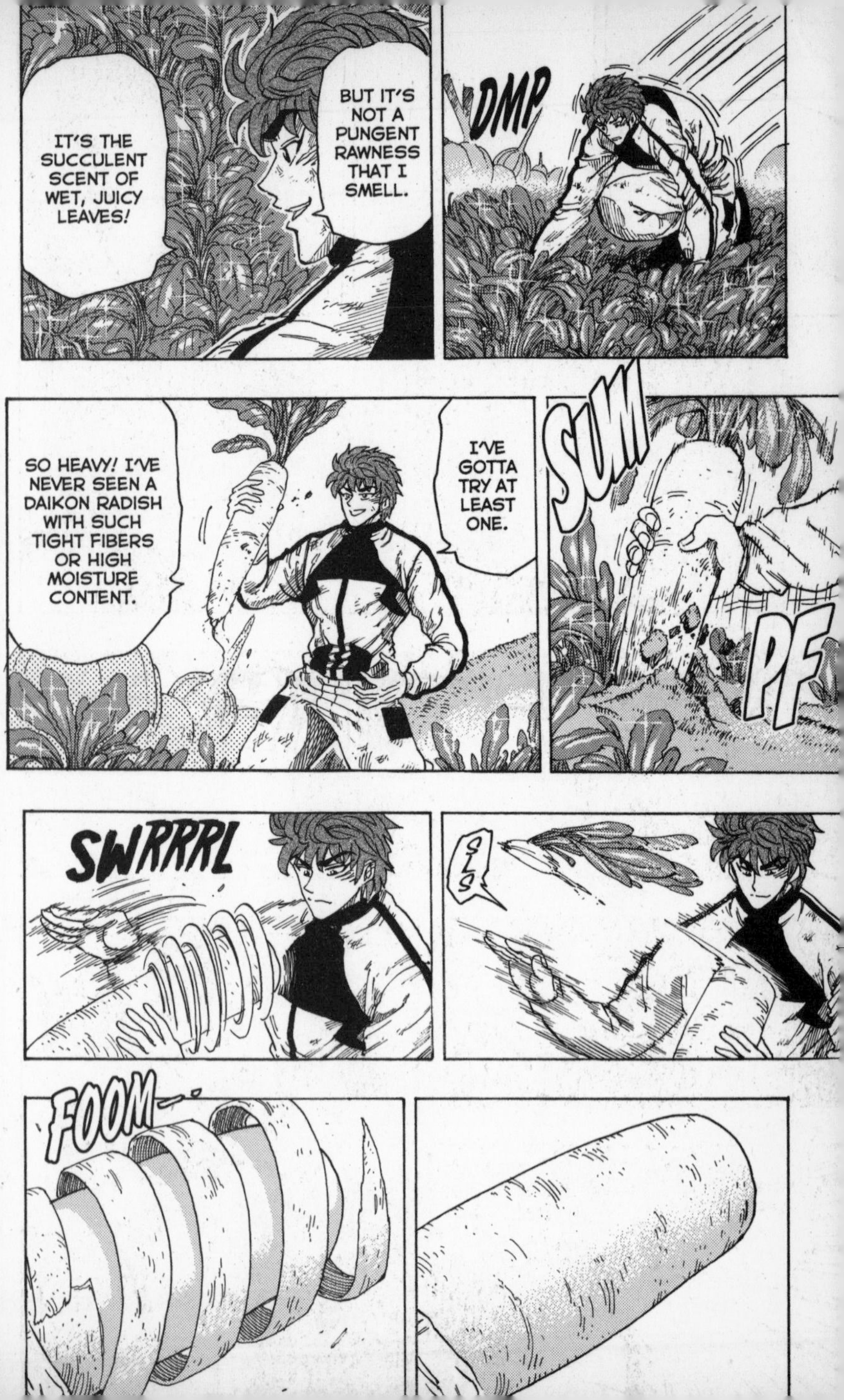
DMP
BUT IT'S NOT A PUNGENT RAWNESS THAT I SMELL.
IT'S THE SUCCULENT SCENT OF WET, JUICY LEAVES!
SUM
PF
I'VE GOTTA TRY AT LEAST ONE.
SO HEAVY! I'VE NEVER SEEN A DAIKON RADISH WITH SUCH TIGHT FIBERS OR HIGH MOISTURE CONTENT.
SLS
SWRRRL
FOOM

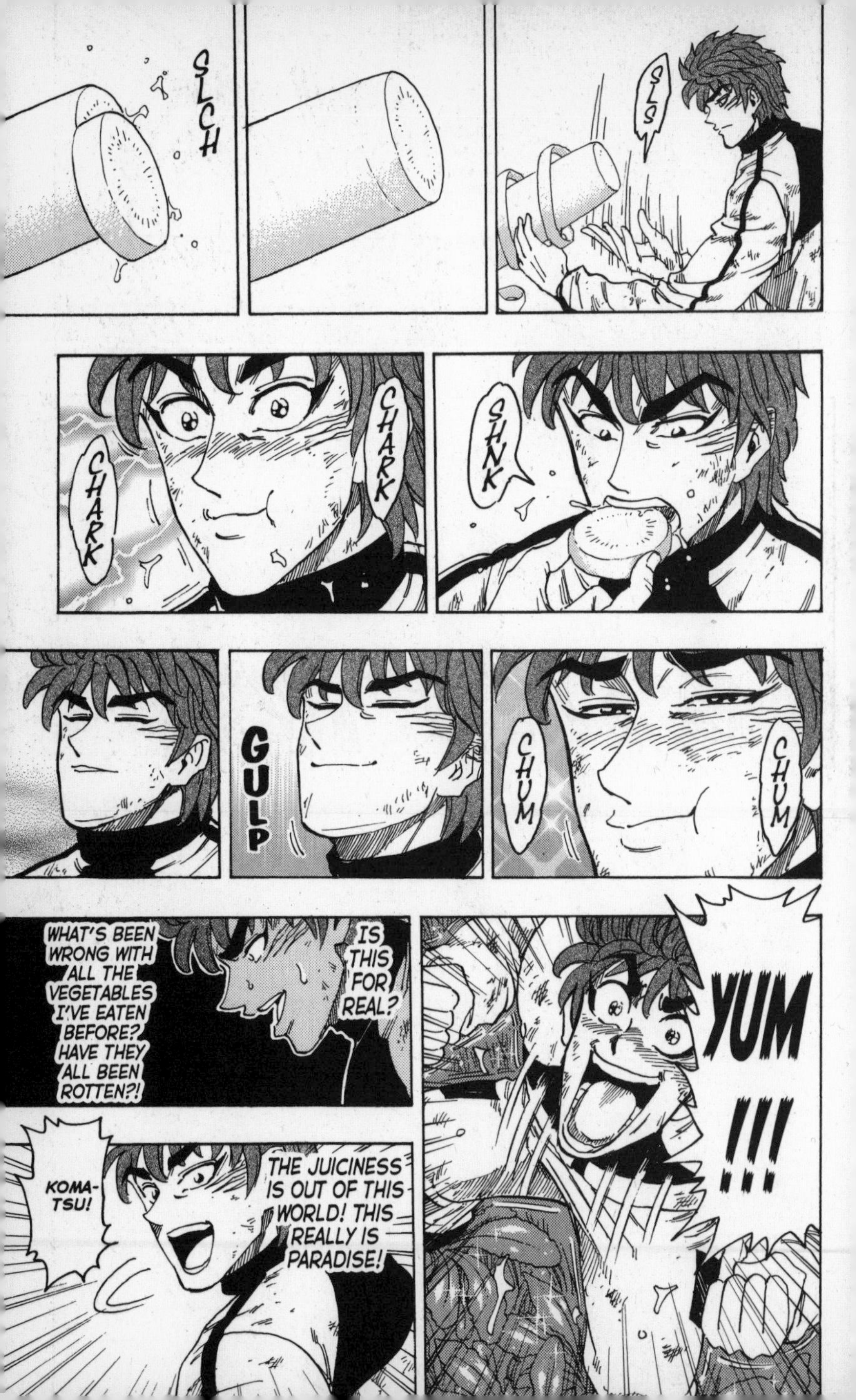
SLS
SLCH
SHNK
CHARK
CHARK
CHUM
CHUM
GULP
YUM!!!
IS THIS FOR REAL?
WHAT'S BEEN WRONG WITH ALL THE VEGETABLES I'VE EATEN BEFORE? HAVE THEY ALL BEEN ROTTEN?!
THE JUICINESS IS OUT OF THIS WORLD! THIS REALLY IS PARADISE!
KOMATSU!

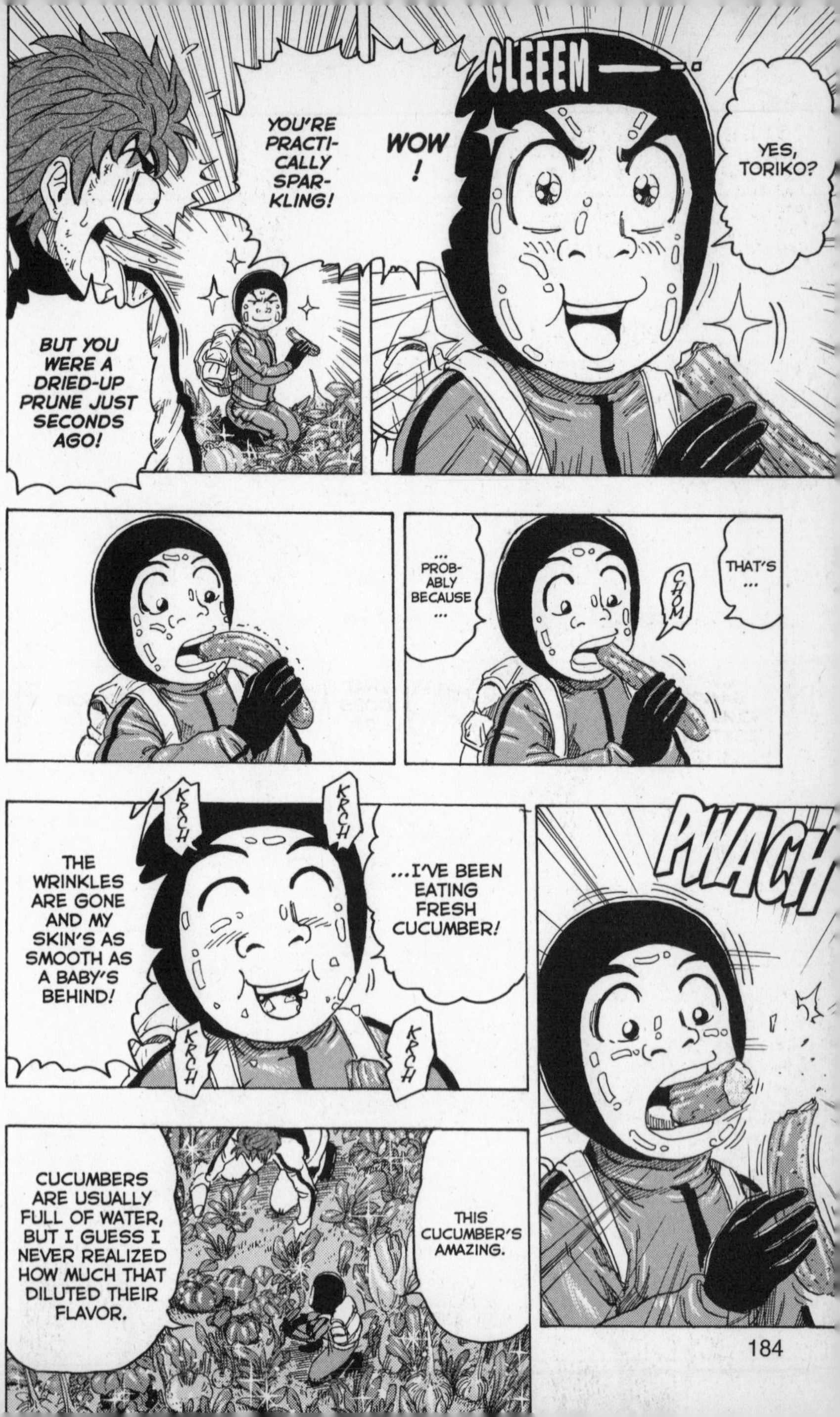
GLEEEM
YES, TORIKO?
WOW!
YOU'RE PRACTI-CALLY SPAR-KLING!
BUT YOU WERE A DRIED-UP PRUNE JUST SECONDS AGO!
THAT'S...
CHOM
...PROB-ABLY BECAUSE...
PWACH
KRCH
KRCH
...I'VE BEEN EATING FRESH CUCUMBER!
THE WRINKLES ARE GONE AND MY SKIN'S AS SMOOTH AS A BABY'S BEHIND!
KRCH
KRCH
THIS CUCUMBER'S AMAZING.
CUCUMBERS ARE USUALLY FULL OF WATER, BUT I GUESS I NEVER REALIZED HOW MUCH THAT DILUTED THEIR FLAVOR.

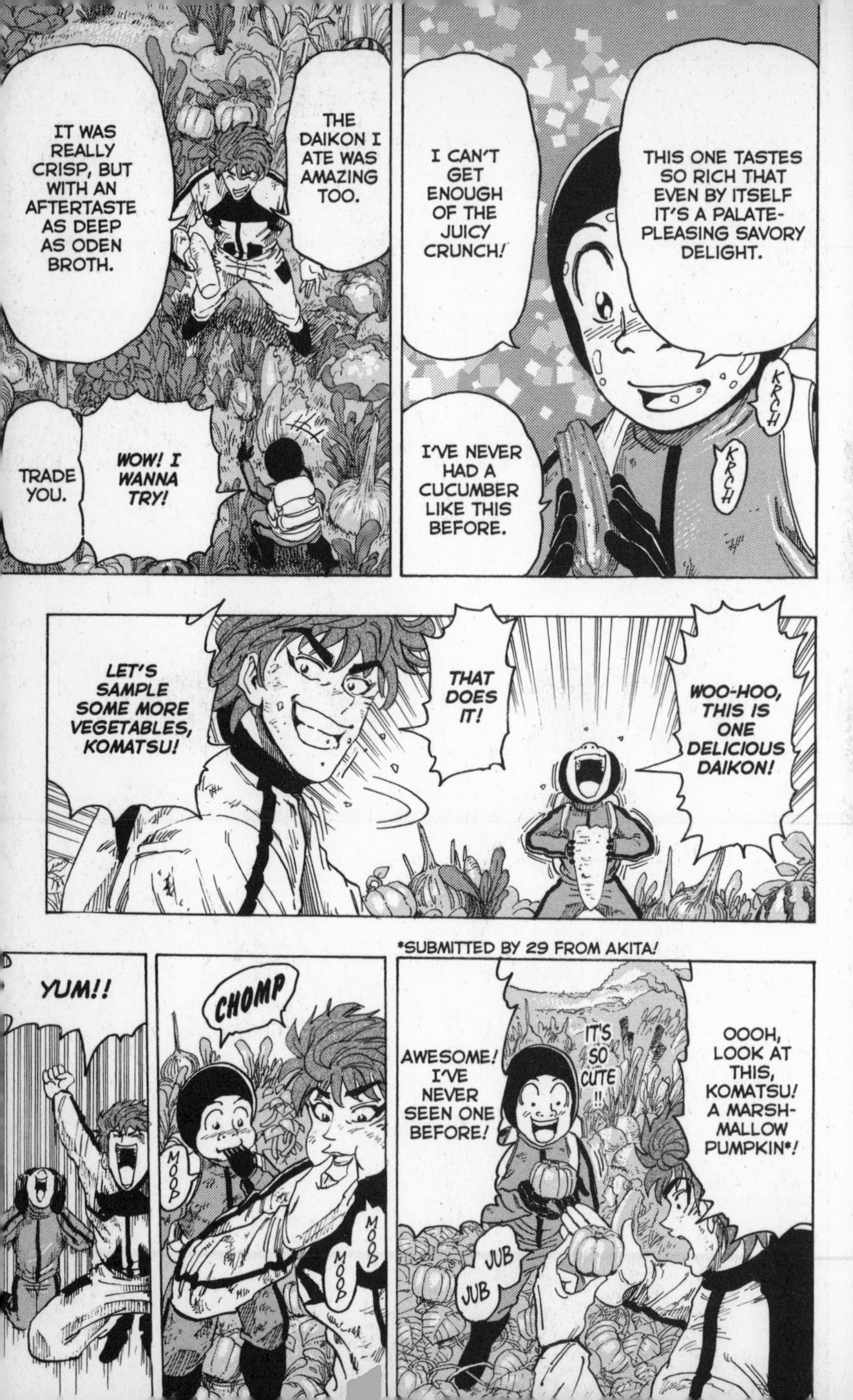
THIS ONE TASTES SO RICH THAT EVEN BY ITSELF IT'S A PALATE-PLEASING SAVORY DELIGHT.
I CAN'T GET ENOUGH OF THE JUICY CRUNCH!
KRCH
KRCH
I'VE NEVER HAD A CUCUMBER LIKE THIS BEFORE.
THE DAIKON I ATE WAS AMAZING TOO.
IT WAS REALLY CRISP, BUT WITH AN AFTERTASTE AS DEEP AS ODEN BROTH.
WOW! I WANNA TRY!
TRADE YOU.
WOO-HOO, THIS IS ONE DELICIOUS DAIKON!
THAT DOES IT!
LET'S SAMPLE SOME MORE VEGETABLES, KOMATSU!
OOOH, LOOK AT THIS, KOMATSU! A MARSH-MALLOW PUMPKIN*!
IT'S SO CUTE!!
AWESOME! I'VE NEVER SEEN ONE BEFORE!
JUB
JUB
CHOMP
MOOP
MOOP
MOOP
YUM!!
*SUBMITTED BY 29 FROM AKITA!

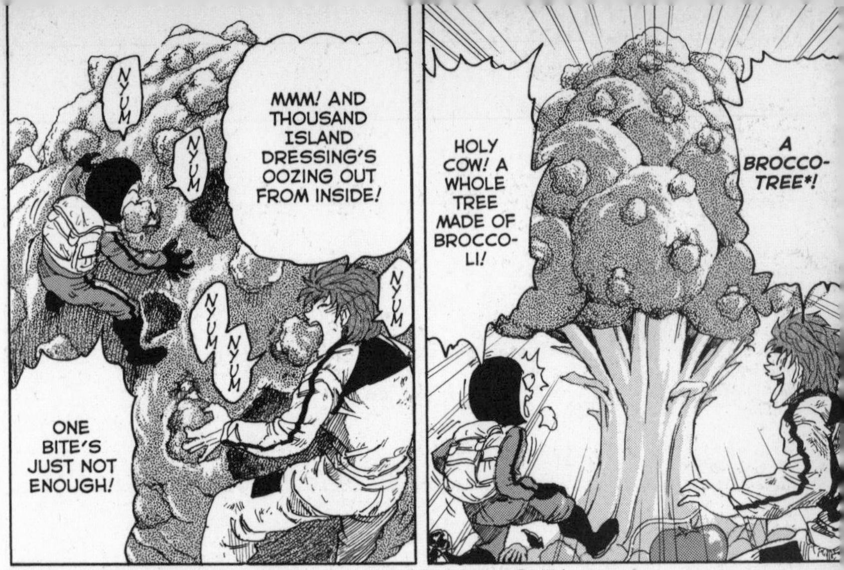
A BROCCO-TREE*!
HOLY COW! A WHOLE TREE MADE OF BROCCO-LI!
NYUM
NYUM
MMM! AND THOUSAND ISLAND DRESSING'S OOZING OUT FROM INSIDE!
NYUM
NYUM NYUM
ONE BITE'S JUST NOT ENOUGH!

*BROCCOTREE SUBMITTED BY TSUNA KIMATSUKA FROM KANAGAWA!

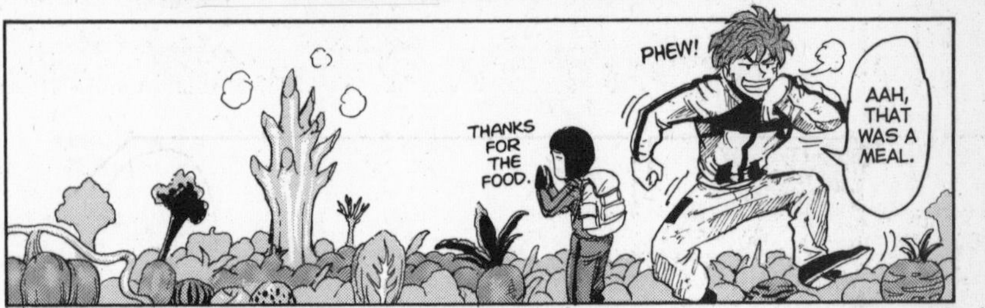
PHEW!
AAH, THAT WAS A MEAL.
THANKS FOR THE FOOD.

*POTATO SPRING SUBMITTED BY SANTA FUKAMI FROM AICHI!

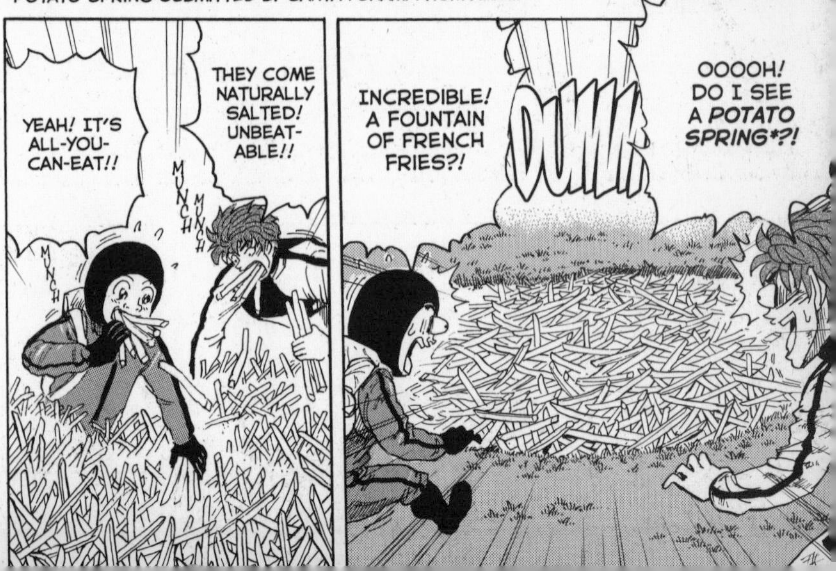
OOOOH! DO I SEE A *POTATO SPRING**?!
DUMM
INCREDIBLE! A FOUNTAIN OF FRENCH FRIES?!
THEY COME NATURALLY SALTED! UNBEAT-ABLE!!
MUNCH MUNCH
YEAH! IT'S ALL-YOU-CAN-EAT!!
MUNCH

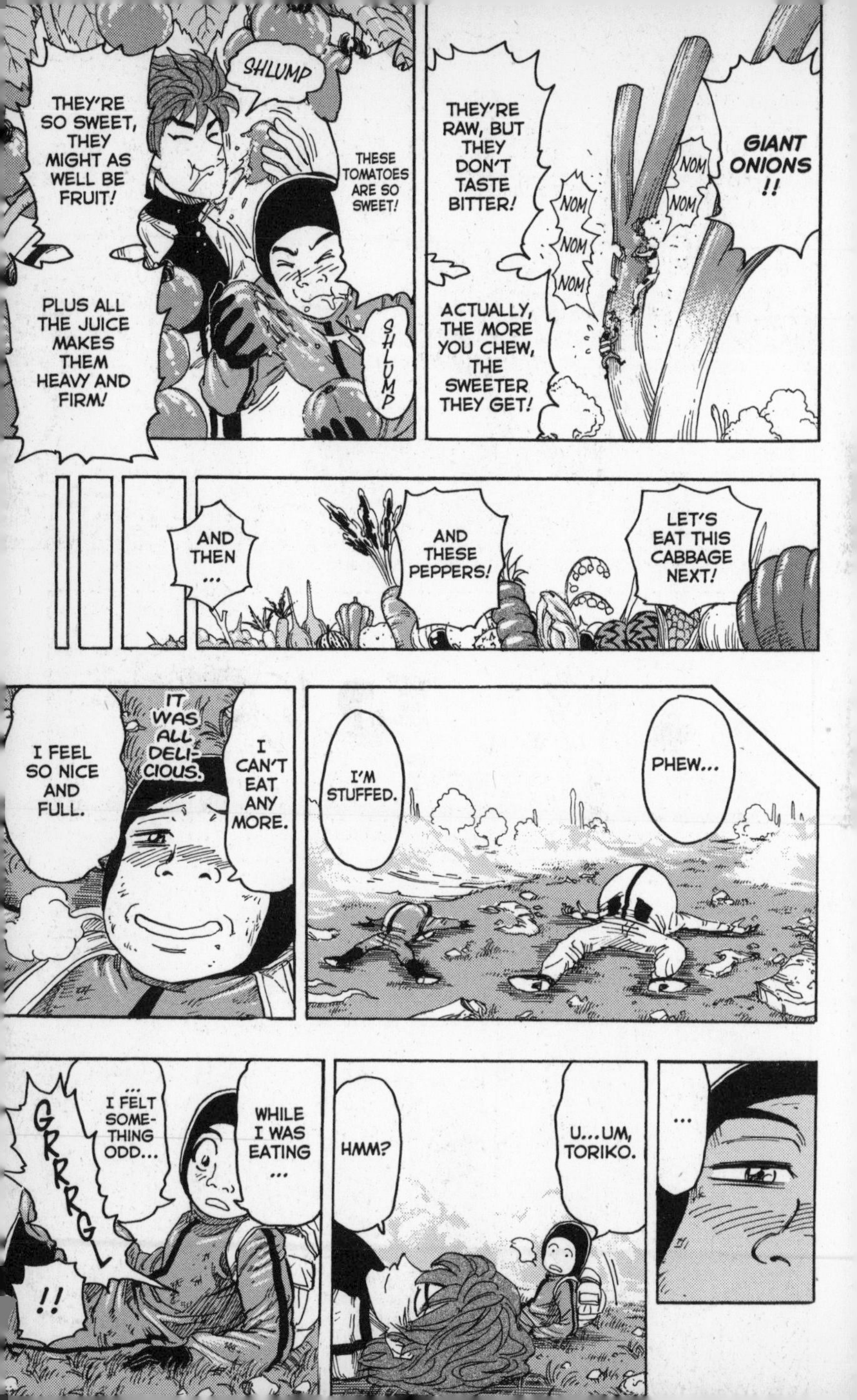
GIANT ONIONS!!
NOM NOM
THEY'RE RAW, BUT THEY DON'T TASTE BITTER!
NOM NOM NOM
ACTUALLY, THE MORE YOU CHEW, THE SWEETER THEY GET!
SHLUMP
THESE TOMATOES ARE SO SWEET!
THEY'RE SO SWEET, THEY MIGHT AS WELL BE FRUIT!
SHLUMP
PLUS ALL THE JUICE MAKES THEM HEAVY AND FIRM!
LET'S EAT THIS CABBAGE NEXT!
AND THESE PEPPERS!
AND THEN ...
PHEW...
I'M STUFFED.
I CAN'T EAT ANY MORE.
IT WAS ALL DELI-CIOUS.
I FEEL SO NICE AND FULL.
...
U...UM, TORIKO.
HMM?
WHILE I WAS EATING ...
... I FELT SOME-THING ODD...
GRRRRGL
!!

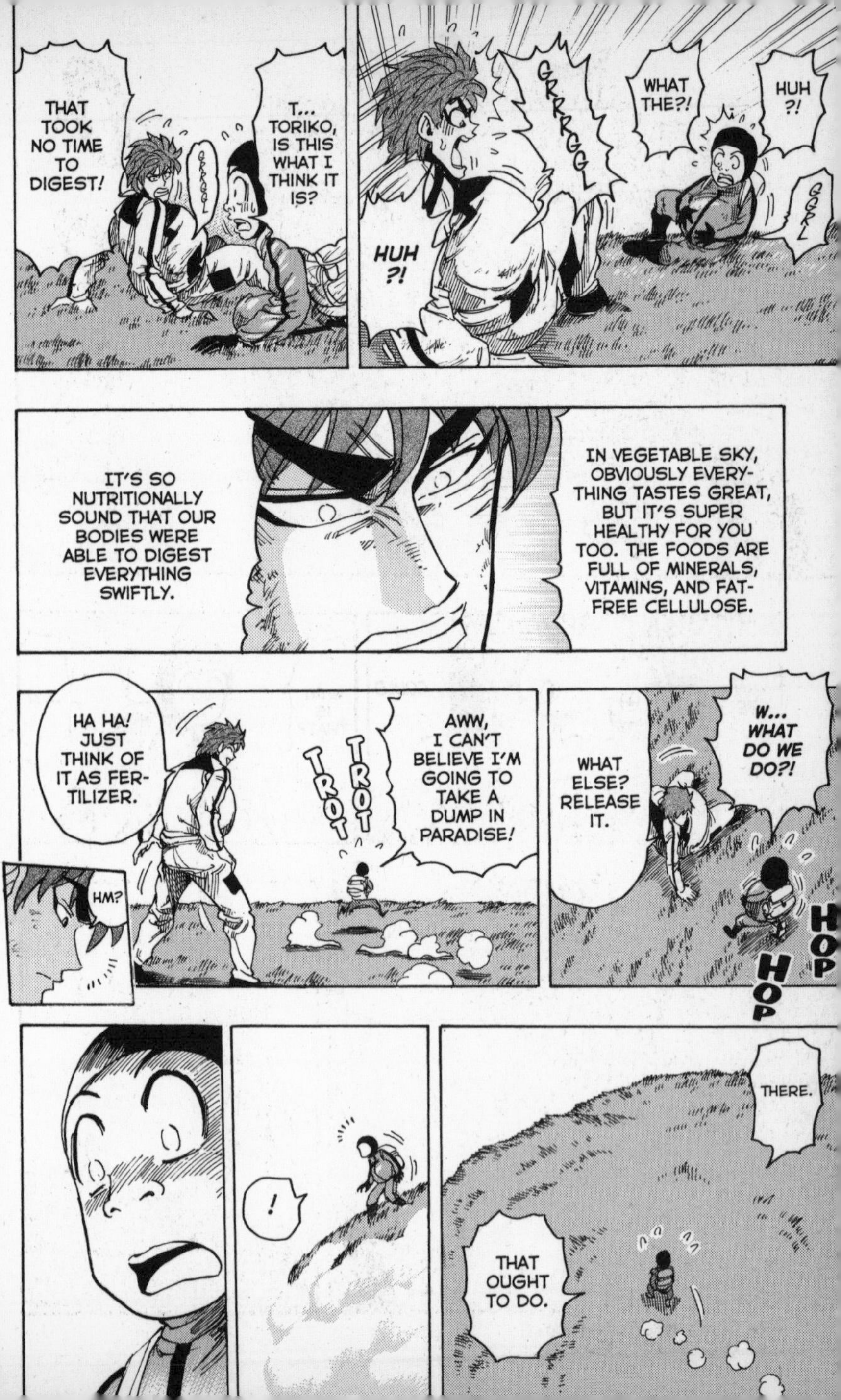
HUH ?!
WHAT THE?!
GGRL
GRRRGGL
HUH ?!
T... TORIKO, IS THIS WHAT I THINK IT IS?
GRRRGGL
THAT TOOK NO TIME TO DIGEST!
IN VEGETABLE SKY, OBVIOUSLY EVERY-THING TASTES GREAT, BUT IT'S SUPER HEALTHY FOR YOU TOO. THE FOODS ARE FULL OF MINERALS, VITAMINS, AND FAT-FREE CELLULOSE.
IT'S SO NUTRITIONALLY SOUND THAT OUR BODIES WERE ABLE TO DIGEST EVERYTHING SWIFTLY.
W... WHAT DO WE DO?!
WHAT ELSE? RELEASE IT.
HOP HOP
AWW, I CAN'T BELIEVE I'M GOING TO TAKE A DUMP IN PARADISE!
TROT TROT
HA HA! JUST THINK OF IT AS FER-TILIZER.
HM?
THERE.
THAT OUGHT TO DO.
!

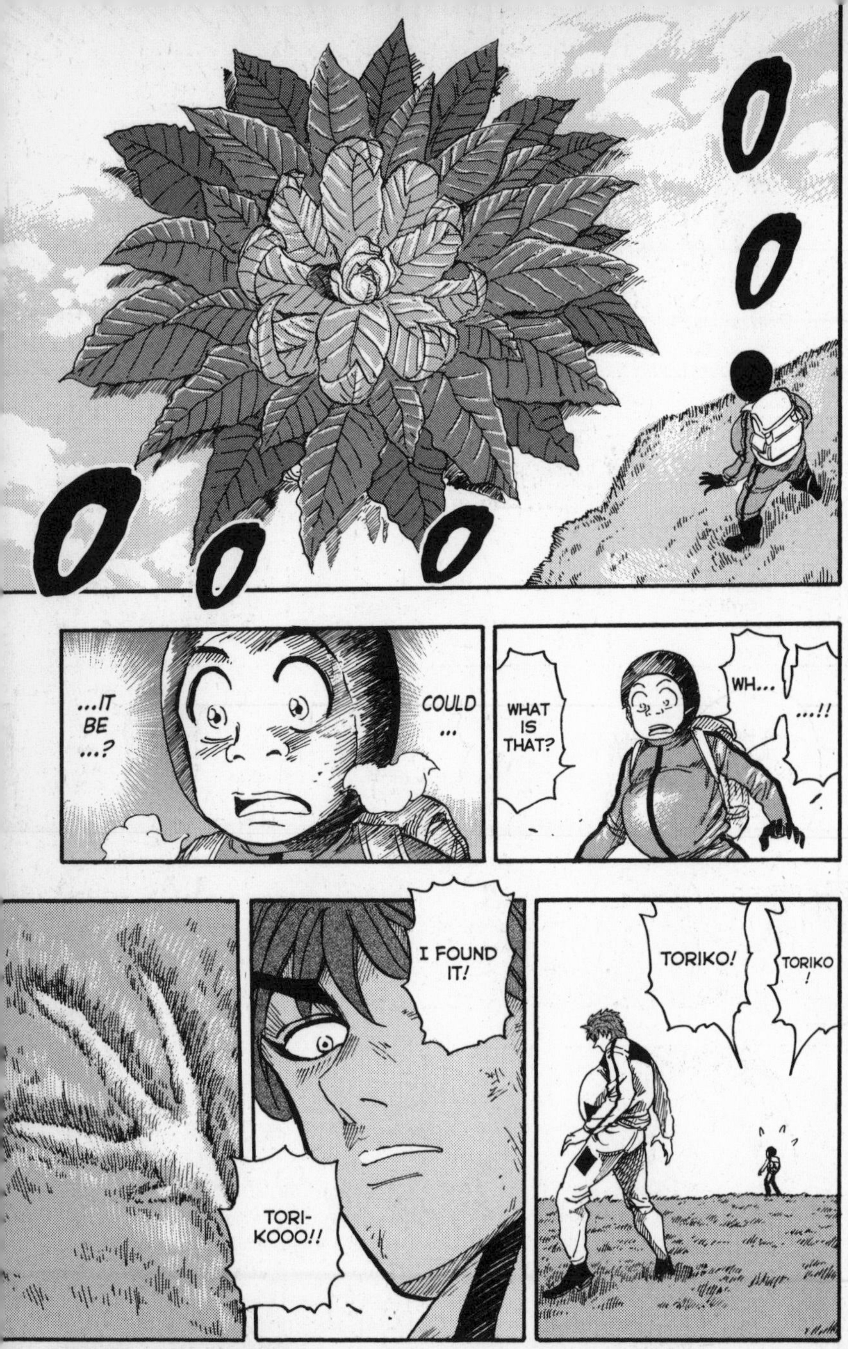
WH...
...!!
WHAT IS THAT?
COULD ...
...IT BE ...?
TORIKO!
TORIKO!
I FOUND IT!
TORI-KOOO!!

TO BE CONTINUED!

TORIKO

GOURMET CHECKLIST

Vol. 117

DOCTOR FISH

(FISH)

CAPTURE LEVEL: 1-30 (DEPENDS ON SPECIES)

HABITAT: LIFE

LENGTH: DEPENDS ON SPECIES

HEIGHT: ---

WEIGHT: ---

PRICE: DIET FISH = 1,250,000 YEN PER FISH; MELANIN GRAMMY = 500,000 YEN PER FISH; BLOOD TETRA = 20,000,000 YEN PER FISH; TUMOR FISH = 100,000,000 YEN PER FISH

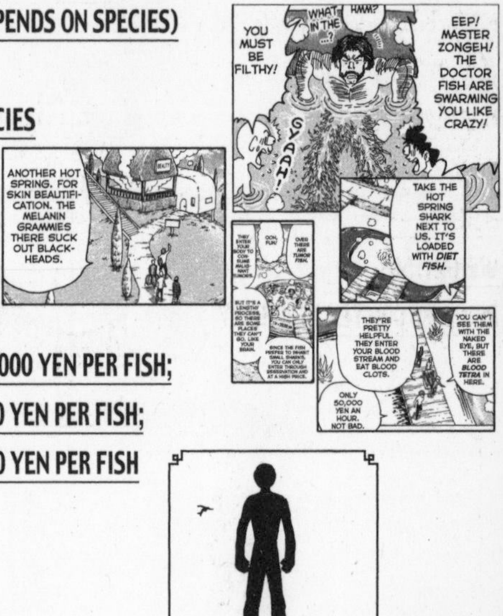
EEP! MASTER ZONGEH! THE DOCTOR FISH ARE SWARMING YOU LIKE CRAZY!
HMM?
WHAT IN THE ...?
YOU MUST BE FILTHY!
GYAAH!
ANOTHER HOT SPRING. FOR SKIN BEAUTIFICATION. THE MELANIN GRAMMIES THERE SUCK OUT BLACKHEADS.
TAKE THE HOT SPRING SHARK NEXT TO US. IT'S LOADED WITH DIET FISH.
OVER THERE ARE TUMOR FISH.
OOH, FUN!
THEY ENTER YOUR BODY TO CONSUME MALIGNANT TUMORS.
BUT IT'S A LENGTHY PROCESS, SO THERE ARE SOME PLACES THEY CAN'T GO, LIKE YOUR BRAIN.
SINCE THE FISH PREFER TO INHABIT SMALL SHARKS, YOU CAN ONLY ENTER THROUGH RESERVATION AND AT A HIGH PRICE.
YOU CAN'T SEE THEM WITH THE NAKED EYE, BUT THERE ARE BLOOD TETRA IN HERE.
THEY'RE PRETTY HELPFUL. THEY ENTER YOUR BLOOD STREAM AND EAT BLOOD CLOTS.
ONLY 50,000 YEN AN HOUR. NOT BAD.

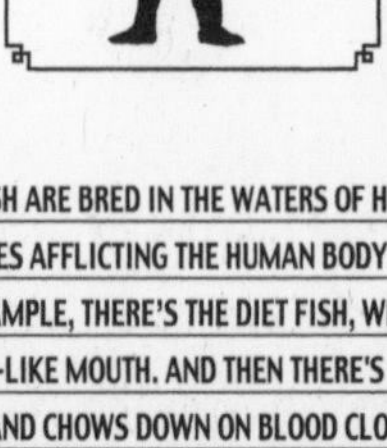

SCALE

AS MENTIONED IN THE PREVIOUS ENTRY, DOCTOR FISH ARE BRED IN THE WATERS OF HOT SPRING SHARKS, AND WILL EAT AWAY MALIGNANCIES AFFLICTING THE HUMAN BODY. THERE ARE MANY SPECIES OF DOCTOR FISH. FOR EXAMPLE, THERE'S THE DIET FISH, WHICH SUCKS UP SUBCUTANEOUS FAT THROUGH ITS STRAW-LIKE MOUTH. AND THEN THERE'S THE BLOOD TETRA, WHICH INVADES A HOST'S ARTERIES AND CHOWS DOWN ON BLOOD CLOTS. TUMOR FISH FEED ONLY ON TUMORS, AND MELANIN GRAMMIES SLURP UP THE BLACKHEADS OF BEAUTY FANATICS LIKE SUNNY. AND THAT'S ONLY A SMALL SAMPLING! THE COST OF BATHING WITH DOCTOR FISH VARIES BY SPECIES, BUT IT'S ALWAYS WELL WORTH THE PRICE.

TORIKO

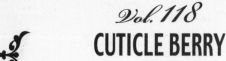

GOURMET CHECKLIST

Vol. 118

CUTICLE BERRY

(FRUIT)

CAPTURE LEVEL: 20 IN THE WILD
(CAN BE CULTIVATED)
HABITAT: RICH SOILS
LENGTH: 5 CM
HEIGHT: ---
WEIGHT: 50 G
PRICE: 80,000 YEN PER BERRY

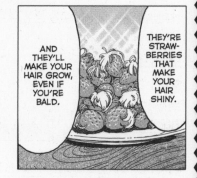

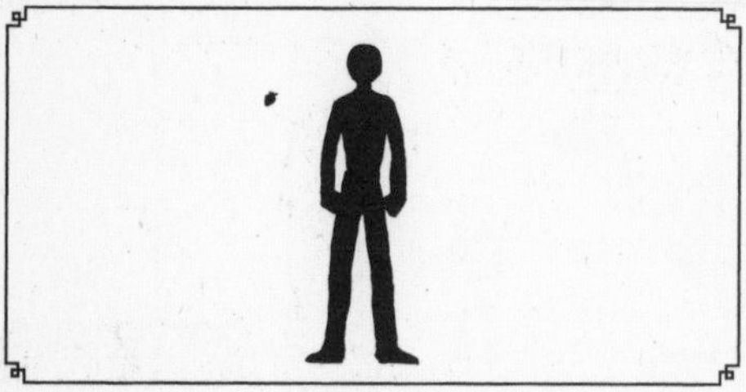

THEY'RE STRAW-BERRIES THAT MAKE YOUR HAIR SHINY.
AND THEY'LL MAKE YOUR HAIR GROW, EVEN IF YOU'RE BALD.

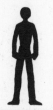

SCALE

EAT THIS STRAWBERRY IF YOU WANT LUSCIOUS LOCKS! NO HAIR? NO PROBLEM--EVEN IF YOU'RE BALD, THEY SOMETIMES CAUSE HAIR TO SPROUT. IT'S NOT UNCOMMON TO SEE A MIDDLE-AGED MAN CHOWING DOWN ON A PILE OF CUTICLE BERRIES...BEFORE HE FINALLY GIVES UP AND BUYS A TOUPEE.

TORIKO

GOURMET CHECKLIST

Vol. 119

CHACO BIRD
(BIRD)

CAPTURE LEVEL: 51

HABITAT: DENSE FORESTS

LENGTH: 3 METERS

HEIGHT: ---

WEIGHT: 400 KG

PRICE: NO VALUE AS A FOODSTUFF (LEAVES SELL
FOR 30,000,000 YEN EACH)

`SCALE`

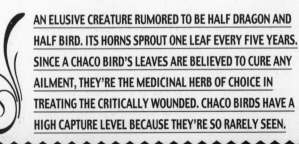

AN ELUSIVE CREATURE RUMORED TO BE HALF DRAGON AND
HALF BIRD. ITS HORNS SPROUT ONE LEAF EVERY FIVE YEARS.
SINCE A CHACO BIRD'S LEAVES ARE BELIEVED TO CURE ANY
AILMENT, THEY'RE THE MEDICINAL HERB OF CHOICE IN
TREATING THE CRITICALLY WOUNDED. CHACO BIRDS HAVE A
HIGH CAPTURE LEVEL BECAUSE THEY'RE SO RARELY SEEN.

TORIKO

GOURMET CHECKLIST

Vol. 120

MORNING ROSE
(PLANT)

CAPTURE LEVEL: 5

HABITAT: NO SPECIFIC HABITAT

LENGTH: 22 CM

HEIGHT: ---

WEIGHT: ---

PRICE: 5,000,000 YEN PER FLOWER

SCALE

WHEN DAWN BREAKS AFTER A FULL MOON, THIS ROSE BLOOMS. BUT BY NOON, ITS FLOWERS HAVE WILTED. IT IS SAID THAT DRINKING THE DEW FROM A MORNING ROSE'S PETALS WILL RESTORE YOUR YOUTH AND GIVE YOU LUSTROUS SKIN. FEMALE CELEBRITIES FROM ALL OVER THE WORLD WHO COVET THE MORNING ROSE'S AMAZING EFFECTS DISH OUT HUGE SUMS OF MONEY TO PURCHASE THEM, SO THE MARKET PRICE SOARS YEAR AFTER YEAR. CURRENTLY, IT COSTS THE SAME TO BUY ONE MORNING ROSE AS TO BUILD A HOUSE IN THE COUNTRYSIDE.

CHARACTER PROFILE

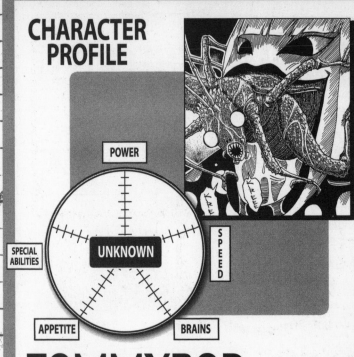

POWER

SPECIAL ABILITIES

UNKNOWN

SPEED

APPETITE

BRAINS

TOMMYROD

AGE: UNKNOWN		**BIRTHDAY:** UNKNOWN	
BLOOD TYPE: UNKNOWN		**SIGN:** UNKNOWN	
HEIGHT: 175 CM		**WEIGHT:** 200 KG	
EYESIGHT: 20/8		**SHOE SIZE:** 27 CM	

SPECIAL MOVES/ABILITIES:

● Bomb Eggs, Parasitic Insects

A Vice-Chef of Gourmet Corp. He houses approximately 10,000 insect eggs inside him, hatching them in his esophagus, and vomiting them forth from his mouth to attack his target. He's especially proficient in aerial battles thanks to the wings on his back, and when he allows himself to fight at full strength, he packs an unparalleled punch. However, Tommyrod expends over half of his physical strength preventing his ultimate weapon, the Parasite Emperor, from being born.